TRACK'S GREATEST CHAMPIONS

by Cordner Nelson

Tafnews Press

Published in 1986 by Tafnews Press, Book Division of Track & Field News, Box 296, Los Altos, CA 94023 U.S.A.

Copyright © 1986 by Cordner Nelson. All rights reserved. No part of this book may be reproduced in any form, by mimeograph or any other means, without permission in writing from the publisher.

Previous edition published in 1970 in Great Britain by Michael Joseph Ltd under the title *Track and Field: The Great Ones*.

Standard Book Number 0-911521-19-4

Printed in the United States of America

Cover design and layout: Teresa Lee

To
BERT

Contents

Illustrations	iv
Foreword	vi
Publisher's Introduction	vii
Paavo Nurmi	1
Jesse Owens	15
Cornelius Warmerdam	27
Harrison Dillard	39
Emil Zatopek	49
Bob Mathias	65
Parry O'Brien	77
Rafer Johnson	91
Glenn Davis	105
Al Oerter	115
Herb Elliott	129
Valeriy Brumel	141
Peter Snell	151
Viktor Saneyev	165
Lasse Viren	177
Alberto Juantorena	183
Yuriy Syedikh	189
Daley Thompson	197
Sebastian Coe	219
Edwin Moses	241
Carl Lewis	257
Profiles of Other Track & Field Champions	281
Athletes of the Year, 1947-85	385

Illustrations

Subject	Photographer	Page
Paavo Nurmi		4
Paavo Nurmi		9
Jesse Owens		19
Cornelius Warmerdam		31
Harrison Dillard		38
Emil Zatopek, Helsinki 5000		48
Emil Zatopek, Helsinki marathon		59
Bob Mathias, with other 1952 decathlon medalists		73
Parry O'Brien		83
Rafer Johnson		101
Glenn Davis, Rome 400H finish		113
Al Oerter 1960		126
Al Oerter 1964		126
Al Oerter 1968	Don Wilkinson	127
Al Oerter 1985	Sailer/McManus Photo	127
Herb Elliott, Rome 1500 finish		139
Valeriy Brumel		145
Peter Snell, with Murry Halberg		159
Peter Snell, Tokyo 1500 finish		163
Viktor Saneyev	Tony Duffy	169
Lasse Viren	Theo van de Rakt	176
Alberto Juantorena	Rich Clarkson	185
Yuriy Syedikh	Don Chadez	188
Daley Thompson	Theo van de Rakt	196
Daley Thompson	Stewart Kendall: Sportsphoto	209
Daley Thompson and Jurgen Hingsen	George Herringshaw/ASP	216
Sebastian Coe	Theo van de Rakt	218
Sebastian Coe, 1984 1500 final	Diane Johnson	225
Edwin Moses	Peter Probst	240
Edwin Moses, 1984 victory ceremony	Diane Johnson	251
Carl Lewis, Helsinki 100 finish	Claus Andersen	256
Carl Lewis, Los Angeles 200	Cor Eberhard	273
Said Aouita	Theo van de Rakt	283
Roger Bannister, the first sub-4 mile		286
Bob Beamon—THE jump		288
Ralph Boston		292
Sergey Bubka	Rhein-Ruhr-Foto/Gustav Schroder	294
Lee Calhoun		296
Henry Carr	Fionnbar Callanan	296

Subject	Photographer	Page
Ron Clarke, the first sub-28 10K	Knut Edvard Holm	298
Steve Cram	John Burles	302
Joaquim Cruz	Jeff Johnson	302
Charles Dumas		309
Adhemar da Silva		309
Lee Evans	Alan Shapiro	309
Anders Garderud	Don Chadez	312
Walter George		312
Gunder Hagg (and Arne Andersson)		315
Bob Hayes		318
Rudolf Harbig		318
Uwe Hohn	Zigurds Mezavilks	318
Michel Jazy	Fionnbar Callanan	324
Matti Jarvinen		324
Bruce Jenner	Dave Drennan	324
Kipchoge Keino	Don Chadez	327
Vladimir Kuts	Ed Lacey	330
Carlos Lopes, the fastest marathon	Theo van de Rakt	334
Janis Lusis	Knut Edvard Holm	336
Dallas Long		336
Jack Lovelock		336
Ralph Metcalfe		344
Randy Matson		344
Bobby Morrow, winning Melbourne 200 (and Andy Stanfield)	Sports Illustrated: John Zimmerman	344
Charley Paddock		352
Steve Ovett	Ed Lacey	352
Eulace Peacock		355
Bob Richards, winning at Helsinki		360
Henry Rono	All-Sport/Tony Duffy	360
Gaston Roelants		360
Jim Ryun, 3:51.3 at Berkeley	Alan Shapiro	363
Josef Schmidt		366
John Pennel and Bob Seagren	Rich Clarkson	366
Eddie Tolan		374
Bill Toomey		374
Tommie Smith	Knut Edvard Holm	374
Mal Whitfield		378
Arthur Wint		380

Foreword

In 1968 I struggled to choose the thirteen greatest track champions of all time for a book called, by its English publisher, TRACK AND FIELD: THE GREAT ONES. Now, seventeen years later, those thirteen are still among the great ones, but other magnificent athletes have joined them in this new book.

The years have not made our choices any easier. We track fans still have the problem of ranking an athlete who set several world records which are not as good as the marks of some of today's non-winners. We still argue the relative merits of a world record and an Olympic championship. We try to compare the relative merits of superiority in a single event against superiority in two related events. We cannot accurately measure the importance of one phenomenal season compared with several years of merely outstanding performances. And, possibly most difficult of all, we struggle with weighing losses in unimportant meets. Our problem is truly complex.

I know I am not perfect in my choices, and I can only apologize for not including more great athletes. You can make your own choices from more than 200 athletes in the alphabetical Supplement. The most outstanding of those are given extra space for their successes, and you can compare them to some extent by looking at the Honors Line.

This new feature summarizes, on one line, a whole career in terms of Olympic medals, world records, and World Ranking. Another improvement is the addition of vital statistics. For help in this compilation of facts, I want to thank Dave Johnson, Garry Hill, Jon Hendershott, Ed Fox, Bill Mallon, and Bert Nelson.

Publisher's Introduction

Track's Greatest Champions is an expanded and updated version of *Track and Field: The Great Ones,* which was published in England in 1970. The original 13 chapters have been left untouched, except for addition of a paragraph or two to update the careers of those athletes who were still active after 1970. There are eight new chapters in this book—so Cordner Nelson now offers us his 21 "greatest champions" of track and field, those 21 men whose athletic achievements stand preeminent in the sport.

In addition, the book has a revised and updated Supplement containing more than 200 profiles of other worthy track and field champions. The information provided in the Supplement provides a uniquely valuable reference source for every track enthusiast.

We are happy to help give Cordner Nelson's classic work new life.

PAAVO NURMI

Around the Olympic stadium they ran, the two of them drawing steadily away from fourteen other 5,000 meter finalists. The taller man set the pace inside the white picket fence, but the little man was poised confidently near his shoulder, ready to strike.

On the last lap the little man bided his time, past the covered stands on the backstretch, around the last curve along the standing-room section beneath the white colonnade. Then the little man sprinted furiously and it was soon over. He established his superiority within a few yards and the other man was forced to let him go.

It was Antwerp, August 17, 1920, the last time for many years the taller man would lose an important race, for his name was Paavo Nurmi.

He wanted, more than anything else, more than almost any other man, to be a great runner. His desire began when he was nine, peering wistfully through a wooden fence at a boys' club track meet. Later, when he joined, he usually finished ahead of the other boys. At ten he ran 1,500 meters in 5:43, and he ran 5:03 at eleven.

When he was twelve, tragedy struck. His father died and the the family of six lived in one room while little Paavo worked as an errand boy, pushing a cart up hills. He was a vegetarian, not, as some historians say, because he believed in it, but because of necessity. Poverty helped make Paavo Nurmi a grave, unsmiling, silent man who knew no other way except hard mental and physical discipline.

In the 1912 Olympics, Hannes Kolehmainen won four races and became fifteen-year-old Paavo's idol. Inspired, Nurmi joined a club and began the training which carried him to fame.

'All my spare time was used in walking through the woods or in running.'

At seventeen, he won the 3,000 meter race in the junior nationals in 10:06.5, but he attracted little attention otherwise. In 1917, at the age of 20, his 15:47.4 was only the fifth fastest 5,000 meter time in Finland, and in 1918 he ran only 15:50.7. As a mechanic in the army, he rose at 5:00 a.m. to walk the icy roads, then ran in the afternoon.

In 1918, on the Russian front, legend has it that he ran 15 kilometers in 59:24 with full equipment, including a knapsack containing 55 pounds of sand. He won a 20 kilometer race by over ten minutes. He received letters from Kolehmainen advising him to vary his training with speed work, but Nurmi did not absorb this advice immediately.

In 1920, he ran to a Finnish record of 8:36.3 for 3,000 meters. On the sea voyage to Antwerp for the Olympics, he was miserably seasick and some blame this for his defeat, but Nurmi offered no alibi. Even then he was beginning to practice non-communication, even by smile or frown, which was to help weave a legend among the strands of fact.

One legend, based on fact, was Nurmi's invincibility. Some say he could run faster if he wanted to. Three days after his defeat at Antwerp, that legend began. A frustrated Nurmi his blue eyes hiding his disappointment over his 5,000 meter loss to Joseph Guillemot of France, trailed the little man to the homestretch of the 10,000 meters.

Then the legend became reality, and all of Nurmi's desire and talent and hard training burst out into one massive show of strength. He rushed past Guillemot and won by eight yards in 31:45.8.

Three days after the 10,000, the sandy-haired Nurmi ran his third Olympic race. He was behind in the last 200 meters of the 9,000 meter cross country race, but once again he thrilled the crowd with a strong finish. He won by four yards.

Nurmi returned to Finland as a minor hero, but he was dissatisfied. He continued his morning walk of at least an hour, with a few spurts of running. He continued his afternoon workout of long, slow running from April through September. In his eagerness to improve, he added pace training.

He began to carry a stopwatch in his right hand, cocking his head to read it as he passed the posts along his training runs. His running style became a long, pleasing stride, heel touching first, his body and head erect and still, his elbows held high and wide.

It was his remarkable knowledge of pace which enabled him to set his first world record, in 1921. He ran 30:40.2 for 10,000 meters at Stockholm. Testing himself at the short end of the scale, with no speed training, he lost the 800 meters in the Finnish Championships by one yard in 1:58.4. He also ran a mile in 4:13.9, third fastest ever run.

In 1922, he forced the track world to take notice. He traveled to England to win AAA championships in the 4-mile and steeplechase. He went back home and delighted the Finns with three world records on consecutive weekends – 3,000 meters (8:28.6) on August 27, 2,000 meters (5:26.3) on September 4, and 5,000 meters (14:35.3) on September 12.

In 1923, a slender Swedish school teacher named Edvin Wide developed into a great runner and Swedes clamored for a race against Nurmi. Finns wanted Nurmi to ask for a distance of 10,000 meters to be safe, but Nurmi surprised them by asking for Wide's best distance – one mile. The classic race was seen by 18,000 spectators on August 23, at Stockholm's Olympic stadium, a long, low, gray-violet horseshoe with covered stands and two square watch towers at the north end.

According to legend, Nurmi had run a practice mile in 4:11 at a pace of 63, 63, 63, and 62, under the world record of 4:12.6, and he wanted to run such a pace here, but Wide had other plans.

The tow-headed Swede ran the first 440 yards on the 383-meter track in 58.6. Nurmi, stopwatch in hand, knew better than to follow such a suicide pace, but the excitement drew him down to 60.1.

With Wide ten yards ahead, Nurmi calmly continued his long straight-backed stride, making his own pace as if Wide did not exist. Wide led in 2:01.9, still eight yards ahead of Nurmi's 2:03.2.

The absurd pace began to take its toll. Wide slowed to 64.9 for the third quarter, and Nurmi moved ahead in 3:06.7. Then the gallant Swede forged ahead. With the few Finns unheard in the din, Nurmi raced past Wide on the backstretch and pulled away. At 1,500 meters, on the last curve, Nurmi was eight yards ahead and he won the mile by 18 yards.

Jubilant Finns ran from the stands to congratulate him, and

When day is done: Nurmi prepares to leave the stadium after winning the 1924 Olympic 1500 and 5000 within a 75-minute period.

then the announcer called out through a megaphone the electrifying results: Nurmi had run 1,500 meters in 3:53.0 and one mile in 4:10.4, both world records.

Legend has it, substantiated by those last 120 yards in a comfortable 17.4, that Nurmi could have run faster. Indeed, a year later, Nurmi's terse estimate of his own capability was 'Four minutes, four seconds, maybe.'

Whatever his capability, Nurmi helped build the legend most admirably the very next day. He set a world record for 3 miles (14:11.2) while defeating Wide by 90 yards in a 14:39.9 5,000. Then, on September 10 in Copenhagen, he lowered the 3,000 record to 8:27.8.

As world record holder at six distances from 1,500 to 10,000 meters, he was an outstanding favorite for any race he ran in the 1924 Olympics at Paris. He firmly believed he could win five races, but everything conspired to frustrate him.

First, the IAAF printed a schedule calling for the 5,000 meters to follow the 1,500 by half an hour. Outraged Finns protested and the schedule was widened to a hardly generous 55 minutes.

Second, he fell on an icy road on Easter Sunday and his knee was injured on a sharp stone. He could not walk for two weeks and then only with a stiff leg. When he attempted to run again he was shocked. He could not better 2:12 for 800 meters.

Third, Willie Ritola returned from the United States, where he had approached world record time at 4 miles and 10 miles. In the Olympic Trials in May, Ritola broke Nurmi's world record for 10,000 meters (30:35.4) and won a fast 5,000. A perturbed Nurmi could only win the 1,500 and 3,000 in slow times, and Ritola replaced Nurmi as Finland's current hero.

Grimly, Nurmi went to work, harder than ever. After his morning walk of 10 to 12 kilometers and some gym work, he rested an hour before going to the track. There he ran four or five furious sprints of 80 to 120 meters, then a fast 400 to 1,000 for time, followed by 3,000 to 4,000 meters with 'the last lap always very fast'. In the evening he ran 4,000 to 7,000 meters across country, punishing himself at the finish. He closed with four or five sprints.

'This daily training helped me to attain the condition I had at the 1924 Olympic Games.'

His condition became exciting in June. On the Helsinki track,

June 19, six days after his twenty-seventh birthday, he made a spectacular effort to prove he could run two races in one day.

He started the 1,500 meters with a deliberately reckless lap in 57.3. He passed 800 meters in 2:01 and 1,200 in 3:06. He finished comfortably with a new world record of 3:52.6. Fifty-five minutes later, he started the 5,000 meters and he ran 14:28.2, another world record.

Nothing like it had ever been done before, but still he was not permitted to run the Olympic 10,000. Finland did not want Nurmi and Ritola running each other into the ground in the first event. But if Nurmi would allow Ritola to win ... No!

Nurmi, who had coached Ritola on pacing methods, now fumed in silence. He was king of the runners. Why should he take a back seat to Ritola?

Legend has it that on the first day of Olympic competition in Paris, Nurmi ran 10,000 meters in 29:58 in solitary splendor on a training track while Ritola was winning the gold medal with a world record 30:23.2. One Finnish expert, Lauri Pikkala, denies there was such a run, but he believes Nurmi was capable of 29:30.

Two days later, Nurmi was untroubled in a heat of the 5,000 and the next day he won a mild 1,500 heat. The following day, July 10, he was determined to win the finals of both events.

The track in Stade de Colombes was 500 meters around and Nurmi aimed for 75 seconds for each of the first two laps, a bold pace of 60 seconds per 400 meters. Cocking his head toward the right to read his watch, he passed 400 meters in 58 seconds, 500 meters in 1:13, and 1,000 meters in 2:31, at least 15 yards faster than in his 4:10.4 mile.

Coolly, he tossed the watch aside and looked back. The nearest runner was 40 yards behind. Satisfied, Nurmi coasted the last lap in 82 seconds to win by nine yards in 3:53.6. Except for his need to save strength, he could have smashed the world record.

Excited thousands stood and cheered, but Nurmi ignored them. While some of his opponents collapsed, he stopped only to snatch up his sweat clothes. Then he jogged off to the dressing-room. He had expected victory; his concern was for the 5,000.

He rested on a mattress in the dressing-room and received a massage. Legend has it that he slept.

In less than an hour he was back on the track, running the 5,000 final. Ritola and Wide set out at a fantastic pace of 2:46.4

for 1,000 meters and Nurmi trailed by 40 yards. The spectators knew Nurmi was attempting an unreasonable double and they were not really disappointed. Only Nurmi knew what he was doing. Calmly, glancing at his stopwatch, he gradually caught up.

They passed 2,000 meters in 5:43.6, and after another lap Nurmi took the lead. After 3,000 meters in 8:42.6, a suddenly discouraged Wide dropped far behind, but Ritola, who had set an Olympic record for the steeplechase the previous day, was determined to beat Nurmi.

Nurmi increased the pace by two seconds per lap, passing 4,000 meters in 11:38.8, but Ritola stayed on his heels. At the bell, Nurmi took one last look at his time and tossed the watch aside. The crowd stood, cheering.

Ritola fought alongside in the home stretch while Nurmi remained the gracefully erect stylist with long, bounding, hip-rolling strides, his arms carried high. Nurmi's blue eyes were coldly calculating as he looked over at Ritola, spurted ahead, and kept him a frustrating meter behind all the way to the tape.

This was the day Nurmi earned such nicknames as 'The Flying Finn' and 'The Phantom Finn'. As great as his double victory was – and it is not likely to be equalled – the strife between Ritola and Nurmi was not yet settled. Each had won two gold medals and Nurmi's close margin in the 5,000 left many fans unsure of his superiority over a longer distance. Two days later, a ruthless Nurmi set out to remove all doubt.

After a day of rest (nothing to do except run a heat of the 3,000 meter team race in 8:47.8 while running up and back to urge his team to a qualifying effort), they lined up for the start of the 9,000 meter cross country race under a blazing sun. It was the hottest day Paris had known in many years – 102 degrees.

Ritola set off at a vicious pace, obviously out to run away with it. Nurmi, knowing the pace was foolish, stuck with Ritola anyway. He had plans for Ritola.

After 3,000 meters, along the Seine, Wide let go and it was between Nurmi and Ritola on the cobbled streets. For four miles Nurmi stayed with this man who most seriously challenged his superiority. In that oppressive heat, behind such a fast pace, only 15 of the 39 starters finished, and many of them went to the hospital, but Nurmi prepared to go faster.

He felt as tired as Ritola looked, but he intended to crush him. Suddenly, Nurmi surged away. Quickly, he gained 100 yards. Ritola gave up and finished almost a minute and a half behind although still a minute ahead of the bronze medalist.

A great roar of cheering greeted Nurmi's entrance into the stadium. He ran to the finish magnificently serene, in sharp contrast to the staggering, collapsing runners who followed.

Nurmi had changed his shoes before Ritola entered the stadium and now a close friend, Hannes Kolehmainen, saw Nurmi do something he almost never did in public. He saw Nurmi inspect the bedraggled Ritola and smile.

Nurmi had run six times in five days, but one more day remained. Running against a much-subdued Ritola, Nurmi won the 3,000 meter team race by 50 yards in 8:32.0. It was his fourth individual championship of the 1924 Olympics and he was further honored with two more gold medals as a member of Finland's winning teams in the 3,000 and cross country.

At this point in his career he was the proud owner of eight gold medals and one silver, plus six world records, and he was hailed as the athletic wonder of the world. Anyone except Nurmi might have been satisfied, but he knew he could have won the 10,000. He had lost his world record to Ritola, and he wanted it.

At Kuopio, Finland, on August 31, he shattered the unfortunate Ritola's 10,000 meter record with 30:06.1. Nurmi also collected official records for 4 miles (19:18.7), 5 miles (24:13.1), and one-half hour (9,957 meters). Unhappily, his 29:07.1 for 6 miles was not official.

A month later, at Viipuri, October 1, Nurmi added to his renown. He broke his 4-mile record with 19:15.6 and went on to 5 miles in 24:06.2. His collection of world records stood at the magnificent total of ten.

Nurmi had a good job as a paper-hanger, hired by the best families in Finland so they could point with pride to his work, but he gave it up to tour the United States in 1925. Americans stood in line and thousands were turned away without seeing the Olympic hero. Some American bankers appraised the good will Nurmi won for Finland as worth ten million dollars.

On January 6, at the Finnish-American Athletic Club Games in Madison Square Garden, Nurmi was first seen by the eager American public. They were shocked when he ran $2\frac{1}{2}$ miles to

Paavo Nurmi

warm up. They were enraptured when the balding, stolid man in white shorts and blue jersey set a pace of 59.0 and 2:02.5 trying to escape from Joie Ray in the mile.

They were excited when Ray passed Nurmi in the third quarter. But with 250 yards to go, Nurmi raced past Ray and won by three yards in indoor record time of 4:13.6, collecting the 1,500 meter record as well.

The crowd was surprised to see Nurmi on the track eating a large red apple shortly afterward. And they were amazed an hour and a half later when he defeated Ritola with an indoor record of 14:44.6 for 5,000 meters.

The spectators here, as everywhere, were most impressed because Nurmi never appeared to extend himself. And yet he broke seven indoor records in five races in his first 12 days.

He ran at least 68 races in the United States, setting records in many of them. Some, at odd distances, only bore the name 'Noteworthy Performances' in the record books, but they had the Nurmi quality. For example, his $1\frac{7}{8}$ miles in 8:29.0 was 20 yards farther than 3,000 meters, making his time superior to his outdoor record.

Enthusiastic crowds saw him circle the small tracks in record time for 2,000 meters (5:22.4), 3,000 meters (8:26.4), and 2 miles (8:58.2), all faster than the outdoor world records. He excited them with a mile record of 4:12.0 on Buffalo's flat floor on March 7. He disappointed them only twice. He failed to finish behind Ritola in a 5,000 when he suffered stomach cramps, and he lost a close 880 challenge to three-time AAU champion Allan Hellfrich.

Nurmi's tour was a great success athletically, but it was bad for him. His already withdrawn personality was further affected by ugly accusations of exorbitant expenses, later disproved. His health deteriorated. He suffered from shin splints and several other injuries. One historian wrote, 'It took Nurmi three years to regain his style.' Another, more gloomy, said Nurmi never fully recovered. In any case, Nurmi set no outdoor records in 1925.

But he once said, 'I love to run. It is my life. As long as I can run I shall do so.' And in 1926 he was good enough to lower his 3,000 meter record twice, to 8:25.4 and then to 8:20.4 at Stockholm, July 13. Four days later, at Viborg, Finland, he anchored a 6,000 meter relay team to a world record 16:11.4, breaking their own 16:26.2.

He was in Berlin on September 11 for the greatest 1,500 meter race ever run. Edvin Wide was there, better than ever, and Dr Otto Peltzer of Germany was to be feared. Peltzer was the world record holder for the 880 and so fast he had set a world record for 500 meters in June. Nurmi's only hope was to set a fast pace.

He passed 400 meters in 61 flat and 800 in 2:02.2, but he was not the magnificent champion of two years ago. His pace slipped to 2:34.4 at 1,000 meters, three seconds slower than his Olympic pace.

Wide and Peltzer passed him in the last stretch and Peltzer's finishing speed lowered Nurmi's world record to 3:51.0. Wide, only three yards behind, was given 3:51.8, while Nurmi approached his world record with 3:52.8.

The next day, Nurmi knew he was not right and he endured another rare defeat. He lost the 2-mile race by 20 yards to Wide's world record 9:01.4.

Further deterioration of Nurmi's supremacy came in 1927. He regained the world 2,000 meter record from Wide with 5:24.6, but he lost it later when Eino Borg ran 5:23.4. (Borg's time was not as impressive as Nurmi's indoor record 5:22.4.)

Now Nurmi concentrated his ambition toward the Olympic Games. On July 29, 1928, he started off with 23 hopeful 10,000 meter runners on the 400 meter track in the Grand Stadium of Amsterdam. Around they went, past the covered stands on each stretch, separated from the cheering spectators by a 500-meter cycling track and a moat. At 5,000 meters in 15:11, all had dropped back except Nurmi's two dangerous opponents, Ritola and Wide.

On the 18th lap, Wide began to fall behind and once again Nurmi was alone with Ritola. He kept the pace fast, but Ritola would not let go. On the last lap, Nurmi began a long kick. He built up a lead of four precious yards over Ritola. Around the curve he held it. Down the homestretch he held it, all the way to the tape. His time of 30:18.8, good on the soft track, broke Ritola's Olympic record.

Two days later, Nurmi ran a comfortable heat in the 5,000, but on the next day he bore the indignities of the steeplechase. A novice hurdler, he fell heavily in the water jump. Wet and shaken, he climbed out and resumed running, and he managed to qualify for the final. Two days later they ran the 5,000 final.

Once again the three veterans ran together until the last two crucial laps. Then Wide dropped back. With 600 meters to go, Ritola began a long drive. At the bell, Nurmi was on Ritola's heels, 15 meters ahead of Wide. But on the last curve, with Ritola running hard for the tape, Nurmi could not keep up. He had to strain to hold off Wide by seven yards. He finished 12 yards behind Ritola and fell on the grass, exhausted.

The next day, Ritola dropped out of the steeplechase. Nurmi trailed early, but he moved up to a comfortable second place at the finish. Sports writers stated positively that Nurmi let his friend, Toivo Loukola, cross the line first, but once again this must be classified as interesting legend.

Nurmi, very disappointed, said later, 'If I had not been ill, my success at Amsterdam would have been as great as at Paris in 1924.'

Nurmi's dazzling collection now contained nine Olympic gold medals and three silver. As far back as 1925 he had declared his ultimate goal to be a victory in the 1932 Olympic marathon, and so now he was eager to run longer distances. On October 7, in Berlin, he ran one of his greatest races.

Circling the track at a steady pace, he probably bettered Shrubb's world record for 8 miles, but, unfortunately, no time was recorded. At 9 miles his pace was still fast and he was undoubtedly under Shrubb's record of 45:27.6. Lack of official timing deprived him of another world record. He ran past 15,000 meters (124 yards longer than $9\frac{1}{4}$ miles) in 46:49.6, 29 seconds under Jean Bouin's 15-year-old record.

Continuing his severe pace, Nurmi passed 10 miles in 50:15.0, 25 seconds under Shrubb's 24-year-old record. He increased his pace only slightly near the end, but he collected his third world record of the day by covering 11 miles 1,648 yards in one hour.

German observers were astonished because Nurmi showed no sign of distress, and yet his 10-mile and one hour records were to last 17 years.

In 1929, Nurmi was talked into another sea voyage to the United States for indoor racing, but he was in poor shape and after losing a slow mile to American indoor champion Ray Conger, he returned home, embittered. It appeared to be the end of the road for the 32-year-old Nurmi, but he still liked to run.

In 1930, he travelled to London, and on June 9, after a half-hour nap on a table, he added to his glory with the world 6-mile record in 29:36.4, a time he had beaten in the 10,000 meters without official recognition. Afterward, in the shower, he commented, 'Not a good time; the track was bad.'

He won the Finnish 10,000 meter championship in 31:04.6. Then, in Stockholm on September 3, his relentless pace carried him to another world record. His 20,000 meters in 1:04:38.4 knocked a minute and 51 seconds off the old record.

In 1931, great young Finnish runners were maturing while Nurmi's age and recurrent rheumatism were weakening his fierce claim to the number one position he had held for 12 years. On July 24 in Helsinki, he ran an exciting 2-mile race against Finland's three best: Lauri Lehtinen, Lasse Virtanen, and Volmari Iso-Hollo, who were to win a total of eight Olympic medals between them.

Nurmi, not one to give up easily, ran with his young rivals for lap after lap and they actually pulled away from Iso-Hollo. On the last lap, with the crowd cheering wildly, Nurmi was second behind Lehtinen, but Virtanen was on his heels. It looked bad for the old champion as they ran past 3,000 meters.

Suddenly, Nurmi electrified the crowd by passing Lehtinen. They pulled away from Virtanen. Then the old master gradually widened his margin over Lehtinen. All three finished under Wide's world record: Virtanen 9:01.1, Lehtinen 9:00.5 and Nurmi 8:59.5.

After such a triumph, Nurmi's chances in the 1932 Olympics seemed good at his regular distances, but he was determined to run the marathon and, possibly, the 10,000. Then the IAAF shocked Finland by doing what no runner could do. They barred Nurmi for alleged violations of his expense accounts during the 1929 season.

'My heart bleeds to end a career by winning the marathon.' And the stoic Finn had tears in his eyes.

Never a quitter, Nurmi hoped he would be reinstated and so he continued to train. In a marathon race on June 26 in Viipuri, Finland, he led by a mile and a quarter over Armas Toivonen before he ran off course. His time for 35 yards short of 25 miles was 2:22:03.8. Six weeks later, Toivonen finished only 36 seconds behind the Olympic marathon winner at Los Angeles, but Nurmi's suspension was not lifted and his great international career was ended, with nine of his world records still in the books.

Since 1920 he had won seven Olympic races and set world records in the astonishing total of 16 individual events plus one relay, even though collecting records did not seem important to him. At least six times he lost the enjoyment of world records at intermediate distances because they were not timed officially. Seven other times he broke his own world record, and he bettered outdoor records in at least five indoor races. Thus, astounding as it may seem, he ran faster than an existing world record at least 35 times.

He lost three Olympic races, under extenuating circumstances, and only two other races of consequence – on consecutive days during a bad year. He was never beaten in a race longer than 5,000 meters. No runner before or since has been so successful over such a wide range of distances.

His imprint on the track world was greater than any man's, before or after. He, more than any man, raised track to the glory of a major sport in the eyes of international fans, and they honored him as one of the truly great athletes of all sports.

Even at the age of 36 he loved to run. In 1933 he was still an amateur in Finland and he entered the Finnish Championships at Turku. To get the maximum competition, he ran in the 1,500 meters against Lehtinen, who was now the Olympic champion and world record holder at 5,000 meters.

Calmly, Nurmi followed Lehtinen to the homestretch. Then he burst past with impressive power. The old man won by nine yards.

Nurmi's farewell comment was typically tart: 'I thought Lehtinen was better than that.'

Nineteen years later, when visiting spectators went into the stadium for the 1952 Olympic Games in Helsinki, they were stirred by a bronze statue of one of Finland's great heroes, Paavo Nurmi. Inside, the highlight of the opening ceremony was the appearance of the torch bearer, whose identity was kept secret until the gigantic electric scoreboard produced goose pimples, lumps in throats, and wild cheers from 80,000 people with the single word ... NURMI.

JESSE OWENS

Right from the beginning, anyone who watched Jesse Owens run could see his unmistakable quality, both in his beautifully fluid grace and his sheer speed.

The first track coach who saw this graceful speed, in a game of tag, felt a surprise and pleasure like the first expert to recognize the Koh-i-noor diamond.

This obvious talent was properly motivated in 1928 when Charley Paddock, 'The World's Fastest Human,' stood on the stage in Cleveland, Ohio, and inspired the junior high school students.

'I met him later in the coach's office,' says Owens, 'and I was so impressed that I decided right then that I would become The World's Fastest Human by winning the 100 meters championship in the Olympic Games.'

Coach Charley Riley recalls, 'Jesse ran so fast I thought my stop watch was out of order.' As a high school junior at Cleveland East Tech in 1932, Jesse Owens hit the tape first in both sprints and won the broad jump in Ohio's state meet. His best jump was 24' 1¼", less than 1½ inches from the national high school record.

On June 11, he took his marks in a district Olympic qualifying meet in Cleveland. Local spectators were not surprised to see him win, but his time, even with wind, brought forth a surprised cheer. It was 10.3, equal to the world record.

Even though he failed to qualify in the regionals, track fans thought he was a remarkable prospect, but they had not seen anything yet. As a lithe, mature senior, Owens sailed through the air for a startling high school record of 24' 11¼". Only the best 15 men in history had jumped farther.

In the state meet, he won three events again, speeding gracefully along the track for a national high school record of 20.8 in his heat of the 220. On June 17 at Chicago's Stagg Field, he ran wild in the national interscholastic meet against the best available high school athletes. He broad jumped 24′ 9½″ and sped to amazing high school records of 9.4 and 20.7, compared with the world records of 9.4 and 20.6.

As the greatest high school star of all time, he returned to Chicago two weeks later for a hectic weekend in the national AAU meet. He ran behind Jimmy Johnson in the junior 100. He leaped to victory in the junior broad jump at 24′ 2⅛″. In heats and final of the senior 100 meters he ran against the great Ralph Metcalfe, the current Fastest Human. Metcalfe pulled away to win and Johnson also beat Owens. Then, easing his disappointment, Owens became a national champion with a broad jump of 24′ 6⅜″.

Some twenty-eight colleges and universities sought Owens and he chose Ohio State. When he was born J. C. Owens on September 12, 1913, in Danville, Alabama, one of eight children of a cotton picker, his chances for a university education were limited. When he was six, he had to pick cotton to help out, and he was run over by a cotton drag. But his family moved to Cleveland ... and opportunity. He worked in a gasoline station as a freshman at Ohio State, became a good student, and developed his track technique.

Track coach Larry Snyder made some interesting discoveries: Owens' arm action was too short. Owens's broad jump run was 14 feet too short. Owens needed a hitch kick to maintain balance in the air. And surprisingly enough, Owens waited at the start of a race until he saw the others move.

'Jesse Owens listens,' Snyder said, 'and then he tries to put the suggestions into practice. He is so well coordinated that even a radical form change ... becomes part of his style after a very few practice sessions.'

Early in 1934 Owens opened a few eyes in New York with a world indoor record of 25′ 3¼″ in the AAU broad jump. He placed third in the 60 meters behind Metcalfe and Ben Johnson. Owens came back in exciting fashion to beat Johnson in the NYKC Games. He equalled the indoor record for 60 yards with 6.2.

Outdoors, he ran another 9.4 and defended his AAU broad jump championship with 25′ ⅞″, but in the 100 he again had to run against Metcalfe, the greatest sprinter in history. Owens had

Jesse Owens

hopes all the way to the last 20 yards when Metcalfe's big figure powered past.

Thus, Owens entered his sophomore year as a renowned broad jumper, but he had yet to win a major sprint race. Working as the most popular page boy in the legislature, he competed in several indoor meets. He won the Millrose 60 in 6.3. He set a record of 6.6 for 60 meters in an AAU semi-final, but he lost to Johnson's incredible start in the final. He lost a dual meet 60 to Willis Ward in 6.2, but he avenged that defeat in the Big Ten Championship on a dirt track with the first 6.1 ever run.

The broad jump at the 1935 indoor AAU meet was fierce competition. Eulace Peacock broke Owens' indoor record with 25' $3\frac{1}{2}$''. Owens retaliated with remarkable jumps beyond 25 feet, including 25' 9'' and 25' $7\frac{1}{2}$''. Later, in the NYKC Games, Owens lost to Peacock by $1\frac{1}{4}$ inches.

Owens worked hard in training. He began a session with comfortable striding. He ran a 50 to 75 yard dash five or six times from the starting gun. He toiled over three low hurdles, straining his natural 7-foot stride in order to clear the first hurdle. Three times a week he ran the first 300 yards with 50-second quarter-milers, then burst into an astounding 15 or 20 yard lead at 440 yards. He took a few carefree practice jumps three times a week.

Outdoors, he covered 100 yards in 8.4 with a running start. At the Drake Relays he ran 9.5 and broad jumped 26' $1\frac{3}{4}$'', third best of all time. Only $\frac{3}{8}$'' short of the world record, Owens took off seven inches behind the board. An enthusiastic coach Snyder said, 'Owens can jump 27 feet.'

Owens breezed to four victories in a quadrangular meet, including sprints of 9.4 and 20.7. The next meet was a day to go down in history.

Ten thousand people went to the Big Ten meet at Ferry Field in Ann Arbor, Michigan, on May 25, 1935, hoping to see a new broad jump record. But Owens was worried about his sore back, injured while rolling down stairs in a playful scuffle.

'I had to be helped to the automobile that took us to the field, and my teammates practically dressed me into my track outfit.'

It was the first really hot day of spring, with a wind under 3 m.p.h. At 3:15 p.m., when he was supposed to run the 100, he says, 'I could hardly go to my mark at the start ... but when the starter said, "Get set," my pain left.'

The gun cracked and Owens was off fast. He pulled away steadily and beat Bob Gieve, one of the nation's best college sprinters. The time was 9.4, equalling the world record, but it was a yard or more faster than any modern 9.4.

The Michigan officials were more reluctant than any known timers to give fast times. They actually timed 'the center of gravity' instead of the first part of the torso to reach the line, as the rules specify. Secondly, the watches stopped surprisingly close to 9.3. Thus, Owens' time was certainly as worthy as a present-day 9.3 and probably 9.2.

Ten minutes later Owens half crouched at the head of the runway, ready for his first broad jump. In the sand near the world record distance, he had optimistically placed a piece of paper as a marker. Other athletes gathered to watch, and the avid spectators were so silent they could hear his footsteps as he sped toward the white board.

The steel spikes in his left shoe hit the board with a rousing sound heard high in the stands. Owens' left leg went forward once in a full stride as his body rose awesomely high. His feet thrust out ahead and cut into the sand, leaving the marker undisturbed.

After the suspenseful measurement, the announcer led Owens to the edge of the track and said, 'Ladies and gentlemen, I wish to introduce a world's champion.'

Owens' mark was 26' 8¼". It was the only jump he took that day, but it remained as the best in the world for 25 years.

At 3:45, far down at the end of the straightaway, Owens took his marks in the third lane, eager for a 220 record. At the gun he was off so fast he never saw his opponents. No longer worried about his back, he shot down the long straightaway, his lithe body erect, his legs flashing swiftly back and forth in beautiful strides.

As if two world records were not enough, his time here set the fans to shaking their heads in open-mouthed wonder. His 20.3 was a new world record for both 200 meters and 220 yards.

Fifteen minutes later, the now delirious crowd watched in tense silence as Owens ran as hard as he could, sweeping over the low

Jesse Owens

hurdles on the now unkempt track. He was happy with his time, a world record 22.6, although two of the three official watches showed 22.4. Both the 200 meter and 220 yard records lasted 12 years.

Within one glorious hour, Owens had squeezed in a whole career of superlatives – six entries in the world record book.

'When the meet was over the pain returned to my back and I had to be practically carried to the dressing-room.'

After winning three firsts in the Central Collegiate meet and four in a dual meet against Southern California, Owens attempted the unprecedented feat of winning four events in the National Collegiates at Berkeley, California.

He jumped 26′ 1¾″ in the trials on Friday. Then, running against a 9 m.p.h. wind on June 22, the 5′ 10″, 160-pound 'Ebony Antelope' thrilled the crowd with his graceful speed. He defeated Peacock by a surprising two yards in a 9.8 100. He beat George Anderson by two feet in a 21.5 220. He rested while the 2-mile was run, and then he beat the great Glenn Hardin by three yards in a 23.4 low hurdles race.

No other man has ever won more than half as many events in one NCAA meet.

After the meet, coach Snyder told Owens, 'So far as we are concerned, the keyed-up, highly competitive track season is over.' He advised Owens to make no particular effort 'to keep in strict training.'

A relaxed Owens beat Peacock again in the Far Western AAU. In the national AAU, before 15,000 people at Lincoln, Nebraska, he faced Peacock, Metcalfe, and George Anderson, who had been timed in an unbelievable 9.2 by seven timers in May. Peacock beat Owens in a heat in 10.2, fastest on record, but it was disallowed because of wind.

In the final, Owens ran well for half the distance, but an inspired Peacock pulled away and Metcalfe passed Owens. Peacock won in 10.2 with a wind of 7.76 m.p.h., 3¼ m.p.h. too fast for a record.

In the broad jump, Owens came through in a courageous defense of his championship with a good 26′ 2¼″, but Peacock leaped ¾ of an inch farther.

Owens needed his best to win in that company, and Peacock edged him out twice more in 100's in the next week. Thus, three

Jesse Owens

of Owens' four failures since high school came at the end of a hard season after his coach told him to ease off.

He went back home for a well-earned rest. He resumed his $3 a day job in the Ohio State House, and he was married. One reporter described him as a 'mannered, suave college student'.

Owens was ineligible for indoor collegiate competition in 1936. He lost to Peacock by one foot in the Cleveland 50 yard dash. Outdoors, in practice, he ran 300 yards in 29.5, a remarkable time when compared with the official world record of 30 seconds flat.

He won four events in three dual meets and he was well on his way to repeating his four Big Ten championships when disaster struck. He fell in the low hurdles, and at the halfway point he was far behind Bob Osgood of Michigan, a 23.5 man. Owens began to run as he never ran before.

Coach Snyder raved about it: 'Jesse gained the 19 plus one yard to win by a yard. I think it was the fastest 100 yards ever run by any human being and he cleared five hurdles while doing it.' Owens' time was 23.5.

He defended his three Central Collegiate titles. His great performances for the season included another 9.4 100, a 9.3 with wind, the second fastest ever 220 in 20.5, and an American record 21.1 220 around a turn.

The important NCAA meet was at Stagg Field, Chicago, June 19 and 20. In a heat of the 100 meters, Owens ran a puzzling 11.2. The distance turned out to be 110 meters, and so Owens had the finest time ever recorded for 110 meters or 120 yards.

In the final, Owens flashed past 100 yards in another 9.4 and won in 10.2, a world record good enough to last 20 years.

Owens defended his broad jump title at 25' $10\frac{7}{8}$", glided around a curve to win a 21.3 200 meters (and 21.4 220), and completed his second brilliant quadruple victory with a 23.1 in the 220 low hurdles.

Next came the AAU meet at Princeton, N.J., on a hot July 4. Owens regained his broad jump title with only two jumps, reaching 26' 3", but his most significant event was the 100 meters where he had yet to win an AAU championship.

He was behind Sam Stoller at 50 meters, but he led Metcalfe by a safe three yards. He ran away from Stoller, while the powerful

Metcalfe could gain only four feet on him. Owens had his first victory over Metcalfe, in 10.4.

The suspense-filled Final Trials for the Olympic team, held on the following weekend in the humid, 100 degree heat of Randall's Island, New York, was the most important meet yet for Owens. He broad jumped 25′ 10¾″ to win. The way he was running this season, he was favored in the 100 and he beat Metcalfe by five feet in 10.4. He was now on the team in two events, but the 200 promised trouble.

Coming off the curve into the homestretch, Metcalfe was leading, but Mack Robinson was catching him. Owens was challenged for the third spot on the team by Bobby Packard. For a moment Owens was in danger, but he turned on his smooth power and swept past spectacularly to win by two feet in 21 flat, an American record around a curve.

Next came a sea voyage to Germany with a dangerous loss of conditioning. Owens seemed vigorous in Berlin, but then came Hitler's 'Aryan superiority' and some unexpected German triumphs on the field. It was a nervous Jesse Owens who took his marks for the 100 meters heat on August 2.

The expectant morning crowd of 80,000 was far larger than any track crowd Owens had seen. No runner in Owens' heat could threaten him, but he ran fast anyway, winning by an extravagant eight yards. His Olympic record equalling time of 10.3 was not allowed because of wind.

He had left the village on the bus early that morning, and he had to wait nervously for the 12th heat. Now he was afraid he would miss the bus back for lunch. After this first day, coach Snyder arranged for a cot in the peaceful quiet of the dressing-room, and Owens carried a cold lunch.

Owens 'ran scared' again in the quarter-finals that afternoon before 110,000 spectators including Adolf Hitler, rocking with frenetic excitement in a box jutting out from the second deck. Owens ran 10.2 again with wind.

On August 3, Owens was more composed, and he breezed home confidently in 10.4 against Frank Wykoff and Lennart Strandberg in the semi-final. But in the final he was anxious to win, and, as coach Snyder says, 'He was always best when the blue chips were down.'

The big German starter in his white coat raised his pistol and said, 'Get set,' in German. Owens came to the set position. Then the anxious wait. Two seconds seemed like ten. The gun fired. Owens shot out of his holes with a good start. With one of the fastest accelerations ever seen, Owens drove to a startling 10-foot lead over Metcalfe in the first 25 yards.

Then the powerful Metcalfe began to reach full speed, and he cut down the distance between them alarmingly. Owens ran smoothly through the tape, four feet ahead of Metcalfe and he was an Olympic champion, exactly as he had planned eight years before. Only he was not quite through yet.

With the theory of Aryan supremacy crumbling before his very eyes, Hitler was seen to make a hasty exit before Owens mounted the victory stand for his gold medal. Der Führer presented no more medals.

August 4 was a busy day for Owens, with four appearances. In the morning he sped around the curve and qualified safely for the 200 meter quarter-finals in Olympic record time of 21.1, but the broad jump qualifying was exciting.

He jogged unsuspectingly to the broad jump runway and awaited his turn. Still in his sweat clothes he ran down the runway to check his step. To his horror, an official waved a red flag, signalling a foul jump. Owens' protest was to no avail. He had one foul against him and he still did not have his step.

Hopefully, he sped down the runway, but his left foot hit two inches beyond the board and again the ominous red flag waved. Now he was within one jump of being eliminated from his best event and all he needed was a jump of 23' 5½".

Worried now, Owens walked away from the pit. Someone put a hand on his shoulder and said hello. He turned to see a smiling Luz Long of Germany, his chief rival for the broad jump championship. Long, a blond Aryan in plain view of about 70,000 Germans, offered advice to his black rival. Gratefully, Owens drew a line a foot behind the line and moved his takeoff back accordingly.

Faced with disaster, he raced down the runway, holding his stride in so he would not foul. He overdid it and took off two feet behind the board. It was not a good jump, for him, and he watched anxiously while the officials measured a mark perilously close to the qualifying standard. His jump measured 23' 5 9/16". One eighth of an inch less would have meant shocking failure.

In the afternoon, a strong wind came up, and all the jumps in the final were wind-aided. Almost casually, Owens sandwiched in a quarter-final of the 200 meters in 21.1, aided by a wind of 8.27 m.p.h.

Owens' first jump was 25' 4¾". It was a relief to be in the lead, but Luz Long came back on his second trial to tie. Owens, who had expected this to be his easiest event, had to draw upon his competitive courage. On his second jump, his heels cut the sand at 25' 9¾". Long's third jump fell an inch short, but it was a threat. Owens jumped 25' 5¼" and then fouled his fourth trial.

Long's fifth jump was 25' 9¾", an exact tie, and the German crowd roared. Now Owens felt the pressure, but to him that meant a better effort. He sprinted down the runway, leaped high into the air, and whipped his legs in a graceful running motion to keep from falling to his left. His jump was 26' ½".

Long fouled his last jump and Owens was the champion, but he increased his Olympic record to 26' 5¼" on his last attempt. Long was the first to congratulate Owens and they walked arm-in-arm.

Owens bubbled with joy. When photographers asked for a jump for the cameras he agreed readily. Fully warmed up, he streaked down the runway and gave it all he had. The jump was not measured, but Brutus Hamilton is sure it was over 27 feet and he told Owens so.

'I wouldn't be surprised,' Owens agreed. 'I felt good, hit the board just right, and thought for a moment I wasn't coming down.'

That was his last broad jump. Hamilton says, 'I'm certain in my own mind that Jesse could have leaped at least a foot farther had he taken a few weeks to concentrate upon his event in his prime.... He didn't care much for the event and never practiced.'

August 5 was 200 meters day. Owens coasted prettily through his semi-final in 21.3, saving himself for what he knew would be a difficult race. His team-mate, Mack Robinson, had finished only two feet behind Owens in the Final Trials and today Robinson won the first semi-final in an alarming 21.1.

The wind let down a little for the final and a light drizzle began to fall. Owens kept a wary eye on Robinson ahead of him to the right, and he ran the curve to catch him. Into the stretch he led Robinson satisfactorily by two yards, but he was tired from four days of competition. He forced himself down the home-stretch as the rain fell harder, and he gained another yard.

He hit the tape three yards ahead in 20.7, a time superior to his straightaway record of 20.3.

Row upon row, the spectators rose to their feet before Adolf Hitler and paid tribute to this Negro youth whose talent and competitive courage were unsurpassed. Owens stood in the rain for a moment of wonder. He had come a long way from Alabama.

He was bothered constantly by autograph hunters and photographers – at the stadium, at the dormitory, at meals. On August 8, after two days of 'rest', Owens ran the important leadoff leg in a heat of the 400 meter relay, followed by Metcalfe, Foy Draper, and Wykoff. They ran 40 flat to equal the world record.

Next day, in the final, Owens showed his marvelous pickup. He blasted out in front and beat his nearest opponent by about six yards. His team-mates increased the lead to 11 yards and they set a new world record of 39.8.

On the victory stand, with a laurel wreath on his head, a diploma in one hand, a tiny potted oak tree in the other, and his fourth gold medal around his neck, Owens felt wonderful. 'That's a grand feeling, standing up there. I never felt like that before.'

He was the toast of the athletic world. Invitations poured into compete all over Europe, and the AAU, in need of money to pay for the Olympic trip, signed contracts for his services without his knowledge.

He had to run a 100 meters race the very next day at Cologne. He was more than two yards ahead of Metcalfe with 20 meters to go but he eased up to let his friend win. When Metcalfe's time was announced as 10.3, it was obvious Owens had given away a world record. Tired, he also lost the broad jump for the first time that year, to Wilhelm Leichum.

Owens ran several times, including 10.3 at Bochum, August 12, and then his last competition was in a relay in White City, London, on August 15. The AAU had rented him out for more races in Sweden, but he was tired. Telegrams had been coming in streams, offering money, and Owens was advised to take what he could and set himself up for life. He returned to New York on the Queen Mary instead of going to Sweden, and he was suspended by the AAU even though he had never signed an entry blank for a Swedish meet.

'I've lost six pounds,' he explained, 'being circused and pushed all over Europe. I'm burned out and tired of being treated like a head of cattle. I'm turning professional because I'm busted and know the difficulties encountered by any member of my race in getting financial security...because if I have money I can help my race like Booker T. Washington...because I owe it to my wife...and because after I have made some money I hope to go into politics and do something for my people.'

He still had a year of college eligibility and wonderful potential, but the most sensational career in track history came to an abrupt end. Ironically, none of the 'fabulous' offers were acceptable.

Owens had stopped the watches at 9.4 five times; only Frank Wykoff had ever done it twice. No other man had cleared the uncommon distance of 26 feet more than once; Owens did it seven times. He never lost in outdoor college competition; in only two years he won more events than any other collegian. His indoor and outdoor world records in the broad jump and his Olympic record each lasted an astounding 25 years, longer than any other records in modern history.

He set official world records in seven events, plus two unofficial records and three indoor records. He never lost at 220 yards or 200 meters.

Sportswriters and fans, individually and in polls, have proclaimed Jesse Owens the greatest track and field athlete of all time. Certainly, he accomplished more in two years than any other athlete...or in one week...or in one hour...

CORNELIUS WARMERDAM

Greatness comes in many forms. It can appear in a single moment or accumulate over a long career, but all great athletes have one thing in common... an unquestioned superiority over their opponents.

In the entire history of track and field, no athlete's superiority has been so unquestioned as Warmerdam's.

To Cornelius Warmerdam, bright, tow-headed third son of an American immigrant from Holland (and thus affectionately known as 'Dutch'), the concept of himself as a superior athlete was distressingly slow in coming. Modesty is not an outstanding characteristic of the very great, but Dutch Warmerdam was different. He was unassuming to an unusually pleasant degree.

In his early years as a vaulter, he had something to be modest about. A fine student who skipped the third grade, he received his diploma from high school in Hanford, California, before he was seventeen. Handicapped by his tender age, his vaulting progress had reached only 12' 3" from his eight feet at age 12 and nine feet at age 13. His greatest triumph was a tie for third in the 1932 California state high school meet.

College coaches did not clamor for his services. 'The opportunity of going on to school was limited in those days. Junior colleges did not exist and money was scarce.' Dutch farmers work like beavers, and Warmerdam had worked hard from the age of ten on his father's 40 acres of peaches and apricots. Now he worked on the ranch for a year and a half instead of attending college.

He liked to pole vault, however, and he had built his first uprights at the age of ten. Now his runway and pit were on their fruit drying field.

One summer day in 1933, a curious salesman, tipped off by the high school track coach, stopped his car on the road and watched with amazement as a lean, fair-haired youth sprinted on the other side of a spinach patch carrying a long pole. He saw the boy vault over a crossbar more than twice his own height. Soon after, the excited salesman was talking to Fresno State track coach Flint Hanner.

'I just saw a kid jumping well over 13 feet... in a spinach patch.'

Hanner said, 'That's not much of a broad jump.'

Soon after being corrected on that point, Hanner hastened to the ranch. Warmerdam was happy to begin Fresno State in the spring of 1934, when he vaulted a promising 13' 6".

In 1935, still not quite twenty years old, Warmerdam squirmed over the bar at 14' $1\frac{7}{8}''$ in a dual meet, less than five inches from the world record. In the West Coast Relays at Fresno, he tied for first at 13' $6\frac{1}{2}''$ with five men, including Earle Meadows and Bill Sefton.

Warmerdam's progress was now satisfactory, though hardly world-shaking. Unfortunately for his track career, his personal philosophy prevented him from faster development as a vaulter. He valued other things in life besides pole vaulting. He never trained in the summer, as all successful athletes must do now. In the fall, he trained only when he wanted to prepare for indoor meets, and those did not begin until 1939. In college, he enjoyed bastketball during the winter months, and he was good enough to be a high scorer and captain of the team.

In 1936, he raised his personal record only one inch, hampered by a bad ankle. 'I missed several meets because it hurt to jump.' His only triumph was a tie for first in the Drake Relays at 13' 8". At the end of June, he competed in the Far Western semifinal trials for the Olympic team. Only two men at the Los Angeles Coliseum meet were to qualify for the Final Trial in New York.

Suffering from his sore ankle Warmerdam struggled over 13' 6". After one miss at 14 feet, he had to stop. The next day his ankle was swollen to twice its size. 'I could hardly walk.'

Instead of competing in New York, he picked cotton in the hot San Joaquin Valley. His father told his unhappy son, 'Don't quit; keep at it.' He had a tooth pulled and the ankle gave him no more trouble. 'It appears that the abcessed tooth had caused the irritation in the ankle joint.'

Weight training was not used by athletes then, and Warmerdam's only strength training came from wielding heavy pruning shears three months a year. He helped develop his speed and an even step by training over the low hurdles.

'It's practically all speed. If you can't get up speed on the runway, you can't get your weight up the full 80 degrees.'

In 1937, his last season as a collegian, Warmerdam was free from injury and he vaulted well. In the dual meet with Southern California, he flew over the bar at 14 feet to tie for second with Sefton behind Olympic champion Meadows. At the Pacific Association AAU meet, he was pleased to swing over 14' 4" even though he lost on fewer misses to Jack Mauger. He also lost ground on the world record, for Sefton and Meadows had raised it to an awesome 14' 11".

At the famed Princeton Invitational, he won at 14 feet over Mauger. In his first national AAU meet, at Milwaukee, Wisconsin, on July 3, Warmerdam became embroiled in a long and exciting competition against the co-holders of the world record, plus former record holder George Varoff.

Warmerdam and Varoff missed once at 14 feet. None of the four missed again until the bar reached 14' 7⅝". All four missed on their first attempts. In the second round, Sefton and Warmerdam sailed over. Meadows and Varoff cleared on their third jumps to make it the greatest 4-way vaulting ever seen. Warmerdam thus defeated Meadows and Varoff, but he lost to Sefton because of his single miss at 14 feet.

The Pan-American Games were held in Dallas, Texas. On July 17, Warmerdam won his first major championship by clearing 14' 3" and defeating Varoff and Meadows. Then Warmerdam enjoyed his first trip to Europe and he cleared 14' 3" in Stockholm.

In 1938, he graduated from Fresno State. In the spring he won the Compton Invitational at 14' 6". He cleared 14' 6" again, in the Princeton Invitational, but Meadows beat him with the same height after Warmerdam had loaned him his spare pole.

Warmerdam soared over 14' 5½" to defeat Varoff for his first victory in the national AAU. He beat Varoff again in Berlin during USA's first international dual meet. He set a British All-Comers record of 14' 3" at Glasgow, vaulting from a runway on a soccer field into a pile of sand.

He was now good enough to be sought after for indoor meets.

On February 11, 1939, in Boston, he propelled himself over the bar at 14′ 6⅛″ for a world indoor record. He added the indoor AAU championship to his small collection of honors, but he lost his outdoor title in Lincoln, Nebraska. At 14′ 4″, he knocked the bar off and lost to Varoff. He still had much to be modest about.

In 1940, he was teaching history and geometry in a mountain high school. Pole vaulting, in his philosophy, was something he did for fun, and training was more difficult now. As his weight went near 180 pounds he added more tape to his old bamboo pole, 'picked out of the Stanford University discard rack.'

He did not compete in the indoor meets, and Meadows took over as indoor champion. Warmerdam's first meet, in the cool spring air of the Long Beach Relays, resulted in a ridiculous 12′ 6″. 'I was in fairly good shape but I was eliminated before really getting warmed up.'

Dutch Warmerdam had a quiet maturity which put pole vaulting in its proper place, but he also had some pride. He took sprint starts, worked on the parallel bars, and vaulted tenaciously until dark. His weight was down to 170 pounds.

Now a member of the San Francisco Olympic Club team, he won at 14′ 4″ at Stanford on April 6. On April 13, he drove to an insignificant meet with California and Washington State in Berkeley. 'I knew I was in good shape.'

Down on the runway at Edwards Field, he lifted over 14 feet easily, on his first attempt. He felt good clearing 14′ 2″. The bar was raised to 14′ 5″ and he missed. On his second attempt he cleared easily. Exhilarated now, he had the bar raised to a personal record height of 14′ 8½″. Why not? He had nothing to lose.

When he shot over the crossbar on his first vault, he was a little puzzled. It seemed too easy. Quietly excited, he asked the officials to raise the bar to 15 feet. He had wondered what it would be like to attempt a world record.

He soon found out, for he missed. But he was far from discouraged. 'I knew I could make it after the first miss because it was a close miss and fairly easy for me.'

The few spectators watched silently as he stood 140 feet from the pit, holding the heavy bamboo pole in front of him. They saw the lean, broad-shouldered man start his purposeful run, lop-sided because of the pole on his right side. His left elbow

Cornelius Warmerdam

pumped in lieu of an arm swing as he gathered speed. He approached the pit at a dangerous pace and lowered the tip of his pole until it jarred to a halt in the box. Simultaneously, his arms went high, transferring forward speed into upward energy with a sudden shock.

For a moment his body was alongside the pole. Then he lifted his feet, turned on his side, and pushed his body upward, feet first. It was a hard, struggling effort, but his body flew off the pole, and he was above the bar, wonderfully free. He pulled his hands up barely in time. Then he concentrated on landing safely in the low pile of shavings.

It was the world's first 15-foot vault.

The cheers were loud, joyful, and not a little surprised. Even Warmerdam, known as a calm, quiet individual, expressed his pleasure. In one marvelous second over that crossbar came his transition from good vaulter to world record holder.

The AAU meet was held in Fresno and Warmerdam knew that pit well. They started vaulting at 6:30 p.m. on the warm evening of June 29, at a height of 12′ 6″.

Warmerdam cleared each height with calm confidence, on his first attempt. Meadows and Bud Deacon went no higher than 13′ 6″, leaving Ken Dills, a 14′ 8″ vaulter, as Warmerdam's only threat. Dills cleared 14′ and 14′ 4″. On his first trial, Warmerdam sailed skillfully over 14′ 8″, and Dills failed. Warmerdam was the national champion, breaking the 4-way meet record, and now he wanted another world record.

The people in the two long stands on either side of the track watched keenly as Warmerdam raced unevenly down the runway. There was the smooth pole plant, taking some of the shock out of his sudden halt, and then he was up, arching over the bar. He landed in the shavings with the satisfaction of another world record – 15′ 1⅛″.

'It was big for me because it was in Fresno and my folks were there to see me.'

He took no European trip in 1940. He was married in August and he did not compete indoors in 1941, but he ran with a dedication and he kept up his strength. His training now required almost no vaulting.

On April 12, in a dual meet with Stanford, he was ready. Starting at 12′ 6″ again, he cleared each of six heights through

14′ 8″ on his first attempt. Then, with the bar at 15′ 2⅝″, he missed. He missed again. A third time he charged at the bar with determination, and this time he went over the record height.

Without doubt, he was vaulting better than ever, but two weeks later, in Los Angeles, he lost at 14′ 6″. 'Officials asked me to jump at 15 feet anyway. I did, and cleared on my first attempt. This was not an official jump.'

Two days after that, in Visalia, California, he cleared 15 feet. On May 24, in the Coliseum Relays, he cleared 15 feet. He was now consistently better than the best of all the other vaulters in history.

At the invitational in Compton's little stadium on the night of June 6, he zoomed over 15 feet for the fifth time in 1941. Few, if any, track and field athletes had turned in so many performances better than all other men, but it seemed as if he had reached his ceiling.

Still, he was hopeful as he attacked 15′ 4¼″, more than an inch and a half above his world record. Seven thousand alert specators in the old wooden stands watched the lean 6-footer in his red shorts and his white shirt with its red winged O. Warmerdam seemed perfectly calm as he peered down the runway, then launched into his loping run.

He missed.

In pole vaulting, a miss is not a tragedy; you keep on trying. Warmerdam, who had kept trying for 11 years, tried once again, and this time he sailed over. The crowd's roar shattered the silence. He put on his red sweat suit and tried to be patient during the long process of measurement, with an official holding a tape high up on a ladder.

The crowd cheered when the announcer confirmed the new record, but Warmerdam felt too good to stop. The bar was raised another inch and a half, but he knocked it off, of course. The crowd could not reasonably hope for another world record the same night, but they enjoyed watching. On his second miss they applauded his effort and prepared to go home.

After a short rest, he tried again, racing hopefully down the runway, shooting toward the dark sky. A sudden surprised roar burst upon him as he fell triumphantly to the pile of shavings. He had cleared 15′ 5¾″. The crowd was delirious. Two world records in one meet!

The rest of the season was disappointing by comparison. He won twice more at the now disdained height of 15 feet. Then, at the AAU, after winning at 15 feet, he had 'Three very good attempts at 15' 7".'

In the fall, he taught at Piedmont High School, near Berkeley. On December 28, in New Orleans, he won at the Sugar Bowl with 15 feet and he was ready for an even greater season. His presence was desired in the Millrose Games and he wrote out a telegram to the meet director:

'There is no use crossing the continent to vault 14 feet. But if you will extend the runway from 125 feet to 137 feet, I can almost guarantee you a fifteen-foot jump.'

The eager director granted his request, but on his flight to the February 7th meet, Warmerdam had to change airplanes in Chicago. To his dismay, his pole was lost. Vaulting with Milt Padway's pole, two feet shorter than his own, he cleared 14' $8\frac{5}{8}$" to regain the indoor record Meadows had taken from him in 1941.

'Then, with the bar at 15' $\frac{3}{8}$", he sped down the board runway, unsure of his borrowed pole, and sailed over. It was the first 15-foot vault indoors, and 16,000 fans went wild. Hats sailed into the arena. Promoter Fred Schmertz says, 'I think it was the greatest ovation ever given to a single individual.'

Warmerdam stayed in the east for the Boston AA meet. Using his own pole, he cleared the first five heights, through 14' $8\frac{3}{4}$", without a miss. He wanted a new indoor record height of 15' 2", and he made it on his second attempt.

After the cheering and measurement, the bar was set at 15' $7\frac{1}{4}$", an inch and a half higher than he had ever vaulted outdoors. The crowd in the double-decked Boston Garden watched intently while he held his pole in the box, adjusting the standards. He missed, but he was confident tonight.

He went back to the far end of the runway. When he started his second run he could hear nothing except his spikes pounding into the wooden runway like a suspenseful drum roll.

He watched with satisfaction as his left foot hit his check mark at 120 feet and again at 70 feet. He slid the end of his pole into the slot and swung up smoothly. 'A vaulter must have a body as hard as a prize fighter's to absorb the shock.'

He rode the straight pole patiently for a moment, then twisted and shot his feet toward the roof. His left leg bent under his right in a scissors motion and he struggled to a face-down position as he went over the bar sideways. His 167 pounds landed on his hands and knees in a dangerous pile of shavings only as high as the runway. 'Once, in an indoor meet, my knee went through and hit concrete.'

The spectators left their seats in a frenzy of admiration. Two hundred youngsters pursued him. Everybody wanted to shake his hand and congratulate him. Even a quiet Dutchman had to smile with pleasure, but he wanted to vault some more.

The bar was raised to 15' 10". He missed the first attempt, but he felt good. He missed the second, but he knew the height was possible. On his third trial, his remarkable shoot lifted his body cleanly over the bar, but he did not bring his left elbow up in time and it knocked the crossbar off. After the meet, the crowd pursued him out of the building and he almost missed his plane.

With almost routine skill, he left the crossbar on at 15 feet to 15' 2" in four more meets. Then, at the district AAU meet in Berkeley on May 2, he went over 15' ¾" without a miss and he asked for an outdoor record height of 15' 6". He missed twice. Then, as on his two previous world records, his third jump brought triumph.

The bar was measured carefully at 15' 6⅛", and he had the satisfaction of his fifth world record.

He bettered 15' 1" in Memphis, Tennessee, and Fresno. On May 23 he went to the town of Modesto, 90 miles north of Fresno, where eager local people promoted a new meet called the Northern California Relays. The spectators in the low wooden stands were pleased when he vaulted 15' 3" without a miss. Few big meets had such a fine meet record.

Delayed an hour because one 14-foot standard fell from its improvised perch on a wooden crate and had to be taken to a shop and welded, the vault lasted long after the meet ended, but Warmerdam wanted to try 15' 8".

On his third attempt, his faithful bamboo pole, heavily taped, rode high ahead of him, then dipped and thudded into the deep slot. His left hand shifted up to his right, an extraordinary 13' 11" from the end of the pole. He was jerked violently upward, then swung smoothly. He twisted over and thrust himself skyward.

'No athlete has much left after sprinting 50 yards at top speed, yet I still have to figure on the body shock that comes when the pole strikes the ground. The pole vibrates, jars your whole system. It can tear loose the grip of your right hand. It can do something to destroy the physical coordination so necessary to finish the job after momentum ends at the crossbar.'

He arched sideways over the bar and dropped free.

The small crowd roared. An excited official knocked down the crossbar. Measured again, it was only 15' 7¾", but it was a world record by ⅛ of an inch. Another roar of pleasure and admiration, but Warmerdam seemed almost embarrassed.

Next came a trip to Pocatello, Idaho, for the Intermountain AAU and a victory at 15' 1⅛". 'This vault was very difficult, running into a wind.'

On June 20, he was in New York for the national AAU. He won at 15' 2½" and stood alone on the victory stand in his bare feet to receive his medal from Mayor Fiorello La Guardia.

For his unprecedented achievements and his good character, he won the Sullivan Award for 1942.

In 1943, he returned in triumph to the Millrose Games and won at 15' 1½". He repeated his indoor AAU victory, leaving the crossbar undisturbed at 15' 3⅜", and he cleared 15' 1¾" in San Francisco.

On March 20, 1943, as a brand new ensign in the U.S. Navy, he flew to the Chicago Relays for the finest vaulting of his career. He knocked the bar off only once through 15' 3⅝" and it was raised to 15' 8½".

He stood for a moment at the head of the runway, concentrating his desire. Behind him, across the banked board track, the crowd in the triple-decked stands grew quiet with anticipation. When he launched into his loping sprint, his footsteps were the loudest sounds in Chicago Stadium.

He knew he could vault this high, but he had never succeeded a 15' 4" or higher on his first attempt. He swung into his vault at full speed, swung up, twisted, and pulled, then pushed his whole body toward the lights. Elated with his zooming push, he flattened out on top only a little sideways.

He was over! It was the highest vault ever made, and it came on his first attempt. Exhilarated, he had the bar moved to 16' ½".

Three times he raced down the runway and flung himself

hopefully toward the bright ceiling, and three times he missed but two of his jumps were the best ever seen. Of those two, he says, 'I thought I might have cleared 15' 11".'

One writer, years later, called this, 'Perhaps the greatest performance seen on any track at any time.'

Outdoors, Warmerdam vaulted well, soaring over 15 feet nine more times, but he never matched his impressive Chicago vaulting. He won the AAU title again at 15' and later thrust himself over laudable heights of 15' 4" and 15' 3".

In 1944, his duties as a naval lieutenant and his location at Monmouth College in Illinois frustrated further improvement. He cleared only 14' 5" in the Chicago Relays. His only 15-footer came in his farewell appearance when he won his sixth AAU championship in New York. He would have been everyone's favorite for Olympic champion in 1944, as well as in 1940.

Warmerdam's outdoor world record lasted 15 years and his indoor record stood for sixteen years. No other man cleared 15 feet until 1951, but Warmerdam had driven his body over that height an astounding total of 43 times, plus twice in exhibitions.

Bob Richards, the second man to vault 15 feet, said, 'Warmerdam was part sprinter, part shock-absorber, part acrobat, and part strong man. He wasn't human.'

No athlete ever had so many marks so far ahead of the next best man of all time, in any event.

Nat Cartmell, 1904 Olympic double silver medalist in the sprints, summed it up when he said, 'Warmerdam is the only all-time, indisputable, supreme champion the athletic world has ever known.'

Harrison Dillard in 1948.

HARRISON DILLARD

In August of 1936, a skinny black boy of thirteen sat on the curb of Cleveland's Central Avenue watching a parade for a hero. He saw Jesse Owens sitting high on the back seat of an open car, smiling and waving to the crowd. He felt the wonder and awe of Owens' Berlin triumphs. Four gold medals!

'I certainly was hit by the spark that afternoon,' says Harrison Dillard.

His junior high school team-mates laughed at this scrawny, undernourished child of poverty, and they called him 'Bones', and the coach said he was not strong enough to sprint. One man took an interest in the frail boy – his idol, Jesse Owens.

Owens gave him his famous shoes from Berlin, and helped form young Dillard's love of hurdling.

'I've always felt,' Dillard once said, 'that sprinters, including me, are a dime a dozen. That's just running. But when you combine running with the gymnastic ability required in the hurdles, you have a high art in track and field athletics.'

In the spring of 1941, Dillard had begun to develop his art. Proudly, he wore Jesse Owens' shoes and he won both hurdles in the Ohio state high school meet.

Dillard enrolled at Baldwin-Wallace College because of his deep friendship with Coach Eddie Finnigan, and he worked toward filling Jesse Owens' shoes. His only significant competition in 1942 came at the AAU championships on Randall's Island, New York. Dillard did well to place third in the junior high hurdles. He lost the junior low hurdles by only three inches. In the senior intermediate hurdles, the only time he ever attempted that event, he placed fifth in 53.7.

In the spring of 1943, he began to fill those shoes. Although his best time over the high hurdles was 14.8, he won at the famous Penn Relays. In the Ohio Athletic Conference meet, he led little Baldwin-Wallace to a surprising championship by winning both sprints, both hurdles, and the sprint relay. His promising season came to an abrupt end when, at the age of 19, he was drafted into the army.

Army service during a world war is not the ideal training climate, especially when you are under fire in Italy, and Dillard's career could have suffered immeasurably. But when you are trying to fill Jesse Owens' shoes you simply carry on. When the war ended in Europe in that joyous spring of 1945, Dillard began training and he ran in seven service meets. He ran 10.6 for 100 meters, 14.6 for the high hurdles, and he was voted the outstanding competitor of the climactic meet in Frankfort.

In the spring of 1946 there was no longer any doubt about Dillard's future greatness. At the Kansas Relays he flashed over the hurdles in 14.2. In the Ohio Conference, June 1, he won in 9.7, 14.6, and 22.8. In the Ohio College meet, June 8, he ran 9.6 and 14.2. Then he stirred a somnolent track world by equalling the world record of 22.5 for the low hurdles.

He lost only twice in 1946, once while injured at the Penn Relays and once to dangerous George Walker in the Central Collegiate highs.

He went hopefully to the NCAA Championships at Minneapolis and he hit the tape first in both hurdles. His 14.1 was a personal best and his 23 flat was a world record around a curve. Once again he gave Owens credit for changing him to a left-footed hurdler, an advantage in curve hurdling.

In San Antonio, Texas, he won the AAU highs in 14.2 when a charging Walker hit the ninth hurdle. Dillard completed his notable sweep of four national championships with 23.3 for the 200 meter hurdles around a turn.

He was even better in 1947. In Madison Square Garden, he won both hurdles championships in the indoor AAU and completed an undefeated indoor season. Outdoors, he equalled his previous best of 14.1 three times and ran 14 flat five times. Undefeated in the highs, he tied the world low hurdle record again at 22.5. Then he lost his only race of the year to Bill Porter's fine 22.7 in the Coliseum Relays. It was only his third loss in 137 races.

The NCAA meet was at Salt Lake City. Dillard defeated Porter by two yards in 14.1, but he was concerned about the fast low hurdlers he must face. He left nothing to chance. He started as fast as possible and kept going. He never saw his opponents and he beat Porter by over two yards. His 22.3 was a new world record for 220 yards and it equalled Fred Wolcott's 200 meter record. Considering the 6-mile headwind and 50-degree temperature, it may be the best ever run.

The next weekend he was in Lincoln, Nebraska, for the AAU championships. He won both hurdles again, in 14 flat and 23.3, an unprecedented sweep of eight outdoor national gold medals in two years.

'Bones' ranked No. 1 in the world for both hurdles for the second year, but he also began to be recognized as a sprinter. Although his best 100 was 9.6, he ran four commendable 10.4's for 100 meters in Europe. At Stockholm on August 5, he ran 10.3, only one tick of the watch off the world record. He ranked ninth in the world in the 100 and he was good enough for fourth in the 200, where he ran 21.2 twice around a curve.

In 1948, Dillard was phenomenal. He began indoors with a perfect record of ten high hurdle victories and four low hurdles. His 7.2 while defending his AAU title was a record, but he surpassed it with 7.1 at the Chicago Relays.

Outdoors, he ranked No. 1 for the third consecutive year in the lows, his last year of serious competition over the 2′ 6″ hurdles. His excellent record included 22.4 and 22.5, plus a wind-aided 22.3.

On April 17, in the Kansas Relays at Lawrence, Dillard took his marks in the highs alongside Clyde Scott of Arkansas, a hurdler good enough to win the Olympic silver medal four months later. Dillard's new winning streak was up to 53, and he wanted to win this one.

At the gun, his golden uniform flashed to the front sensationally. He charged each hurdle wildly, taking off eight feet in front. As he whizzed over the 3′ 6″ barrier, he brought his right leg forward incredibly fast. His right foot was within 15 inches of the track when his left foot came down a long five feet beyond the hurdle. This was the style criticized by coaches but later used by short, fast men to become great hurdlers.

Now it drove his 5′ 10″, 150-pound body down the Kansas track faster than any hurdler in history. He sat on the sixth hurdle and rode it down but he kept going. He finished an astounding ten yards ahead of Scott in 13.6, a new world record both for

120 yards and 110 meters. One official watch showed 13.5.

He reached the AAU meet in Milwaukee with an incomparable win streak of 82. He wanted to make the Olympic team in two events, but the AAU was still organized under the archaic system which required heats and finals all in one day, and Dillard had to take his marks four times in 67 minutes. His third race was the 100 final and he lost to Barney Ewell. By then he was too tired for the high hurdles final and he lost to Porter's 14.1 by five feet.

In spite of that sobering lesson, he went to the blocks in both events in the Final Trials at Evanston, Illinois, the following week. In both heats he won promisingly, but in the 100 final, hampered by a bad start, he was beaten by Ewell and Mel Patton in a record tying 10.2. But he was on the Olympic team.

The next day, he was at the start of the high hurdles. He was the outstanding favorite to be the Olympic champion and all he needed here was a relaxed third place.

The gun cracked and he left his blocks with his great pickup. He reached the first hurdle ahead of the others, as usual, but he hit it. He almost never hit hurdles, but at this important time he hit the hurdle. To his dismay, he lost stride. Falling behind, he drove desperately to make up the lost ground, but he was not at the right place on the track and he hit another hurdle, and another. Disastrously far behind now, the greatest hurdler of all time came to a helpless stop, his hands against the seventh hurdle.

With his Olympic dream shattered, the shock must have hurt, but the horrified spectators would never know it. Actually smiling, Dillard jogged to the finish and threw both arms around Porter. People were there to sympathize with him, but he kept a tight little smile on his face and said, 'I can run some, too.'

And so he resigned himself to being a sprinter in the Olympic Games in London. Courageously, he prepared to meet those great sprinters on their own terms. Coach Finnigan said simply, 'They'll never meet a guy with a greater desire to win.'

On July 30, Dillard was on the track at Wembley for the first round. He raced resolutely through his heat in 10.4, fastest of the 12 heats. In the afternoon, he ran 10.4 again, matched only by Patton, the favorite. The next day, Dillard won his semi-finals in 10.5.

In the final that same afternoon, before 83,000 spectators,

Dillard fidgeted in the outside lane. He was supposed to finish fourth. At the gun, Dillard sprinted off his blocks and into the pickup admired by experts as one of the fastest ever. While the ill-fated Patton was stumbling far behind, Dillard shot into the lead.

Patton was gaining, but he was too far back to threaten. Lloyd LaBeach was gaining, but not fast enough. Dillard sprinted smoothly toward the tape, his hopes rising, but Ewell was gaining rapidly at the end. Ewell hit the tape, stopped, jumped for joy, clasped his hands in a boxer's handshake, and grinned.

Dillard waited quietly, keeping his thoughts to himself, and his hopes. The silver medal was more than he was expected to win, but a man can't help hoping. Later, he said, 'I never went through anything like that wait.'

Then came the official announcement: First, Dillard, United States. Time 10.3, equalling the Olympic record. Into a wind of five miles per hour, this was a great performance.

'Aw nuts,' Ewell said, 'I thought I had it.'

Dillard patted him sympathetically on the back. Later he said, almost wistfully, 'I won something, anyway.'

Coach Finnigan vaulted the rail on to the field and ran to Dillard. They embraced and Dillard lifted him off the ground. Tears streamed down Finnigan's cheeks. Overcome, he went to his hotel room and wrote a note to Jack Clowser, Dillard's Boswell:

'This was the day we waited for so long. To think it came not in the hurdles but in the event we all thought Dillard couldn't win. Fate is strange and wonderful. I'm going out to find a church somewhere. My heart is bursting.'

Now Dillard was a select sprinter. On the third leg of the 400 meter relay team, he flew around the curve, passing everybody to give the U.S. a commanding lead. In post Olympic meets he triumphed over Ewell three times, in 10.4, 9.6, and 9.5. In Paris he ran 20.8 for 200 meters around a curve, time bettered by only five men in history. He scurried over the high hurdles four times in 13.9. For the year 1948, he was ranked best in the world in the 100 and low hurdles, No. 2 in the highs, and No. 4 in the 200.

A smiling, likeable man, Dillard worked in the promotion department of the Cleveland baseball team. He had not filled Jesse Owens' shoes completely but his name was honored in the world record books for the 120 yard and 110 meter high hurdles, the 220 yard and 200 meter low hurdles, the low hurdles around a curve, and indoor bests in both high and low hurdles. In the hazardous sprints and hurdles, his competitive record stood at 201 races won and only six lost. He could have retired gracefully, content with a collection of medals and clippings surpassed by few athletes.

But the spark inside him, ignited by Jesse Owens, had grown to a raging flame, and he still ached over his failure in the hurdles. Even though he admitted, 'I've lost some of my zest for competition,' he would compromise. He would run indoors and hope to keep in shape for a comeback in 1952.

On the indoor boards in 1949, he won his first five high hurdle races. He seldom hit a hurdle. He had one stretch over 200 hurdles where he knocked down only two. But he ran into trouble in the NYKC Games and finished third, his only failure in ten races. In the Chicago Relays, he beat Craig Dixon by two feet to tie his own indoor record of 7.1 for 60 yards.

He ran very little outdoors in the United States in 1949, but he took two tours. In Georgetown, British Guiana, he ran an excellent 13.8, 10.4, and 9.4, the best time in the world that year. Later in April, in Trinidad, he ran a 9.4 100 with wind. In the fall, not at his best, he ran a 10.4 for third place in the meet against the Scandinavian countries. He also lost in the AAU high hurdles, running 13.9 to Dixon's 13.8. Thus, his World Ranking, in a poor year, was No. 2 for the hurdles and No. 7 for the 100.

In 1950, he ran only indoors (with the exception of a 14.4 in Glasgow, which left him unranked). He tied the board track record of 6.1 for the 60 yard dash at Philadelphia, but he lost the hurdles to Jim Gerhdes. That was his only failure in three indoor seasons, through 1952. Now called, 'Old Bones', he raced over the hurdles to victory in all three AAU championships.

He resumed his quest for an outdoor championship with 14.4 on May 3, 1952, in Berea, Ohio. He flew out to Los Angeles for the Coliseum Relays and ran a first-rate 14.1 for third place after leading for half the race.

Three weeks later, at Compton, he was given third although he ran 14 flat and actually finished second. Having finished behind Billy Anderson, Dixon, and Jack Davis, and with world record holder Dick Attlesey making a strong comeback, Dillard was lightly regarded, but he phoned Jack Clowser:

'Don't worry, I'll be ready. I can feel the improvement with my new double-arm style. It makes up for the trifle in flat speed I may have lost.'

He ran a 14.2 in the Ohio AAU, and then he went out to Long Beach, California, to seek the AAU title on a cold, windy night.

Dillard waited patiently on his marks, head down, while four false starts by Dixon and Davis upset the others. At the gun, Dillard was off fast. Any doubts as to his merit were dispelled in a few seconds. His speed was startling over the first hurdle. At the fifth hurdle he led by four yards. He lost almost half of that to Davis' formidable finish, but he won in 13.7.

A week later, a few miles away in the imposing bowl of the Los Angeles Coliseum, the U.S. team chose itself in the heat of competition. Cold weather and the threat of rain held attendance to 22,000 on Saturday, but the high hurdle field was stronger than it could possibly be in the Olympics.

The tension was so great that the hurdlers went to their marks six times without a start. Dillard appeared cool and calm, knowing his start was faster than any hurdler who ever lived, for he had never been beaten to the first hurdle.

Tense and jumpy, they took their marks for the seventh time. This time, when the gun fired, there was no recall Dillard charged the first hurdle and cleared it safely with a lead of a full yard. He built up a comfortable lead. Then he sat on the seventh hurdle, and it was like four years ago. He was in danger of missing the team, and this year he had no 100 meters to save him.

He was unable to recover his proper stride. Fear ran through him as he hit the eigth hurdle. They were gaining on him now. A man of less poise might have charged desperately, trying to regain speed, but he knew the important thing was to clear the barrier in stride. He adjusted his step and cleared the last two safely. He hit the tape ahead of Davis in 14 flat, and he now had his chance – the one he had lost in 1948.

Now it was the Olympic championship he wanted ... the gold medal. He was favored to win, but he knew better than most the hazards of hurdling. In Helsinki, he went to his marks for the final a determined man, for this was the race 'on which I had set my heart.'

After a false start by Davis, Dillard was more keyed up than he had ever been. He tried to ignore the crowd in the flag-rimmed stadium. On his marks, he looked down at the red brick track. He came to the set position, head down. Suddenly, his nerves failed him and he started to move. He rocked forward. Desperately, he caught himself and pulled back as the gun sounded. His start was poor, for him, but his great pickup carried him to a one-yard lead at the third hurdle.

This was not enough, for Davis was terrifying at full speed. Dillard sped forward, driven by the aching desire from his 1948 failure, his legs a whirl of blurred speed over the obstacles. Three lanes over, to his left, he glimpsed the dreaded figure of Davis gaining on him, but he could not run any faster.

He concentrated on the one thing which could win for him. If he could avoid hitting a hurdle and maintain full speed... All his poise and experience and careful training came into play. It was his competitive skill against Davis', with Davis the stronger runner.

At the ninth hurdle, Davis pulled almost even. Still Dillard could do nothing except his best. Coolly, he flashed over the next to last barrier. Davis, under the same pressure as Dillard, hit the hurdle hard, crashing it down and landing flat-footed.

Over the last hurdle, Dillard flew with bird-like grace. He sprinted for the tape and thrust his head forward in a victorious lunge. He won by more than a foot as both men ran 13.7.

Dillard shed his calm dignity and whooped for joy. 'Good things come to those who wait.'

Few men ever won gold medals in two different Olympiads. Nobody ever did it in two diverse events. After he ran the second leg on U.S.A.'s victorious relay team, he mounted the victory stand in front of the covered main stands and received his fourth gold medal. In world records and gold medals he had done a good job in filling Jesse Owens' shoes.

For all practical purposes, that was the end of Dillard's career as an outdoor runner, although he beat Davis by two yards in 13.9 in the White City meet against the British Empire and ran a commendable 10.4 in Vienna even though slowed by a muscle strain in the last 20 meters. He did not run outdoors again for four years, and he never reached satisfactory condition in his abortive attempt in 1956.

Indoors, however, he ran with distinction. He lost only two indoor races over the next three years. One was to Davis in 1954, but he beat Davis in 1955 for his eighth triumph in indoor AAU high hurdles. He was also ranked No. 1 indoors as a sprinter in 1953. Three times his superior start and pickup won sprint-hurdles doubles.

In 1956, at the age of 32, Dillard slipped to No. 3 in indoor hurdling, placing third in the AAU behind Lee Calhoun and Davis. In his first outdoor competition since 1952, he ran 14 flat with wind, but unusually bad weather and pressure of his job prevented full training.

Explaining sadly, 'I'm a little out of shape,' he placed only eighth in the AAU and seventh in the Final Trials. 'Old Bones' great career was over.

He won four Olympic gold medals. He won an unmatched two consecutive doubles in both the NCAA and AAU, plus one other AAU title. He won nine indoor AAU championships. His name appeared in the record book in all the high and low hurdles available. He approached world records in the sprints and defeated some all-time great sprinters. His won-lost record was almost incredible for such hazardous events. In 1947–48 he built up the longest winning streak of any runner in history.

He was second in the voting for the Sullivan Award in both 1947 and 1948, and he won it for 1955. As somebody said, 'It couldn't happen to a nicer guy.'

Coach Larry Snyder once appraised Dillard's potential as a sprinter, had he not run the hurdles, by saying, 'He might have been the best of them all.'

Jesse Owens showed great perception when he chose Harrison Dillard to fill his shoes.

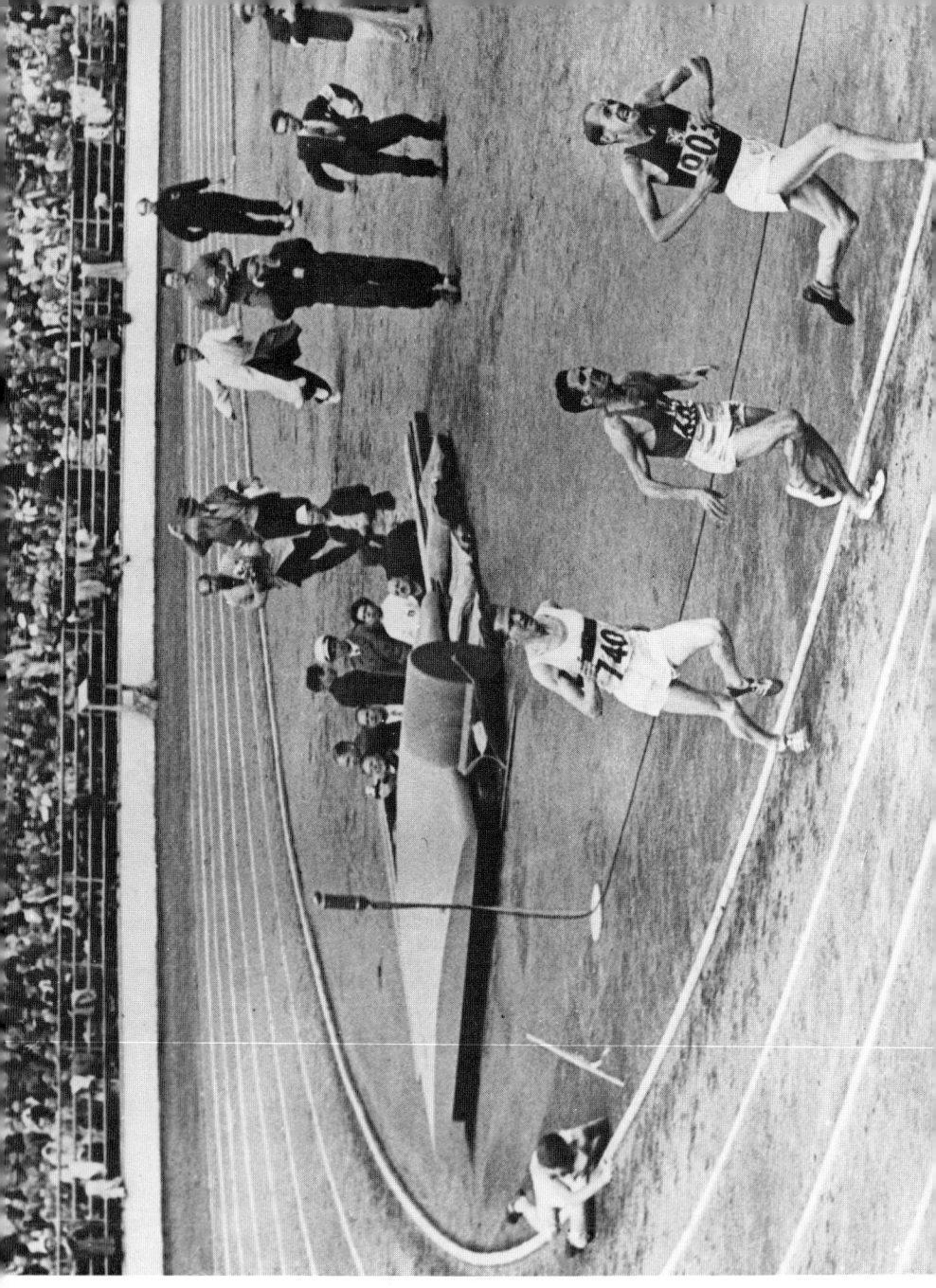

The classic picture: Zatopek races for home in the Helsinki Olympic 5000 ahead of Mimoun, Schade and the fallen Chataway.

EMIL ZÁTOPEK

The crowd of 60,000 at Wembley could scarcely believe their eyes. They were watching the 10,000 meter run of the 1948 Olympic Games, but this Czech, Zátopek, was the worst looking runner they had ever seen.

He was an awkward, scrawny little man, 5' 8½" tall, wearing a faded red shirt of Czechoslovakia, and he seemed to be in pain. Corn silk hair bobbed on his wobbling head. Periodically, his face twisted into an agonized grimace. His tongue flopped out of his mouth. His shoulders hunched grotesquely. He puffed and blew alarmingly. Every few strides his right hand stretched down toward his knee as if to scratch. His heels seemed reluctant to lift behind him, as if they were weighted. He looked, in short, as if he might be having a fit. At the very least, he seemed about to drop out.

Never has a runner been so deceiving.

The crowd had heard little of this awkward runner, even though only last month he had run 10,000 meters in an excellent 29:27 – 1.6 seconds slower than Viljo Heino's world record. A combination of indifferent athletic reporting plus iron curtain secrecy had conspired to deny Emil Zátopek his due publicity.

His position far back in the pack of runners and his apparent exhaustion did nothing to enlighten the crowd. After each lap, he looked alertly at a certain point in the crowd, and each time a rabid Czech held up a white sock. But now, after eight laps, a red vest was held up. The undesired signal meant the pace had slowed below 71 seconds per lap. Instantly Zátopek responded. He moved awkwardly up to fifth place, and now the crowd cheered the ugly duckling, more because he was the underdog than because they fancied his chances against the great Heino. For even though he had edged Heino last year at 5,000 meters, this was twice the distance, where Heino excelled and Zátopek had run only two races.

Little did they know.

A few Czechs in the stands were chanting, 'Zátopek,' and the crowd's excitement grew louder. When he galloped past the light blue vest of Heino to take the lead at 4,000 meters, the applause was great.

Heino passed him, and the crowd responded with excited shouts. The red signal showed and he burst past Heino with a startling spurt. He pulled away to a lead of 30 meters and the crowd joined in the chant of 'Zá-to-pek, Zá-to-pek.'

He began to lap runners, but his pace was slower than his planned 29:35. The red vest kept waving, and he became confused.

He shouted anxiously to an official, 'Where is Heino?'

Came the reply, 'Heino is out.'

Zátopek struggled on in the stifling heat. More confusion resulted from a mistake by the lap indicator, but Zátopek calmly ran the correct distance and ended with a blazing finish. His time was 29:59.6, a new Olympic record, 47 seconds ahead of Alain Mimoun. High in the stands, his joyful countrymen sang their national anthem. No less joyful was Zátopek, whose personality exudes friendly enthusiasm and the joy of living.

The next day the crowd cheered the new hero as he ran 30 seconds faster than necessary in his qualifying heat of the 5,000 meters. Two days later, the exciting final was held on a track drenched by a downpour. Zátopek led the pack into the tormenting wind and rain. His pace was a reliable 68–69 for eight laps and the others were content to follow.

At 3,500 meters, Gaston Reiff of Belgium rushed past. Zátopek, paying for his excesses of the previous days, was too tired to follow and Willi Slykhuis of Holland moved past. The two favorites ran away from Zátopek and he was soon a hopeless 65 yards behind Reiff, with Slykhuis between them.

Zátopek's legs felt heavy and he kept slipping in the slush. He tried to go faster, but the laps went by and he was far behind. On the backstretch of the last lap, still a distressing 30 yards behind Reiff, he felt his courage return.

He began to sprint, awkwardly but fast. He rushed past Slykhuis and the crowd was up and roaring. As Reiff turned wearily into the homestretch, Zátopek was twenty yards behind, charging like a runaway locomotive.

Emil Zátopek

The astonished crowd screamed his name and Reiff heard. Amazed, he turned his head and saw the madman charging down on him. He gave everything he had and barely moved faster, but it was enough. He hit the tape with Zátopek two yards behind.

Zátopek's wild finish seemed to impress observers even more than his overwhelming victory in the 10,000. Now, everybody wanted to know about him. What made him so good?

It began in 1941 when he was 18. He had moved to Zlín when he was 16. Full of ambition, he worked in a shoe factory and attended technical school at night. The shoe company sponsored a race in the streets and young Zátopek was forced to run even though he tried to get out of it and said, 'I'm no good at running.'

That, of course, was not quite the truth, for he had proved himself better than his contemporaries in a few runs for fun, and he finished second out of a hundred boys in this race. During the next year, he ran a few more boys' races, still with no enthusiasm. But when he was singled out for training in 1942 he was happy.

His first formal race was at 3,000 meters. He finished only three seconds back of his trainer in 9:12 and the newspaper reported, 'A good performance by Zátopek.' He read it over and over again.

Now, training became the most important part of his life. Where others searched for races they could win, he searched for stiff competition he would surely lose, and his times grew promisingly faster. In 1943, he began to work at rudimentary interval training, striving to increase his speed.

'You must be fast enough. You must have endurance. So you run fast for speed and repeat it many times for endurance.'

He trained hard and began to break national records each year. When the Russian army drove the Germans from Zlín, Zátopek, enthusiastic as ever, became a soldier and after the war he began officer's training at the Military Academy.

His first race outside Czechoslovakia was in the 1946 European Championships at Oslo. He was enthralled. When he first saw the great Heino he approached him with deference and timidly touched those world-record legs. At the start of the 5,000, his knees trembled.

He ran with Europe's best until Slykhuis pulled away. Then Sydney Wooderson shot away from Slykhuis with dazzling speed.

Over 100 meters behind, Zátopek was narrowly beaten by Evert Nyberg and Heino, but his good 14:25.8 was another national record.

All winter he trained with stupendous energy. He found a quarter-mile path in the woods near the military camp and he labored through rain, mud, snow, and ice... in military boots. Sometimes he had to carry a flashlight to see his way. He said simply, 'There's a great advantage in training under unfavorable conditions.'

He was so fit that his first 5,000 meter race of 1947, against Nyberg in Prague, resulted in 14:08.2, second only to the peerless Hägg's 13:58.2.

Immediately, he had to fly to Finland, where Heino waited for him in Helsinki. Zátopek had lost his freshness and he was nervous, but he tried to run away from Heino. After 3,000 meters it became a fierce battle, with the lead changing on every lap. In the homestretch they fought side by side until Zátopek struggled one yard ahead at the tape in 14:15.2.

Suddenly, everybody wanted him to run. He graduated as an army lieutenant, and his entire month's leave was spent in fiery competition. He was undefeated at 5,000 meters in 1947 and he was No. 1 in World Ranking. At 3,000 meters he ranked No. 3, because of a defeat by Reiff. Zàtopek's 8:08.8 was second only to Hägg's record.

One reason he was not a favorite for the Olympic 10,000 meters was because his first attempt did not come until May of 1948, at Budapest. He had prepared strenuously. He ran as many as 60 runs of 400 meters in one day, with only a 200 meter jog in between. And yet the race was difficult. He ran a good 30:28.4, a national record by two full minutes.

Next came 3,000 meters in 8:07.8, and then his 29:27 at Prague on June 17. Five days later, he ran Slykhuis off the track in a 14:10 5,000. He was in great shape, and yet the track world was not prepared for his triumph in London.

After the Olympics, Zátopek was worn out and his hip hurt, but it was impossible to avoid racing, even though he was badly off form. He lost his second race of the season, to Reiff's 14:19 at Prague.

On October 24, he was married. His wife, Dana, had placed seventh in the women's Olympic javelin at London, and she

Emil Zatopek

shared Emil's superabundance of high spirits and energy. Denied permission by her parents to participate in a handball championship that morning, she went cycling with Emil and they crashed while kissing. Late for their wedding, they made up for it by dancing until dawn, after the other guests had all dropped out.

The combination of marriage, a new job, and his Olympic success would put an end to most careers, but Zátopek only tried harder. His third race of 1949 was 14:10.8 for 5,000 meters, and he knew he was better than ever.

On June 12, he ran in the Army Championship at Ostreva.

'I was in Zlín all day Friday. On Saturday around 11 o'clock I got an express train for the race at Ostreva. I had to stand all the way and had only beer and biscuits to eat. It was a five hour trip. I was dead tired when I arrived and boarded a street car to go to the stadium. I went to sleep and a soldier awoke me just in time to get off at the stadium.'

Naturally, he planned no special effort in the 10,000, but he felt unusually strong. In the seventh kilometer the announcer said Zátopek had a chance for the world record and the crowd began to cheer him on. With a hard finish, he crossed the line in 29:28.2. He was a world record holder!

He ran 14:14.4 and 29:49.6, then he had to stay out of competition for a month with a leg injury. He beat Heino in 29:58.4. On September 1, Heino regained the world record with 29:27.2.

Czechs begged Zátopek to reclaim his record, but he answered, 'Perhaps in the spring,' for his training had suffered from the excess of races and travels. He ran three more 10,000 meter races with one good time of 29:38.2.

Then a world record attempt was organized for Ostreva on October 22 and he had three weeks to prepare. For fourteen days he ran ruthlessly – five times 200 meters at full speed, 30 times 400 meters at racing speed, and five more 200's, with only fast 200-meter jogs for recovery. Then a leg injury slowed him, but he trained carefully, with two days of rest.

A cold wind quieted before the race, but dark clouds threatened. Zátopek wore blue shorts and a white shirt with his army sports club initials, ATK. At 7,000 meters, in 20:35.5, he was well ahead of a record pace when a crisis struck and he slowed. At his new pace he would fail. The crowd pleaded with him.

He fought his weariness with all his willpower. On the last

lap he ran as hard as he could. In the homestretch he suddenly waved to the crowd and smiled. His time was 29:21.2.

The world record was his again. Dana's words describe his feelings: 'He glowed like a meteor and couldn't fall asleep all night for excitement.'

He had finished 1949 undefeated except for one 1,500 meter lark. His next goal was 10,000 meters under 29:15. He had given runners a new philosophy which was building a chasm between those who are great and those who play only for fun.

'If one can stick to the training throughout the many long years, then will power is no longer a problem. It's raining? That doesn't matter. I am tired? That's beside the point. It's simply that I just have to.'

With snow on the ground, Zátopek wore an extra jersey, sweat pants, a knit cap, and heavy boots to protect his ankles. One exercise he invented was bounding exuberantly through the snow with exaggerated knee lifts.

In 1950 he won many easy races in times which would please almost any other runner. In June he increased his training load to its highest intensity. For two weeks he ran at least 40 times 400 meters each day.

On August 2, in Helsinki, he lowered his personal record for 5,000 meters to 14:06.2. He was ready. Two days later, he ran 10,000 meters on the famous track at Turku.

He found himself running exceptionally well. He increased his pace. Heino was there as a spectator, cheering him on. The entire Finnish crowd cheered him. He ran faster and faster, finishing with a wild sprint. His time took a stunning 18 seconds off his world record – 29:02.6.

After two more good 5,000's, he went to the hospital with food poisoning from a goose. His stomach was pumped, and the doctor ordered him to withdraw from the European Championships, but the doctor did not know his patient.

Zátopek went to Brussels anyway, and a crowd of 60,000 saw him run the 10,000 on a puddled track in a foolhardy 29:12.0. He won by more than a minute even though he had to race Reiff in three days.

In the 5,000, he clung grimly to Reiff's desperate pace, then raced past him at the bell. There was a great silence from the Belgian crowd. Reiff almost collapsed and finished 23 seconds

Emil Zatopek

behind. Later, he commented, 'I was beaten by Zátopek's strength, by his courage, and by his amazing energy.'

Zátopek's time was 14:03.0, his fastest ever.

Four days later he ran 29:54.6 and the next day, a fine 14:05.2. Thus, in one great month, the doctor's patient had run the two outstanding 10,000's of all time, plus the second, third, and fourth best 5,000's. Once again he finished the year unvanquished.

That winter he decided to train indoors. His bold experiment in weight training included hours of labored riding the bicycle with 4.4 pound weights on each foot, deep knee bends, and knee raising against the stubborn resistance of a wall exerciser. A near-disastrous ski accident put one leg in a cast for a month, and his desire to run was frustrated until April.

For him, most of 1951 was a bad year. He lost a race at 3,000 meters. He won all his 5,000 meter races, but his times were not sensational and he lost his No. 1 ranking to Reiff. His record remained untarnished in the 10,000 meters, with a best of 29:29.8, but his real honors came at longer distances.

At Prague, on September 15, he set out to break the national record for one hour. He ran his first 10,000 meters in 31:06. Then, 'I knew that I would have no problem in lasting out and so I ran as fast as I could.'

His second 10,000 was a good 30:10. In one hour he covered 19,558 meters (12 miles 268 yards). That, plus his 20,000 meter time of 1:01:16, ruined Heino's world records.

Heino's comment was, 'Believe me, Zátopek could run twenty kilometers in one hour.'

People talked about such a fantastic possibility. Other than Heino and Zátopek, only four men had ever run under 30 minutes for one 10,000. Zátopek was relied upon to do it twice, back to back. Zátopek, himself, was doubtful, but he knew he could do much better than his own record, and so, on September 29 at the excellent track among the trees at Houstka Spa near Stará Boleslav, he tried.

It was a warm, windless day, and he felt fine. He led the other 16 runners from the start, passing the first 5,000 in 14:56. At 10,000 meters he felt confident in 29:53.4. The spectators were agog. He passed 15,000 meters in 44:54.6, a surprising world record.

Suddenly, he felt a painful stich in his side. He knew it came from eating before the race, but he had needed the strength and now he fought against the pain. He passed 10 miles in 48:12, another world record.

The stitch went away after a few minutes, but he had to fight his fatigue. He waited in suspense for the gunshot which would signal 59 minutes. He approached the post marking only 400 meters to go for his 20,000 meters. If only he could run a few yards past that post before the shot, he could finish under one hour.

Still no shot. Puzzled, he entered the curve. Then the shot rang out. He tried hard, all the way around to the finish, in 59:51.8. He had done it! Still the timer had not fired the final gun He had to continue. He ran another 52 meters before the hour ended – his fourth world record in one stunning race.

He sighed. 'Today I really had more than enough.'

He ran three more 5,000's in October. Then he rested and enjoyed ice skating with Dana and running in deep snow. He had to his credit four of the five fastest 5,000's ever run, and six of the seven best 10,000's. It was time to prepare for the Olympics.

In April of 1952, he caught a chill but he ran anyway. He became ill and was confined to bed. After a few days he could stand it no longer. He sneaked away from the doctors and nurses, and he ran.

With the Olympics only two months away, he ran 5,000 meters in a horrifying 14:46.4. In Kiev on June 11, he was badly beaten by two Russians, but his time, 60 yards back, was down to 14:22.0. Two days later, after Aleksandr Anufriev had built up a lead of 120 meters in the 10,000, he gave all he had to win in 29:26.0.

He became depressed, but he won his national championships in 14:17.6 and 30:28.4. After three weeks of preparation, he felt confident of his ability to win the 10,000, but no more.

In the beautiful stadium at Helsinki, 32 intense runners lined up for the start of the 10,000 meters on the first day of competition. Zátopek, in his bright red vest, was in the second row, and he started calmly, letting the others struggle for the lead.

He was a wise veteran now, cool and collected. He ran to his own pace, placidly watching the times on the gigantic electric scoreboard, easily visible from the backstretch. His first lap was in 68.9, in tenth place. He tried to stay in the first lane, for a wiry moss had been built into the red brick and clay track for buoyancy.

Emil Zatopek

At six laps, in 7:02.4, a rousing drive put him in the lead, and he began his effort to shake loose from the others. He increased his pace cold-bloodedly on each curve and his lap times swung between 68 and 72. At 5,000 meters, in 14:43.4, only two brave runners hung on.

After 13 laps, young Gordon Pirie could stand it no longer, and then there was only Mimoun. Since 1948, the courageous little Algerian in the blue of France had lost only to Zátopek. Now he hung on grimly as 70,000 keen fans howled appreciation and advice.

Zátopek increased the pressure for six laps. Then, slowly, the dark little runner faded behind him. Zátopek continued a safe 71-second pace. On the last lap, with the crowd cheering louder than in 1948, he increased to 64 seconds. He won his second gold medal by 90 yards in 29:17.0, his third best time.

He was in high spirits for the third heat of the 5,000 meters two days later. At the start he said, 'Shall I ever get into the final?' but during the heat he was a friendly extrovert. He encouraged Curt Stone of the United States in English: 'Come along, Stone, if you want to qualify.' He spoke in Russian to Anufriev, 'Sasha, come on, we must get a move on.' Desiring to remain on the pole, he gently took hold of one runner's shorts and moved him aside. On the last lap, when only five were left in contention, he lulled them to an easy pace with five fingers held up in front of their faces.

Two days later, the final was serious business. Still, he was smiling and at ease in the dressing room and on the starting line, greeting his opponents in his warmest English, French, and German. Then the gun sounded and a capacity crowd stirred to one of the greatest races in history.

Zátopek was willing to help set the pace, but Herbert Schade of Germany, a threat because of his 14:06.6 in June and his Olympic record 14:15.4 in his heat, wanted to lead. At 4,000 meters it was the bespectacled Schade in 11:24.8, followed by Zátopek and Reiff.

To many onlookers, Reiff was still the favorite, with his smooth stride and great speed, but suddenly he stepped off the track and quit with 500 meters left. Four runners entered the last lap together.

As the bell clamored, Zátopek heaved himself into the lead.

Fighting hard on the backstretch, he was startled to see a red-headed runner appear alongside. It was Chris Chataway, Britain's 22-year-old wonder, sprinting into the lead. To his dismay, Zátopek saw Schade and Mimoun go past. Zátopek, six yards behind, looked a tired and beaten runner, and he was full of despair.

At the same time he was calculating where he would attack. He could not allow himself to be fourth. Into the last curve he suddenly threw everything he had into a straining, heaving, awkward sprint. The crowd roared, almost hysterically excited.

Running in the third lane, he went past Schade. Mimoun swung out to pass Chataway and bumped Zátopek, but Zátopek was once again the runaway locomotive, charging past all of them.

He was not aware of the hapless Chataway's fall behind him. His only thought was to give everything he had. He thundered down the homestretch, pulling away from Mimoun on sheer strength and will power.

He won in 14:06.6. His last furious 200 meters was in 28.3, his last 400 was 58.1. Everybody was surprised by such a glorious finish. Probably, he could not have done it unless it was necessary.

The crowd remained standing in quiet awe. They had witnessed an amazing demonstration of courage.

Exhausted, Zátopek returned to the Olympic village and so he did not see Dana win the women's javelin. When he heard the good news, he said, 'This gold one pleases me more than all the other ones so far.'

Zatopek's double victory in his regular events was no surprise, even though some experts had favored Schade and Reiff. But the marathon was a baffling matter. He had never endured even half that distance. He was uncertain of his training. The whole thing was a gamble, and nobody knew it better than Zátopek.

He had two precious days of rest. He spent some time learning patience at the slow marathon pace. Then, at 3:30 p.m., he took his marks with 67 other runners before an expectant crowd of 80,000. He felt unsure of himself; his three gold medals meant nothing here. This was the strongest field of marathon runners ever assembled.

He started near the head of the pack for three laps around the red track. Then, with a wave to his friends, he left the stadium, keeping a wary eye on Jim Peters ahead of him. Peters,

Emil Zatopek

The 1952 Olympic marathon: Zatopek enters the stadium.

who had the fastest time ever run, feared Zátopek and tried to run away with a long, stretching stride and an awkward head roll.

At 10,000 meters, in the village of Molmi, Zátopek was running comfortably with Gustaf Jansson of Sweden, 17 seconds behind Peters. The next 5,000 meters included some hills, but Zátopek still felt fresh. This was still a familiar distance. Jansson finally spoke to him in Swedish, challenging him to catch Peters. At 15,000 meters in 47:58, they caught the white-clad Englishman, and they ran together amicably for 3,000 meters.

Zátopek asked Peters if the pace was fast enough. Peters, almost out on his feet, said it was too slow.

Incredulous, Zátopek said, 'You say "too slow". Are you sure the pace is too slow?'

'Yes,' Peters answered.

Zátopek shook his head and increased the pace.

'Come with us,' he encouraged Peters. 'It's much easier when there are three together.'

Zátopek and Jansson rounded the turning post side by side, with Peters falling behind. Now they ran into a breeze and running became harder.

At 25,000 meters on the now-familiar road, Zátopek led Jansson by five seconds after the Swede stopped for fruit juice. Zátopek fought down his desire to drink, for liquids did not agree with him when he ran.

Now was his chance. He ran over two hills at a good pace. Then, hopefully, he looked back. He was relieved to see Jansson far behind.

Now it was a question of being able to finish at this pace. Many an unhappy track runner has run well for 20 miles only to fall apart with miles still to go. Zátopek feared this invisible barrier, and he ran carefully.

His feet were beginning to blister, and his legs had lost their spring, but he gritted his teeth and kept running. He knew how to fight.

At 30,000 meters, his 1:38:42 was 12 seconds faster than the world record. His legs ached and he seemed to have a chest full of needles. He relaxed his arms and opened his mouth wider to get more air.

At 35,000 meters, in 1:56:50, he was over a minute ahead of

Jansson. The crowd shouted encouragement, but the clamor only made his head ache.

He ran steadily, fighting the pain, through the outskirts of Helsinki. At 40,000 meters, in 2:15:10, he led by a satisfactory $2\frac{1}{4}$ minutes. Now he knew he could do it. Only eight more minutes to go.

The Zátopek who entered the stadium through the marathon gate to a blare of trumpets seemed frail and timid compared to the man who had charged down the homestretch of the 5,000 meters. His face was ashen, his red vest was soaked and hanging outside his shorts. His legs barely lifted high enough.

The crowd, however, did not notice. All they saw was the most glorious triumph in the history of sport. Wildly, they came to their feet. Whatever their language, they chanted with all the rest, 'Zá-to-pek, Zá-to-pek, Zá-to-pek.'

He pushed himself wearily around the track. He lifted his arms above the tape. He smiled. He had won a triple victory impossible to evaluate. It was certainly the greatest in Olympic history. The crowd loved him.

He sat down. Cautiously, he removed his shoes to examine his bloody feet. He heard his time – 2:23:03.2 – fastest ever run on an out-and-back course. People congratulated him. Not the least of his rewards was a real kiss from the women's javelin champion.

He greeted the other finishers with slices of orange – Reinaldo Gorno, $2\frac{1}{2}$ minutes behind, then Jansson. He munched an apple, smiling and talking. After the victory ceremony he jogged a lap of honor and his ovation has never been surpassed.

After the Olympics he could have taken a welcome rest, but he was reaching top form and he wanted to make use of it. He ran 5,000 meters in 14:06.4 early in October. Then he returned to the forest stadium at Houstka for another record attempt on October 26.

After a hard rain, the track was in good condition. Zátopek ran around and around, monotonously strong. In one hour he had covered 18,970 meters. At 15 miles in 1:16:26.4, he triumphed over the world record by more than a minute. At 25,000 meters, his 1:19:11.8 took another minute off Mikko Hietanen's record. Zátopek seemed fresh. He finished, smiling and waving. His time for 30,000 meters was 1:35:23.8 an impressive minute and a half under the record. Now the Czechs pointed with pride to every official world record from 10,000 meters on up.

Czechoslovakia awarded him the Order of the Republic, its highest honor, never before given to an athlete. But an illness threatened to end his career in 1953. He had his tonsils removed and spent several days in the hospital. His 5,000 meter times were mediocre, for him, and he lost one race at 3,000 meters.

On August 5 he was in Bucharest for the biggest race of the year. Anufriev had run 13:58.8, Kovacs had bettered Zátopek's best time with 14:01.2, and a new threat was named Vladimir Kuts. Zátopek was 30 meters behind with two laps to go, but a savage 800 meters sent him past Kuts on the last turn and he won in 14:03.

He became ill again and he missed six weeks of competition. On October 17 in Prague, he appeared hopelessly beaten, 30 meters behind Kovacs with a lap to go. Once again he won by fighting harder than even he thought possible. He ran the last lap in 57.8 to win in 14:09.0.

On November 11, in good shape again, he ran 10,000 meters in the three-lined Houstka stadium where his tenacious pace had broken six world records. This time he passed 6 miles in a world record 28:08.4. He fought hard during the last lap and ran 10,000 meters in 29:01.6, a full second under his own world record.

He ended the year with a pleasant trip to Brazil for the famous New Year's Eve race. An estimated 800,000 people cheered him along as he won in record time.

In 1954, the world began to catch up with Zátopek. Younger, talented runners used his example to train more intensely. He began the year free from handicaps and ran 14:04.0 on May 14.

On May 30, in Cólombes Stadium in Paris, he roused a small crowd of 6,000 with something special. In a 5,000 meter race, he was 4.4 seconds behind Hägg's world record pace at 4,000 meters, but his last raging 1,000 in 2:43.8 brought him across the line in 13:57.2. He had broken the honored 12-year-old record by one second. He now held the wondrous total of ten world records – everything longer than three miles.

With only one day of rest, he amazed the track world again. Running almost alone in Brussels, he was a man inspried. He pushed himself as if his life depended upon it, and he broke his

Emil Zatopek

records for 6 miles (27:59.2) and 10,000 meters (28:54.2).

A month later, July 3, he ran into trouble against Kovacs before 80,000 partisan fans in Budapest's Népstadion. Zátopek was slightly ill and feverish, while Kovacs ran faster than any other man except Zátopek. At 6 miles Zátopek managed to lead, but Kovacs went ten meters past him on the last curve. All of Zátopek's fighting courage could gain only four meters in the stretch and Kovacs won in 29:09. The Hungarians were overjoyed, for this was Zátopek's only failure in any race over 5,000 meters.

Zátopek went to Bern for the European Championships knowing he was no longer invincible. An eager crowd packed the small Neufeld Stadium, expecting an exciting 10,000 meters, but Zátopek took no chances with tactics. He ran with determination from the start and he beat Kovacs by a satisfying half lap in 28:58.0 on a wet track. Zátopek now claimed seven of the eight best 10,000's ever run.

He had given too much in the 10,000, however, and he allowed Kuts to go far ahead in the 5,000. Kuts won by a shocking 100 meters in a new world record time of 13:56.6. Zátopek was outkicked by Chataway, and he finished a dispirited third in 14:10.2.

He tried to regain his 5,000 meter record at Stockholm on September 3. He came heartbreakingly close with 13:57.0.

In Prague, on October 23, Zátopek's demise was near completion. In the dual meet with the Soviets, he was helpless as Kuts went far ahead. Kuts kept going and set a world record of 13:51.2. Zátopek suffered his worst defeat, half a lap behind.

In 1955, he trained harder than ever, running as many as 90 times 400 meters in a day in a vain effort at improvement. Although he ran 10,000 meters under 30 minutes on seven occasions, in two of them he placed a sad third – against Hungary and against Pirie and Ken Norris in London. He ranked only fourth in the world after seven consecutive years as first, six of them undefeated. He also lost six 5,000 meter races.

His hard training paid off in one great achievement, on October 29 at Celakovice. Albert Ivanov, a Russian friend, had bettered Zátopek's 25,000 meter record by two minutes on September 27, and Zátopek wanted it back. He passed 10,000 meters in 30:24.2. He passed the 15-mile mark in 1:14:01.0, almost 2½ minutes under his own world record. He continued his steady pace and broke Ivanov's record by almost half a minute, in 1:16:36.4.

In 1956, he was definitely poorer, set back both by age and a hernia operation, and yet he ran 29:33.4 in October, approached within 27 seconds of his 25,000 meter record on October 21, and placed sixth in the Olympic marathon at Melbourne. His enthusiastic followers claim he would have won except for his disastrous hernia operation, causing a three-month layoff in the summer.

For most runners, sixth in the Olympic marathon would be a crowning achievement, but to the balding Colonel Zátopek it was the end. Grinning, he said:

'I realized I was licked at the halfway point. I started confident that I could make a good race of it, but I suddenly realized about all that was left was to go out like a champion. That was when I decided it was no use breaking my neck with any more speed and risk collapse. . . . This was my last race.'

Actually, he ran with spirit in 1957, and won half of his ten 10,000 meter races. His times for the last five ranged between 29:47 and 29:25.8, excellent for a man of thirty-five. He lost a 5,000 meter race while running 14:06.4.

Emil Zátopek's problem was that he became a legend before he lost his zest for racing. Nobody can remain the greatest forever, not even with the greatest of courage.

BOB MATHIAS

'Boy,' said Bob Mathias in May of 1948, 'the more I hear of the decathlon, the less I like it.'

Coach Virgil Jackson, however, was determined to prove the worth of his prize 17-year-old. He wanted Mathias to begin training for the decathlon and enter a meet only four weeks away.

'By 1952,' Jackson argued, 'you will have had the benefit of college coaching, and if you keep at it I'll bet you can make the Olympic team then.'

In retrospect, that is quite funny, but it was enough to persuade the boy. On June 10, he was on the field at Pasadena, California, competing against some of the best in the United States in the Southern Pacific AAU decathlon.

He ran 100 meters in 11.3 and broad jumped 21' 4½", not what he had hoped. In the 16-pound shot put, he lost more than the expected ten feet from his high school best, reaching only 43' 1". He high jumped only 5' 10", a disappointment after his second place in the high school high jump at the West Coast Relays. He lifted no eyebrows with his 52.1 for 400 meters.

None of his marks were noteworthy, even for the tender age of 17½, and he was beaten several times by his more mature opponents. Such is the peculiar nature of the decathlon, however, that it pointed out one virtue in young Mathias: he had no weakness. He was in first place.

People who saw him take a cat nap while he waited between events thought he was lazy. They did not know about his anemia at the age of 11, curtailing his beloved sports. They did not know the hours his mother had spent teaching him how to relax.

On the second day, Mathias ran the hurdles in 15.7, no surprise to his opponents, for they knew he was state high school champion in both hurdles. He threw the discus 140' ⅛", more than ten feet short of his excellent personal record.

Now people began to believe he had no weakness. They

did not know he had first attempted the pole vault and javelin only four weeks before. In the pole vault he missed his first two attempts at nine feet although he had cleared ten feet in practice.

He worked feverishly on his step on another runway, and on his third trial he cleared easily. He went on to clear 11' 9", much higher than he had hoped. The dazed observers were discovering one more quality about Bob Mathias: he was something of a genius at rising to the occasion.

In the javelin, the best he could do on his first two throws was 155 feet, good for a beginner. On his last throw, he sent the spear flying out 175' 4⅝", surprising everybody.

For an athlete over six feet tall and weighing more than 185 pounds, the 1,500 meters is a difficult and unpleasant event, but he ran it in 4:59.2.

He had accomplished more than anybody hoped. He won with 7,094 points. As a result of this sensational beginning, he was in Bloomfield, New Jersey, two weeks later for the AAU championships, hoping to be among the first three and represent the USA in the Olympic Games.

Surprising the easterners, Mathias improved on four of his Pasadena marks the first day with 11.2, 21' 6⅝", 6 feet even, and 51 flat. But he was a disheartening 354 points behind three-time champion Irving Mondschein.

One of the few who was confident was the 17½-year-old boy himself. Starting the second day he drove over the high hurdles in 15.1 to put fear into Mondschein. He sailed the discus 139' 7", a disappointment to him, but he gained 124 points. Then a thunderstorm halted competition for an hour and a half.

With the field turned to mud, pole vaulting became dangerous. Al Lawrence, a 13-footer, cleared only 11' 6¼" and the surprising boy tied him. After a mediocre javelin throw of 157' 3" from the muddy runway and a personal record 4:55.2 in the 1,500, Mathias was the national champion.

His 7,224 was the second best score in the world since 1940. And he was on the Olympic team!

He traveled to England by ship as the youngest track and field member of any U.S. Olympic team in history. He knew he needed more training and he worked hard, staying close to the yellow and blue RAF barracks at Uxbridge. His hard work hurt his elbow and his knee. These injuries and the international competition threatened his chances, but he still hoped for a medal.

At seven o'clock on the morning of August 5, Mathias wakened, calmly drank orange juice and ate a steak, and rode the bus ten miles to Wembley, where 70,000 spectators braved the rain. Not allowed to warm up properly, he ran his 100 meters at 10:30 a.m. in 11.2, equalling his best time.

His first broad jump was over 23 feet. Unfortunately, he fell back, and an hour later, when his second turn came, he could jump only 21' 8¼". He was far down in the field of 35, and he had to start gaining.

He put everything he had into his first shot put and the ball sailed over 45 feet. Smiling with satisfaction, he stepped out toward his put. To his dismay, a red flag waved, indicating a foul, and then, for the first time, he heard of the bizarre Olympic rule requiring him to step out of the back half of the circle. He had to settle for 42' 9¼".

He had to wait in the rain, wrapped in his blanket, for the high jump. He missed at 5' 9", an easy height for him in high school. When he missed for a second time he began to worry. If he cleared no height all his chances for a medal were gone.

He remembered a happy day when he was ten. He had tried to jump four feet high with no previous experience and, somehow, his formless dive had carried him over the bar. Now he determined to try the same dive. With everything riding on his gamble, he swung around almost directly in front of the bar. He ran hard and used all his strength. His form amazed everyone, but he cleared the bar.

Up in the stands, coach Brutus Hamilton whacked coach Dink Templeton on the back and cried, 'The kid's going to win it.'

Templeton agreed wholeheartedly and called Mathias a 'competitive genius'.

Mathias went over the bar at 6' 1¼", his best height. He gained on almost everybody, including the stunned Mondschein, a 6' 7" jumper. Ten weary hours after he started competing, Mathias ran 400 meters in 51.7. He was in third place, 49 points behind cocky Lt Carlos Kistenmacher of Argentina.

Kistenmacher boasted to his young opponent: 'Whatever you do in each event, I'll do better.'

Mathias was not worried enough to miss his nap on the bus

back to the Olympic Village. He ate and went to sleep. At seven the next morning, he was disappointed to find it was raining harder than ever and his legs were stiff and sore.

At 10:30 a.m., he ran the worst hurdles race ever. He hit the first hurdle and lost balance and momentum. His 15.7 was a tribute to his ability to come back.

Kistenmacher slipped badly to 16.3 and Mathias passed him, but Simmons, a fine hurdler, ran 15.2 to take the lead. Mathias was a good third behind Ignace Heinrich of France.

Aroused, Mathias threw the discus 145 feet, but Mondschein's discus slid along the wet grass and knocked over Mathias' marker. Half an hour later, frustrated officials placed a marker about a foot and a half short of his throw. Even so, his 144′ 4″ was so good it put him in the lead by 48 points.

It was noon and Mathias wanted to leave the field. He was hungry and he wanted to get out of the rain. An official warned him he might be called to vault at any moment, and so Mathias returned to the meager comfort of his blanket. The competitors were divided into two groups, and Mathias was in the second group. By the time the hungry boy was allowed to vault, six hours had passed.

The other entrants were slipping on the pole and sliding on the runway, but Mathias coolly passed until the bar reached ten feet. He cleared it easily.

Miserably wet and muddy, Mathias continued vaulting. It was dark now and there was unsatisfactory illumination from the flickering Olympic torch and a pitiful string of 50-watt bulbs along the stands. Vaulting was dangerous.

Meanwhile, the more fortunate group finished the competition. Heinrich was the winner, unless Mathias could triumph over the rain, the poor light, and fatigue from the late hour.

Courageously, Mathias kept vaulting. He cleared 11′ 5¾″, near his best height. He missed twice at 11′ 9″. Then he decided to stop. He could win ... if nothing went wrong.

Harried officials used flashlights so the javelin throwers could measure their steps. A flashlight illuminated the foul line. Mathias ran down the wretched runway and threw, but he crossed the line. Another foul would put him in grave danger. On his second throw, he concentrated on avoiding a foul. He put his whole arm into a desperate throw and the javelin disappeared into the night. His elbow hurt, but the javelin stabbed into the mud at 165′ 1″. He was only 189 points behind Heinrich.

Now, if only he could finish the 1,500 meters, he could win. The track was soaked, and he had cramps in one foot and in his empty stomach, but he was not about to give up. He put on a sprint toward the finish line, lighted by flashlights. His time was 5:11, and those 354 dearly bought points boosted his total to 7,139.

He was the Olympic champion... at the age of 17 years, 8 months, and 3 weeks. Wearily, he plodded barefoot to the stands and hugged his mother while his father and two brothers grinned.

At that moment, tired and hungry after 12 hours in the stadium, he did not consider that all decathlons are not conducted under such distressing conditions. He said, 'No more decathlon, Dad ... ever again.'

Reaction to Mathias' cinderella victory was stupendous. President Truman sent him a telegram and, later, greeted him in person. The people of little Tulare, California, erupted in a joyous victory celebration which shut down the town and clogged Highway 99 for three hours. Coach Virgil Jackson 'found myself alone, in a city park, sitting on a park bench for 20 minutes and crying like a baby.'

Mathias was besieged for autographs and interviews. A crowd of 5,000 people met him at the Visalia airport, nine miles from Tulare, and thirty state highway patrolmen handled traffic. At a testimonial dinner the next night, he was praised by Governor Earl Warren and decathlon world record holder Glenn Morris. Mathias was honored the next night in Fresno, and later on 'Bob Mathias Day' at Sacramento's State Fair and in Los Angeles.

He was voted the Sullivan Award for 1948, for his good character as well as his dramatic victory. And still later, the Tulare court reporter stated, 'Bob Mathias' victory in the Olympic Games and his all-around fine sportsmanship in school here have done more to combat juvenile delinquency in Tulare than any other happening.'

Mathias played football that fall at Kiski prep school in Pennsylvania, then started track in the indoor season. In the National Interscholastics at Madison Square Garden, he showed his class by winning the prep high hurdles and placing second in both broad jump and high jump. During the easy spring season he concentrated on the AAU decathlon to be held June 28 and 29. Eager citizens had secured the meet for Tulare.

Mathias' home town numbered 12,000 total population, and each evening 7,000 enthusiastic spectators watched the decathlon. Mathias was second at the end of five events, but he crushed Mondschein the second night and won with 7,556 points, a total bettered by only four men before him. He said, 'It seemed to come a lot easier this time.'

In Oslo, Norway, he won a decathlon with 7,346 points, and then he enrolled at Stanford. In the spring he was all over the track and field. He lowered his best high hurdle time to 14.5, raised his vault to a good 12' 10", and lengthened his shot and discus marks impressively to 49' 6" and 157' 5¼", each one a record for Stanford freshmen.

In the important meet against the California frosh, not content to win those four events, he also won the low hurdles and placed second in the high jump and fourth in the javelin. In a low-pressure practice decathlon he scored 7,602 points.

He sought the national AAU decathlon title again in zealous Tulare on June 27 and 28, and he faced the toughest opponent of his career. Bill Albans, an Olympic hop-step-jumper, was fresh from scoring an amazing 22 points in the NCAA meet.

Mathias was happy with his 100 meters in 10.9, but Albans ran 10.6. Mathias rose to the occasion with a personal broad jump record of 23' 3⅜", but Albans leaped 24' 6⅞". Mathias put the shot 47' 6¼", his best in a decathlon. Albans could do only 39' ⅜" and Mathias passed him, but Albans high jumped 6' 2¾", two inches higher than Mathias, to regain the lead. Mathias ran 400 meters in 51 flat, equal to his best ever, but Albans ran 49.5.

At the end of the first night, Mathias had scored 4,230 points, a total bettered by only three men before this meet. But Albans was 101 points ahead with the highest first-day total in history.

Starting the second night, Mathias ran the hurdles in a good 14.7, but Albans ran 14.1, the fastest time ever recorded in a decathlon. After 6 events, Mathias was 210 points behind and the 6,500 spectators were worried.

Mathias, however, had only begun to fight. He threw the discus a good 146' 5". He set a personal record with a vault of 13' ¾".

Bob Mathias

He threw the javelin for a personal record of 182' 4½". A bewildered Albans said, 'He isn't human.'

Mathias, with the event won, set out after Morris' world record of 7,900 points. The temperature had reached a nearly unbelievable 114 degrees, making distance running most difficult, but he pushed himself around the track in 5 :05.1.

His score was a superb 8,042 points. He was now, at the age of 19, world record holder in the event demanding the most experience.

For the third summer, the teenager toured Europe. On August 6, exactly two years after his Olympic triumph, he won the Swiss Championship with 7,312 points on a wet track.

In the spring of 1951, a muscle spasm in his back limited his action. In the low hurdles, he ran 23.5 and placed fourth in the conference meet. In the shot, he was a highly regarded prospect at 51' 2½". He placed sixth in the NCAA and seventh in the AAU. How won the conference discus, placed second in the NCAA and fourth in the AAU, for a remarkable seventh in World Ranking. In the dual meet against the Big Ten conference at Eugene, Oregon, on June 19, he threw the discus 173' 4" and set another excellent personal record with 24' 5" in the broad jump.

Stanford coach Jack Weiershauser tried to explain Mathias' success without full training in any single event : 'He just does it, that's all. Especially when we need it. It's all in his mind.'

In the fall of 1951, Mathias played football and helped greatly in Stanford's surprise appearance in the Rose Bowl. Then he did some skiing and led his fraternity to the intramural basketball championship. Critics said he was not developing his great track potential. He did no weight training and not enough technique training.

In the 1952 collegiate season, he cut his high hurdle time satisfactorily to 14.3. In the NCAA, he ran 14.2 for a laudable second place behing Jack Davis. He also placed sixth in the discus and seventh in the shot. He competed in all three events in the Final Trials, but his mind was on the decathlon at Tulare, three days later. It meant more than the AAU championship this time. It also served as the Final Trials for the Olympic team.

On the night of July 1, before 6,000 hometown fans, Mathias was invincible. He ran the 100 meters in 10.8, his best time.

He broad jumped 23′ 5¼″, his best decathlon broad jump. He put the shot 49′ 10⅞″, also his best decathlon mark. In the high jump he never touched the bar. After clearing his best ever height of 6′ 2¾″ he stopped to conserve energy.

In the 400 meters, he raced hard against young Milt Campbell and finished in 50.8, his best time. His first-half score was higher than Albans' best-on-record.

He hit three hurdles to begin the second night and the crowd felt disappointed in his 14.6, but it was his fastest time in any decathlon. He threw the discus 157′ 11⅝″, his best in a decathlon. After seven consecutive decathlon bests he vaulted only 12′ 3¾″, but he came back with a personal record of 193′ 10⅜″ in the javelin, He ran 1,500 meters in 4 :55.3, almost his best. He was the only man ever to win four AAU decathlons.

This magnificent world record, under the newly adopted tables, totaled 7,829 points. Under this new system, his battered record of two years ago was only 7,444.

At 21, Mathias stood 6′ 3″ and weighed 195 pounds. He was an outstanding favorite to win the Olympic decathlon when they assembled in the beautiful stadium at Helsinki, but he had butterflies in his stomach. He was experienced enough now to know the hazards of decathlon competition. More than ability was needed. A man had to survive. Any injury or even bad luck could eliminate him from contention. No man had ever won the Olympic decathlon twice.

The bad luck struck him at the very beginning. On his marks for the 100, he heard a click and started running. A camera had set him off, but it cost him a false start. One more and he would lose all of the points from the 100, enough to beat him. He hung back until certain he heard the gun, but even with that bad start he ran 10.9.

On his third broad jump, trying to improve on his 22′ 10¾″, injury struck him. He felt a pain in his left thigh. Worried, he went to the Olympic Village and ate a large steak for lunch.

Somebody asked Brutus Hamilton, now head U.S. coach, if Mathias could continue.

'Yes, of course,' Hamilton said. 'Bob not only is the greatest athlete in the world but he's also the greatest competitor. You watch him now. When the pressure is on, he's at his best.'

A little later, a pressured Mathias stepped into the shot put

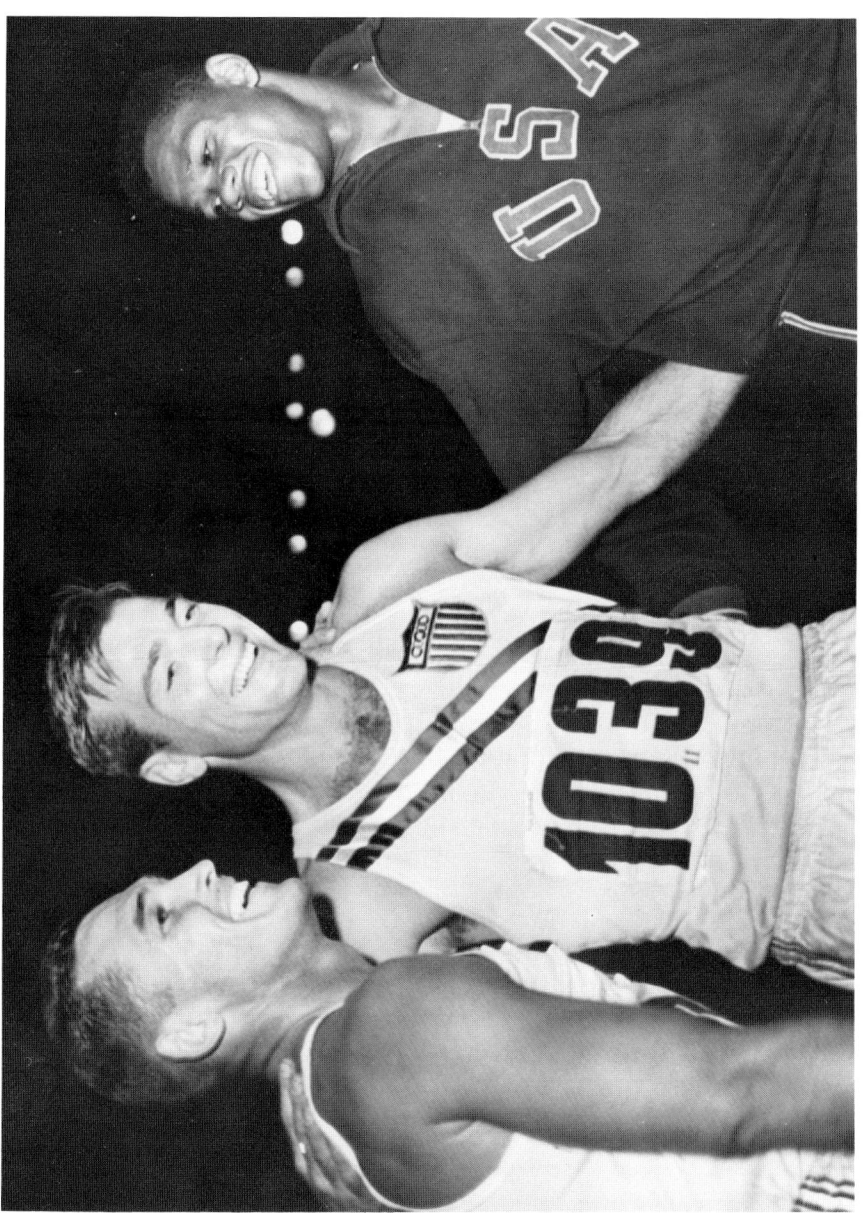

A U.S. sweep in the 1952 Olympic decathlon. Bob Mathias, flanked by Floyd Simmons and Milt Campbell.

ring. On his first put, he sent the ball out 50' 2⅜", his best ever in a decathlon. He overwhelmed his competition by at least five feet and took the lead.

In the high jump he cleared 6' 2⅘", his best ever. Then he studied his decathlon scoring tables. Satisfied, he stopped jumping to rest his sore leg.

It was cold and windy on the field. He took his mattress under the stands and calmly went to sleep. Refreshed, he returned to the field wearing a heavy overcoat under his blanket.

At 8:00 p.m. he ran his 400 meters. He sizzled around the wet track with a 22.5 200 meters, then hung on for 50.2, again his best ever.

Thus, backing up Brutus Hamilton's confidence in him, he had recorded three consecutive decathlon bests. His score was only 27 points behind his recent world record.

After a good night's sleep, he had a rubdown and heat for his injured leg. The trainer put on an elastic bandage. Still, when he tried to lift his leg over a hurdle, the pain was intense. He hit the first hurdle and never regained his timing. He had hoped for 14.2, but his time was 14.7. He was now only 179 points ahead of Campbell, still vulnerable.

During a light rain, he threw the discus 153' 10", an excellent decathlon mark but a disappointment to him. Then he omitted lunch at the Village in favor of another rubdown.

The pole vault lasted five dreary hours, through rain, sunshine, and a cold wind. He cleared 13' 1½", his best decathlon height. Coolly, he examined the scoring tables. His leg hurt more with each vault, and so he withdrew, satisfied to be 26 points ahead of his world record pace.

After another rubdown, he was ready for the javelin. He needed around 195 feet to stay ahead of his record pace, but he had never thrown that far. His first throw fell hopelessly short. His second was also short.

Up in the stands, coach Weiershauser urged some American youths into a rooting section, and they chanted, 'Oh, Bob. Hey you. Don't forget to follow through.'

Mathias smiled, and shouted to his coach, 'I got you.' His last throw brought a different cheer when it landed at 194' 3⅛".

At 10:00 p.m. he paced himself cautiously around the red brick track in the 1,500 meters. His taped leg ached with every

Bob Mathias

stride, but when he was sure of himself he increased the pace and ran his fastest 1,500 meters – 4 :50.8.

For the third time in his unparalleled career, he improved the world record. His 7,887 was equal to 8,450 on the old tables – 550 points better than the second best man of all time. He won his second gold medal by 912 points, largest victory margin in history.

Coach Hamilton was one of the first to shake his hand.

Mathias said, 'I'm glad I didn't let you down, Mr. Hamilton.'

Hamilton, himself a former Olympic decathlon silver medalist, had a film of emotion in his eyes.

'Bob, you'll never let anyone down.'

After the interviews, the remaining 15,000 spectators wanted a victory lap and Mathias jogged around to loud cheers. At the same moment, in a little town so far away it was barely afternoon, the citizens of Tulare paraded and danced in the street.

In a post Olympic meet in Zurich, Mathias was credited with 13.8 for the high hurdles, a time bettered by only eight men before him. 'I felt very good, had an excellent start, and was helped by ideal weather conditions and a very fast track.'

In the 1953 conference meet at Stanford, 8,500 fans were on hand to say farewell to Bob Mathias as a track man. He was cutting his season short to be married, and he had the Marine Corps ahead of him. His last event was a stirring low hurdle race against Jack Davis, one of the world's great hurdlers. Mathias pressed Davis all the way, barely losing in 23.2

Further honors as an amateur ended when he signed a contract to play himself in a film, 'The Bob Mathias Story'. He retired undefeated in the decathlon even though his remarkable potential was never fully developed.

Postscript: in 1956, three years after his last collegiate competition, he competed briefly in the maroon and gold of the Marine Corps. His quite remarkable feats proved better than anything else that his natural ability and competitive genius counted for more of his success than did his training.

After that long layoff, he threw the discus 162′ 5½″, better than most of his throws in his final year at Stanford. In the Marine Corps Championships he won the hurdles in surprising times of 14.4 and 23.4.

In the Interservice decathlon at the Coliseum, he was amazing. He ran 100 meters in 11 flat broad jumped 22′ 8¾″, and put the shot 50′ 4¼″. He was near a world record pace. He fell off a bit in the high jump, to 5′ 11¾″. Not in the best of shape, he ran a good 51.9 for 400 meters.

The next day, he ran 14.9, threw 160′ 2¼″, and vaulted 11′ 11½″. He took only one javelin throw but it sailed 204′ 1¼″, his best ever. The winner at 7,193 points, he was happy to withdraw from the 1,500 meters.

Obviously an Olympic contender except for his professional status, he said somewhat wistfully, 'I'm a little sorry I turned pro.'

PARRY O'BRIEN

Success in athletics, as in many other fields, comes from a combination of natural ability plus hard work, intelligently directed. All great athletes had unusual natural talent, and a few of them tried as hard as humanly possible, but most of them received their coaching from others.

One notable exception, whose creative thinking taught the world's coaches how to coach, was Parry O'Brien.

One night in 1951 at Fresno, California, O'Brien shoved a 16-pound iron ball 53′ $6\frac{7}{8}$″ for second place. This was almost two feet shorter than his best mark and even shorter than his national freshman record 53′ $10\frac{1}{2}$″ of the previous year. He had improved impressively over his 57′ $9\frac{1}{2}$″ with the 12-pound shot in 1949, but he was disappointed.

When the event was over, he stayed at the shot put circle. For two hours, while the meet went on under the lights, he practiced intensely with the help of 1948 Olympic champion Wilbur Thompson. He almost missed his airplane, but he arrived home in Santa Monica at 1:30 a.m.

At 3:00 a.m. his father was startled from a sound sleep by heavy thuds. Sleepily, he investigated and saw his son in the asphalt alley, putting the shot from a chalked circle under the street light. After each put, Parry had to search among the weeds of the vacant lot with a flashlight to find the iron ball.

'I think I've discovered something,' he told his sleepy father. 'I couldn't wait until morning.' And he continued his intense concentration until 4:00 a.m.

His father's affectionate summation was: 'He has more determination than four mules.'

O'Brien hoped he had improved, but in the NCAA meet at Seattle he put only 53′ 10″ and he lost by one frustrating inch to Darrow Hooper, who was the high school record holder two years before.

The defeat hurt O'Brien. He had fouled on puts near 55 feet, and it was his first loss to a collegian. Then, in a mid-week meet at Eugene, Oregon, against the Big Ten conference, he put only 53′ 9½″. Disgusted, he worked out for 2½ hours after the meet.

A week after his NCAA failure, he was in Berkeley for his first national AAU meet, and he had 'psyched himself up' into a heated determination to beat Hooper.

'I try to whip myself into a frenzy. When I'm ready for a toss I'm in a different world.'

He was also competing against world record holder Jim Fuchs, victorious in 88 consecutive meets. Fuchs was not at his best because of a sore back, but he put 55′ 2″.

Without warning, the track world was forced to recognize O'Brien as an unusually reliable competitor, able to focus his hours of strong self-discipline and intense concentration onto the best put of his life at the right moment. For he came through with 55′ 9¼″ to win his first great victory.

Next came a significant trip to Europe with too many meets too close together. 'I was looking for a way to throw that was easier but with which I could get the same results.'

He reached 55′ 5″ at Paris on July 8. Then he began his daring experiment. At the start of a put, he began turning his right foot farther and farther toward the back of the circle, like Fuchs, but he also shocked coaches by turning his whole body so that his back was toward the direction of his throw.

'I was severly criticized by German coaches and other experts who said it wasn't natural for the body to go that way, and it was too unorthodox to succeed. But I was thoroughly convinced that with the orthodox method I was, and always would be, no better than a 56-foot shot putter. I was certain that I could not achieve the kind of marks I had in mind – 59 and 60 feet – with this orthodox technique.'

In the fall of 1951, he gave up football in favor of track. 'I wanted to be able to take the credit or the blame for what I did myself. I always wanted to be a soloist.'

He began training for the 1952 season and he made another important decision. He would go all-out with his new form. He drew a chalk circle under the street light behind his fraternity house and he put the shot into a parking lot. He worked day and night.

His coach, Jesse Mortensen, did not try to restrain O'Brien's experiments. In fact, he pointed out two advantages of O'Brien's discovery: (1) more power from the right leg, and (2) a push of a foot longer, giving O'Brien valuable time to work up speed and force.

'For quite a while I had to be my own coach, work out my own technique, correct my own faults. That's why I wanted to be off somewhere doing it alone where I could get greater concentration.'

About two evenings a week that spring, O'Brien went secretly to the nearby Coliseum. Shamelessly, he tossed his shot over the chain-link fence and climbed over. Down on the field, lighted and inspired by the Olympic torch, he practiced diligently for an hour and a half to two hours.

His work paid off. He beat Hooper by $\frac{5}{8}$ of an inch in a triangular meet. He won at Fresno with 55′ 9$\frac{3}{4}$″, his best yet. The next week, in the Coliseum Relays, he progressed admirably to 56′ 6$\frac{3}{4}$″ but he lost to Fuchs by half a foot. At Compton, O'Brien challenged with 57′ 3$\frac{3}{4}$″, but Fuchs put 58′ 5$\frac{1}{2}$″, only five inches from his own world record.

For two weeks O'Brien kept a picture of Hooper on his desk, concentrating on the moment he would avenge his NCAA defeat of last year. The shot put consists of many arduous hours of training for each split-second explosion in competition, but that explosion is what counts.

O'Brien went to the NCAA meet at Berkeley and exploded with 57′ $\frac{5}{8}$″. He won the shot easily. In the discus, which he threw for fun but with his own peculiar concentration, his unexpected 170′ 4$\frac{1}{2}$″ was second only to soon-to-be Olympic champion Sim Iness.

In the AAU meet at Long Beach, California, O'Brien controlled his explosion perfectly in the cool night air to reach his best distance of 57′ 4$\frac{3}{4}$″. It beat Fuchs by five inches and set a new meet record. Now only two men had ever put farther than O'Brien.

As one of the established favorites, O'Brien ran into the fiercest competition yet recorded, in the Final Olympic Trials in the Coliseum. Hooper came through with a great 57′ 1$\frac{3}{8}$″ on his first put. O'Brien's first put thudded into the turf at 56′ 3⅞″ and he was a vulnerable third, behind Bernie Mayer.

Mayer arched the shot 56′ 7¾″ and O'Brien reached 56′ 9⅜″, but Mayer and Fuchs were still threats. O'Brien had to improve. On his fourth effort, he put all his concentration into it and reached 57′ ½″.

As the Olympic shot put began, clouds as black as ink crowded toward the stadium in Helsinki. O'Brien studied the clouds and 'put everything I had into my first try. I could see it might rain.'

He took his strange position in the ring, facing backward, shot nestled against his neck. He puckered his lips and bent double, left arm high. He shoved across the ring, building up to his explosion. Turning with all his strength and desire, he straightened his right arm behind the shot. He released his pent-up air with a loud 'Pow.' The shot went 57′ 1⅜″, his sixth consecutive meet over 57 feet.

The rain came, hindering his opponents. For a long time it looked as if O'Brien's tactics had won easily, but Hooper was not finished. A crippled Fuchs could manage only 55′ 11¾″, within an inch of Hooper, but Hooper had one chance left.

O'Brien watched tensely as Hooper pushed out his last gallant effort. A roar went up from the crowd. Many were sure Hooper had won. The suspense was almost unbearable. Then the figures went up on the field board.

O'Brien's mark was 17.41 meters. The figure 17 appeared under Hooper's number, quickly followed by 39. O'Brien had won the Olympic championship by ¾ of an inch. He showed little emotion, for his thoughts were on the future. He wanted to reach 60 feet in 1953. 'I feel sure I can do it.'

After a tour of Europe in which he lost only once, in the discus, he returned home and devoted himself to weight training, pioneered by Otis Chandler but never fully exploited. In February, O'Brien flew to New York, curiously examined the leather-covered indoor shot for the first time, and put it 55′ 10¾″ to win the AAU title over Fuchs and Mayer.

His intensive practice lasted three hours a day, with as many as 150 throws. 'I don't quit until my hands are bleeding.' As a result, in April, he increased his personal record impressively, to 57′ 10½″, 58′ 1⅞″, and 58′ 8¼″.

Parry O'Brien

On May 7 he was in Fresno for the West Coast Relays, building slowly to a climax. He wore two sweat suits against the chill wind for his first put of 57′ 5½″. He stripped them off and put 58′ 4¾″. He put them on and moved to keep warm while he waited.

He worked on himself carefully. He took a swig of honey from a plastic bottle. 'The fastest energy there is.' He worked himself into a frenzy at the proper moment. 'The shotputter has to know when to blast and when to rest, when to take it easy, and when to give it all he's got.' For his third put he was fully clad and barely reached 55 feet.

He shed the two sweat suits and stepped into the ring for his fourth put. He was ready. He placed his right toe at the rear of the circle. His 6′ 2½″, 225-pound body bent low. At that critical moment the national anthem began. Spectators and athletes alike came to attention, but O'Brien's concentration was on his effort.

He dipped his body. He shoved his body a foot and a half across the ring, landing in the same position. Then he uncoiled explosively, with the fluid movement of a medium tank. The shot made a silver arc under the lights.

Suddenly, the usually stoic O'Brien was dancing up and down with joy. Abruptly, he heard the national anthem, and he stood at attention, impatient for the measurement.

It was 59′ ¾″, a new world record.

Four weeks later in the Compton Invitational, he raised it to 59′ 2⅜″. A shocked Hooper, beaten by more than three feet, said, 'O'Brien's weight training gives him unbeatable power.'

In the NCAA, O'Brien won at 58′ 7¼″. In the NCAA discus, after upsetting the Olympic champion at the Coliseum Relays and Compton, O'Brien threw a personal record 173′ 8″, but he lost to Iness' world record 190′ ⅞″.

O'Brien pushed the iron ball to a meet record of 57′ 11¼″ in the AAU, and placed fourth in the discus. In an extended tour of Europe, he finished the year victorious in the shot put in more than 45 meets He ranked sixth in the world with the discus.

From his high school marks it seems O'Brien did not have outstanding natural ability, but he did have unusual speed for a big man. He once ran 100 meters in 10.8. In Europe, he ran the first leg in six relays and was never beaten.

He was now the greatest shot putter in history, but he was

only beginning. With his collegiate competition ended, he competed in fewer meets in 1954, but his quality improved.

He began in the indoor AAU meet at Madison Square Garden. His 59′ 4″ was the best in history, indoors or out. His first outdoor meet was the Drake Relays in Des Moines, Iowa, on April 24. He dented the turf at 59′ 9¾″, another world record. His second meet was a special competition in which he bettered all previous records for combined right and left hand – 102′ 1¾″.

His third meet was an added event during a dual meet in the Coliseum. News came that Stan Lampert had put 59′ 5⅛″, second best ever. 'I could just see all my records going down the tubes.'

Fired up, he fouled his first toss. His second went 60′ 5¼″, the first 60-footer in history, two days after the first 4-minute mile.

His third put sailed 60′ ½″. Then he put 59′ 10¼″, foul, 59′ 10¼″ again, and 58′ 10¾″. Thus, his answer to Lampert's threat consisted of the four longest puts in history.

On May 15, at Fresno, he upset the great Fortune Gordien in the discus with a mighty 184′ 1½″. That night, he completed the best double ever with a 59-foot put.

At the Coliseum Relays on May 21, he started with five good puts, all over 58′ 6″. His sixth went 60′ 5¾″, adding another half inch to his world record.

At the Southern Pacific AAU meet in the Coliseum on June 11, he surpassed any shot putting he had done previously. In a period of five minutes he took four puts: 60′ 5½″, 60′ 6″, 60′ ½″, and 60′ 10″.

Only five weeks before, the 60-foot shot put had been rated as an ultimate performance comparable to the 4-minute mile.

O'Brien closed out a short but spectacular season with a new AAU meet record of 58′ 11¾″ in St. Louis, plus a second place in the discus. He ranked third in the world in the discus. No other modern athlete has ever ranked so high in two field events.

He became an Air Force lieutenant and 1955 was a year of poorer performances. He raised the world indoor record to 59′ 5½″ in the AAU. In Mexico City, he won the shot at the Pan American Games and placed second in the discus. In the AAU meet at Boulder, Colorado, he became the first man in thirty years to triumph in both the shot and discus. He was an undefeated first

Parry O'Brien

in the shot, but his best marks were 59' 4½" and 175' 7", and he slipped to sixth in the discus world placings.

O'Brien was still not satisfied with his efforts. He explored every conceivable possibility for improvement, digging 'deep into what you might call an inner reserve of strength.' He investigated the possibilities of physics and aerodynamics, of religions and Yoga, and of self-hypnosis.

Olympic year found him better than ever. He trained at the University of Pennsylvania the week before the indoor AAU at Madison Square Garden. He brought himself to such a pitch that he fouled his first two puts and had to be careful to qualify at 58' 6". His fourth put was 59' 4", still short of his indoor record, and he fouled his fifth.

On his last attempt, the leather-covered ball crunched into the boards farther away than any other throw ever recorded anywhere – 61' 5¼" – and the fans sprang to their feet, roaring with surprise. Most amazing of all, the shot was found to be five ounces heavy.

In early outdoor meets, he threw the discus 184' 10" and put the shot 60' 8½". On May 5, in Salt Lake City for the Intermountain AAU, he raised his world record to 61' 1" and threw the discus 179' 7" for the world's best double.

On the night of June 2, in Stockton, California, O'Brien won the Pacific AAU at 60' ½", then reached a best-ever 61' 8¾" on an unofficial 7th put. He also threw the discus 180' 4½". After raising his outdoor world record to 61' 4" in the Service Championships and doubling in the discus, he seemed to be good enough to make the Olympic team in two events.

Then came disaster. A ganglia cyst in his right wrist cut him down to 58' 11½" in the AAU and he lost to Ken Bantum. The longest winning streak in athletic history came to an end at 117.

He also slipped in the discus and placed fourth. After a week of concentrating on the shot to the neglect of the discus, he finished only fifth in the discus in the Final Trials, but he was successful in the shot at 60' 10".

He had the cyst removed, gained to 235 pounds with intensive weight training, and after seven weeks he returned to competition in great shape. He added a quarter of an inch to his world record with 61' 4½" at Pasadena on August 18. On September 3, in Eugene, he went wild.

Parry O'Brien

His first put was a mighty 62′ 3″, the tenth time he had broken the world record. His second put was 62 feet even. His third left the fans dazed. It was 62′ 6⅜″, another world record. As if the three longest puts of all time were not enough, he threw the discus 181′ 7¾″, second to Al Oerter by four inches, giving him another best-ever double.

His great condition was proved at Santa Ana, California, on October 27 when sloping ground invalidated a world record 62′ 8½″ and a series of six throws all longer than 60′ 11″. But that was nothing compared with his next meet.

It was November 1, in the Los Angeles Coliseum, and the U.S. Olympic team was in its final meet before leaving for Australia. An eager O'Brien put 62′ ½″ on his trial and 62′ 2¼″ on his second. His third measured 62′ 8″, the twelfth time he had bettered a world record. His fourth went 62′ 5¾″.

When his fifth throw left his finger tips he knew it was a good one. He thrust both arms into the air and jumped slightly off the ground – his equivalent of the mad leaps of other triumphant athletes. The throw measured 63′ 2″, almost three feet farther than the next best shot putter in history.

His sixth put was 62′ 1″, completing the greatest series of marks anyone had ever accomplished in track and field.

He appeared to be the surest favorite of the 1956 Olympic Games, but in the huge, round Melbourne Cricket Grounds anything could happen. He was up against the only other 60-footers in history – Bill Nieder and Ken Bantum.

'You wouldn't think I'd be nervous, but man, I really was.'

He stepped into the unfamiliar concrete circle for his first put. He moved well across the ring, but the shot slipped off his fingers and went only 58′ 9½″. 'The shots were new and there was nothing to grip on.'

He had to wait a long time between throws, and twice more the shot slipped off his hand. His best mark was only 60′ 11⅛″, but five of his puts were better than the best of his competition and he was still Olympic champion.

For the fifth year in a row he ranked as the world's best shot putter and he was fifth in the world among 1956 discus throwers. At the end of 1956 he had made the twenty-one best winning puts in history, plus almost as many other puts longer than Nieder's best of 60′ 3¾″. He could have retired then as one of the greatest athletes of all time, but competition was in his blood.

In 1957, after he put 62' 2" in an exhibition in Manila on January 11 and won his fifth indoor AAU championship at 58' 8", he neglected the shot in an effort to reach the top in the discus. Even so, he lost only once in eight meets, to Nieder's great 62' 2". He ranked second behind Nieder in the world ratings.

In the discus, his efforts were rewarded with the coveted first in World Ranking. He was undefeated, with a best mark of 183' 3".

His true love was the shot put, however, and in 1958 he hardly threw the discus. Indoors, he won the AAU shot at 60' 1¼" then traveled to Frankfort, Germany, and set an indoor record of 61' 8½". He regained his first ranking with an undefeated season, including a 63' 1" put in the California Relays.

In 1959, O'Brien was honored as first in the shot for the seventh year, although a young giant named Dallas Long beat him twice and broke his world record with 63' 7". O'Brien had fine exhibition puts of 63' 6" and 63' 8", but his best official mark was 63' 4". He won against Long at Compton (62' 7"), in the AAU (62' 2¼"), and in the Pan American Games (62' 5½"). Track fans shook their heads in wonder. He had lost only four times in 7½ years.

In the discus, O'Brien ranked seventh in the world with a best of 185' 1½". He sailed the platter far enough for second in the AAU and third in the Pan American Games.

O'Brien made a real effort for his third Olympics, ignoring the discus. He won the indoor AAU again, at 61' 8". He put 63' 5" and 63' 1¼" in early meets. He won at the California Relays and Compton. He won an AAU victory at 62' 6¼". He made his third Olympic team with 62' 3¾" for second place in the Final Trials. He had good puts of 63' 2" and 63' 3¼" in two more meets before the Olympics.

Down on the green turf of Rome's Stadio Olimpico, Parry O'Brien stalked about, waiting his turn. No man in track and field had ever tried harder to win than he had, and almost nobody was so successful, but now he had reached his limit. Now, at the age of 28, he had ceased improving and others were better.

The Europeans had cracked badly under the stress of Olympic

competition, but he worried about Nieder and Long. Nieder, with a brace on his right knee, had raised the world record to 65′ 7″ in April and again, to 65′ 10″ on August 12. Long, 6′ 4″ and 260 pounds, had put 64′ 6½″ in March, before he was 20, and he had a much greater potential. All O'Brien could do was his best.

He led off with 61′ 7″, possibly good enough for the bronze medal now that Britain's Arthur Rowe had failed to qualify. Nieder put only 61′ 3″ and Long's first effort was a poor 55′ 1⅜″.

O'Brien stepped into the ring for his second trial. He knew exactly what to do. He had more throws over 62 feet than everybody else in history combined. If he could get off a good one, the others might fold. He bent low, shoved off, and pushed the shot 62′ 8¼″.

Nieder followed with 61′ 7″. Long, with shoulders like a block of granite, moved to second with 61′ 11¼″. Now O'Brien could do nothing for himself. He stalked grimly back and forth, flexing his muscles and manipulating a white towel. He neither spoke nor smiled.

They all failed to improve on their third round and in the fourth. The suspense was almost frightening. O'Brien's game fight thrilled onlookers as he led against overwhelming odds.

Then Nieder did everything right and the shot sailed 64′ 6¾″ and O'Brien's dream was over. He stayed ahead of Long and won a silver medal, but on the victory stand his eyes were on Nieder's gold. He announced his retirement and he was hailed for his great competitive ability.

He could not stand retirement, though, and in February of 1961 he won his ninth consecutive indoor AAU title, at 61′ 3″, then upgraded the indoor record to 63′ 1½″. Outdoors, he lost only to Long, put 62′ 3″, and placed second in the AAU. He was ranked third in the shot put world ratings, and he threw the discus 188′ ½″, plus two over 189′ on sloping ground.

In 1962 he concentrated on the discus and ranked tenth in the world in both events. His best shot put was only 61′ 4½″, but he threw the discus 193′ 2″.

In answer to a pertinent question, he said, 'Quit? What for? I'm as good as ever. . . . You may see me in Tokyo.'

In 1963 he improved to fourth in World Ranking, the same as in 1951, but this year his best was 62′ 8″, almost seven feet farther than in 1951. He was second in the AAU and in the meet against Russia.

In the seldom seen two-handed shot put he raised the unofficial record to 106′ 10¼″, reaching 45′ 9½″ left-handed.

After an absence of two years, he competed in the 1964 indoor AAU. His 62′ 10″ was good, but he lost to Gary Gubner's 63′ 2½″. Outdoors, he raised his personal record, astonishingly, to 63′ 10″, but he lost the Southern Pacific AAU to Long's world record 66′ 3½″. In the AAU, O'Brien placed third, but his best distance was the same as John McGrath's fourth place and only two inches ahead of Dave Davis.

Like Zátopek, O'Brien was honored as a living legend while still competing far beyond his time. His opponents respected his achievements and they used his methods, but none of that counted for him in the heat of competition. They were passing him by.

The Final Trials, to choose the U.S. Olympic team, were held in the Coliseum in mid-September. Long was considered certain to make the team. Randy Matson, off his 64′ 11″, seemed sure. O'Brien was everybody's favorite for third although he was threatened by 63-footer Davis, by McGrath, and by Gubner, off form from his 64′ 11″ of 1963.

Matson led at 63′ 10″ with Long second. Davis's second put went 62′ 8″, placing him third. O'Brien could do only 61′ 5″. With only four men qualifying for another three puts, Gubner stepped into the ring for his last chance and put one out near O'Brien's mark.

The crowd, pulling for O'Brien as they never had when he was king, waited in suspense until the measurement showed Gubner half an inch behind.

Now as nervous as he had ever been, the 32-year-old O'Brien took his place on the concrete for his fourth put. His desire to beat Davis's 62′ 8″ burned inside him. He went through the familiar movements. Carefully, using all the wisdom he had accumulated in 17 years of effort, he directed his body toward one perfectly-timed instant of explosion.

The round ball made an arc and landed heavily. The measurement – 63′ 2″ – delighted the crowd, but O'Brien worried about Davis. He paced about beyond the 70-foot line until Davis's last chance was gone. Then, and only then, did he shed his reserve and flex his biceps for the crowd. They gave him the loudest cheer of the meet.

He was on his fourth Olympic team. At Tokyo, he had no hopes for an upset victory. All he could do here was hope for a medal. He shoved the weight a full 63 feet, his longest Olympic put, but he placed only fourth. Time marches on.

He retired again, but not from the discus. 'Traditionally, the careers of discus throwers last longer. Some of the greatest have hit their peak in their late 30's or early 40's. A throw of 200 feet will win a lot of meets in this country and abroad, and I have a career best of 193' 7".'

He sent the platter spinning out over 190 feet several times in 1965 and he improved his record to an excellent 196' 10".

In 1966, he retired from the discus. Nobody should have been surprised when he made a comeback in the shot at the age of thirty-four. Nor should they have been surprised at his performances. But they were.

Now successful in the banking business, he had the time and opportunity to train in the new UCLA gymnasium, and new weight equipment also helped. He began indoors with 62' $9\frac{1}{2}$". Then, at Seattle, he threw 63' 9", only an inch short of his best ever.

In Canada for the Achilles Invitational at Vancouver, February 19, O'Brien trailed a new star, Neil Steinhauer, on his last put. The amazing O'Brien came through with 64 feet, his best ever.

'I used to compete against the lines, but now I can throw against somebody and it's stimulating. I'm in it for what I can get out of myself. I don't need the trinkets ... just the satisfaction of knowing I've produced my maximum.'

Outdoors, he increased his personal record to 64' $2\frac{3}{4}$" at the Coliseum Relays. Then, on May 28, in Honolulu, he arched the heavy ball 64' $7\frac{1}{2}$". This greatest put of his life contained an element of sadness, for it was his farewell to striving.

In addition to his contributions of a new technique, proof of the value of weight training, and new ideas in mental preparation, O'Brien had now showed the world something new in the field of longevity.

'It's gratifying to know I have contributed something to the sport that has done so much for me ... travel, friends, education.'

In 1967, he placed third in the indoor AAU with 61′ 9″, but he did almost nothing outdoors. His bests were 60′ 2″ and 175′ 2″. Old soldiers never die.. They just fade away.

During his unparalleled career, O'Brien placed high in World Ranking more often than any other man. He scored more points in U.S. national meets than any other athlete. In addition to his two firsts, a second, and a fourth in four Olympics, he won two firsts, a second, and a third in Pan American Games. He triumphed in more than twenty major relay meets. He won five medals in NCAA meets and thirty in AAU meets – eighteen of them gold.

In no other athlete has so much quality come in such quantity.

RAFER JOHNSON

About the time the little town of Tulare, California, was going wild in celebration of 17-year-old Bob Mathias's Olympic victory in the decathlon, a 12-year-old boy in Kingsburg, twenty-five miles south, was painfully trapped in a peach cannery conveyer belt. The front half of his left foot was 'hanging by the tissue near the toes.' He needed twenty-three stitches and he was on crutches for eight weeks.

Almost four years later, high school coach Murl Dodson took the same unfortunate boy to Tulare to watch the incomparable Mathias break the world record in the AAU decathlon championships.

When the excitement was over, the boy thought about the 26 contestants in the decathlon and said, 'I could have beaten most of the guys in that meet.'

And so Rafer Johnson decided to be a decathlon man.

One of five children of a family which knew real poverty, Rafer Johnson liked sports and he was good at them. After his visit to Tulare he began to work four hours a day at whichever events he fancied.

Two years later, Johnson was giving Kingsburg something to talk about with Tulare. Johnson was a football star, averaging more than nine yards per carry for Kingsburg High. In basketball, he averaged 17 points per game. In his one season of baseball, he batted a phenomenal .500. In track, he lettered all four years and won the state high hurdles championship in 14.3, almost won the lows in 19 flat, and broad jumped 23' 1".

Already recognized as a fine prospect, he went south to Pasadena and won a high school decathlon for the second year. He ran 14.3 over the high school hurdles and threw the high school weights 51' 10¾" and an eye-opening 174' 4¼", only ten feet behind Oerter's national record. He bettered Mathias's 1948 marks with an 11 flat 100 meters, a 22' 10½" broad jump, and a good

6′ 3″ high jump. He was weak only in the vault, javelin, and 1,500 meters.

He traveled across the country to Atlantic City, New Jersey, for the national AAU decathlon, July 2 and 3. He improved in his three weak events, raising his vault to 11′ 4″, but he slipped in other events. His score was only 5,874, good for third place.

Of all the colleges to seek his services, he chose UCLA. After freshman basketball, he began a great 1955 season. He trained as a hurdler and worked on two or three field events every day.

At 6′ 3″, with the slim legs of a sprinter and the agility of an all-round athlete, Johnson had the makings of a great hurdler. He ran his heat in the West Coast Relays in 14 flat, tying the U.S. freshman record. He won the Compton Invitational low hurdles in 22.9, fastest time in the world for 1955. In the AAU meet at Boulder, Colorado, he was narrowly eliminated in the highs, but he almost won the lows. Running the unfamiliar curve race, his time was 23.6 in fourth place to 23.5 for the winner.

Meanwhile, he was improving in other events. In a dual meet on March 25, in which he won six firsts, he raised his best marks in each throwing event to 46′ 3″, 145′ 3″, and 191′ 11″. Later, he threw 154′ 11″ and ran a 220 in 21.5 and a relay leg in 48.5.

But his true love was the decathlon. He once said, 'The decathlon is easier than some other meets,' and with the exception of the 1,500 meters, it was. On February 18 and 19 at Occidental College, in the Southern Pacific AAU decathlon, he hoped to qualify for the Pan American Games.

He improved tremendously over his third place in the 1954 AAU. He ran 100 meters with the wind in 10.6 and broad jumped 23′ 11½″. He cut his 400 meter record to 49.3. His second day was weaker, but his total was 7,055 points, ninth on the all-time list.

The 1955 Pan American Games were held in Mexico City one month later. Johnson's marks for the first day were disappointing, 147 points below his wind-aided marks at Occidental, and he was expected to lose to Bob Richards.

Johnson came through like a champion on the second day with personal records in the first four events, and he won with 6,994.

On June 10 and 11, Kingsburg (with a 1950 population of

only 2,303 people) tried to rival nearby Tulare by holding the Central California AAU decathlon.

Johnson ran 100 meters in 10.5, great time for a 200-pound non-specialist. He raised his broad jump record to 24' 6⅞". Both marks put him in the top 20 on the 1955 world list, to go with his fifth in the high hurdles and first in the lows. He put the shot 45' 3¼", high jumped 6' ¾", and ran the 400 in 49.7. His 4,537 points gave him the highest first-day score in history.

He started the second day with a good 14.5 in the hurdles, then threw the discus 154' 10¾", only a quarter of an inch short of his best. He had gained on Mathias's world record in both events, but now he was facing his three weakest events.

In the pole vault, even experienced specialists have bad days. In the decathlon, one bad part can ruin the whole. Johnson boosted his heavy body over the crossbar time after time. He surpassed his own personal record. The small crowd became excited as he continued to clear. Finally, he was over 12' 8½", and he was still ahead of Mathias.

In the javelin, Johnson gave further evidence that he was a competitor equal to Mathias. He threw a personal record 193' 10⅜". Now he needed to run 1,500 meters in 5:18 to break the world record.

His personal best was 5:23, and he disliked the event, but he ran hard, and with the hometown crowd cheering all the way he finished in 5:01.5.

His 7,985 points bettered Mathias's world record by 98 points. At the age of nineteen, he was the world record holder. His future seemed unlimited.

In 1956, he was pointing for the Olympic decathlon, but during the college season he competed with distinction in the hurdles and broad jump. Even without any such event as the decathlon, he would have been regarded as an exceptional sophomore.

In dual meets he ran the hurdles in 14.1 and 22.7 (22.6 with wind). Against Stanford, he broad jumped 24' 10¼" and against Southern California, 25' 5¾" (sixth best in the world for the entire year). He also ran a 220 in 21 flat.

At the West Coast Relays, his 14.2 earned him fourth place. He won the broad jump at 25' 2¼". His 47.4 helped UCLA win the mile relay.

The next week, in the conference meet at Berkeley, Johnson

lost the 100 yard title by an inch. Trying to hurdle only ten minutes later, he ran into the same trouble as Dillard in 1948 and he finished third. He placed second to a team-mate in the broad jump without taking his final jumps. He won the low hurdles. His 16 points enabled UCLA to defeat USC for the first time in history.

Johnson won the broad jump at the California Relays. At Compton, he won the lows in 22.8 and ran 14 flat in the highs behind Davis, Calhoun, and Campbell.

In the NCAA meet at Berkeley, the low hurdles were eliminated in favor of the intermediates and so Johnson entered only two events, but his international class was evident.

In the high hurdles, he ran against Lee Calhoun, one of the greatest of all time. Johnson showed his unusual competitive ability by leading Calhoun over the last hurdle, but he lost by $2\frac{1}{2}$ feet. His time of 13.8 against a wind of 1.3 m.p.h. was remarkable. Only four men ran faster in 1956 and Johnson was sixth in World Ranking. Only two hurdlers in history, Wolcott and Dillard, had faster times than Johnson in both hurdles races.

In the broad jump, Johnson competed against Greg Bell, soon to be Olympic champion. Johnson led with his preliminary jump of 25' $\frac{1}{4}$", but Bell won with 25' 9" on his first jump on Saturday. Johnson fought back with 25' 4" for second place.

Johnson's 16 points made him runner-up to Bobby Morrow for high-point honors and enabled UCLA to win its first NCAA title.

In the AAU meet at Bakersfield the following week, he tried only the low hurdles. He ran his heat in 22.7, then lost the final by one foot in 22.8.

The Final Trials followed a week later in the Los Angeles Coliseum. Overly eager, Johnson hit two hurdles early in his heat and rode the fifth one down. Even so, he missed his chance in the final by mere inches. In the broad jump, his struggle was against five 26-footers. He jumped 24' 10" in the preliminaries, good for third. He lost it to a 25' $1\frac{1}{2}$" jump, but he came back gamely with 25' $1\frac{3}{4}$" and 25' $3\frac{1}{4}$" to make the Olympic team. He ranked sixth in the world in the broad jump.

Two weeks later, on July 13 and 14, he tried for the decathlon team at Wabash College in Crawfordsville, Indiana. Heavy rains had softened the track and runways. He ran 10.6 in the 100, but his broad jump was a poor 23′ 2½″.

He came back powerfully, with a personal record of 49′ 8¾″ in the shot. In the high jump, his football knee bothered him, but he cleared 6′ 1″. Then, with darkness falling, he put on a sprint finish to catch Aubrey Lewis in the 400 meters. Their 47.9's were the fastest ever run in the decathlon.

Johnson's first-day total of 4,640 was the highest ever, and he started the second day with a fine 14.4 in the hurdles. He was on his way to a world record and a probable Olympic title.

Then came the trouble all decathlon men fear. In the discus, he reinjured his knee. He threw 149′ 5″, but he could vault only 11′ 5¾″. He threw the javelin 182′ 4½″ and ran 1,500 meters in 5:12.4. His 7,755 points, fourth highest ever, beat Milt Campbell by 196 points.

Johnson reinjured his knee practicing the pole vault in Melbourne and he had to withdraw from the Olympic broad jump.

He began the Olympic decathlon with a 10.9 in the 100, while Campbell ran 10.8. In the broad jump, Johnson tore a stomach muscle. Earlier in the season, he had said, 'The decathlon is actually not as difficult as people think,' but now he was changing his mind. A decathlon man must also contend with injuries, fatigue, long hours, and the weather.

His 24′ 1″ left him behind an improved Campbell and he was not in any condition to catch Campbell. His first-day total of 4,375 left him 191 points behind.

Dispirited, knowing he could not win with his injuries, Johnson lost his rhythm and ran only 15.1 in the hurdles. Campbell ran 14 flat and his lead increased to 525. Johnson lost more points with a poor discus throw of 138′ 4½″. Now he was 612 points behind. What was worse, he led Kuznetsov by only 266 points.

Every vault was painful. Lifting his legs tore at his wounded muscles. He struggled desperately over height after height, failing only after he had raised his decathlon best to 12′ 9½″.

In the javelin, Kuznetsov neared his best mark with 213′ 8″. Johnson responded with a personal record 197′ 9″.

In the 1,500 meters he had to run fast enough to maintain his lead over Kuznetsov. Suffering with each stride, he struggled around in 4:54.2, his best ever.

A sympathizer asked if his injury hurt during the race.

'Sure it hurt, but what was I going to do? Quit?'

He had lost the gold medal everybody thought was his, but under the circumstances he said the silver medal 'was very gratifying to me'.

Later he said, wistfully, 'I'd sure like to win at Rome in 1960.'

The year 1957 was almost lost to Johnson. He could not sprint nor jump because of his injured knee. He worked on the weights and improved to 159' 7½" with the discus and a good 228' 1" in the javelin. Early in June he was able to run a relay leg from the blocks in 48.6

He was a busy young man at UCLA. As if a decathlon man does not already have too much to do, he lettered in basketball, worked enthusiastically as student body president, spoke before youth groups, and began his acting career.

In 1958 he started as a weight man, and a badly pulled thigh muscle kept him at it. His results bore no similarity to the international class hurdler and broad jumper he was in 1956. He raised his shot put record to a creditable 54' 5", threw the discus 166' 4½", and reached 227' 8" with the javelin.

Then, on April 26, in a dual meet with Stanford, Johnson completed the greatest weight triple in the history of the sport. He put the shot 54' 11¼", far enough to make the top 20 in the U.S. for 1958. He threw the discus 170' 9½", making him tenth best American. He threw the javelin 237' 10", good enough for No. 10 on the U.S. list.

At the West Coast Relays, he won the javelin at 238' 11". In the Coliseum Relays, he ran a fine 47-flat relay leg. In the conference meet, he won the javelin at 243' 10". In his first broad jump since the Olympics, running at less than full speed, he cleared a promising 24' 10" on a narrow foul. He qualified in the hurdles with 14.7, his first flight since 1956. Then a sprained ankle put him out of the meet.

The AAU meet in Bakersfield was a disappointment to him. He placed ninth in the discus and sixteenth in the javelin at 212' 11½". He qualified for the low hurdle final, but he did not finish.

Track fans were surprised when he recovered fast enough to compete in the Kingsburg Invitational decathlon the next weekend. He risked only one attempt in each of the three jumps, recording 23′ 3″, 5′ 2½″, and 10′ 11⅞″, but his other marks were noteworthy. He ran the 100 in 10.6, put the shot 50′ 5″, and ran the 400 in 48.9.

His high hurdle time was a surprising 14.2. He threw the discus 157′ 10½″, and the javelin 209′ 9″. His 5:02 for 1,500 meters brought his total to a good 7,780.

Greatly encouraged, Johnson entered the national AAU decathlon at Palmyra, New Jersey, eight days later. He had to run 5:14.7 in the 1,500 to beat C. K. Yang by 62 points. His 7,754 was exactly the same as his 1956 score.

He went to Moscow for the important meet with Russia 22 days later. On the first day, 75,000 people in the Bolshoi arena anticipated a great duel between Johnson and their new world record holder, Kuznetsov.

Johnson again ran 10.6, but Kuznetsov excited the crowd with a jump of 24′ 7″ while Johnson managed only 23′ 6¼″. Johnson was weak in the shot with 48′ 2¼″, and in the high jump at 5′ 10⅞″. After four events, to everyone's surprise, he was ten points behind.

In the 400, Johnson ran 48.2 and finished the first day with 4,529, a lead of 119 points in spite of his mediocre field performances.

The second day, Monday, was cool, and the track was heavy from an overnight rain. Johnson ran a disappointing 14.9 to Kuznetsov's 15.1.

Johnson threw the discus 160′ 11½″ and gained a little more, but now he had to hold Kuznetsov in his strong events. Typically, Johnson came through with his best decathlon pole vault, 12′ 11½″, only two inches lower than Kuznetsov.

After two throws of the javelin, Johnson's best mark was under 205 feet while Kuznetsov had one of 214′ 6½″, bringing him within striking distance. Johnson could recapture the world record by running 1,500 meters in 5:05, but Kuznetsov could break it by running 4:47.4.

It seemed easier to improve his javelin mark. Johnson concentrated hard as he ran down the runway and whipped the javelin into the air. A mass exclamation of awe sounded from 30,000 people. The javelin was amazingly high in the air when it passed Kuznetsov's marker.

Johnson's throw was 238′ 2″. The world record was his again, even before the 1,500 meters. He disliked the 1,500, but now, with every second worth five or six points, he tried fairly hard. His 5:05 picked up 225 points. His second-day total of 3,773 was the highest ever scored.

His total was 8,302 points, even though half his marks had been mediocre, for him. Kuznetsov kissed him on both cheeks. He was given a bouquet of flowers, and the Russians tossed him in the air while the crowd applauded. *Sports Illustrated* named him 'Sportsman of the Year'.

He had finished his college competition, although he was still at UCLA, and 1959 was a bad year. Leg trouble kept him out of the running and jumping events, although he raised his discus record to 171' 7½" and threw the javelin 240' 7". Once again Kuznetsov took the decathlon record away from him, by 55 points. Worst of all, his season was cut short just before graduation by a serious back injury in a head-on auto accident.

It was now obvious that only injuries were keeping him from being the greatest all around athlete of all time, but the winter of 1959–60 was one of suspense and despair.

He could not so much as jog until February of 1960. Then he spent two months of torturous conditioning. He walked and jogged as long as six hours a day. Not until April did he try sprint starts. When he first tried to broad jump, in June, he and Coach 'Ducky' Drake were as tense as bomb disposal men expecting that fatal explosion. When Johnson landed without strain, he began to hope again for his gold medal.

He had his best discus throw, 172' 3", and he ran the hurdles in an encouraging 14.1. He won the javelin at the California Relays with 249' 10", and at Compton with 251' 9½". His excellent throwing fell off in the AAU to a sixth-place 233' 1", and he placed only seventh in the Final Trials with 240 feet.

But to him, the only important event was the AAU and Final Trials decathlon held at Eugene, Oregon, July 8 and 9. He was threatened by Yang, the great Chinese, now a UCLA student who trained with Johnson.

Johnson began with his old familiar 10.6. In the broad jump, off a helpful board runway, he jumped 24' 9" and had a foul well over 25 feet. He put the shot 52 feet, his best in a decathlon, but he cleared only 5' 10" in the high jump. In the 400, he started too slowly and his frenetic sprint finish made it only 48.6.

His total was 4,750, better than any other first-day score, but he led Yang by only 195 points and Yang was dangerous in the hurdles, vault, and javelin.

Johnson ran over the high hurdles in 14.5, but Yang set the 4,500 spectators buzzing with his 14.1. Johnson was now only 62 points ahead.

Johnson needed a come-through, and so he spun the discus 170′ 6″. 'That really gave me confidence.'

Next, he raised his personal record in the vault to 13′ ¼″ and moved to the javelin runway. 'I worked hard all last week, and I knew I'd have to put everything into my first throw.'

He sent the silver javelin into the air and stopped his forward momentum as he watched it land far out on the turf. The crowd cheered. Delighted, he broke into a run toward his javelin. Then he stopped and knelt on one knee and offered thanks, his face wet with tears. The announcer verified the distance – 233′ 3″ – and once more the world record was his.

When he ran 1,500 meters in 5:09.9, his total rose to 8,683, a startling 300 points over the world record. Added to his best-ever first-day total was a second-day score of 3,933, also the best ever made.

Then he encouraged Yang in his heat and supported his tired team-mate after it was over. Yang had scored 8,426, also over Kuznetsov's record.

Admiring Johnson, Oregon coach Bill Bowerman said, 'I don't think anyone doubts for a minute that Rafer Johnson is the best athlete in the world.'

At Bern, Switzerland, land of fast hurdle times, Johnson ran 13.9 behind Calhoun's world record 13.2. On August 30 he had the honor of carrying the American flag in the opening ceremony of the Olympic Games.

The Olympic decathlon at Rome included the five highest scorers of all time, with Dave Edstrom's 8,176 fourth, and Yuriy Kutyenko's 7,989 fifth. Johnson's analysis: 'I'm prepared to win, whatever that takes.' Even the jinx of having his picture on the cover of *Time* magazine did not worry him.

Competition began at 9:00 a.m. on September 5 in the flag-decked stadium in Rome. Running in the fourth heat of the 100 meters on the red track, Johnson had to start four times. On the third false start, he ran 40 meters at full speed before the recall gun stopped him. With this handicap, he ran only 10.9, 132 points worse than his usual 10.6.

Jumping into a headwind, Johnson reached only 23' 7¾" on his first trial, to 24' 5¾" for Yang. Johnson jumped only 22' 8½" on his second. Alarmed, he powered his 196 pounds out to 24' 1¼".

Competition resumed after lunch, at 3:00 p.m. Johnson's first put thudded down only 47' 8¾" away. Exasperated with himself, he exploded to 51' 10¾". He gained 273 points in Yang's weak event. Now he had a lead of 143 points. Edstrom dropped out with a groin injury, and the two Russians were obviously not at their best. It was a battle between the two UCLA men.

At 5:45, during the high jump, Johnson and all the others received another bad break.. The clouds burst open above the stadium with a downpour which surely set an Olympic record. All competition stopped and everybody scurried for cover. The athletes waited, cooling off physically and mentally, while the downpour lasted an hour and 20 minutes. So remarkable was the drainage system, however, that competition resumed 20 minutes after the rain stopped.

Johnson had to be satisfied with a high jump of 6' ¾", while Yang went over 6' 2¾". Kuznetsov made only 5' 8¾" and he was no longer a threat... if Johnson could avoid injury.

Johnson received a soothing rubdown before starting the 400 at 10:50 p.m. He wanted to increase his narrow 75-point lead, and he set a stiff pace. Yang was inspired, though, and he rushed past Johnson into the last curve and built up a five-yard lead. Desperately, Johnson fought back to within four feet. His 48.3 was not his best, but it was now fourteen hours since competition began that morning.

Wearily, Johnson returned to the Olympic Village with 4,647 points, not up to his potential. He had lost four of the five events to Yang and yet, without a weakness, he led Yang by 55 points. Somebody said, 'That's what the decathlon is all about.'

'The pressure is unbelievable,' Johnson says of Olympic competition. 'It can really get to you. Some athletes tense under this sort of pressure. Others rise to it and perform even better.'

After an inadequate sleep they assembled at 9:00 a.m. for the high hurdles... and near disaster for Johnson. Off to a good start, eager for a fast time, he hit the second hurdle with a sicken-

Rafer Johnson, in the 1960 Olympic Games.

ing thud. A smaller man might have gone down, but Johnson crashed through and ran on, raggedly. 'I lost rhythm completely, same as at Melbourne.'

The big danger, especially to a hurdler who had not been able to practice much in four years, was the possibility of being so far off stride that he could not clear the next hurdle. Somehow, he regained his stride but not his speed. His time was a shocking 15.3.

Now Johnson was in a desperate situation. Instead of leading Yang by 62 points as in his world record at Eugene, he was 138 points behind – a total of 200 points worse.

When his discus throw sailed only 146' 1½" he knew defeat was more than possible. He came back with 158' 3" and 159' 1", but he was 11 feet shorter than in his great world record performance. Still, he gained 272 points on Yang and took a lead of 144. (At Eugene he had led by a comfortable 402 after seven events and he won by only 257.)

They began vaulting at 2:30, with Yang in good position to become the Olympic champion because he could vault a foot higher than Johnson. After all these years the gold medal was slipping away.

But Rafer Johnson was a great one. He simply vaulted higher than ever before. His 13' 5¼" lost to Yang by eight inches and he still had a perilous 22-point lead.

He had said, 'I hope it's all wrapped up before the 1,500 meters. I never want to settle one in that thing.'

But Yang was a fine javelin thrower. At Eugene they had both reached 233 feet. If Johnson allowed that to happen again, it would be settled in the 1,500, and Yang would win.

They had to use the yellow Seefab javelin, unfamiliar to them. Johnson, with a best of 251' 9½", suffered the most loss, but his first throw stuck in the turf at 228' 10½". Yang threw 223' 9½" on his second throw. Johnson did not improve, and he watched tensely on Yang's last throw.

Yang did not improve, but Johnson had a lead of only 67 points. He had to stay within ten seconds of Yang to win. Yang had run 4:36.9, 17.3 seconds faster than Johnson's best. And Johnson's best had been forced out of him at Melbourne when he went all out to retain second place.

At 9:20 p.m. the tension rose as they started the last heat

together. Up in the stands, their coach, 'Ducky' Drake, was asked how it would come out. He could only praise Johnson's courage.

And that was what Johnson needed now. Doggedly, he followed Yang at a pace he had never run before. He held on, with all his strength and courage and pride. Into the homestretch he was still on Yang's heels. 'I wavered in the stretch.' He finished six yards behind, losing only nine points with a time of 4 :49.7, by far his best ever.

He won the gold medal he wanted so much by 58 points, with a score of 8,392. In the locker room, he was mobbed while Yang sat alone and wept. Yang had made a glorious effort, but Rafer Johnson was not to be beaten. Yang struggled to his feet and clasped Johnson's hand. 'Nice going, Rafe.'

Johnson said, 'Tonight I'm going to shower and then just walk for about four hours and look at the moon. I don't know where – just walk, walk, walk. I've got to unwind. I'm through, man. I'm through.'

He was voted Track & Field Athlete of the Year, and he won the Sullivan Award. No athlete has been more deserving, for in addition to his unsurpassed achievements in track, he has led a life of service to humanity. (His goal : 'Eventually, I'd like to work for the state department'). The Reverend Louis Evans said of him : 'This is a most remarkable human being.'

Certainly he was a most remarkable athlete. Although handicapped by injuries throughout most of his career his achievements in a wide range of events bordered on the fantastic :

Sprints – 10.5 for 100 meters and 21 flat for 220 yards. He came within one inch of victory in the Pacific Coast Conference 100 yard championship. In an 880 relay, he ran surprisingly close to international sprinters with a 20.7 leg.

440 – He ran 47.9 for 400 meters in a decathlon and ran a 440 relay leg in 46.9.

High hurdles – he was a rousing second in the NCAA behind eventual Olympic champion Lee Calhoun with a time of 13.8, truly outstanding against the wind. He was No. 6 in World Ranking in 1956, his one year of hurdling.

Low hurdles – in 1956 he ran under 23 flat five times, won at Compton, and placed second in the AAU. His 22.7 was the fastest time in the world.

Broad jump – in his one year before injuries stopped him, he bettered 25 feet five times. He placed second in the NCAA, was successful in making the Olympic team, and ranked sixth in the world.

Shot put – his 54′ 11½″ put him among the twenty best on the 1958 U.S. list.

Discus – he threw 170′ 9½″ in 1958 as part of the greatest weight triple of all time, and he made the U.S. top ten. He threw 172′ 3″ in 1960.

Javelin – his victories included the 1958 West Coast Relays (238′ 11″) and Pacific Coast Conference (243′ 10½″), and the 1960 Mt. San Antonio Relays (236′ 11″), California Relays 249′ 10″), and Compton Invitational (251′ 9½″).

Decathlon – after losing in the national AAU as a high school boy in 1954, he triumphed in all except one other decathlon out of a total of 11. His 'failure' came in the 1956 Olympics while badly injured. He surpassed Mathias's world record at the age of 19, and he raised the record twice more.

One track enthusiast summed it up when he said simply, 'No other man ever had the all around ability of Rafer Johnson.'

Russian head coach Gabriel Korobkov said, 'America has so many great ones to choose from, but I think Rafer Johnson was the best I've seen.'

GLENN DAVIS

Great champions are a special breed. The proof of their greatness is in rising to new heights in the face of ruthless competition, and rare is the man who does it consistently.

Such a rare man was Glenn Davis.

His first significant test was witnessed by 34,000 enthusiasts in the Los Angeles Coliseum, on the warm evening of June 29, 1956. This meet to choose the U.S. Olympic team was the greatest track and field meet yet contested, and Glenn Davis was up against the fastest 400 meter hurdlers ever assembled in one race.

Davis, a muscular six-footer wearing the red and gray of Ohio State University, had raced a full circuit of the track while leaping over ten dangerous hurdles for the first time only two months before. Until his name appeared in headlines three weeks before this meet, he had never aroused interest as a possible Olympian.

As a high school boy he liked to compete, and in 1954, despite a brace for his dislocated shoulder, he sped victoriously down the track in 9.9 seconds for 100 yards and 21.1 for 220. He chopped pugnaciously over the high school hurdles in 14.7 and 19.1. He flung his body over a crossbar six feet above the ground. He landed in a sand pit an exhilarating 23′ 6″ beyond the white takeoff board. He caused a sensation by winning the Ohio State meet all by himself, but his best 440 time was only 52 flat and he received more acclaim as an all-state football player.

As a freshman, in 1955, he was more concerned with his books than track, but in the early 1956 season Davis swarmed eagerly over the track and field for Ohio State. He stopped the watches at 9.7 and a fine 20.9 in the sprints, and 23.3 in the 220 yard low hurdles. He ran his first intermediate hurdles in an unpromising 54.4. Six days later, on April 27, at Franklin Field in Philadelphia, he won at the famed Penn Relays in 52.3. He spent most of May running in dual meets, and in the Big Ten meet on May 26 he flashed around a curve full of low hurdles in 23.5 to equal a conference record good enough to last twenty-three years. He also earned thirds in the 220 and long jump and fourth in the hundred.

He did not excite international interest, however, until the Central Collegiate meet on June 9 in the hot, humid climate of Milwaukee, Wisconsin. He barely reached the safety of the tape ahead of another sophomore, Aubrey Lewis of Notre Dame. Davis's 50.8 was impressive as the fifth fastest ever, only four tenths off the world record, and both sophomores became exciting prospects in that Olympic year.

A week later, on the grey track at Berkeley for the National Collegiate championships, Lewis caught Davis off stride at the last hurdle and beat him by three yards in 51 flat. Six days after that disappointing 51.5, Davis showed another flash of potential might by winning the AAU in 50.9 with Lewis absent.

Now, in the Final Trials, he was cautious while taking his marks in the sixth lane. Lewis had hit the last hurdle in his heat and was out of the final, but this only intensified Davis's awareness of the hazards of those three-foot hurdles. He, himself had lost the NCAA race at that last hurdle and he knew the danger.

Eddie Southern was to his left in lane five. Southern, only eighteen, had frightening talent. In lane seven was Josh Culbreath, the amazing little Negro marine who had never lost a race until this year when he began his training late. Culbreath had won the AAU three years in a row, plus the Pan American title in 1955.

As the gun sounded, Davis was off his blocks fast, hurdling left leg first. At the third hurdle he saw Southern's dark hair and white shirt already even with him. Startled, he increased his speed, but the young Texan gained another yard around the last curve. To an apprehensive Davis it seemed as if Southern was the one touched with greatness.

But Davis had that special desire champions use to tap an extra reserve of strength. He dug desperately into this reserve, running not smoothly but with great power, and he began to gain precious inches on the white shirt. Into the homestretch he was still two yards behind, and he was reduced to seventeen strides between hurdles.

Glenn Davis

At the last hurdle his superior power pulled him even. Southern was running hard, far faster than any previous runner in history, but Davis crushed him in the last 40 yards. As he hit the white yarn five feet in front, he was smiling.

When the announcement came, the crowd roared with amazement. Davis wiped his eyes, hung his head, and smiled. He had run 49.5, almost a second under the world record. The stamp of greatness was on him.

Five months ahead, in Melbourne, were the Olympics – the Holy Grail of track athletes. Davis wanted to keep in shape, but an Achilles tendon injury slowed him ominously. In the first meet after the team assembled in Berkeley, six weeks before the Olympics, Davis limped a pitiful 54.2, almost out of sight behind Culbreath's 51 flat.

A week later in Ontario, California, Davis barely won by the width of his chest in 51.1, and the following week he ran only 51.9. In the final tune-up meet, he lost to Culbreath by three yards, tying up dismally in 52.1.

In Melbourne, his legs sore and tight, Davis expected serious competition from Southern and Culbreath, plus impressive Yuriy Lituyev, an undefeated Russian who had equalled the pre-Davis world record.

Davis breezed through his heat in 51.3, but Culbreath looked formidable in 50.9. In the semi-finals, early the next afternoon, Southern struck fear into Davis with a strong 50.1 while Davis had to struggle to finish second in 50.7. Culbreath seemed perilously effortless in winning the second semi in 50.9.

Two and one half hours later they were on the track again, with the tension mounting, before 100,000 in the round, three-tiered stadium of the Melbourne Cricket Grounds. Davis felt nervous in lane four, between the all-green of South African Gerhardus Potgieter and the red-shirted Lituyev.

Afraid of Southern, Davis started too fast, and he had to chop his stride at the second hurdle, but fear made him hurry and he was only two yards behind Southern over the fifth hurdle. Then he gave the cheering crowd a glimpse of his stunning power. While the others were struggling to run as fast as in the earlier semi-finals and all except Lituyev were failing, Davis used his remarkable reserve.

He ran scared until the eighth hurdle. With a small lead over

Southern, he kept driving his powerful legs in a frenzy. He led by two yards at the ninth hurdle, by three at the tenth, and he hit the tape an impressive five yards ahead in 50.1.

In his first year as an intermediate hurdler he could take pride in being both the world record holder and Olympic champion. When he crossed the line he looked toward the sky and said, 'Thanks.'

After such a year, 1957 was a great disappointment. He competed in five to seven events in each indoor meet, but a bad case of bursitis in his left thigh bothered him all spring, and he could not run in the National Collegiate championships because Ohio State had been banned for overzealous recruiting.

By such misfortune he was limited to two major meets. On June 8, at the Meet of Champions in Houston, Texas, he triumphed in his first important 440 yard race, reaching the tape ahead of Southern in 46.8. Then he hurried over the low hurdles in 22.7. His times in that admirable double were fifth and sixth fastest in the world for 1957.

In the AAU championships, held in Dayton, Ohio, Davis wanted to defend his championship, but he had not practiced since the Olympics and he missed his step shockingly in his heat.

In the final, he was yards behind Culbreath on the poorly lighted backstretch, but once again his desire pulled him through. A foot behind at the last hurdle, he hit the tape $2\frac{1}{2}$ yards ahead in typical all-out effort, head twisted high to the right. His 50.9 was a new American record for 440 yards, and he was honored as first in World Ranking again.

The next night, on a dark straightaway, he finished his competition for the year with a close fifth place in the low hurdles against the fastest field ever assembled. He was still troubled with bursitis in his leg when the 1958 indoor season began, but he wanted to compete in every event possible. In one dual meet, he took only one high jump, and cleared 6' 2", tying for second. He also achieved enough in the long jump to rank eighth in Indoor Ranking for 1958.

But his main triumphs came in the hurdles. Running from one event to another, he managed to win enough hurdle races to rank third in Indoor Ranking in 1958. On March 21, Davis met the celebrated Hayes Jones in the 50-yard hurdles at the Cleveland K.C. Games. Jones was a 13.7 hurdler, destined to be best in the world for 1958, but Davis's big chest hit the tape first in an amazing 6.1 victory.

Then, outdoors at the Quantico Relays on April 11 and 12, after winning the 440 hurdles and long jump on Friday, Davis met Elias Gilbert in the highs on Saturday. Gilbert had run a fantastic 13.4 at Compton last year, but Davis beat him in 14.3.

He lost races to both Jones and Gilbert later, but now he was interested in converting to the 440 flat race, and on May 14, in a dual meet with Ohio Wesleyan, he circled the track in collegiate record time of 46.1, completing a fine double with a 21-flat 220. In the Big Ten meet at Lafayette, Indiana, on May 24, he ran a sensational 440 against the speedy West Indian, George Kerr, and he stopped the watches on the world record time of 45.8.

The National Collegiates did not schedule the intermediate hurdles then, and so Davis sought his first NCAA championship in the 440. In the meet at Berkeley he was up against Eddie Southern, who was undefeated with a pair of 45.9 times to his credit.

Taking his blocks, Davis worried about Southern once more and he knew he must run his best to win. In lane eight, he could not see his opponents, and so he ran in blindness and suspense, reaching the 220 in 22 flat. Around the last turn he ran powerfully but as they rounded into the homestretch he was dismayed to see Southern's black hair to his left. For a moment the issue was in doubt, but then he began a powerful drive which all but destroyed Southern. Davis's red-clad barrel chest reached the tape five yards ahead in world record time of 45.7.

Later, Davis said, 'I had a lot left.'

Someone asked Southern, 'Have you ever tied up like that before?' His grim answer was, 'Yes... the last time I ran against Glenn Davis.'

In the AAU meet in the hot California valley city of Bakersfield, six days later, Davis left the 440 to Southern, who won in 45.8. Davis wanted to run the intermediates against Josh Culbreath, the world record holder, and he ran with the marvelous power of a panther. He led Culbreath by four yards into the homestretch and he won by five yards in 49.9, his third world record.

The next night, a confident Davis took on the world's best 220 runners. He won his heat and semi-final, both in 21.4, but before the final he asked coach Larry Snyder, 'Do you think those guys are as tired as I am?'

Davis sped around the curve and finished powerfully, as usual, only two yards behind Bobby Morrow, then the world's most acclaimed sprinter. Davis's second place beat out such favored sprinters as Ed Collymore and Ray Norton, who had finished one-two in the previous week's NCAA and who were good enough to rank third and fourth in the world for 1958. Davis ranked seventh. If you add a surprising 100 meters he ran later in 10.3, you can make an interesting case for Davis as a world class sprinter.

In truly astonishing condition, Davis went to Europe for a series of triumphs which proved his greatness beyond all doubt. After some comfortable warm-up races came three weeks of the most sensational 400 meter running ever seen, with and without hurdles.

At Oslo on July 17, Davis raced around 200 meters in 21.1 and over the 400 hurdles in 49.8. Not content, the next day he ran his 10.3 100 meters and a 45.6 400 meters, and the excited Norwegians made him jog a lap of honor.

In the dual meet against Russia, Davis impressed the Moscow crowd with 45.6 and 50.4 on a wet track. At Warsaw, Davis flashed across the line a full second ahead of Southern in a stirring 45.5, second fastest 400 ever run. The next day he hurried around the track twice more, over the hurdles in 49.8 and on a 45.1 relay leg.

He completed his glorious string on August 5 and 6 at Budapest in the meet with Hungary. The first day he squished around a disappointingly wet track in 45.6 and commented, 'If it had been dry, I think I could have clocked a time of 45.2.' Even so, he could smile with pride at having run seven of the thirteen fastest 400–440 races ever run.

The next night, in the hurdles, a determined Davis started like a sprinter, but he was thwarted by hitting the last hurdle and he lost valuable yards. Still, the watches showed 49.2, three tenths under his own world record, and he grinned about his third record of the year.

He lost a slow, careless 400 to Southern on the sharp-cornered track in Athens for his only 400–440 loss of the year. He was paid homage as first in World Ranking for that event, plus the intermediate hurdles, an unprecedented honor. Add his seventh in the 200, his tie for seventh on the 100 meter list, and his early triumphs over Hayes Jones and Elias Gilbert in the high hurdles, and it was a gratifying year of unparalleled achievement in quantity, quality, and versatility.

The 1959 season, however, was a disaster for Davis. A chronic back injury hurt him and his doctor cut his season short. Running in the AAU at Boulder, Colorado, Davis missed his step miserably over the first four hurdles. He pulled up within a tantalizing yard of Dickie Howard with 20 yards to go but his effort had depleted his entire reserve and he lost in 50.9 to Howard's 50.7. It was his first loss in his specialty in three years, but even in such deplorable condition he ranked fourth in World Ranking for 400 meters and sixth for the hurdles.

Now a school teacher, Davis began 1960 in poor condition. In three frustrating 440 races he saw a different runner finish ahead of him each time. Then he began to run himself into shape. In the Coliseum Relays he edged his barrel chest ahead of Howard in 51 flat, and he beat him by two yards in 50.3 at the Meet of Champions. In the AAU at Bakersfield, he needed his rousing finish to beat Howard by five feet in 50.1.

A week later, July 1, at Stanford, California, Davis took his blocks for the Final Olympic Trials, his most important race since the 1956 Olympics. He was in the slow curb lane, threatened by the fastest field of hurdlers of all time. Once again it was a test of true greatness.

He ran satisfactorily around the curve and down the backstretch, but others were ahead of him. Not until the 8th hurdle was he within striking distance of Southern. Resolutely, Davis began his powerful drive and nobody could resist him. He hit the tape in 49.5 while a shocked Southern ran 49.9 and lost to Davis, Howard, and young Clif Cushman.

In significant tune-up meets before the Olympics, he outpowered future Olympic 400 meter champion Otis Davis in two out of three races, including a notable 45.5. He was ranked fifth in the 400 meters for 1960. Then, at Bern, Switzerland, in chilly twilight, he raced furiously around a curve to equal the official record of 22.5 for the 200 meter low hurdles. The next night he won the intermediates in 49.7. He was ready for the Olympic test.

On September 2, in Rome, Glenn Davis walked uneasily through the dark tunnel from the warm-up track in the Marble Stadium into the bright sunlight of Stadio Olimpico. Proudly wearing the deep blue of the U.S.A., Davis was the sixth runner in single file, marched in by gray-clad officials like doomed gladiators in ancient Roman times.

Davis was fearful. He knew the possibilities of losing and it was on his mind when he knelt on his blocks in lane six. The orange-coated starter raised one of his two pistols and called, 'Via.' Davis rose to the set position. Then the gun sounded and he was running wildly, afraid of what might happen in this last and greatest test.

He led over the first hurdle but in his tension he was overstriding and he missed his step at the second, losing precious yardage. To his dismay, he could not regain his step, and after the fifth barrier his worry increased. Then, with the poise of a true champion, he regained his step.

He had to drive hard, but he gained satisfactorily on the curve, and he moved to second place in the homestretch. At the last hurdle he caught Howard. Only then did he feel confident. His powerful legs pounded viciously down at the track and he won by almost three yards in 49.3.

On the victory stand, between Howard and silver-medalist Cushman, a jubilant Davis received his second Olympic gold medal from the 1928 champion, David Burghley, Marquis of Exeter. They turned and watched with feeling as three American flags ran up the poles behind the Olympic torch. A happy group of Americans in the crowd sang their national anthem and Davis nudged his teammates and they smiled and waved. Davis said, 'This is a greater thrill than winning at Melbourne.'

Davis's track glory was almost ended, for he signed a professional football contract the next month, but he had still to run the third leg on U.S.A.'s 1,600 meter relay team. He took the baton barely ahead of Germany's dangerous team and then waited coolly until the homestretch before turning on his power. In the stretch he gained four precious yards, exactly the winning margin, and he collected his third gold medal and fifth world record as the U.S. team ran 3:02.2.

The finish at Rome: Glenn Davis wins another gold medal.

In his remarkable career, Davis lost only four out of forty intermediate hurdle races. One loss came in those uncertain first two months, and the other three when he was out of condition – two of them in unimportant races. When his career ended he had to his credit six of the nine fastest intermediate times ever run. He bettered 49.9 ten times. No man has ever had such a superb record in this event, and few, if any, have proved such astonishing versatility on the track. Above all else was his rare ability to win.

The highest possible tribute came from Larry Snyder of Ohio State, who coached them both: 'Glenn Davis is possibly a greater talent than Jesse Owens.'

AL OERTER

Among the people who like track and field athletics, an argument rages: Which is more desirable, a world record or an Olympic gold medal?

One athlete who favors the gold medal is Al Oerter.

Breaking a world record, he says, is like 'trying to catch leaves'. Records fall unexpectedly, to discus throwers who happen to be at the right 'wind alley' at the right time. But when Oerter talks about the Olympic Games his green eyes light up with a glow unusual in this big, shy man.

'The Olympics are unique, a world community...what men have been trying to achieve for centuries. There is no job, no amount of power, no money to approach the meaning of the Olympic experience. It's unfortunate they only happen once every four years. They are so special....'

Al Oerter is two men in one. He is the solid citizen who does a difficult job well, who loves his wife and two daughters, and whose values are the kind the world needs. On the other hand, he is a soaring, creative, competitive genius, the like of whom has seldom been seen at any time, or any place, in any sport.

The remarkable story of Al Oerter's experiences at the Olympic Games breaks down neatly into four acts.

ACT I, 1956: The scene was the Melbourne Cricket Grounds on Tuesday, November 27. The curious shape of the round field left huge half-moons of grass on either side of the track, and the triple-decked stands, built piecemeal at various periods in the past, were filled with 100,000 enthusiastic Australians.

Young Al Oerter was nervous. Barely 20 years old, the 6' $3\frac{1}{2}''$, 220-pounder with a bushy blond crew-cut hoped for an Olympic medal, but his competition was strong and he was so tense that failure would be only natural. Sitting on the bench or keeping limber, he watched his opponents.

First, he watched Adolfo Consolini of Italy who was Olympic champion in 1948, long before Oerter wanted to throw the discus. Consolini was second in 1952, the year of Oerter's first interest in the high school discus. Now thirty-nine Consolini had a fine practice throw of 194 feet a few days before, but a cut on his index finger threatened to hamper him. His first throw went only 170' 4".

Next, Oerter watched dependable Ferenc Klics of Hungary, thirty-two years old and fifth in the last two Olympics. The discus throw is a good event for older athletes, and young Oerter knew he had a lot of improvement ahead of him. He watched Klics throw 169' 9"

Next, Oerter feared Gordien. Fortune Gordien, thirty-four, was bronze medalist in 1948 and fourth in 1952. He broke the world record in 1949 and raised it to 194' 6" in 1953, a year when Oerter could manage only 153 feet with the high school discus. In 1954, Oerter set a high school record of 184' 2¾", but Gordien surpassed that by eight feet with the heavier discus.

In 1955, while Oerter threw the heavy discus to a freshman record 171' 6" in a postal meet, Gordien let down to 180' 11". But this year Gordien was coming back strong. He threw a frightening 198 feet in practice at the Olympic Village and Oerter did not expect to beat him even when Gordien's first throw sailed only 179' 7½".

The important thing was to throw his best. His previous best, at the moment when he stripped off his blue USA sweat suit and stepped onto the concrete circle, was 183' 5", made with the help of a wind. After that he was only fourth in the NCAA and an unpromising sixth in the AAU. But he had made the team with 178' 7½" and he had four throws over 180 feet in tune-up meets, and he had a chance for a medal if he did not tie up.

'Everything built up inside me. I really was keyed up and inspired.'

He looked out toward the flag marking the Olympic record of 180' 6½". Then, carefully, he went into his windup, spun powerfully, and sailed the discus up the center.

That was a moment to remember. Nervous and inexperienced as he was, he came through with a personal record of 184' 10½", a new Olympic record. About 100,000 people roared approval.

Al Oerter

'I don't know how I did it. Somehow or other everything just went right and this throw came out.'

Now he was even more tense. 'I had a hard time even raising my arm after that.' Still, he managed two more throws over 180 feet.

All he could do was watch Gordien. None of the others came close, but Gordien was always a threat. 'Naturally, I kept my fingers crossed. I was always afraid Fortune would beat me. I knew he could.'

Gordien's last throw made Oerter hold his breath, but it slapped down at 179′ 9½″. Oerter, aged 20, was the Olympic champion. The three Americans threw their arms around each other and they stood on the victory stand and watched their flags and heard their music. Oerter liked it. Quietly, he started thinking about 1960.

FIRST INTERMISSION: In 1957, Oerter showed unsatisfactory improvement. He was badly beaten in the Coliseum Relays and the Compton Invitational, and he had only one throw beyond the 180-foot line prior to the esteemed NCAA meet. Characteristically, he came through as collegiate champion with his longest throw yet – 185′ 4″. The next week, in Dayton, Ohio, he threw 181′ 6″ to win his first AAU victory. Then he lost four times in Europe and ranked only fourth for the year in the world rankings.

1958 was not much better. After Rink Babka shocked discus throwers everywhere with a throw over 200 feet on March 22 only to have it ruled invalid because it landed in a ditch, Oerter threw 202′ 6″ into a good Arkansas wind on April 5, but a slope of 2½% ruined his chance for a record.

Oerter raised his personal record by 3½″ at the Drake Relays and to 188′ 2″ at the Central Collegiates. In the NCAA, his good 186′ 2″ was tied by Babka, who beat him soundly for the AAU title a week later. Oerter lost to Babka a second time in Moscow in late July, and he ranked second in the world.

Oerter was a promising shot putter, too, with a best mark of 56′ 11″ in 1959, when only four men were over 60 feet. He renounced the shot because the lateral hip shift confused his training for the hip twist in the discus.

In 1959, Oerter was out of college, working for Grunman Aircraft in data processing. Most athletes are unable to handle the pressures of job and family in addition to training, and so they surrender their chance for success, but Oerter was well organized. He alternated weight training with throwing practice, and he competed in only a few meets, but he improved noticeably.

He won the AAU at 186′ 5″, raised his personal record to 188′ 9″ against the Soviets in Philadelphia. He improved again, to 190′ 8½″, in his Pan American Games victory at Chicago. He was first in World Ranking for 1959.

ACT II, 1960 : The scene, on September 7, was Rome's beautiful, flag-rimmed Stadio Olimpico with its background of hills and monuments. Oerter had a good season behind him with most meets over 190 feet and a new personal record of 194′ 1½″, but he was afraid.

The reason for Oerter's fear was big Rink Babka, now weighing 267 pounds, with an awesome practice throw over 200 fee. Babka had given Oerter his first downfall in two seasons at the Final Trials in Palo Alto. And on August 12, Babka had sailed the platter to an impressive record of 196′ 6½″.

Oerter had made an exciting warmup throw around 198 feet the day before, and then he qualified easily with an Olympic record of 191′ 8″, but none of that counted. Only the gold medal counted and Babka threw 190′ 4″ on his first attempt.

Oerter stepped onto the concrete circle determined to win it right away. As he spun, his foot slipped and his plan failed. Even so, his throw went 189′ 1″. On his second throw, he reached only 186′ 1½″, and his tension grew. Babka, too, failed to improve and nobody else had a chance. Oerter threw only 185′ 5½″ and he became more nervous. His fourth throw landed at 186′ 1½″ again.

'I was so tense I could barely throw.'

He entered the ring for his fifth throw. All his hopes and dreams were going for naught unless he could control his tension. A champion must, most of all, control himself when the pressure is on. He had done it in 1956, and now it was necessary again.

He spun slowly, carefully, powerfully. His hip came around first, then his body untwisted ahead of the discus. Last came his hand, whipping the discus around violently and spinning it off into space. It rode high and kept sailing, floating down reluctantly. It bit into the turf 194′ 2″ away.

Once again he had come through with a personal record where

Al Oerter

it counted most. And after Babka's threat ended, Oerter mounted the top step of the victory stand again.

INTERMISSION: Oerter had another good throw, 194' $\frac{1}{4}$", against the British Commonwealth in London, September 14. Then, true to his philosophy, he became semi-retired in 1961. He threw the steel-rimmed platter in only four meets. His best mark of 190' $5\frac{1}{2}$" came, typically, in the AAU meet, but he lost to Jay Silvester.

Silvester raised the world record to 199' $2\frac{1}{2}$" on August 20, 1961. Not satisfied with himself, Oerter worked harder on his strength and built his weight up to 250 pounds for the 1962 season. He began with his best ever throw, 198' 6", at the Mt. San Antonio Relays.

In the Los Angeles Coliseum Relays, throwing at night under bright floodlights, Oerter set out to better 200 feet. On his second throw he sailed the discus 198' $7\frac{1}{2}$" for a personal record, but he was still dissatisfied.

On his fourth throw, 'The ring was so slippery I nearly fell,' but the discus hit the green turf 200' $5\frac{1}{2}$" away, first official throw over the glamorous 200-foot mark.

Asked to compare this world record with his Olympic championship, Oerter answered in the glow of the moment, 'This is more satisfying because it was so long in coming.'

Seventeen days later, he lost his world record to Russian Vladimir Trusenyov's unexpected 202' $2\frac{1}{2}$". Seventeen days after that, in the AAU meet at Walnut, California, June 23, Oerter put on the greatest exhibition of throwing to date. His first throw sailed 200' $3\frac{1}{2}$". His worst was 195' 5". His best was 202' 2", only half an inch short of the world record.

On July 1, Oerter was supposed to compete against Poland in Chicago, but on Monday he strained a muscle lifting weights. He tried diathermy treatments and on Saturday he flew to Chicago, determined to compete against former world record holder Edmund Piatkowski, undefeated since 1960.

Oerter's second throw spun through the air for a long time and when he saw it land he raced after it to watch the measurement. It was 204' $10\frac{1}{2}$", a world record.

'I had to get it early because I didn't feel strong. I really didn't expect to do it. The wind wasn't really the way I like it.'

Three weeks later, at Stanford University's huge bowl, a crowd of 81,000 watched the dual meet with Russia. Oerter was up against Babka and the only other 200-footer, Trusenyov.

Oerter threw 199' 8½" on his first throw, and he won overwhelmingly, with a best of 200' 1". He now had made five of the six throws in history over 200 feet. Undefeated, he was an easy choice as first in the world for the year.

In 1963, his first meet was the Mt. San Antonio Relays in Walnut, April 27. He said: 'Because of my job I got a late start getting into condition. I planned it that way because I didn't want to be burned out and stale for next year. I have been working out off and on since January. Mostly off. Only the last two weeks did I get down to some serious work. I still am not in top condition.'

In such deplorable condition it is small wonder he failed to better 200 feet on one throw. His series was incomparable: 201' 5", 205' 5½", 199' 3½", 204' 1½", 203' 3", and 202' 10". He had raised the world record a third time and increased his 200-foot throws to ten.

'I was the most surprised man at the Mt. San Antonio Relays. I'm not in very good shape.'

Jay Silvester became a strong threat, with a warmup toss of 215 feet and a foul of 207 feet, but Oerter came through when it counted. 'The more you strain, the less distance. It has to be a very relaxed type of motion.'

Silvester said, 'When you throw against Oerter, you don't expect to win. You just hope.'

Nevertheless, Oerter beat Silvester by an insecure foot with 202' 11" in the California Relays, and his 202' 8½" lost to Silvester's 204' 4" at Compton. But Oerter was suffering from a slipped disc and he could not enter the AAU meet. Every throw caused a pain to shoot down his left arm.

Back at the Mt. San Antonio Relays in 1964, Oerter was not at his best but a wind, strong enough to force him to throw wearing a ski jacket, held his discus up for the two longest throws of all time. His first sailed 206' 6" and his sixth was 206' 4".

This was gratifying in more ways than one, for Oerter's attitude toward his sport is more amateur than most. He believes some athletes do too much training.

'Technique and strength can be maintained over prolonged periods of time with minimum effort. As I become older, it becomes more satisfying to be able to maintain a world class condition while having a wife and family and a job that's rather demanding.'

Now weighing 260 pounds, he went to the AAU meet at New Brunswick, New Jersey. He threw with a homemade brace around his neck, made with two towels and a belt. This helped stop a whiplash action of his head, which pinched a nerve and hurt in his left arm. His first throw was a winning 201′ 1½″ and he had two others over 200′.

The next week he insured his place on the Olympic team by winning the semi-final trials in New York with 201′ 11″. In spite of his neck brace, he said, 'I'm throwing better than ever.'

He won against the Soviets in Los Angeles with a throw of 200′ 5¼″, but then things began to go wrong.

'My neck still bothers me. I tried to throw without the brace but it still hurt, so I put it back on. I'll have to live with it for awhile, I guess.'

Next, Ludwig Danek of Czechoslovakia broke Oerter's world record with an amazing throw of 211′ 9½″ on August 2. Then Oerter threw poorly in the Final Trials. His 193′ 4″ lost to Silvester.

'Honestly, I couldn't get up for this meet. There was every reason to be high, but subconsciously I didn't have it. I've always advocated the team trials should be settled in just one meet.'

ACT III, 1964: The scene was Japan's National Stadium in Tokyo, filled with 75,000 attentive spectators and rimmed with flags of all nations. Oerter could hear a peculiar metallic rhythm as wind whipped the ropes against the tall flagpoles.

Oerter was in trouble on the concrete circle. He wore no neck brace, for the pain from that injury was nothing compared with his new problem. Six days ago he had torn some cartilages in his lower rib cage. He had to stop exercising. His ribs were heavily taped. His right side was periodically packed in ice to prevent internal hemorrhaging. Doctors told him to rest for six weeks to heal his wounds.

But to Al Oerter, the Olympic Games are too important to consider quitting. Now he spun slowly in a warmup throw. The pain cut into his side like a knife and he doubled over. 'I was thinking of dropping out.'

He only thought it, though. When his turn came, he was in the circle, trying for his third gold medal. He spun around and let go, grimacing with pain. 'It felt like somebody was trying to tear out my ribs.'

The discus went only 189' 1½". Danek, the tall, lean record holder, threw 195' 11½". Oerter's second throw hurt again and he improved only to 191' 5" while big Dave Weill moved ahead of him to second place with a throw of 195' 2".

The nightmare contined, with the wounded champion spinning the discus only 180' 9½" and 178' 4½". Danek moved nearer to victory with 198' 6½" on his fourth throw. Oerter watched helplessly as Silvester knocked him back into fourth place with 193' 10½" on his fifth throw.

Of his own fifth throw, Oerter says, 'I was using a slow spin and trying to stretch the tendons to get a little higher. I had been throwing too low and I was trying a very easy turn to correct the problem. The sixth was to have been my best effort with a faster turn.'

He spun easily and lifted the back of his hand high, looking toward the sky as he whipped the discus into its whirling flight. Spectators held their breaths, watching the discus settle toward the grass. Then a mighty roar rose from the stadium. Oerter's throw was 200' 1½". He had done it again.

A stunned Danek failed on his last throw and Oerter passed. He was still champion.

He was praised all over the track world. Coach Payton Jordan called it the gamest performance he had ever seen. Track fans noted that no man since 1908 had won the same Olympic event three times. But Oerter could throw no more. He had to rest his injuries if he expected to defend his title in 1968.

INTERMISSION: With no competition at all in 1965, Oerter built his strength up to its highest ever. In 1966, after a mediocre beginning because of rusty technique, he met Danek at the California Relays. Danek threw 205' 9", and Oerter threw 207' 5", a personal record. 'I'm so strong it scares me, but I'm a year away in technique.'

He won the AAU for the sixth time, threw 205' 6" and 205' 7" in two other meets, and ranked first in World Ranking for a sixth year.

Even with such success he gave three reasons why he expected to improve: (1) 'Slight changes in my technique, allowing for a better turn. (2) My mental attitude is better than it has ever been. (3) I am able to increase my strength each year without maintaining a severe weight training program.'

One secret of Oerter's longevity is that he enjoys throwing the discus. He considers physical conditioning important to him and to his family. 'Throwing is my recreation. I compete because I love competition.'

But in 1967 he had his worst year. He threw 203' 6" in one minor meet but all his others were under 200 feet and he placed a dismal fourth in the AAU. When 1968 began cheerlessly, it seemed as if time was bringing to Al Oerter, as it must to all men, a gradual extinction.

He did not believe it himself. Carefully, he prepared for October and his fourth Olympics. Before the AAU meet in Sacramento, he explained he was bringing himself along slowly. All he wanted to do here was qualify. He threw 194' 6" and finished nine feet behind Silvester. In the semi-final Olympic Trials in Los Angeles he was little better. He threw 197' 10" and lost by almost eight feet.

'I'm fairly satisfied. This was my fifth competition of the year and I figure that I am coming around. It just takes longer to get in shape now.'

Meanwhile, Silvester had broken the world record with an awesome 218' $3\frac{1}{2}$" at Modesto, California, and had several other throws far longer than Oerter's all-time best. Four other throwers had bettered Oerter's 1966 mark of 207' 5", and his chances had all but disappeared.

Back home on Long Island, Oerter was getting ready. 'One of my games in track is preparing. I can't compete every week and be adequately prepared. You have three good workouts in between at most. It just isn't enough.'

He returned to California late in July, better prepared. Among the trees at the Echo Summit track, near South Lake Tahoe, on July 27, he threw 205' 10" to hand an unsuspecting Silvester his first defeat of the season. On August 10, at Walnut, he had five throws over 200 feet with a best of 205' 9", but he lost to Silvester by almost four feet.

After a disappointing third place at 196' 4" in Houston, Oerter went all out to win the Final Trials at Echo Summit. He threw

204′ 8″, but he lost to better throws by Silvester and Gary Carlsen.

A week later came the final blow. Silvester threw at Reno, Nevada, and raised the world record to an unreachable 224′ 5″ with a strong, favorable wind. In addition, Silvester had an overpowering series of throws, including 223′ 4″, 219′ 3″, and a foul of 230′ 5″.

But Al Oerter did not reach the peaks of true greatness by conceding defeat. He knew only one way to compete in the Olympic Games, and that way required an all-out effort, physically and mentally. He worked harder than ever, even though he said, 'I didn't think I had a chance this time.'

ACT IV, 1968: The scene was Mexico City's Estadio Olimpico. Down the wide ramp onto the field marched the expectant discus throwers in their colorful sweatsuits. They broke ranks and each selected a discus and awaited his turn in the high green cage.

They were frustrated in their efforts to prepare for competition by a light rain. One by one, as the rain grew heavier, the competitors reluctantly took shelter under umbrellas at the edge of the field. Only Oerter continued to throw. He was beginning to gain on them.

'Once in the Olympic Village you can't improve on your strength or speed. The only thing still possible is to improve your mental attitude. In the weeks before an Olympic competition, I mentally simulate every conceivable situation for each throw. For example, I imagine I'm in eighth place, it's my fifth throw, and it's pouring rain. What do I do? An inexperienced thrower might panic or be thinking, "Gees, I hope I don't fall down." I know ahead of time what I will do under every condition.'

After twenty minutes, the concrete circle was hopelessly wet. They all retired into the warm dressing room and relaxed – except Oerter, who paced purposefully, keeping himself ready.

After another 25 minutes the unwelcome rain stopped and they were hurried into competition without a satisfactory warmup. Oerter was not wearing his neck brace nor his sweat clothes. With a towel around his shoulders, he paced back and forth like a caged tiger. His first throw went 202′ 8″, farther than any of his previous Olympic throws.

He fouled his second throw. He was now in fourth place, but

Al Oerter

he knew he could do better. He had been throwing better than ever in practice. Now he needed the longest throw of his career.

He walked into the big cage, discus in one hand, towel in the other. He wiped his feet carefully and threw the towel aside. He stepped onto the pale green concrete.

'The circle was still wet from the rain, so I eliminated my preliminary warm-up swings. All that rocking back and forth upset my balance.'

He looked out toward his goal – the white sign marking Silvester's qualifying-round Olympic record of 207′ 9¼″. He swung the discus back once, coiling for his throw. He started his spin, slowly, carefully, with great discipline and power.

He let it go, high and spinning. He recovered on his right foot and watched hopefully as the discus soared toward the dark sky. He knew it was a good throw and he watched the flying saucer hold a good flight position all the way down, past the markers of Silvester, Losch, and Milde, beyond his own best, beyond Silvester's Olympic record.

He heard the roar of joy and amazement from the crowd, and he felt a keen satisfaction. He had done it again.

He was careful to step out of the rear half of the circle. He picked up his towel and peered expectantly at the electric field board. The yellow lights appeared – 64.78. He had thrown 212′ 4½″, almost five feet farther than ever before.

Now the others could start worrying. Silvester, without a favorable wind, pressed too hard and fouled. Danek came through with his best throw of the year – 206′ 5″. Silvester continued to press and fail, and the others could not gain, but Oerter threw 204′ 9½″, 212′ 4½″, and 210′ 1″ – giving him the three best throws of his life.

That fourth gold medal was his.

Out of the myriad of praise for what is possibly the greatest feat in the history of the sport, came two concise explanations by coaches who know him well.

Bill Easton, Oerter's college coach, said, 'He has the most concentration of any.'

And head U.S. coach Payton Jordan said, 'He's all heart and guts.'

Or, as Silvester once said, 'He's the toughest man to beat in track and field.'

Track's Greatest Champions

1960   *1964*

Al Oerter

1968    *1985*

Act 5 in the Oerter drama never happened, but there was a sequel. He threw 203' in 1969, ranking only No. 10, and he retired to family life and his job as a computer engineer.

In 1977, to the surprise of the track world, he began a comeback by throwing 205-1. He threw 205-5 in 1978, not bad for a legendary champion now 41 years old.

But he was building his strength privately and revamping his technique. In 1979 he put a little fear into more than one discus thrower by throwing farther than ever. His best sailed 221-4 and he ranked No. 9 in the world.

Oerter's goal, of course, was the Olympic Games of 1980. He sailed the discus 227-11 during the season, but in the Final Trials, knowing there was no Olympic competition for Americans, he placed only fourth. He threw 225-7 in 1981, at the age of 44. In 1982, he slipped to 216-11, still better than his PR during his glory days. He wanted to make the USA team for the World Championships in 1983, and he threw 222-9 but an injury ended his hopes. He threw 209-8 in 1984 and didn't seriously challenge for a spot on the Olympic team. In 1985 he reached 211-3 (No. 8 on the U.S. list) and it still may be a while before the four-time Olympic champion decides to throw his last discus as he obviously still enjoys the sport and the competition.

HERB ELLIOTT

Few men are born with the natural ability of Herb Elliott. Still fewer punish themselves so hard in training. And nobody ever had a greater will to win.

The result? : A short, brilliant career as the greatest miler of all time, ending at the age of twenty-two.

Elliott's prodigious talent was in evidence from the beginning, in Perth, Western Australia. His parents valued physical fitness highly, and at an early age he liked to run, row, swim, cycle, and play football and hockey. While he was still eight, he won age-group sprint championships.

He triumphed in his first half-mile race, from handicap, at the age of ten. At fourteen, he ran his first mile, in 5:35. He lost only once in the mile, an unfair match against a boy three years older. At fifteen, he won the state schoolboy 880 in 2:10.4.

At sixteen, he was phenomenal. He won the junior national 880 by inches in 1:55.7, an Australian junior record. Two days later, he crushed Ron Clarke by 20 yards in 4:20.8, another junior record.

At seventeen, a greedy Elliott won six events in his school sports : 100 in 10.6, 220 in 23.4, 440 in 51.0, 880 in 1:59.4, mile in 4:22.0, and the broad jump at 19′ 7½″. One impressed witness was a skinny, tanned, white-haired man named Percy Cerutty. The famous coach told Elliott :

'There's not a shadow of a doubt that within two years you will run a mile in four minutes.'

That was in October, 1955. Later in the month, a willing Elliott won the state mile in 4:20.4. In December, he let a piano fall on his foot, breaking two metatarsal bones, and he missed the 1955–56 season. Discouraged, he did little training and smoked thirty or forty cigarettes a day.

Then, with another great prospect about to go under, Elliott's parents took him across Australia to the Olympic Games in Melbourne. Inspired by Vladimir Kuts in the 10,000 meters, Elliott's interest rose again. He spent three hours in Percy Cerutty's little house and the enthusiasm of the coach ingited Elliott's will to run.

They visited Cerutty's training camp at Portsea, and Elliott says: 'I took one look at glorious, God-kissed Portsea and wanted to run through the sand from sheer joy and exhilaration.' After the Olympics, Elliott joined Cerutty at Portsea and began to work.

Cerutty ran Elliott around the dirt trails through the trees and up steep sandhills until Elliott dropped. He shamed Elliott into lifting heavier weights. He force-fed Elliott his own philosophy, such as: 'Thrust against pain. Pain is the purifier. Walk toward suffering. Love suffering. Embrace it.'

Elliott did as he was told, including fixing a goal: 'I wanted to be the best miler in the world.'

He had only two months of such intense work on his still painful foot, plus one 880 race, when he entered the mile at Olympic Park Stadium on January 12. He ran a startling 4:06.0, breaking Clarke's world junior record, and John Landy commented: 'Elliott is the most fantastic junior I have ever seen. He looks as though he's been running in top company for years.'

The next day, Elliott exhausted himself in a long run on the Portsea golf course. 'Most athletes imagine themselves at the end of their tether before they're even 75 per cent exhausted. I was so determined to avoid this pitfall that if at any time I thought I was surrendering too soon to superficial pain, I'd deliberately try to hurt myself more.'

In the next few weeks he started the track world buzzing by breaking all world junior records from the 880 to 3 miles. His 880 in 1:50.8, mile in 4:04.3, and 2 miles in 9:01 were especially noteworthy.

On February 25 he had his nineteenth birthday and ceased to be a junior. He was thrown to the lions at the Australian Championships against Merv Lincoln, an experienced 4:01.8 miler on his way up. Elliott trailed for three laps, then burst into the lead.

'I felt like a frightened bunny running for dear life.' He led Lincoln by five yards at 1,500 meters and dazed him by 15 yards in 4:00.4.

Two days later, Elliott added the 880 title to his collection with a topnotch 1:49.3. His season was over. Barely nineteen, he ranked sixth among the world's best milers for 1957. He had succeeded without sufficient background, but on May 1, he began his preparation for 1958. During the Australian winter and spring he ran 2,500 miles and lifted tons of weights.

His first mile race of 1958 came on January 25 in Melbourne. He ran 3:59.9, but it did not excite him. He had bigger goals in mind.

The next day he saved a girl from drowning in the rip tide at Portsea, his second rescue. Four days later he raced Lincoln at Olympic Park. Lincoln was favored, off his best time of 3:58.9, and Elliott did not shake hands.

'To shake hands with one's opponents before a race and wish them luck is hypocritical. I don't want to talk to them and the last thing I want to do is shake their hands because it would break down my purposefulness.'

Elliott took the lead after the half and led at the bell in 3:02.6. He poured on all he had over the last lap, but Lincoln came up to his shoulder in the homestretch. Elliott fought him off to win by two yards in 3:58.7.

Elliott barely survived in his next race as his desperate sprint barely caught Lincoln at the tape in 3:59.6. He broke the Australian 1,000 meter record with 2:21.0, then ran in the Australian Championships in Brisbane. He sped the last lap in 52.8, last 880 in a stunning 1:52.8, to win in 4:08.8. Once again, he completed a fine double by winning the 880 in 1:49.4.

His Australian season was over, but 1958 was to be a four-part season. Before the second phase began, he created a sensation by rescuing Cerutty from drowning in the Portsea surf.

Still regarded as an exciting prospect not yet arrived, he was invited to California in May for a series of four races. When he announced he would not go without his coach, Cerutty was invited along.

He lined up for his first race, in the Coliseum Relays at Los Angeles, a strong, lean, 5' 11½", 150-pounder with a hawk nose broken in three varied violences. He took the lead in 3:00.3 and then turned on his amazing speed. For half a lap it looked like a world record, and 34,000 fans cheered him on. But he won by only 20 yards.

'My last 50 yards were my poorest, but that may be due to the fact that there was no one at hand to push me.'

His time was 3:57.8, faster than the official world record and second only to Derek Ibbotson's pending 3:57.2. Elliott went sightseeing, trained, and played golf. His next race was in the California Relays at Modesto, May 31.

When he first saw the hard clay track, he exclaimed, 'Gor blimey, it's like a bloody brick.' Nobody pushed the pace, and he won easily in 4:02.7. He said, 'Some nights you have it, others you don't. Cerutty's comment was made with fingers delicately patting a yawn.

The next weekend, Elliott was in the little stadium at Compton for the Compton Invitational. He led at three-quarters in 3:01.8 with Olympic champion Ron Delany on his heels all the way. Now Elliott turned on his dazzling speed, his elbows flying like a sprinter's.

On the backstretch he was four yards ahead and Delany had to let him go. Elliott ran his last 120 yards in an eye-popping 14.7 to win by 15 yards in 3:58.1.

Delany came up and said, 'Well, me boy, you may have beaten me here now, but sure I'll thrash the pants off you in Dublin town.'

Two weeks later, Elliott ran in the U.S. AAU Championships in Bakersfield. Jaded from his social activities but full of run, he sped an unnecessary 4:01.4 in his heat.

In the final, he pushed hard on the last lap and won by four yards over Lincoln in 3:57.9.

'I have never been in such bad physical shape in my life. I felt weak. I haven't eaten well and I ran too fast last night.'

With his U.S. season ended, he had five weeks before the most important meet of the year – the Empire Games in Wales. He did more sight-seeing and 'indulged my long-neglected taste for high living.' He relaxed his training, and placed only third in the British AAA 880.

Preparing to meet Brian Hewson again in the Empire 880, he practiced sprints and ran 100 yards with a running start in a lively 9.6.

The Empire 880 championship at Cardiff came on July 22. Elliott allowed a slow pace, trying different tactics on Hewson. They passed the 440 in 58.8. Suddenly, Elliott sprinted and opened a gap. Hewson recovered and sprinted after him. In the stretch, Hewson came dangerously close, but Elliott gave a little more and he won by two yards in 1:49.3.

Four days later, in the rain, he triumphed over Lincoln by almost 20 yards in 3:59.0 to complete his Empire double. Delany had promised to 'Thrash the pants off' him at Dublin on August 6, but Elliott enjoyed champagne and rich food, and he spent his time sight-seeing.

On August 4, when he should have been concentrating on the Dublin mile, he ran a remarkable half mile in London's White City stadium. He felt no seriousness about the race, but he led Hewson and Rawson, who had beaten him in the AAA. On the second lap he suddenly felt invincible. At the peak of condition, his mighty kick beat Hewson by ten yards in 1:47.3.

Then, on the same day, he had to run another half mile. With Cerutty loudly cheering his opponent, Elliott came from behind on the last curve to win in 1:50.7. Added to his Australian and Empire victories, this day's work earned him first in World Ranking.

Two days later, Elliott rode a bus with Lincoln through the gates at Santry and into a crowd trying to buy seats in the low stands already packed solid with 20,000 people. Elliott dressed with the others in a strange mood.

'No butterflies, no tingling. Nothing. I'm dead.'

He jogged and talked with Alby Thomas, the 3-mile record holder, then rested until half an hour before the race. He put on his spikes and began his serious warmup. The air was moist and cool from rain and there was no wind.

When the runners lined up on the red track it was raining. Elliott was in the third lane, next to Delany, and somebody in the partisan crowd shouted, 'Do him, Ronnie.'

At the gun, Thomas, a 5' 5", 126-pounder, set off at a fast pace. Lincoln followed, five yards back. Elliott was fourth, behind black-shirted Murray Halberg. 'They got off a little too fast for me.'

Chesty little Thomas passed the 440 in 58 flat and the crowd roared. Elliott passed Lincoln and ran up to Thomas's shoulder, but the little man kept going. He passed the 880 in 1:58.0 with Elliott on his heels. Elliott thought, 'I don't even feel I've been running.'

With a record in mind, Elliott charged past Thomas on the backstretch. 'I knew I was running the fastest race of my life.' Into the curve he heard foosteps and Lincoln shot past. 'I was thunderstruck.'

Elliott followed Lincoln down the homestretch. The bell sounded its warning, in 2:59, and Elliott ran past Lincoln into the turn. Three others were threatening behind Lincoln. To the screaming Irish crowd it was still anybody's race, and their boy Delany was still in it.

But Elliott had that invincible feeling again. He could hear Lincoln behind him, with all the frenzied uproar, and he drove hard down the backstretch. On the turn he was timed in 3:39.6, second best ever for 1,500 meters. He sprinted home ten yards ahead of Lincoln.

An excited timer rushed to Elliott. 'Fantastic,' he said. 'It's just fantastic. Your time is 3:54.5.'

Lincoln, who ran 3:55.9, asked Delany if he felt like taking up tennis. Delany, third in 3:57.5, was violently ill, but he said later, 'There is only one way to beat Elliott. That's to tie his legs together.' Halberg kept shaking his head and muttering about running 3:57.5 and placing only fourth. And Thomas, fifth in 3:58.6, was exuberant.

Elliott went to a pub, phoned his fiancee in Australia, 'and then I sat down and got a little drunk.'

The very next night, Elliott helped Thomas in his 2-mile race. He set the pace until the sixth lap when Thomas went past and kept pulling away. 'It was hopeless.' Thomas set a world record of 8:32.0. Elliott's 8:37.6 was bettered by only two runners before this race.

Thus ended the third phase of Elliott's magnificent year. He was due in Stockholm in eighteen days. Denied expense money by international rules, he joined other carefree athletes in driving Gordon Pirie's Volkswagen bus to Sweden. They camped out nights and relished large quantities of beer and ale. They trained sporadically along the way. 'It provided the relaxation that was desperately needed before I could train intensely again.'

He was a spectator at the European Championships and stayed at an athletic camp outside Stockholm. Refreshed and enthusiastic again, he trained hard with Ibbotson for several days.

On August 25, at the 385-meter Stora Mossan track, he ran

Herb Elliott

his first 1,500 meter race, winning easily in 3:41.7. Three days later he was in the new stadium at Göteborg, running 1,500 meters against a great field.

The race started at 7:24 p.m. with world record holder Stanislav Jungwirth setting a mad pace of 56 for the first 400 meters. Elliott was seventh, in 58 seconds. Thomas took over the lead, but Elliott caught him in 1:57.5. 'Suddenly my limbs and lungs were being tortured no longer. I felt strong and confident.'

He ran the third lap in an awe-inspiring 58 flat, scattering the great field of runners behind him. He increased his pace in a long hard drive to the finish. His last 400 meters took only 54 seconds and he won by 18 yards. His 3:36.0 broke the world record by 2.1 seconds.

The crowd of 35,000 continued to applaud for a full minute after the race. Elliott was given a bouquet. He jogged a lap of honor, then tossed the flowers to the crowd.

He was scheduled to run a mile the very next night in Malmö. He objected strenuously to plans for a sub-four-minute race. 'I'm not a machine that can be wound up every day.'

Cerutty calmed him down and raised his confidence in his fitness. Elliott followed the 3:02 pace, feeling tired, but when he turned on his power he ran the last lap in 56 and beat Dan Waern by 25 yards in 3:58.0.

He was tired of racing again, after nine months, but he agreed to run an invitational mile in London's White City on September 3. In a daze, he did not realize his time for three laps was 2:59.8. Hewson was at his shoulder and he was having a crisis, but he would not quit. On the backstretch he pulled away and broke Hewson, but he pushed himself all the way to the tape.

He celebrated at a night club that night, got to bed at 3:30 a.m., and did not hear his good time until the next noon. It was 3:55.4, second best ever.

He flew to Oslo, feeling listless. On September 5, in Bislet Idrettsplass, he ran his last race of the year. After 800 meters in 1:59, he tried to run away on the third lap. His lap was a fantastic 56.5 and put him 30 yards ahead of an astounded Halberg.

Elliott was 'flagging badly at the end.' He lost 20 yards of his lead. His head throbbed and his whole body ached. His time was 3:37.4, second best ever, and yet the crowd of 33,000 applauded only mildly. 'I'd strained my body to the bounds of endurance and running had become a nightmare.'

And small wonder, for in the past nine days he had run four quality races against the best runners of Europe and Australasia, outclassing them completely. His four races included the two fastest 1,500 meters ever run, the second fastest mile, and another mile in 3:58.0, tenth fastest of all time. No other man had ever run such fast races in a lifetime. No other man has ever run so close to his best so many times in so few days.

Within the past thirty-two days he had also run his 3:54.5 mile, the fourth fastest 2-mile in history, and the third fastest 880.

In 1958 he ran under four minutes a total of ten times, plus three 1,500 meter races of equal value. He ran six of the eleven fastest miles ever run, plus the two fastest 1,500s. He richly deserved the title of History's Greatest Miler.

And he was only twenty years old.

To prepare for Cambridge, he began a first year science course at Melbourne University and crammed four years of Latin into nine months. On May 2, 1959, he was married. He also spent time talking to groups of boys. The result was a lack of training.

'The old dedication to running had vanished.' Sometimes he played golf at Portsea instead of running.

He raced only a little in 1959. 'I was amazed that I continued to win races, though only half fit.'

His most severe test of that short season came on March 14 in Brisbane. He rode with Lincoln of the five-hour journey. Carelessly, he drank a bottle of beer and smoked several cigarettes.

Lincoln's hopes were aroused and he pushed the pace on the grass track. He passed three quarters in 3:01 and gave it everything he had into the last curve. Suddenly, Elliott exploded and ran away from him. Lincoln, beaten by 30 yards in 3:58.9, saw Elliott dry-retching. Completely shocked at this burst from a man obviously out of shape, Lincoln never ran well again.

As 1959 ended, Elliott realized the Olympic Games would be held in eight months. 'On 26th December I stopped smoking and started serious training at Portsea.'

So great was his natural talent, however, in spite of two losses in shorter races, he ran 3:59.8 on Bendigo's grass track, and won the Australian Championship at Perth in 4:02.1, distressed by the heat.

'The pain was excruciating. My stomach was convulsing and I felt every moment that I would vomit.'

He won the 880 title from Blue and beat him again in April. On April 2, at Bendigo, he ran 5,000 meters in 14:09.9. At the end of the month he punished himself in a 33-mile run. In May he went to California for three races.

He won the Coliseum Relays 1,500 in a lazy 3:45.4. Then a sore knee developed and doctors advised him to withdraw from the California Relays. At the last moment he told meet director Tom Moore, 'You'll have to count me out, Tom.' Depressed, he broke into tears.

But at the Compton Invitational on June 3 he was able to win in 3:59.2. He returned to the Australian winter, knowing he had to improve in the three months remaining. 'There were days when I was filled with self doubt.'

For a few weeks he ran before daybreak in the streets of Melbourne. He cut short his lunch hour so as to train earlier in the afternoon, but darkness caught him. Twice a week he lifted weights instead of eating lunch, and he listened to Cerutty now.

'He is like an oasis in the desert of my lost enthusiasm.'

On July 23, his wife and baby son left for Rome. Elliott received a leave of absence from Shell Chemical and joined Cerutty at Portsea. 'I needed Percy's inspiration more than I could remember needing it when I was a young and dedicated athlete.'

He trained hard once more, but he ran two bad races, and he arrived in Rome far from confident. On September 3 he could not restrain himself from winning the fastest Olympic heat – 3:41.4 – and now he felt confident. But the next day his throat was sore and his glands swollen. It took all his effort to obtain a penicillin shot.

On the morning of September 6, he attended early mass. Then he ate breakfast and tried to sleep, but the prospects of an Olympic final were too exciting. He tried to read, but he could not concentrate. For an hour and a half he considered race tactics. At 11:30 he went out and jogged easily on grass. He ate a light salad and tried to sleep. He lay awake, with his eyes closed, until 3:00 p.m.

'My nerves and muscles were screaming for action.'

He rode a bus to Stadio Olimpico and went to the dressing-room. He still had half an hour before his warmup. 'Even the worst pain of a mile race is preferable to the two hours anxiety experienced beforehand.'

It was a relief to start the race. He bungled along in the midst of eight other runners. At 300 meters: 'I feel as though I've run two laps already. I'm more tired than I should be.'

He ran wide around the curve. Michel Bernard, in the blue of France, led the pack in 58.2. Elliott ran down the backstretch in sixth place. Around the bend, he moved to fourth, breathing hard. 'I shouldn't feel as tired as this.'

At 800 meters he was a close fourth behind Bernard's 1:57.8. He had wanted to make his break here, but now he felt too tired. Only his long practice at punishing himself enabled him to try. They had been averaging 14.7 seconds for each 100 meters. Suddenly, he ran the next 100 in 13.2 and he was ahead of a strungout line of discouraged runners.

He eased up a little for the next 200 meters, running 28.8 with Rozsavogyi and Jazy on his heels. The bell sounded with a long clanging and he spurted. He ran the curve 100 meters in 14 flat. His crushing lap had taken only 56 seconds and now there was a three-yard gap back to Rozsavolgyi.

To Elliott, running scared, three yards were not nearly enough. On the backstretch 100, he punished himself to 13.6 and his lead became eight yards.

There, on the edge of the track, was Cerutty, wildly waving a white towel, his signal to sprint. Not knowing how close his pursuers were, Elliott forced his protesting body around the curve 100 in 13.6, increasing his lead to 15 yards.

He began to tie up slightly. Try as he might, his last 100 meters slowed to 14.4, but he won by an overwhelming 20 yards in world record time of 3:35.6. His last 800 meters was in 1:52.6, truly astounding after a fast start.

On the victory stand, seeing his flag and hearing his national anthem, his sophistication gave way to pride. 'The tears welled up....'

Outside the stadium, he saw Kuts, who had inspired him four years before in Melbourne. The Russian champion spoke in halting English: 'It was a wonderful run.'

Rome 1960: Elliott takes the gold and the world record.

After the Olympics, Elliott ran eleven races in nineteen days, losing only in an 880 race behind Peter Snell, Delany, and Blue. He ran four good mile races with times from 3:59.8 to 3:57.0. He barely beat Waern in two races, including a fine 3:38.4 1,500. His last race was at 1,000 meters against Waern, the official world record holder. Elliott powered ahead to win by two yards in 2:19.1, seventh fastest ever run.

Elliott completed the year having run the three fastest 1,500's of all time. He ran under four minutes in the mile seventeen times, plus six 1,500s better than a 4-minute mile. His 1,500 meter record lasted nine years.

Although he made a half-hearted effort to run in 1961 and placed fifth with a 1:52.5 half-mile, he actually retired as a miler at the age of twenty-two with the best possible competitive record – undefeated.

VALERIY BRUMEL

There is a wonderful moment in the life of each great athlete when his superiority shows through the darkness of past struggles and frustrations with the suddenness of a flash of lightning.

Such a moment in the life of Valeriy Brumel came near the climax of the high jump competition at Moscow on August 13, 1960.

Only eighteen years old, Brumel had been selected to the Soviet Olympic team in spite of a disappointing season. Only the confidence of his coach, Vladimir Dyachkov, had secured Brumel's place on the team in discussions within the council, and there were many who criticized Brumel's mediocre record. True, he had cleared the bar with a personal record in each of the first three meets of the 1960 season, reaching 6′ $9\frac{7}{8}$″, but then a hip injury set him back and he jumped a poor 6′ $6\frac{3}{4}$″ in the two big meets.

Now he had two misses and he stood with Dyachkov, eager for advice. Dyachkov, his eyes always calm behind his spectacles, said, 'Technically, everything seems to be correct.'

Then he gave Brumel the advice which brought the boy to his moment of break-through into greatness: 'You are too strained at the start. Run in more freely... don't tense up.'

Good advice to any athlete, but Brumel proved himself to be one of those rare ones who can do it. He ran relaxed, and he jumped relaxed, and his third jump was good. The height was a new European record of 7′ $1\frac{1}{2}$″, an astounding improvement.

Brumel's next effort was in Rome's Stadio Olimpico, wearing one blue shoe and one red shoe. In the gathering dusk, he no longer read the mystery story which occupied his time during the long competition. He had cleared the bar satisfactorily at 6′ $10\frac{1}{4}$″ and now he watched the bearded Swede, Pettersson, miss on his third attempt.

After a miss by the crippled defending champion, Charley Dumas, Brumel was now fourth. Only his two red-shirted teammates remained, along with the tall American world record holder, John Thomas. Brumel did not expect to win, but he had hopes of beating his teammates for the silver medal.

At 6' 11½" he tumbled the bar into the pit. Sick at heart, he watched Bolshov straddle easily over the bar. Next came mustachioed Shavlakadze, wearing white bandages on his right calf and wrist. Shavlakadze floated over on his stomach with dismaying ease.

Thomas passed. The confidence of the giant American was formidable. Brumel knocked the bar off again. One more miss and he would not win a medal. He concentrated on relaxing for his last attempt.

He ran hard toward the pit, kicked into the air, and folded himself over the crossbar and into the pit full of shavings. He was saved, for the time.

The bar was raised to 7' ¼". He had to jump first again, and he hit the crossbar too hard. Only Shavlakadze cleared on his first jump.

Carefully relaxed, Brumel cleared on his second trial and grinned as he ran out under the crossbar. Thomas sailed over, spread out like a huge bird. The bar was raised to 7' 1", and Brumel had to clear it or he would win no medal.

It was now too dark to see well, but he made the effort and missed. Bolshov also missed, and now the lights were turned on. Shavlakadze seemed calm as he floated over the bar, but Thomas missed badly.

Once again, Burmel concentrated intently on the paradox of exploding with all his strength and yet relaxing all unnecessary muscles. Somehow, he did it, clearing the bar at 7' 1".

He saw Bolshov miss and he was suddenly third. Now he watched Thomas. The tall, blue-clad Negro looked worried and he dragged the crossbar off with his left leg.

Brumel was now second. He saw Bolshov and Thomas miss a third time, but he did not dare show his joy. The bar was raised to 7' 1¾". He had to clear to win, but he could not come close. He had second place already, and that was enough for an 18-year-old.

He stood on the victory stand alongside Shavlakadze and received his silver medal. He listened to their national anthem. He marched solemnly off the field, hiding his pleasure. Then, inside the tunnel, Bolshov and the others were there and he jumped with sheer joy and there was much hugging and grinning and excited talk.

This was the first tangible reward for all the truly hard work – the heavy weight lifting, springing from his toes while carrying heavy weights, the sprinting, the gymnastics, the dull hours developing rhythm in the runup and takeoff. 'Speed-strength', Dyachkov called it, and Brumel agreed.

'The higher the jump the more speed is necessary, and the more strength.'

For an 18-year-old boy, an Olympic silver medal is a rare achievement, but Brumel did not bask in his glory. On September 17, in Odessa, he raised his European record to 7' 1⅛". He had them raise the bar a centimeter higher than Thomas's world record of 7' 3¾" and he came surprisingly close.

Now his confidence grew, but he cleared only 6' 11¼" and 7' ⅝" in his next meets. At Lugansk, on October 9, he cleared 7' ⅝" without a miss. Then, on his second trial, he cleared 7' 2¼", his third European record since August.

On October 15 at Kiev, he proved he was only human, losing to Shavlakadze and Bolshov. At Uzhgorod, on October 23, he cleared only 7' ⅝", but two days later in the same city, he improved his record to 7' 2¾".

He travelled to China and jumped 6' 10⅝", 7' ¼", and 7' 1⅜" in three meets. Back home, he prepared for the indoor season. On January 28, 1961, he was in Leningrad's glass-roofed Winter Stadium. He was jumping from a dirt takeoff, using his regular shoes, and he had never felt so strong.

The bar was raised to 7' 3", higher than he had ever cleared, and he missed. On his second attempt, he cleared, and the bar was raised to 7' 4⅝". It was an unrealistic height, but he felt no concern.

'I just wanted to jump like the devil.'

He cleared on his first attempt.

It was the highest jump ever made. He was so excited he could not sleep all night long. To be the best in his event in the entire history of the world at the age of eighteen was more than he, or any other mortal, could comprehend.

'It did not feel like anything really great. It was just like any other jump. I expected to make it.'

Thomas still threatened, having cleared 7' 3" that same night, in Boston. Brumel flew to New York for a series of three summit meetings.

They met first at the New York Athletic Club Games in Madison Square Garden. Unused to a board takeoff, Brumel warmed up with graceful ballet leaps, then missed once at 6' 8", carelessly. Then he made every height until he won at 7' 2". He missed twice, then dove over 7' 3". At 7' 5", all three jumps were good misses.

A week later, they met again in the AAU meet. Brumel had hurt his toe, but he won at 7' 2". Their third meeting, on March 3, came in the Knights of Columbus meet, and Brumel established himself as superior with a new American indoor record of 7' 3½".

He went home and trained hard and he did not jump again until after his nineteenth birthday on April 14, 1961. In his first outdoor meet, he leaped higher than Shavlakadze and Bolshov with 7' 1⅞" and he had a good jump at a world record.

On June 18, in Moscow, Brumel seemed hopeless, missing twice at 6' 9⅞". Then he succeeded at five heights without a miss. The last clearance was 7' 4", a new world record. He tried 7' 6½" three times, with one good effort.

Brumel's intense competition with Thomas was resumed in the dual meet with USA at Moscow's Central Lenin Stadium on July 16. Brumel was superb, clearing 7' 2¼" without a miss, but Thomas also cleared. The bar was raised to a world record 7' 4¼" and rain began to fall. Thomas came startlingly close on his third attempt. Then Brumel dove over, elbows held high behind him, his mouth wide open, and a crowd of 70,000 thundered approval.

'The thing you have to understand is that I have been working very hard at this jumping – longer and harder than Thomas. You may not have heard of me until Rome, but it has been a long time for me.'

In Sofia, Bulgaria, at 6:40 p.m. on August 31, Brumel stood with his back to half a dozen rows of curious people in front of a large building. He had missed twice at 7' 4⅝", but now he ran fast and twisted successfully over the bar for his third world record jump of the year.

He used excellent jumps of 7' 3" against Great Britain, 7' 3⅜" in the USSR Championships, and 7' 2½" in Tokyo to finish the

Valeriy Brumel

season undefeated. Somewhat incidentally, he had a good broad jump of 25' 1¼" in the qualifying round of the USSR Championships.

Brumel, who had made only 362 practice jumps in all of 1961, gave up jumping for the winter and worked for 'speed-strength.'

'The barbell and I are particular friends. Weightlifting develops practically the same muscles which send a jumper up.'

In April of 1962, when he took his first jumps, his sense of timing was off and he was discouraged. In his first meet, on May 21, he jumped only 6' 9⅞" and Bolshov beat him with fewer misses, but in June Brumel was better, sailing over seven feet in all three meets. Before their trip to Palo Alto, for the dual meet with the United States, Dyachkov told him, 'Now you are ready for a new record.'

The esteemed meet was held in Stanford's huge stadium and Brumel jumped before 81,000 people from the same grass takeoff where Thomas had set his world record of 7' 3¾". Brumel had been swimming that morning, but he won with flawless jumps through 7' 1". He missed once at 7' 2", but he cleared 7' 3" on his first attempt with apparent ease. The bar was raised to 7' 5", a record height he had missed many times.

Now he hesitated. The crowd grew silent, wondering at this slim, dark-haired youth in red vest and blue shorts who could seriously attempt to throw his entire body over a crossbar almost a foot and a half above his head.

He started walking toward the bar, casually relaxed. Then he jogged a few steps. Suddenly purposeful, he crouched and ran fast in an awkward way, his elbows leading his armswings. Smoothly, he leaned back, stretched his left foot forward, and kicked his right leg with savage power.

He shot upward, legs spread. His right arm and leg went over easily, then his head. He dipped his head and tucked his left arm close to his side, safely out of the way. He twisted over the bar, hitting it hard enough to make it move. Recoiling with a fright reaction, he thrust his left leg high toward the sky and dropped into the pit.

He thought, 'Will it stay up?'

Before he could look, a tremendous roar of pleasure from 81,000 Americans told him the bar was still there.

'I was filled with inexpressible joy.'

Valeriy Brumel

He bounded to his feet and faced the nearby crowd. He threw both arms straight up and grinned. Bolshov kissed him. Thomas hugged him. 'This was a marvelous moment for me.'

Nine days later, in Helsinki, he barely missed 7' 5⅜". He won the USSR Championships at 7' 3½". Suffering from a cold, he won his greatest title yet, the European Championships, at 7' 3".

On September 29 in Moscow, Brumel, who likes books, plays, and chess, visited an art gallery in the morning before an unimportant meet for physical education students. He did not jump as well as usual. He missed once at 6' 8¾" and at 6' 11½". He missed twice at 7' 3" and so an attempt at 7' 5½" was not seriously regarded. It was something of a surprise when he cleared cleanly on his first jump.

At the end of his 1962 season, Brumel had made the six best jumps of all time and twenty-one of the twenty-three highest ever.

He cleared 7' 2¾" indoors in Leningrad. Then he left his wife Marina, a gymnast, and flew to New York to challenge Thomas in the 1963 indoor season. On February 1, he cleared 7' 2". On February 9, in Los Angeles, he injured his foot and jumped in great pain. He cleared 7' ¼", same as Thomas, but he lost on more misses. On February 15, he raised his board record to an excellent 7' 4", and he won the AAU at 7' 3½".

He was apparently not at his best in the dual meet with the USA at Moscow on July 21. He disappointed once at 7' ⅝" and he missed twice more before diving over 7' 3¾". The bar was raised to 7' 5¾", but his first jump was poor and his second was only fair. On his third attempt he flopped over for his third world record made in meets against the USA. The huge crowd, including Premier Khrushchev, were delighted.

He had cleared the bar at a height more than 16 inches above his head. This recalled a conversation when he was fourteen. A coach asked why he was so anxious to high jump and Brumel answered:

'I read somewhere that there are people who can clear the bar raised higher than their own height. I'd like to do the same thing.'

Brumel was undefeated outdoors, but no other jumps were higher than 7' 1¼", almost a mediocre height for him.

He started out in 1964 as if he would continue in triumph indefinitely. He won at 7' 3¾" and 7' 3¼" in June. In July, he won against the USA in Los Angeles with 7' 3½", but he missed badly at 7' 6". He flew over 7' 4¼" at Kiev on August 8.

Then came a decline which neared disaster. No word of an injury leaked out through the iron curtain until the next indoor season, but suddenly Brumel was no longer the super athlete. In the five meets before the Olympics he lost twice to Shavlakadze at 7' 1½" and 7' ⅝".

At the Olympic Games in Tokyo, he was obviously off form, although his injury was never mentioned. In the qualifying round on October 20 he had two shocking misses at 6' 9¼". In the final the next day he had some shaky takeoffs, but he cleared 6' 11¼" without a miss and there were only five jumpers left.

On his first jump at 7' ¼" he again had takeoff trouble. He hardly left the ground, and he grabbed the crossbar with his hand. On his second jump, he missed badly.

Now came another moment of truth. He could not afford another bad takeoff. He could not afford the fear of imminent failure. He concentrated on form and relaxation. Everything had to be right. As he faced the bar, a whole career seemed to hang in the balance and the suspense was enough to defeat almost anybody.

Brumel approached the bar fast but carefully. His foot-plant was precise and he threw all his extraordinary power into his kick and spring. He was over the bar. He did not touch it. He was still in.

The bar was raised to 7' 1". He was now in fourth place, and his next jump was as important as the one he had just made. Any miss now could be the one to defeat him.

He cleared the bar on his first jump.

Now he sat quietly while the others missed. As suddenly as that he was back in first place. Thomas, again dangerous, cleared on the second round and Brumel ran over to shake his hand as he left the pit. On the third round, big John Rambo of the USA went over, but Pettersson and Shavlakadze missed, assuring Brumel a medal.

The bar went to an Olympic record height of 7' 1⅞". Once again, a miss would give Thomas a chance to take the lead. After Rambo missed, Brumel went about his jump with the care and precision of a jeweler. He did everything exactly right and he left the bar on the uprights.

Valeriy Brumel

Thomas cleared impressively on his first jump, but Rambo went out. Now there were only two of them as the bar was raised to 7′ 2⅝″. Now the tension reached Brumel. His cortical nerve cells were tired, and he jumped poorly, for him, limited by his mysterious disability. But Thomas could not clear either.

Even off form, Brumel won the gold medal he wanted so much.

At the end of the 1964 season, he had the ten highest jumps of all time and eighteen of the nineteen jumps better than 7′ 3″. He had cleared 7′ 2″ 43 times, compared with fifteen by all other jumpers.

He did not jump again until February, 1965, when he again tried some U.S. indoor meets. He had to withdraw from a meet at Philadelphia on February 5, and then it was disclosed he had a bad knee before the Olympic Games. Six days later, in the NYAC Games, he was successful at 7′ 3″, and he won the AAU at 7′ 2″. In San Francisco, February 26, he won at seven feet on fewer misses, then withdrew in pain.

His knee was so bad he had to miss two months of training. He did not jump in competition until July 18. Still hampered by his bad knee, he could jump no higher than 7′ 2¼″ in 1965. But he was good enough to be undefeated and he ranked first in the world for the fifth consecutive year.

In his five great years since his first Olympic year, no man jumped higher than Brumel in the same meet, although he suffered defeat four times, one of them indoors.

Four days after jumping 7′ ⅝″ against France on October 3, he was riding behind a friend on a motorcycle late at night. Going through a dangerous underpass, the driver veered sharply to make an unsuspected turn and lost control.

When Brumel regained consciousness he examined himself for injuries. Everything was all right except his right leg. He could see white bone sticking out. In the hospital it was discovered that he had two simple fractures below the knee and one multiple fracture of the ankle.

He was in surgery for five hours. At first, doctors feared they would have to amputate, because of gangrene. He ran a high temperature for three weeks.

Coach Korobkov was in tears. 'I can't believe that such a stupid accident can interrupt the career of the greatest athlete we've ever had in the Soviet Union. We were expecting even more from Brumel.'

Later, Brumel said 'I'll never give up sports. It is my passion. It is my life.'

His leg was in a cast for almost three years. He used crutches thirty-one months. He tried to exercise too soon, and the leg gave way again. He endured six operations. His leg had to be stretched to restore its proper length. Three years and eleven days after the accident, he began to walk without crutches.

He began training – gymnastics, swimming, running. Once, he ran 100 meters in 10.6; now he set a goal of 12 flat. In the early spring of 1969 he jumped 6'7", but he could add no more glory to a career already among the great ones.

PETER SNELL

For some reason the winner of the Olympic 800 meters has always been from an English-speaking nation. Perhaps this is no more than coincidence, but athletic enthusiasts from Great Britain and her former colonies have accepted this tradition as their just due.

Thus, it was a great disappointment to these devotees when the heats and semi-finals at Rome in 1960 saw the elimination of all their hopes.

Among the six finalists who took their marks on the curved starting line forty-five minutes after Glenn Davis had won the 400 meter hurdles were some of the fastest runners of all time.

The only finalist acceptable to Anglophiles was an unknown novice named Peter Snell.

He was a muscular 6-foot, 176-pounder in the all-black of New Zealand. He had already shocked spectators at the Olympics by qualifying for the final. The day after running two heats, Snell surprised them by winning his semi-final in 1:47.2. At twenty-one, he certainly lacked experience, and his hard semi-final had probably expended all his reserves. Almost everybody picked him to finish last.

When the starter in his orange coat fired his starting gun, Snell ran hard, staying in the sixth lane around the curve. Into the backstretch, he cut sharply to the curb and found himself fourth. The pace was fast – 25.4 for 200 meters and 51.9 for 400 – and Snell had no inclination to move up. He alternated between fourth and fifth with Roger Moens, the confident world record holder.

The crowd roared so loudly Snell could barely hear the bell and he heard no lap time. Around the curve, into the backstretch, he was satisfied to stay close, but at 600 meters in 1:19.1, a wall of runners blocked him off.

He faced the choice of running extra yards around the curve

or staying inside in fifth place. He chose to stay on the pole.

'I felt this meant abandoning the chance of winning the race, but there was the hope that the front runners would split and I could get through into a place.'

Turning into the homestretch, Moens went into the lead, followed by George Kerr, whose 1:46.4 was the fastest time of the year. Snell saw his chance and burst through alongside Paul Schmidt, a 1:46.2 man. 'Here was a chance for third.'

Snell continued his determined drive, past Schmidt, past Kerr. Now only Moens was ahead of him, on his right.

Twenty yards from the tape, Snell fought even with Moens, between the unsuspecting Belgian and the curb. His legs pounded powerfully with every bit of strength he had. As Snell pulled ahead, Moens looked over at him in shocked bewilderment.

Snell stretched his arms out and threw back his head as he reached the tape, but he did not know he had won. 'I was so delighted with my own performance I didn't care whether I was first or second.'

Exhausted, he held onto a metal post outside the track until he recovered enough to walk back. Then Moens, who had been on his knees in despair, came over and congratulated him.

Snell was still in the stadium when the 5,000 meters was run. He cheered mightily as his teammate, Murray Halberg, gave New Zealand a second gold medal in half an hour.

Now came a deluge of interviews. Everybody in the track world wanted to know about Peter Snell:

At the age of twelve, he was successful in both the 440 and 880 in school record time. He set a junior cross country record at thirteen. He set a school mile record of 5:21 at fourteen, and he cut his times to a good 2:01.6 and 4:48.4 in his last year.

All this was done casually, with no specialization. His best sport was tennis, where he was good enough to reach the quarter finals of the national under-17 tournament, but he also liked cricket, the high jump and broad jump, golf, badminton, rugby, and hockey.

One teammate discouraged even that much running, telling Snell, 'Pete, you'll never do any good. You haven't got a finishing sprint.'

At eighteen, selected to run against an Auckland team, he surprised everyone with a 1:54.1 victory. That triumph led to a meeting with Arthur Lydiard, and he began following Lydiard's training with enthusiasm. He gave up tennis and placed third in the national championships in 1:52.9.

When that 1958 season ended, he began full-scale training under Lydiard, although he had to spend two evenings each week at night school preparing for examinations in quantity surveying. At first, he had difficulty doing the long distance training Lydiard advocated. After his first agonizing run over Lydiard's hilly, 22-mile course, he burst into tears.

Later he cut his time from over 3 hours to 2:40 and ran well in cross country. In the 1958–59 season he made a national reputation. He beat Halberg at 2,000 meters in 5:15.8 and won two Auckland titles in 1:51.6 and 4:12.4. At the national championships, he won victories in both events.

If such progress had continued in the 1959–60 season, Snell would have been known in Rome, but after a good fourth place in the national cross country, he suffered a stress fracture of the tibia with total inactivity for two months.

By Christmas he was running again, but he lost twice and ran only 1:53.9 in the national 880. On March 14, he ran in Melbourne against Herb Elliott and Tony Blue, a promising 1:48.9 man, soon to run 1:47.8. After a slow start, Snell outsprinted them in 1:51.3.

In good practice runs at Rome, he ran three-quarters in 2:57, an 880 in 1:48, and 400 meters in 48. Lydiard told him, 'This is going to be a test of stamina and you are probably the only athlete sufficiently prepared to stand four races in three days.'

After his Olympic triumph, the next question in the minds of track fans concerned Snell's future. Twelve days after, he answered decisively in a 2-mile relay against the USA at London.

Snell took the baton three yards behind, ran a lap in a sensational 50.5, and finished with an amazing time of 1:44.8. Even if his running start added a full second to his time he was far superior to the world record of 1:46.8.

'In Rome, I realized I just hadn't appreciated my own capabilities.'

Eight days later, in Dublin, Snell ran against a crack field in a night meet at the famous Santry track. He ran away from Ron Delany, Blue, and Elliott with 300 yards to go and held on to win in 1:47.9. The next night he ran his first good mile, in 4:01.5, but he finished fifth behind Elliott's 3:57.0.

Snell ended the 1960 season five days later at White City stadium in London when he smashed Kerr by 15 yards in 1:47.5.

In November, another leg injury interrupted his training for six weeks, but by January 21, 1961, he was good enough to beat Kerr and Moens in 1:49.0. He lost four races after that, partly from poor tactics, but he needed a rest and he did not race again until June 28 in London, where he beat Schmidt in 1:48.4.

In Helsinki's Olympic stadium, Snell won the World Games 800 in 1:47.6 and in Dublin he beat Kerr by a foot in 1:47.2, fastest of the year. He ranked first in the world for the second year.

An hour after his 1:47.2 880, his rousing 4:01.2 anchor leg gave New Zealand the world record in the 4-mile relay. That run 'proved to me what an athlete is capable of doing in an inspired moment', and for the first time 'steered my thoughts toward more concentration on mile running'.

The next day he placed third in the mile, in 4:10.0.

In Sweden, two days later, Snell beat Waern over 1,000 meters in 2:20.4, third fastest of the year. After a 1:48.8 880, he went home to rest.

It was six weeks before he resumed hard training. Then he ran four miles to work and four miles home. In November, he ran the 22-mile course in 2:11, then a full marathon in 2:41. The afternoon of the marathon he tried to play cricket. That evening, worn out, he went to a party where he met Sally Turner, later to be his wife.

In December he was in great shape, running ten miles every morning and doing speed work at night. 'I have several of my races on tape. When training gets tough and discouraging, it helps to go in my room and listen to the Rome 800 broadcast.'

On January 1, he lost a handicap mile, but his time was 4:01.3, with an impressive last lap of 56.3. On January 20, he ran 1:48.2, and four days later, 1:47.1.

Snell's next race was to be a mile run at Wanganui on January 27. He intended to run New Zealand's first sub-four-minute mile, and he had secret hopes of bettering Halberg's national record of 3:57.5. As for Elliott's world record of 3:54.5, 'I shrugged the suggestions off as being ridiculous.'

Peter Snell

On the morning of the race, he jogged for half an hour. He flew to Wanganui, had afternoon tea with relatives, and sought the privacy of a hotel. He stretched out while he ate a package of barley sugar and worried about Lydiard's prediction that he would run 3:55. At six o'clock he went out and looked at the grass track, bare in spots. At 8:55 he began to warm up, nervously. At 9:30 they lined up on the backstretch of the 385-yard track.

When the gun sounded, he started poorly. He was seventh at the 220, in 31.7. Too slow. He moved to third at the 440 in 60.7. He moved to second at the 880 in 2:00.6, then took the lead.

His goal was to reach the three-quarter mark in three minutes With nobody helping him, he reached the mark in 2:59.6. 'I was still moving comfortably.'

In the homestretch, approaching the bell, Bruce Tulloh sprinted past. Snell moved confidently to Tulloh's shoulder around the curve. Then he burst into a hard drive and ran away from Tulloh.

'At this point I abandoned the studied relaxation. This is the moment when you stop consciously controlling what you are doing and pour everything into driving out the utmost speed.'

The crowd exploded into a roar of joy and excitement. On top of his 2:59.6, this speed meant a fast mile. 'I don't think I've ever felt such a glorious feeling of strength and speed without strain.'

Around the curve he raced, and down the stretch. He was still running hard and fast when he hit the tape. The crowd poured down onto the field. After several minutes of utter confusion came the exciting announcement. His time was 3:54.4, one tenth of a second under Elliott's world record.

A week later, after an easy half-mile in 1:52.2, and two pleasant days of sightseeing, he was in Christchurch for a half-mile race before only 12,000 people. 'I was definitely going for a world record.'

Snell had the pole lane, with seven runners outside him. At the gun, he started fast, but quarter-miler Barry Robinson went out too fast. His time was 50.7 and Snell ran 51 flat. Then he saw Robinson move out to the second lane.

'I was feeling as good as or better than I had in many of my other races.'

Instead of coasting, he began to push the pace. He knew he was far ahead of world record pace, and he had the necessary courage. 'It was only a matter of being able to continue.'

All around the curve and down the backstretch, 'I felt myself travelling fast.' At the end of the straight his time for 660 yards was a fantastic 1:16.9.

Around the curve he fought to keep going. 'I felt myself slowing.' Now came the physical and psychological benefits of Lydiard's hard work. He was able to keep moving, but when he reached the straightaway his legs tied up and he wobbled. 'I felt that I had come to the end of my run.'

He was running much slower now, and he had to struggle against his inclination to slow down even more. He forced himself all the way, through the tape at 800 meters and on to 880 yards.

'I knew I must have gone inside the records.' Half dazed, he watched the other runners finish. Then, without knowing his time, he jogged a victory lap. He recovered quickly from his violent effort, especially after he heard his amazing times.

He had passed 800 meters in 1:44.3, 1.4 seconds faster than any other man. His 1:45.1 for the half-mile broke the old world record by 1.7 seconds. He was now the first man in twenty-five years to hold both the 880 and mile records, and he had accomplished the feat in eight days.

His 220 splits were an unusual 24.8, 26.2, 25.9, and 28.2. Thus, his final 120 yards took at least a full second longer than in his world record mile.

In Los Angeles, on February 10, he had his first look at an indoor track. That evening, when he appeared before his race, 13,000 fans gave him a thundering ovation for his recent records.

He led from the start. He passed the 880 in 1:50.2, the fastest time ever run on a 160-yard track. His time of 2:06.0 for 1,000 yards was almost two seconds under the world indoor record.

But the award to the outstanding athlete went to Jim Beatty for a record 3:58.9 in the mile, and Beatty's prancing joy soured Snell. 'If I ever meet him on the track, it will be my pleasure to beat him.'

Back in New Zealand, he ran a mile in 3:56.8, the sixth fastest ever run. He needed to rest, but he had more commitments.

Peter Snell

He won the national championship on March 10, running 1:53.9 in mud. A week later, he ran in the Metropolitan Gymnasium, near Tokyo's familiar Olympic stadium. He beat Halberg in a good 4:06.7. The next night he set a world indoor record of 1:49.9 for 880 yards on the 160-yard track.

Now he was happy to rest four days. After a short period of winter training, he ran a mile in 4:00.5 on April 23. On his way to California, he stopped in Hawaii and ran 1:47.8. While there, he learned New Zealand had lost their world record for the 4-mile relay to the University of Oregon. Dyrol Burleson had anchored Oregon with a formidable 3:57.9, all alone.

When Snell learned Burleson was a late entry in the Coliseum Relays mile, he was stunned. Burleson had beaten him twice last year, and Snell was unsure of his own fitness.

They ran before 40,000 enthusiasts. Snell stayed off the 3:02.1 pace and Burleson stayed on his heels. Into the last curve, Snell started his sprint, and behind him, Burleson followed purposefully.

Burleson finished as fast as any previous miler, but Snell simply ran away from him with the fastest finish ever seen. The crowd was gasping in admiration as he ran the last 120 yards in an amazing 13.4. Nobody had ever run faster than 14.2.

He won by 12 yards in 3:56.1, fastest ever in the United States. Now he was regarded as the best mile racer of all time.

On June 5 he began training for the Commonwealth Games to be held in Perth in November. He won the Auckland cross country championship from Bill Baillie by three yards in a strenuous battle over 10,000 meters. Three weeks later, he won the national cross country title by a remarkable 41 seconds.

He suffered his inevitable slump in August. In September he broke a bone in his foot and had to rest for a month. On October 22, he ran a hard 880 in 1:56.0, losing to Philpott's 1:53.4. Unlike some champions, Snell used minor races as workouts and he did not mind losing many of them.

On November 26, he ran in the 880 final of the Commonwealth Games. After a slow pace, Kerr pulled alongside in the homestretch. Snell 'gave it everything I had', and finally cracked Kerr 20 yards from the tape in 1:47.6.

On November 29, Snell qualified for the mile final with an easy 4:02.4. 'It was just no trouble at all.'

On December 1, he ran a hard 440 in a futile attempt to qualify in the relay. In the afternoon he had to meet a dangerous field in the final of the mile.

A crowd of 45,000, including the Duke of Edinburgh, were disappointed with the pace. After three-quarters in 3:09, Snell won by four yards in 4:04.6.

Snell ran poorly, for him, during the 1962–63 season. His best effort was a hard 3:58.6 mile which barely beat Davies. Then he eased off to a long, slow type of training. 'I was concerned to put something back into the bank to wipe out the overdraft on which I had been operating.'

He was married in May and left for America the next day on a honeymoon which was to include three races in California.

The first was the Los Angeles Coliseum Relays on May 17. He did not feel well, even with a 3:06 pace, and Burleson gained on him in the stretch. Snell won by only four feet in 4:00.3. 'The final sprint was an effort.'

Beatty, who looked great in the 5,000, apparently thought the time was ripe and he announced he would run the mile against Snell in the California Relays the following week. The publicity build-up was the greatest Snell had ever seen, and 40 million people were to watch the race on television. 'If he won, I felt, I was done.'

On Saturday morning, in Modesto, he jogged for twenty minutes, ate lunch, and sat in his room worrying. Cary Weisiger had said, 'If we can't beat this guy on his honeymoon, we never will.'

On the way to the track an hour before the race, Snell heard the opening ceremony on the car radio. The New Zealand anthem was played, and he felt emotional. He was tense and he never felt right until the gun sounded. 'I was so nervous I couldn't finish my warmup.'

Snell, wearing the New Zealand all-black, was fourth at three quarters in 3:00.2. He moved easily past Beatty on the backstretch, then waited for Beatty to move, but Weisiger and Grelle were pulling away dangerously. Snell forgot about Beatty and went after the other two.

Suddenly, just before the last turn, he exploded into a sprint the likes of which nobody had ever seen. He flew past the astonished Americans into a 10-yard lead at mid-curve. Into the

Peter Snell receives congratulations from Murray Halberg after the World Record mile race at Wanganui in 1962.

homestretch he looked back, saw a 15-yard gap, and was satisfied to ease off a little.

His time was 3:54.9 and it was obvious he could have broken the world by starting sooner. He was surprised at how fresh he felt. 'I felt like a crisp apple right off a tree.'

At Compton, on June 7, Snell was the target of all the best American milers except O'Hara. After three quarters in 2:58.7 Snell caught Weisiger at the last curve, but he slowed to stay on Weisiger's shoulder. 'I found I couldn't sprint as I wanted to.'

He trailed Weisiger past 1,500 meters in a new American record of 3:39.3. Then he surged past Weisiger and opened a gap. He was surprised his time was as fast as 3:55.0. 'I didn't have my usual kick. I had more left but I couldn't use it. It was a real hard race.'

The place times of his competitors were faster than any in history: Beatty 3:55.5, Burleson 3:55.6, Grelle 3:56.4, Weisiger 3:56.6, Bobby Seaman 3:59.1. This gave Snell three of the four fastest miles ever run.

His 1963 season ended there, and he should have started his long, slow conditioning for the 1964 Olympic Games. But the adjustment to married life, a break with Lydiard, and an understandable need for rest all contributed to a less-than-promising winter.

In October he lost twice, but on January 1, at Wanganui, he ran 3:57.7. He was rounding into shape. 'That mile put me right again.'

Another illness set him back and he lost again. Although he won the national 880 in 1:53.2, people began to believe he was through and he resolved to show them 'I was still around and still dangerous.'

In March he ran well in South Africa with a 3:59.6 and championship victories in 1:50.4 and 4:06.2. On April 11, he raced Davies at Auckland and barely succeeded in 3:58.5.

Then he settled down to serious training for Tokyo. Never before had he been able to maintain a schedule of 100 miles a week for more than three weeks but now he did ten weeks. Every Sunday night he ran the difficult 22-mile course.

Next, he labored through six weeks of hill running. His goal at Tokyo was the 1,500 meters because, 'I felt that some of my sharpness, which was necessary for 800 meters, had gone.'

He began his track work with 20 quarters averaging 62.5, and his speed work went well. For the first time in his career he trained straight through Lydiard's program the way he wanted.

Then, at Tokyo, he caught the 'flu, but he ran three quarters in 2:56 and a mile in 4:02. In an important trial against Davies and O'Hara, Snell ran 1:47.1 for 800 meters. Encouraged, he decided to run in the Olympic 800.

A week later, on October 14, he ran the first heat of the 800. Those who were uncertain of his condition saw him win easily in 1:49.0. In his semi-final the next day, he again won, with 1:46.9. He 'still had something in reserve'.

In the second semi-final, Kerr and Wilson Kiprugut of Kenya broke his Olympic record with 1:46.1. 'I was shocked.'

On the third day, Snell lined up for the final in the pole lane. The weather was perfect and he felt fine. He started fast, but into the backstretch he was third. At the bell, in 52.0, he was in a dangerous box, and he was in it all around the curve to the last backstretch. 'I was very worried. I hadn't been boxed as badly as that before.'

He dropped back, swung wide, and shot past everybody with unmatchable speed. On the curve, he gained, but down the homestretch 'I subconsciously held just a little back for the 1,500.'

He won by four yards over Bill Crothers in 1:45.1, second only to his own world record. Considering the box he'd been in and the fast semi-final the day before, this was truly a great time.

On the victory stand he received his gold medal suspended by a ribbon of Japanese silk. He walked across the track, below the Emperor's box, and gave it to his wife.

The very next day, he had to run the first heat of the 1,500 meters. His aim was to conserve energy, and so he claimed the last qualifying spot in 3:46.8, only two yards ahead of the next man. 'The crisis was now happily over.'

He had a day of rest before he ran his semi-final. He won without trying to in 3:38.8, his fastest 1,500. The others in Snell's heat all ran slower in the final and he, too, was to feel its effects.

He had a day of rest. 'In no circumstances would I attempt to run a record. It was going to be a matter of waiting as long as possible and concentrating purely on winning.'

And in the final he did exactly that, staying off the pace of

58.0 and 2:00.5. At the bell he was boxed, but John Whetton, 'with the manners of a true Englishman', moved aside and let him through on the curve.

Davies led the expectant pack at 1,200 meters in 2:59.3. Snell, in third place, looked awkward, as usual, running at a 60-second pace. Dramatically, he exploded into a beautiful stride, long, fast, and powerful, and he shot into the lead before the curve. They had been running at an average pace of 14.5 for each 100 meters. Snell ran that 100 in an astounding 12.7.

The crowd's roar increased with no surprise whatever. Snell's bold move was entirely predictable, but not his speed. He shot around the curve 100 in an unparalleled 12.3 and opened a gap of six yards, and the crowd expressed amazement and admiration.

He looked back in the stretch. 'I felt that I could renew my effort if I needed to.' He saw no challenger behind him. 'My run down the straight was a little easier than it had been in the 800 meters.' His last 100 meters was only 13.6, but he pulled away to win by 12 yards.

He is the only middle distance runner who ever won three Olympic gold medals.

His amazing finishing speed, especially the middle 200 meters in 25 flat, gave him a last lap of 52.7, a last 300 meters in 38.6, and a final time of 3:38.1.

Back home, instead of being able to rest from his strenuous efforts, Snell found himself in demand during the New Zealand racing season, and he had to do some training for his farewell appearance in Europe in 1965.

At Auckland, before 12,000 people on November 12, Snell made an attempt on the world record for 1,000 meters. At 200 meters he heard a call of '26' and he thought he was running faster than he was. He relaxed and passed 400 meters in 55. 'Immediately I had to put on the pressure.' He passed 800 meters in 1:49.5 and barely broke the record with 2:16.6. He now held the world record at four distances.

Five nights later he planned to break his mile record on the same track. He knew the pace was too fast but he made the decision to follow, and he passed the quarter in 56.4. The pace slowed before the 880, but 'I yielded to an urge to continue at the same rhythm.'

He led at the half in 1:54.1. Thinking of a really fast time, he

Peter Snell

kept the pressure on, but with a lap and a half to go he could feel his legs begin 'to cry out for relief.'

He passed three-quarters in 2:54.3. He forced himself, trying to run faster. His rhythm was gone, along with his energy reserve, his concentration, and his leg speed. All he had left was his will to fight. 'The reserves had already been expended. There was nothing there.'

With the crowd screaming encouragement, he was able to finish, but without any increase in speed. 'It was mechanical desperation running, completely without inspiration.'

His time was 3:54.1, a new world record, but still disappointing. 'I felt really good during the fast early stages. My legs shouldn't have gone so dead later.'

He finished the year with an Australian all-comers record of 3:57.6. He received many awards for his achievements, including an O.B.E. For all practical purposes, this was the end of his great career, for his farewell tour was a disaster.

He barely won the Compton mile from Grelle in 3:56.4. He lost a 1:48.4 880 to Crothers. Then, in Vancouver for a mile on June 15, he suffered from gastritis and ran last.

He recovered, somewhat, in time for the U.S. championships in San Diego on June 27. He ran a strong 3:55.4, but he lost a bitter stretch battle with 18-year-old Jim Ryun.

Then came a series of defeats. The races came too close together to allow him to recover from his illness. Most of all, he lacked the incentive of an Olympic Games.

He retired.

Snell's phenomenal competitive record in big meets was untarnished by his last disability. In addition to his three Olympic championships and world records in four outdoor and two indoor events, he was the best in World Ranking seven times. In 1962 and 1964 he was first at both distances.

His accomplishments alone labeled him the world's greatest middle distance runner, but it was his habit of winning in such convincing style which prompted one otherwise cautious track fan to exclaim : 'When he's right, Snell is unbeatable.'

VIKTOR SANEYEV

In the Black Sea coastal city of Sukhumi in Georgia on October 5, 1945, the Saneyev family brought forth an infant destined for greatness. They named him Viktor.

Nobody knew Viktor had wonderful abilities in track & field, for he never saw a track meet until he was almost 17 years old. But something remarkable was hidden inside him, and the skilled movements of Brumel and Ter-Ovanesyan sparked the tinder of his talent. Working as a machine fitter for money and playing basketball for fun, he began training with homemade weights for his future glory.

Then luck took a hand. A track coach named Akop Kerselian saw young Saneyev's speed and strength, his coordination and rhythm, and in a flash of near-genius suggested the triple jump.

In his first year, 1963, still an eager 17-year-old, Saneyev won the Georgian championships in the 100 with 10.9 and the long jump at 22'9¾", but his third title promised the most, for he won the triple jump at 48'9¾".

In only his second year of competition, he widened some eyes with two silver medals in the European Juniors at 24'4¼" and 51'6½". Later he jumped 51'9¼" and was one of the most promising young athletes of the year.

Then came bad luck, threatening to ruin all of Saneyev's hopes and promise. In 1965, he raised his personal records to 24'8½" and 51'10", but a severe ankle injury put him out of competition and it was so severe he missed all of 1966.

Many athletic careers end with such disappointments, but Saneyev was made of sterner stuff. Even though he could not run for most of the year, he worked doggedly with weights and he made himself stronger than ever for 1967. Still not yet 22, he became a decent long jumper with 25'11" and his triple jump best of 54'8¼" took him all the way up to No. 2 in the entire world.

Thus, in 1968, before the age of 23, he became one of the favorites for an Olympic medal. He raised his personal record to 54'11¾" and again to 55'4¼". He added a 55'3" jump and the USSR title, but what he wanted most of all was an Olympic medal.

Now a handsome 6'1½" and 180 pounds, with straight, sandy

hair, Saneyev went to the Mexico City Olympics undefeated, with the second longest jump of the year, the fourth best of all time. In the qualifying round he was shocked by a world record 56'1¼" from Italy's Giuseppe Gentile, not one of the favorites. With help from the springy Tartan runway and the high altitude, Gentile, the new record holder, became the favorite for the gold medal.

Saneyev reached only 54'1¼" on his first jump in the final, while Mansour Dia of Senegal surprised everybody with 54'10" and Gentile sent more shock waves through the other jumpers with another astounding world record of 56'6"!

Now the gold medal was out of reach, but Saneyev still wanted to prove himself as the competitor by winning the silver. On his second jump, he reached 55'3", but again he received a shock. Nelson Prudencio of Brazil, competing in only his third international meet, jumped 55'11¼".

In the third round, while others fouled or jumped short, Saneyev dug deep inside his reservoir of talent and proved something about himself as a competitor. Bounding with controlled power in nearly even jumps, he cut into the sand at 56'6¼", the third world record of the meet. The new record holder smiled, but he wondered whether even this "ultimate" effort would hold up in such a competition.

In the fourth round, with the field reduced to eight jumpers, Saneyev reached 55'10" while Gentile and Prudencio fouled. And so he still clung to his precarious lead. A 55'10" by Phil May of Australia in Round 4 proved the danger was not over.

Saneyev's teammate, Nikolay Dudkin, frightened him with 56'¾" in Round 5. Then Prudencio sailed an astounding 56'8", and with that one leap, Saneyev lost his world record and the Olympic championship.

For a 23-year-old, barely beginning his international career, an Olympic silver and a brief time as record holder were certainly sufficient glory. But Saneyev had already proved he was a competitor, and he would not concede now. In his last attempt, he sped along the runway with full power, but his step was short and he took off a foot behind the line, surely too great a handicap.

His technique was the best ever, and his jump brought a roar from the crowd and a tense wait until the electronic scoreboard showed 17.39. He won, with a new world record of 57'¾"!

Even Saneyev was amazed. "Results at altitude should be considered as separate records from those at sea level."

Many Olympic champions fade away after their moment of glory, and so those who did not know of Saneyev's dedication had no special hopes for him, but in July of 1969 he showed he was still a great jumper. He won three meets over 55 feet, including a personal best at low altitude of 55'5¾".

He was undefeated before the European Championships at Athens in mid-September and favored to win, and so the pressure was great. For his first attempt, he felt a wind at his back and he made a full effort. He sailed 56'10¾", a foot farther than anybody had ever jumped outside of Mexico City, but the wind was above the permitted limit.

The wind died, but he kept trying. His last two jumps, both legal, were 55'7". Only three other non-altitude jumps in history were farther. He was a true champion.

"The wind didn't bother me at all. The weather in Athens was much like my home in Georgia, very warm. I am accustomed to wind and the gusts never bothered me. I never missed my check marks. I felt there was no difference between Athens and Mexico City as far as external conditions were concerned." Then he joked, "Of course, in Mexico the level of competition was much higher—and I don't mean the altitude."

A month later, at Sukhumi, he cleared 56'3¼", the longest legal jump ever ouside of Mexico. He completed an undefeated season, his second year as best in the world.

In 1970, Saneyev continued to excel, starting with a world indoor record of 55'7¼" in the European Championships.

In the semi-finals of the European Cup on August 2, he made the best non-altitude jump in history—56'7¼"—even though he fell back on landing. He was unquestionably on top of the triple jump world, holder of all the records and championships, but in the finals of the European Cup on August 30, his 55'9¾" was beaten by East German Jorg Drehmel's 56'2½".

A week later, in the Universiade at Turin, Italy, Saneyev faced the strongest threats to his crown. He wanted to avenge his loss to Drehmel to retain his No. 1 ranking, but he was concerned with the other two Olympic medalists, Prudencio and Gentile, plus his dangerous teammate Dudkin.

Sayenev bounced 54'6¼" on his first attempt. Then, after Drehmel took the lead with 54'11", Viktor fouled. Drehmel soared 55'6½" in the third round, and Saneyev's No. 1 ranking began to totter. He came back with 55'5½", but he still trailed.

Drehmel fouled his fourth jump and Saneyev once again showed his true character. His 55'9¾" took the lead and barely held off Dudkin's 55'9¼".

Saneyev was learning how precarious is the title of World's Best. With intense concentration, he drove his legs hard on his last jump and reached 56'6". He earned his No. 1 ranking for the third straight year.

Track's Greatest Champions

After two more victories, at 55'3¾" and 55'8½", he finished a great year on October 18, at home where his fans called him "The Kangaroo of Sukhumi." He gave them nothing less than the longest non-altitude jump ever—56'10¾". Their pride was unbounded, for their Viktor proved himself to be the greatest triple jumper in history.

Beginning the 1971 season, Saneyev owned the four best jumps ever made outside of Mexico City. After a near-record 55'6½" indoors, he added a fifth-longest non-altitude jump on July 17 when he leaped 56'3½" at the Spartakiad in Moscow. His record was far superior to any other triple jumper, but August was a disaster.

Early in August, he lost his world record by a quarter inch to Cuban teen-ager Pedro Perez, jumping at Cali, Colombia (altitude of 3290 feet). Then, with a helpful wind in Helsinki, dangerous Jorg Drehmel cleared 56'3½" on his first trial in the European Championships. Saneyev made an effort worthy of a champion, but his best was 56'1¾". Once again, Drehmel frustrated Saneyev with a personal record.

Saneyev was not a man to give up easily. On August 28, he challenged Drehmel in a triangular meet. Drehmel jumped 55'4¼", but Saneyev soared 55'9" to win.

Still in dnager of losing his No. 1 ranking, Saneyev went all out at Madrid on September. His remarkable sereis—55'8¼", 55'6¼, 55'11", 56'¾", 56'8¾", and 56'5¼"—averaged 56'½", better than all except two legal non-altitude jumps by all the other triple jumpers in history.

Ranked No. 1 in the world for the fourth consecutive year, he now had to his credit seven of the eleven best jumps of all time. Subtracting the four altitude-aided jumps, Saneyev owned the six longest jumps in history.

The all-important Olympic year saw Saneyev disappointed by an indoor loss at the hands of Carol Corbu of Rumania. But Saneyev had not lost two in a row since 1967, and in the European Indoor Championships two weeks later, he started with 55'1½". Corbu dismayed him with 55'5" on his fifth jump. Facing defeat, Saneyev calmly bounded 55'8¼" for a new indoor record.

A week later, in Richmond, Virginia, Saneyev placed an alarming third against the United States. Outdoors, after a 55'¼" victory, he suffered an injury to his Achilles tendon and lost in three straight meets with no jumps over 55 feet. Such dismal jumping, especially in an

Viktor Saneyev

Viktor Saneyev, history's finest triple jumper.

Olympic year, called for desperate measures. Saneyev stayed out of competition for a month and then tested himself. His leap of 56'7¼" was more than adequate proof of his return to condition, but at the Olympics in Munich he would face the best jumpers in the world.

Saneyev concentrated intensely, saving any smiles and conversation for later. He took no practice jumps, favoring his sore tendon, but when it came time for his first jump he put all his talent, training, and competitive ability into it. With a wind of 4.92mph, he sailed 56'11", third longest jump ever.

Shocked, Drehmel fouled his first attempt. Pressing hard, he reached 55'10" on his second jump, then fouled twice. Seemingly the winner, Saneyev knew better than to begin his celebration. He jumped 56'4¾" on his third trial, but Drehmel came through on his fifth jump with three long bounds. Tensely, Saneyev watched the electronic board until Drehmel's mark showed 56'9½". When Drehmel pressed too hard on his last jump, Saneyev had his second gold medal and he sighed with relief. Olympic championships do not come easily.

Later, Saneyev said, "I think something in the range 17.70-17.80 (58'1"-58'4¾") might have been possible even today with stiffer competition and a harder runway."

Saneyev's wind-aided mark gave him eight of the 13 longest jumps in history. Most impressive, he was the only 1968 Olympic champion to defend his title, and he was honored with the Order of Lenin.

But he was not satisfied. He meant what he said about a longer jump being possible, and he wanted to do it on October 17 at the annual "Saneyev Cup" meet before his fans in Sukhumi.

He fouled his first jump, but his second soared 56'9¼" and his hopes rose. But he fouled again and leaped only 55'10¾" and 55'10", and his fans were disappointed.

With only one jump remaining in 1972, he put all his concentration into it, all his skill and experience and intense desire. He hit the board and made his three bounds to perfection. His 57'2¾" was a new world record and his fans exploded with delight.

Now he smiled with satisfaction. "It just happens I reach my top form, my best condition, around September or October each year. It's a natural progression and adaptation of my body."

For the fifth year in a row he ranked best in the world.

In 1973, with the next Olympics a distant goal, Saneyev rested on

Viktor Saneyev

his laurels, but he jumped with remarkable consistency. Unfortunately, consistency sometimes means a lack of exceptionally long jumps, too, and so Saneyev lost once to an exceptional jump by countryman Mikhail Bariban, 55'9¼" to 56'4¼".

The most important meet of the year was the European Cup on September 9. Drehmel had beaten Saneyev before in this meet and he jumped 55'5". Saneyev barely won by half an inch, but he overpowered Drehmel in three other meets by impressive margins.

And once again he came through with his best jump of the year, 56'2", before his fans at Sukhumi. With only one loss, he ranked best in the world for the sixth consecutive year.

A dismal 1974 indoor season saw the low point of Saneyev's career. In the European Championships, a sore foot held him to a poor 50'4" while losing his world indoor record to Michal Joachimowski's 55'10½".

Outdoors, he failed to reach 55 feet in four meets, but he was undefeated going into the European Championships in Rome's Stadio Olimpico. Saneyev was serious about this meet, second only to the Olympics in importance. He lost his title to Drehmel in 1971 and his archrival had the longest jump of 1974 so far.

Strong winds swirled unpredictably, making good jumping nearly impossible. But Saneyev was now an accomplished master of all conditions. Always a competitor, he wanted a winner at the start.

"I knew the other jumpers were being affected mentally by the wind, so I figured a good jump would ruin them."

And ruin them he did, with a legal second jump of 56'6¼". While the others struggled against that mark and the wind, Saneyev had two more fouls and two jumps over 55 feet. The silver medal went to Corbu with a come-through 54'8¾", almost two feet behind the winner!

Saneyev won twice more in 1974, with good jumps of 56'1¼" and 56'5¼". His undefeated season ranked him No. 1 for the seventh straight year. He now held 11 of the 17 best jumps in history. Of the 13 longest non-altitude jumps, he owned the remarkable total of ten. He could retire as the greatest triple jumper of all time, but he was only 28 years old and the flame of ambition still burned in him.

The 1975 European Indoor Championships were held in Poland, and indoor record holder Michal Joachimowski, the Polish favorite, led into the last round with 55'5½". But Saneyev, the consummate competitor, once again geared himself up for his final jump and sailed

55'9¾", only ¾" short of the indoor record.

Outdoors, Saneyev was undefeated for the second straight year, with three meets over 56 feet. His best was 56'10¼" in the USSR Championships. This gave him the three longest non-altitude marks ever, and four of the five best of any kind.

But security is a joke in the triple jump. On October 15 a blow fell on all triple jumpers. Jumping in the Pan-American Games at Mexico City, a 21-year-old Brazilian newcomer named Joao Oliveira soared 58'8¼"!

Since Oliveira's next best meet was almost four feet shorter, Saneyev gained his eighth consecutive No. 1 in World Ranking. But his hopes for another world record were shattered.

"To beat a world record is one thing. To win an Olympic title is quite another. He has given me something to work for. I will prepare to win in Montreal. I would very much like to be the first Soviet athlete to win three Olympic titles."

He wasted no time. On February 2 in the USSR Indoor Championships, he sailed 56'1½" to regain his world record. Not content, he bounded 56'3½" later in the evening.

In the European Indoor Championships in Munich, with Oliveira filming the action, Saneyev showed him something to worry about. His series was 55'3¼", 55'7", 56'1¼", foul, foul, and 55'11¼", giving him the four longest indoor marks of all time. Oliveira was impressed.

Disaster threatened when Saneyev's tendon trouble flared up again. "I didn't compete in our nationals because my Achilles tendon hurt so bad. I thought it might even snap, but it would happen only at the Games. All my thoughts were about the Games. I never thought about what I would do after."

Saneyev coasted carefully, leaping no farther than 55'5½". He went into the Olympics as the favorite because of his awesome competitive record, but mystery man Oliveira was a threat and there were many good jumpers who might defeat him with one exceptional jump.

Conditions in the Montreal Olympic stadium were not good. There was no wind, but they jumped in the shade and the runway and board were hardened by the cold. Saneyev, who liked to win early, put everything he had into his first jump. He hit the board and bounded about 57'9", but the red flag was waving. He fouled the best jump of his life by the length of a short spike.

After former world record holder Pedro Perez took the lead with 55'1¾", Saneyev again had trouble with his step on the slow runway. "I had to hold myself back because I was too nervous and trying too hard." Still he managed to go into second place with 54'10". However, James Butts, a threat from the United States, immediately cleared 54'11¾".

Oliveira, who had led all the qualifiers with 55'1¾", looked bad on his first two attempts, but on his third he bounded into the lead with 55'3½". Saneyev still had step problems, but his technique was otherwise perfect and his 55'11¾" took the lead.

Then came the exceptional jump Saneyev feared. Butts, who came into the meet with a best of 55'2½", shocked the crowd with a soaring leap of 56'4½".

Saneyev had won championships with a great early jump, or by coming from behind. Now it had to be the latter. He concentrated as never before. He had to straighten out his step, and he adjusted it carefully. Then he sped down the runway with his typical overstriding action, and he hit the board perfectly. His technique never in doubt, he sliced into the sand at 56'8¾".

Butts had two jumps remaining, but he was obviously shaken, and he came no closer than two feet. Oliveira improved to 55'5½" for third place, and Saneyev became only the second man in modern Olympic history to win three gold medals in the same individual event. Only Al Oerter had a superior Olympic record.

"A week after the competition, I couldn't sleep well. I was so excited. It was just like winning the first time, just as exciting. I had prepared for Montreal for four years, so succeeding at something after working for it for that long is something to be excited about."

He was undefeated outdoors for the third straight year, and he won the No. 1 ranking, of course, becoming the first man in history to do so in any event for nine consecutive years.

Early in 1977, while winning in two U.S. indoor meets, Saneyev said, "An athlete cannot win forever."

He had two sore ankles, and although he won the European Indoor Championship again with 54'7½", his tendon trouble was too much for him and his four-year outdoor winning streak ended in May.

Almost a cripple, he jumped 55'5½" against the United States on July 1, but he placed only third and his season ended. In October, usually his best month, he had surgery on his Achilles tendon.

Even as a cripple he ranked No. 4 in the world.

Saneyev's tendon healed slowly and he missed the 1978 indoor season. His comeback was slow as he lost in three meets, but he reached 55'8½" on August 18 and he hoped for a third European title in Prague on September 3.

His first jump was 55'3", but he had to improve to retain his lead. He sailed 55'6¼" in the third round and added a quarter-inch in the fourth. Then came the unexpected jump which is always a threat in his event. Milos Srejovic, whose personal best was 54'11½", bounded 55'7" on his last jump to take the lead by an infuriating half an inch.

Saneyev had one more chance, but a 2.1mps wind hurt him and he could reach only 55'1". "Were it not for the wind, I would have won."

He won the USSR title with 55'10½" and closed his season a week later in Tokyo, where he won with 55'10". He ranked no higher than No. 3 for the year, but his goal was 1980.

Saneyev's 1979 season was poor, for him. He jumped 55'9¼", but eight others leaped farther and Saneyev ranked only No. 11 in the world, his first season out of the top ten since 1966.

Still, Saneyev was not through. The tough old competitor wanted to match Al Oerter's record of four Olympic titles in one event. "I'm not prepared to cede my title yet."

His prospects were poor in June of 1980 when he jumped only 53'11¼" and placed sixth. He improved a foot in July, but he placed only fourth. His longest jump was 55'¾" and there were four Soviet jumpers with better marks. It was a tribute to his past heroics when the Soviets selected him to compete in the Olympics.

The Olympic competition stirred Saneyev as nothing else could. He had struggled for four more years with only this day in mind. He wore a bandage below his right knee and he limped after every jump, but he put all his experience and competitive desire into each jump.

Jumping last of the 12 finalists, he bounded 55'3½" on his first attempt, second only to Oliveira's 55'7¾". There was life in the old master yet, but he limped out of the sand, and his second jump was only 54'2¾".

In the third round, Saneyev reluctantly bowed his head to younger men. His teammate, Jaak Udmae, shot out 56'11" and Oliveira jumped 56'6". Still, he would fight for the bronze medal, but even that seemed hopeless, for the surprise come-through jumper appeared to be Ian Campbell of Australia. Robbed of a 57'5" jump (a step-phase foul, the officials said), Campbell had three more chances and he seemed certain to beat Saneyev's 55'3½".

Viktor Saneyev

Saneyev ignored his sore legs and swept down the runway, bounding through the three leaps with his old skill. His mark was 55'11". His hold on the bronze medal was stronger, and while both Campbell and Oliveira had fouls called on their next two jumps, the old master improved another inch to 56 feet even.

Campbell and Oliveira were called again and Saneyev stood at the end of the runway for the last jump of the competition—and the last important jump of his career. He needed a longer jump than any he had made for years, and nobody thought his tired old legs had anything left. But his heart was the same, and he took dead aim on the gold medal.

He loped along the runway, ignoring the pain, concentrating on his markers. He hit the board and swept into the technique he had perfected over so many years. A tremendous roar rose in the old stadium when his feet cut into the sand near Udmae's leading distance.

Saneyev knew he had failed but he watched intently until the scoreboard showed 17.24. He won the silver medal, losing the gold by less than five inches.

Saneyev smiled at last. "I tried to coax out one final effort, but my legs couldn't be urged to do more."

Still, his last jump, a foot and a half farther than his best pre-Olympic jump and his longest jump in four years, stands as a monument to one of the greatest competitors in the history of the sport.

Viktor Saneyev was honored by *Track & Field News* as "Athlete of the Decade."

Lasse Viren, twice an Olympic double gold medal winner.

LASSE VIREN

The people of Finland love track, especially distance running. In six Olympic Games through 1936, their runners won four Olympic gold medals in the steeplechase, and five each in the 5000 and 10,000. But they won none at all in the next 35 years. Against this historical background, 16-year-old Lasse Viren won the 1965 Finnish junior championship at 3000 meters in his first year of serious training.

He progressed slowly and in 1970 recorded a 13:43 5000. His improvement in 1971 piqued interest in Finland as he ran the fifth best 5000 in the world with 13:29.8. His second-ever effort at 10,000 meters resulted in 28:17.4. Viren could manage only seventh place in the European Championships 5000 and 17th in the 10,000, while all Finland rejoiced at Juha Vaatainen's double victory.

At the beginning of the Olympic year of 1972, the 23-year-old Viren was not highly regarded, therefore, not even by the Finnish faithful. Nor did his early races turn many heads. After a 28:39.0 victory on May 27, he placed only third three days later in 28:52.0. On June 8, he ran only 13:45.8 for fourth at Helsinki, and he lost twice more, with 13:37.0 and 13:33.8. None except his closest associates were prepared for his astounding transformation.

Viren denies gaining his fame from using the not-illegal miracle of blood boosting, but circumstantial evidence over the years points a finger in his direction. Whether boosted to excellence by reinsertion of his own blood or by an incredible ability to peak at the proper time, Viren suddenly became one of the great runners of history.

Six days after his last mediocre race, he won the 5000 in a meet against Great Britain and Spain in 13:19.0. The Finns were elated, for now only two runners were above Viren on the all-time list and Viren's Olympic stock had suddenly soared. Two days later, he won a 3000 in 7:43.2, another Finnish record, only four seconds from the world record. One week later, in the Bislett Games, he won the 10,000 in 27:52.4, again a time bettered by only two others in history. And in another 11 days he brought his remarkable three-week surge to an end with a world record 8:14.0 in the 2-mile. Finnish hopes were high when he began his Olympic quest 17 days later.

Heats were run in the Olympic 10,000 for the first time since 1920 and all 15 qualifiers in Munich's modern stadium broke the Olympic record. Viren ran a calm fourth in 28:04.4 and finished amazingly fresh, with a pulse rate of only 120.

The final, three days later on September 3, remains a classic race in track history. The second fastest runner in history, England's Dave Bedford set off on a suicidal pace with a 59.9 400 meters and at 2000 his pace was 28 seconds faster than world record time. And yet only four runners stay with him.

On the backstretch of the 12th lap, Viren suddenly stumbled and fell and 1964 silver medalist Mohamed Gammoudi fell over him. Few television watchers in Finland took a breath in the next second, but Lasse regained his feet and ran in pursuit, ten meters behind seventh place. "I got up instinctively, but at no time did I think I had lost the race."

Viren caught up and after 6000 meters he passed Bedford. At 7000 meters, Bedford lost contact with the pack and Viren led, 4.8 seconds slower than Ron Clarke's record. With 1000 meters left, Viren's pace was 10.2 seconds slower than the world record and four runners threatened on his heels.

The lead changed like people caught in a revolving door during the next lap, but with a lap and a half to go the Finns went wild, for Viren launched an unearthly finishing drive. At the bell, he led Belgium's Emiel Puttemans by three meters and Miruts Yifter of Ethiopia by ten. His two opponents rate among the best in history, and yet Viren gained even more in the homestretch to win in world record time of 27:38.4. Finland's long wait ended at last.

Viren's last lap in 56.4 was not as good as a few in much slower races, but his final 800 in 1:56.4 and his final 1000 in 2:29.2 were the best ever. Track experts shook their heads in wonder, while down on the track two youthful Finns delighted their whole nation by prancing behind Viren on his victory lap while carrying a huge blue and white Finnish flag.

Four days later, in his heat of the 5000, Viren wanted to rest, but he was forced to a winning 13:38.4. In the final, he ran calmly behind a slow pace, confident of his remarkable finishing speed.

Lasse Viren

After circling 8½ laps at an average pace of 66.65, American Steve Prefontaine accelerated with laps in 62.5, 61.5, and 60.3. Gammoudi took the lead on the last backstretch, but Viren strode easily ahead around the last curve and pulled away by six meters in Olympic record time of 13:26.4. There was more joy in Finland that night.

Once again, Viren had astounded everybody with his finishing speed. His last lap in 55.8 was only part of a final 800 in 1:56.1, 1000 in 2:26.5, 1200 in 2:57.3, 1500 in 3:44.7, 1600 in 3:59.8, one mile in about 4:01.2, and 2000 in 5:06.0. In a month and a half, Viren had moved from so-so status to the fastest distance racer in history.

Only a week after his Olympic 5000 triumph, Viren treated 42,000 admiring Finns in Helsinki to a world record in the 5000. He ran away from Bedford after half the distance and won by 80 meters in 13:16.4.

For his two gold medals and three world records, Viren was acclaimed Athlete of the Year by *Track & Field News*.

In 1973, Viren fell back into the pack as fast as he rocketed to the top in 1972. His best 5000 meters was 13:28, but he went unranked. He ran 28:17.8 in May, but he finished 11th in one race and lost two others. Even two victories could boost his 10,000 ranking no higher than No. 7.

He began his 1974 season with 13th in a 5000 and then sixth in a 10,000 in June. He ran faster in August, but he lost more than he won. In the European Championships, he ran 13:24.6 for third and 28:29.2 for 7th. For the year, he ranked No. 5 in the 5000 and No. 9 in the 10,000.

His 1973 disappointment was blamed on a training letdown in the winter and a bad knee. After the 1974 season, he had an operation on his left thigh, but in 1975, Viren ran 13:34.6 and 28:11.4, unranked in both. After finishing fifth in the European Cup 5000, he was asked what was wrong by winner Brendan Foster. Viren merely smiled and said, "Wait until next year."

Viren began the Olympic year of 1976 as mediocre as in the past three years. He placed a miserable 11th in a race on June 3 and lost a 5000 five days later with 13:44.4. But on June 23 in Helsinki, he ran 27:43.0, and track experts nodded knowingly and changed their predictions for Montreal. And once again, hopes rose in Finnish hearts.

Viren ran only once more before the Olympics, a 13:24.8 victory in the Finnish Championships.

In his Olympic heat at Montreal on July 23, he coasted in with 28:15.0. In the final, Carlos Lopes of Portugal pushed the pace from 3200 meters, gradually accelerating until only Viren could follow. With 450 meters to go, Viren moved smoothly past Lopes and with no discernible effort he pulled away to win by 30 meters in 27:40.4. His last lap in 61.5 and last 800 in 2:05.4 were unimpressive, but his last 5000 in 13:31.5 proved he had some of his old magic.

After a day of welcome rest, Viren qualified in fourth place with 13:33.4, and he had only one more rest day before his difficult task in the final. No man had ever won two Olympic 5000's, and Viren faced three powerful finishers in Rod Dixon, Dick Quax, and Brendan Foster.

The pace was slower than the Finnish fans wanted and Viren did his part to slow it down, even though it seemed to make him vulnerable. Accelerating the last four laps, Viren led at the bell, but six runners were tightly bunched behind him, ready to pounce. Four of them were ominously faster quarter-milers than Viren.

A hard drive began with 300 to go, but Viren merely lengthened his smooth stride and held off all challengers down the backstretch. "I was afraid with 200 meters to go, because there were so many good milers in this race."

Around the curve, the fast finishers bunched, ready to blow him away. In the homestretch, Viren showed no real sprinting form and yet, miraculously, he stayed in front, and he won in 13:24.8. Track observers smiled and shook their heads in wonder.

Viren's last 800 in 1:57.5 was slower than in 1972, but his final 55.4 under pressure surprised everybody. Dixon said, "I was really amazed that Viren had that kind of speed over the last 400 meters."

His back-to-back Olympic doubles surpassed every other runner in history, but Viren wanted more. The very next day, he entered the marathon without time to replenish his reserve glycogen, so precious to marathon runners. It would be his first marathon, and he said, "I just hope I will finish honorably."

And honorably he did. In contention for a medal for 35 kilometers, he fought through the wall and finished exhausted in fifth place. His excellent debut in 2:13:11 lost only to the four runners who broke the Olympic record.

His Olympic magic completed, Viren reverted to his mediocre ways. He won only one of seven more races in 1976, a slow 13:49.2.

Lasse Viren

Even so, his near-miraculous Olympic victories ranked him No. 1 in both events, and the single marathon of his life gained him No. 7 in World Ranking.

No one else had ever won two consecutive Olympic 10,000's or two Olympic 5000's. His "double double" certainly stamped him as one of history's greatest distance runners.

The remainder of Viren's career was fairly undistinguished. In December, 1976, Viren stepped in a hole while moose hunting and tore a ligament in his left ankle. Missing his winter training, he ran poorly in 1977. In June of 1978, he ran 13:33.8 at Helsinki for fourth place, and Finns hailed his comeback, but it was his fastest time of the year. He also ran 10,000 meters in 28:11.8 later at the World Games.

In 1979 he ran 28:04.7. "Slowly but surely I am returning. If I am able to train normally for Moscow, anything is possible."

Viren won the honor of Athlete of the Decade in voting by *Athletics Weekly*. Unranked for three years, he appeared through as a champion, but fans who remembered his Olympic triumphs did not count him out in 1980. He trained well during the winter, and he went to Moscow with a 28:10.95 to his credit.

He ran his heat during a killing temperature and showed none of his former magic. He finished fourth in 28:45.8 only because John Treacy collapsed on the track. "This heat is atrocious. It will be terrible to have to run a long distance in heat like this. Near the end of the race I felt like I was breathing fire. I needed oxygen and my head felt like it was in a vise."

In the final, three days later, on July 27, he ran with the pack until only five were left. In the last three laps, Finns hoped he might produce some of his magic of 1972 and 1976. He took the lead before the bell and those who remembered, felt a thrill of recognition. But he could not do it again in such hot weather, and all four runners pulled away from him. He finished fifth in 27:50.5.

"I don't know what I'll do next. A marathon in this heat? I don't know if I'm daring enough . . . I deceived myself enormously." He did attempt the Olympic Marathon five days later, but had to drop out at 27 kilometers.

And so the most spectacular Olympic distance career in history came to an end. He ran three more 10,000's after a month's rest, but failed to finish one and lost badly in the others. He ranked No. 8 for the year.

Viren ran little or nothing in 1981, and his 1982 comeback failed. Hoping to run 13:50 in August, he ran only 14:34.05. His career as a super-champion ended in 1976, but he talked of running the marathon in 1988 and Finnish fans keep a small flame of hope burning. They remember his splendor.

ALBERTO JUANTORENA

Born at Santiago de Cuba on December 3, 1951, Alberto Juantorena grew to be 6'2" tall, and in his teens he raced up and down the floor for the national Junior basketball team until a local track coach marveled at his running ability. At 185 pounds, they called him "El Caballo" ("The Horse"), and he improved remarkably in 1971—from 400 meters in 51.0 wearing tennis shoes, to a most promising 48.2. His Polish coach said, "I have never seen such raw power."

In 1972, Juantorena improved astoundingly. In the Olympic Games at Munich, he surprised everybody in his heat with 45.94. He qualified in his quarter-final with 45.96, but he ran only 46.07 in his semi-final and he missed the final by 0.05.

In 1973, his irresistible improvement continued with a series of local victories and a best time of 45.8. At the World University Games, he strode past European Champion David Jenkins in 45.36 to gain No. 3 ranking in the world.

Racing on the tracks of Europe for most of his 1974 season, Juantorena continued his powerful surge to the top of World Ranking. Undefeated for the entire year, he ran 45.3 three times, lowered his personal best to 44.9 at Siena on July 21, and three days later at Turin, he ran 44.7. "I see 44.0 at Montreal."

Foot surgery slowed the runaway horse in 1975, but he came back in August with some good races. On October 18, in the high-altitude Pan-American Games at Mexico City, he lowered his best to 44.80 for second place, losing to American Ronnie Ray's sizzling 44.45. Even in a disappointing season, he ranked fourth best in the world.

Juantorena returned better than ever in 1976. In May he lowered his best to 44.72 and made a promising breakthrough in the 800 with three races in the low 1:46's. Touring Europe, he ran an eye-opening 1:45.2 and another PR 44.70. Back in Havana on July 10, sharpening for the kill, he lowered his 800 best to 1:44.9. He went to Montreal as one of the most exciting prospects in the Olympics, undefeated in both the 400 and 800.

Few experts gave him a chance in the Olympic 800, but he ran impressively to win his heat (1:47.2) and his semi-final (1:45.9). In the final, he took the lead in 50.9 and led world record holder Rick Wohlhuter around the curve toward 600 meters. "I wasn't doing too well on the backstretch."

Most experts expected Juantorena to fade in his third consecutive day of racing at his longer distance, and Wohlhuter expected to outkick him. But into the homestretch it was the big Cuban with the lunging stride who poured on the power and pulled away. "I depended on my sprinting in the final 200."

With his final 100 in a sizzling 11.9, Juantorena changed his status from good to great. He set a new world record of 1:43.5.

In his difficult double, he was forced to run two heats in the 400 meters the very next day. After a welcome day of rest, he returned refreshed and won his semi-final in 45.10, toying with his opponents in the homestretch.

He took his blocks for the final in lane 2, just inside Herman Frazier and Fred Newhouse. "I knew Frazier and Newhouse were the most dangerous, so I kept close to them." He ran three meters behind Newhouse at 200 meters and two behind at 300. In the homestretch, he gained slowly but he did not edge ahead until 20 meters from the line. "I always try to save a little strength for the finish."

His 44.26 broke the low-altitude record. After seven races in seven days, he said, "I'm tired." But the next day he ran an anchor leg in 44.1 to qualify Cuba's team for the final. On July 31, he anchored Cuba to seventh place with 44.7, his ninth race in nine days.

His was the greatest exhibition of speed and durability in Olympic history. For his undefeated season in both events, he ranked No. 1 in the world and he won the ultimate honor of the Olympic year—Athlete of the Year.

In 1977, Juantorena ran best as an 800-meter man, even though he trained on the amazingly low total of ten or 15 miles per week. "I think I am the only 800-meter runner to have only 1000 kilometers in a year. *Only.*"

After two 1:45.8's, he competed eagerly in both events. In East Berlin, on June 15, he won in 1:46.1 and the next day in 44.98. Two days later, he won the Kusocinski Memorial in 45.73, and the following day he wanted to race Mike Boit, second fastest of all time in the 800.

Alberto Juantorena

But Boit ran the 1500, and Juantorena won in 1:43.66. "If Boit had been in he race, no doubt the record would have fallen."

After his victorious European tour, he carelessly lost the Central American 400 Championship by 0.02. Perturbed, he ran a 44.49 and returned to Europe for the climax of the year.

In the World University Games in Sofia, Bulgaria, the post-graduate student in economics ran past the bell in 51.4 then powered around with nine-foot strides to lower his own world record to 1:43.4. "I didn't think I would be in such good form right now. I expected to peak at the World Cup."

Three days alter came the showdown against Boit. A little too excited, Juantorena led at 400 in 49.7, held Boit on his shoulder at 500, and passed 600 in a sensational 1:15.6. Juantorena's strength lasted to the line, while Boit faded six meters behind. Juantorena actually apologized for his 1:43.6 which tied Boit for the third fastest 800 ever run. "Winning was the only thing for me."

In the first ever World Cup, in Dusseldorf, Juantorena raced Boit again on September 2. This time, Juantorena ran only 52.6 and 1:18.9, with Boit threatening. Boit pulled even in the homestretch, but Juantorena won in the last few strides in 1:44.0. "I was confident of winning in the last 100 meters."

In the 400 the next day, Juantorena stood up at the gun, glanced back to see if the recall gun would fire, then chased after the others. He finished third with 45.83 and stomped off the track. "I was furious."

He appealed, and it was decided to rerun the race the next day. He won in 45.36. "It was a very hard race for me."

He finished the year with 44.65 in Havana. Again he ranked best in the world in both events, and again he won the honor of Athlete of the Year.

Juantorena won every 400 he ran in 1978 and defeated some of the best in the world, but his fastest time was 45.17 except for 44.27 at high altitude. In the 800, he continued undefeated with a best of 1:44.4 on June 22, but in the Weltklasse on August 16, disaster struck. Boit passed him on the final curve and he could not keep up. Not caring now that he was losing the first 800 of his career, he let up and finished sixth. "I wasn't at all at ease during the race. I did want to run like usual but I didn't have the means."

Then he made a remark which must have been news to some of his opponents:

Alberto Juantorena

"I am not a superman."

As a result of his one bad race, he ranked only No. 6 in the 800, but he ranked No. 1 in the 400 for the fourth year.

In 1979, Juantorena ran little. He lost two of his four 400's, with a best of 45.24, and he ranked only No. 5. He ran only 1:46.4 and went unranked in the 800.

Voted the third best athlete of the decade, Juantorena wanted to win in the Moscow Olympics, but physical problems stopped him. He suffered from an ulcer and a pulled hamstring. No sooner did he recover than he had surgery in East Germany for his heel.

He arrived in Moscow in dubious condition, with no racing behind him. "I'm nervous about my return. I need the rhythm of competition."

He could not run the 800, and he did not look like the powerful "horse" of old in the 400. He barely squeezed into the final with 0.02 to spare.

In the final he ran hard but he lacked his former power in the stretch and faded to fourth with 45.09. He ranked No. 10 for the year.

He tried to compete in 1981, but he ran poorly. "After my tendon operation in 1980, I felt good. Then pain appeared in the other foot and I had to rest again." He returned in 1982, saying his future was as an 800-meter runner. His times were slower than in the past, but he kept winning.

His best time was 1:45.15, but he lost only his last race, a lackluster 1:49.26. His days of glory seemed gone, and yet he ranked No. 2 in the world.

In 1983, he arrived in Helsinki for the first World Championships with a best time of 1:44.6 and his opponents feared him. In his heat, he looked as strong as ever, qualifying easily in second place, but disaster struck.

At the finish line he swerved to avoid another runner and stepped over the curb with his right foot. He fell in agony with a broken bone and two torn ligaments. Recuperation would take five months, but he said, "I will begin training as soon as I can. I want to go to Los Angeles next year."

And the old warhorse did train again. In 1984 he ran 1:44.88, but the Soviets kept him out of the Olympics. Thus ended the reign of one of the greatest of all champions, a victim of time, injuries, and politics.

Yuriy Syedikh, hammer thrower par excellence.

YURIY SYEDIKH

Yuriy Syedikh's first experience with the hammer, at the age of 12, was nearly disastrous. Chasing a soccer ball, he missed being hit by inches. His response to the angry hammer thrower: "What *is* that, anyway?"

He tried to throw the heavy ball and chain, but reached only about 40 feet. "I was nothing out of the ordinary in strength. In fact, my health was poor." He liked the hammer, but he would rather be a swimmer, and for awhile he ran and jumped, but gradually he turned more to the hammer. "I liked the very process of working out. When I began to train seriously with the hammer, it began to fly right. Physical preparation at an early stage in one's career is the key."

In 1968, around his 13th birthday on June 11, he threw the 11-pound hammer 124'8'" Four years later and much more serious, he entered the Academy of Physical Culture in Kiev. As a promising 17-year-old who threw 205'1", he shook hands eagerly with Anatoliy Bondarchuk, the 1972 Olympic champion.

"I wanted to train with, and learn from, the best hammer thrower in the world. Anatoliy was that, but he was uninterested in my pleas to start with. But he came around slowly, and we began working an immense amount. Anatoliy laid prime emphasis on developing physical strength. I needed this, initially being relatively weak."

A year later, he threw 226'6" for a world junior record and he won the European Junior Championship. In 1974 he improved his best to 232'6", tenth on the Soviet year list. "I was invited to train with the USSR team."

In 1975, he continued his impressive improvement and threw 246'2", ninth on the yearly world list at the age of 20, and he ranked No. 11 in the world. "I was to wear the national vest for the first time."

After his fine breakthrough in 1975, Bondarchuk told me that we were going to train for the Olympics. My first reaction was one of complete surprise. I hadn't even thought of it yet. I was just 20."

In the Znamenskiy Memorial at Sochi in April, 1976, he was not expected to be a contender. In an exciting competition, he threw 253'5", within seven feet of West German Walter Schmidt's world record. His victory over Bondarchuk and former world record holder Aleksey Spiridonov startled all his competitors.

Two weeks later, now the center of attention, he began with 248'6", improved with 251'4" and threw a personal best of 253'9". As if that did not worry Spiridonov enough, Syedikh then whirled the ball and chain 258'9", second longest in history and a USSR record. He finished with 250'10" and 252'11" for the best series ever. All over the world, other hammer throwers had a sinking feeling.

He thew 255'8" on May 23, then gained his coveted place on the Olympic team by winning the USSR title with 257'6". Eagerly, he went to Montreal with his teammates to compete against Schmidt and Karl-Hans Riehm, a 257'7" thrower in May. Any of the five might triumph, depending upon competitive ability, but Syedikh was relatively untested.

In the Olympic final, Bondarchuk took the lead with 247'8", but Syedikh stepped into the circle and threw 248'2". Three throws later, Spiridonov took the lead by four inches. Riehm was a close fourth at 246'1".

Syedikh entered the circle in Round 2 determined to prove himself. He whirled and sent the ball thudding into the turf at 254'4". Even Bondarchuk winced a little.

Syedikh tried even harder and stepped outside the circle on his next two throws. Still almost two meters in the lead, he finished with 247'11" and then 250'8", the second best throw of all. Less than a year after making the Olympics his goal, he mounted the highest step of the victory stand.

"It was uncomfortable when I appeared higher on the victory stand than my old comrades. I apologized to my coach, but he said, "You're still stupid. Your gold medal is mine, too. Today I'm prouder than ever."

Bondarchuk gave him a bear hug, and Syedikh said, "Thank you, chief. You helped me follow in your footsteps."

Syedikh was calm during his interviews. "I have prepared very well, so my victory was, actually, no surprise to me at all." Balancing his youthful pride, he commented upon his hopes for 1980: "I'm not sure I'll make the team. There are a lot of candidates back home."

Asked why he used only three turns, he said, "Why should you need more than three turns? That's quite enough. Enough for me, in any case, to reach 80 meters (262'5") in 1977."

After the Games, he lost to Spiridonov twice. "I hate losing as much as the other guy. My result was not too bad though, for the time of the year. I am tired, and can hardly wait to get back to my beat records, friends, and a bit of rest. Next season I'll be all out to beat the 80m mark, but now I have already relaxed my schedule and am winding down." Despite his late-season losses, Syedikh was ranked first in the world in 1976 by *Track & Field News*, which headlined "Syedikh Undisputed Leader." Explaining the defeats which would occur in the future Syedikh said: "In the USSR we are lucky to have a whole bunch of world-class hammer men, and you simply can't count on winning every time."

Unfortunately, Syedikh's philosophy proved to be wisdom in 1977 when he concentrated on his exams and lost seven meets. His best throw went 247'8", 4½ meters short of his prediction, and he ranked only No. 7. "The main thing is always to peak for the most important championships, such as the Olympic Games. In that sense, the best example is Al Oerter."

After his letdown year, Syedikh came back impressively in 1978, winning Znamenskiy with 254'1". Then, in Zurich on August 16, he threw with intensity against Riehm, who had raised the world record to 263'6" only ten days before. Riehm averaged 254'2" for six throws, with a best of 257'8", but it was no more than the best losing mark ever. Syedikh threw 261'8" on his first attempt, third best in history. He followed with 259'8", 259'4", 258'9", foul, and 258'8", by far the best series of all time.

And yet, two days later, he threw a poor 243'7", 15 feet behind Boris Zaichuk, who had held the world record at 262'11" for 28 days before Riehm's throw. He entered his second most important meet, the European Championships in Prague, as only one of several good throwers.

In a tense competition, Syedikh won by an inch with 253'6". "I haven't been in good form lately, and I didn't feel I was throwing well. Everybody was so close that I didn't really relax until after Riehm's last throw."

He continued to throw below his great Zurich form, but he won the USSR title with 252'7" and ranked No. 1 in the world.

He followed with another poor year as he pointed for the Olympic Games. His best 1979 throw came in May, at 254'6", and he lost several times, ranking only No. 6. Even more threatening to Syedikh's career, a 21-year-old countryman, Sergey Litvinov, threw

261'10" and ranked No. 1.

Syedikh began 1980 by losing twice to Litvinov in cold winter meets. He suffered a defeat by Igor Nikulin, who was only 19, and barely beat Juri Tamm, who was only 23. His young countrymen threatened to displace him on the Olympic team.

Spurred to greater efforts, as though in the Olympics, Syedikh went to the Black Sea training camp at Leselidze to throw against Litvinov and Tamm. The results were sensational.

Syedikh, looking very quick in the circle, began with 256'11", but Tamm threw 258'7". Syedikh roared back with 261'2", fifth best ever, but Tamm then topped it by four inches. Litvinov could throw only 259'. Syedikh whirled one out 263'8", adding two inches to Riehm's world record, but once again Tamm topped him, by one tiny inch. Two world records in minutes.

Syedikh, upset at losing the record, came back in the next round with furious power and sent the ball flying 264'7". The third world record in a few minutes ended the fireworks, with Syedikh on top of the world, momentarily.

Eight days later, at Sochi, Syedikh threw 262'5" and it gained him only the best third place in history. Zaichuk threw farther on three throws, with a personal best of 264', but he, too, lost. Litvinov threw 267'11", destroying Syedikh's world record.

Syedikh beat Tamm on June 12 with 260'10", but at the Znamenskiy on July 5, just a few weeks before the Games, his 259'1" placed third behind Tamm's 263'9" and Litvinov's 262'. Syedikh's cherished Olympic crown teetered precariously.

In the Olympic qualifying round at Moscow's huge stadium, he broke his own Olympic record with 256'7". In the July 31 final, he drew the first throw in the hot sunshine. "I concentrated hard on being the first thrower. I warmed up for a long time. I put all my determination into it and was successful."

Something of an understatement, for his first throw flew 268'4", a new world record! "I was relieved, because I knew through experience that the psychological impact of my first throw would be considerable."

Another understatement, for the pressure crushed Litvinov, who fouled five times. Syedikh threw 267'3", 261'5", foul, 265'8", and 264'9", the best series ever, with four throws better than Litvinov's. As a competitor, Syedikh reigned supreme.

And yet he endured defeat in his very next meet, in Rome.

Yuriy Syedikh

Against Riehm, best of the Olympic boycotters, who threw 265'1" at the time of the Olympics, Syedikh's good 264'3" lost by 9 inches. Syedikh won the USSR title easily, with 265'3", then lost again to Riehm by one inch in a late September meet in Tokyo. But his Olympic championship and world record still ranked him as best in the world.

Syedikh kept the pressure on his opponents in 1981. He lost no meets even though his best throw was "only" 263'1" He threw only 254' in the World Cup, but he took vengeance on Riehm, defeating him by six feet. He ranked No. 1 for the fourth time in six years, and he was only 26.

He continued triumphantly in 1982, even in the winter. He threw over 260' in four meets, but Litvinov broke his world record with a frightening 275'6" on June 4, and Nikulin threw 274'1" in Athens on September 2. Desperate measures were needed to defend his prestigious European championship in Athens.

Syedikh used his knack for the overwhelming assault and his first throw sailed 267'11". That shocked his countrymen, the two longest throwers in history. Only Syedikh's shortest throw failed to beat the best of his opponents, by three inches. His series of 267'11", 264', 265'7", 260'4", 267'9", 265'7" surpassed everything ever seen. His average of 265'3" outshone all except two throws of all time.

He triumphed over Nikulin four times in 1982 and Litvinov five times, and he lost none. For the third consecutive year, and for the fifth time in all, he ranked best in the world.

Syedikh began 1983 at less than his best, losing twice in February meets in the south. He won twice in May, with 263'4" and 263'10", but misfortune struck in the Spartakiad on June 21. He threw only 258'2", while watching Litvinov set a world record of 276'9". Then at Leningrad on July 28, his 260' lost to Nikulin, who threw a disheartening 272' on June 4.

Thus, he felt doomed to defeat at Helsinki for the first World Championships, far behind his two teammates. In fact, two other Soviets had better marks than Syedikh and so he was chosen solely on his great competitive record. He was also behind Juha Tiainen of Finland and about equal to Zdzislaw Kwasny of Poland and Riehm. The world was ready to humble Yuriy Syedikh.

Unlike his glorious performances in past big meets, Syedikh began with 259'11", whike Litvinov's first throw sailed 271'3". Battling valiantly, Syedikh improved three times, to 265'7", a fine performance but far behind the world record holder. Under the circumstances, he took a certain amount of pride in his silver medal.

Syedikh threw well in his only other meet, winning at 260'9", and he ranked second best for 1983. His resounding defeat at Helsinki appeared to mark the end of his glory.

Syedikh lost another February meet in 1984, but he was training for the summer season. He wanted Litvinov's world record. In June, he tipped his hand with victories at 267'5", 266'10", and then a personal best of 271' which beat Litvinov only by the length of his second best throw, 270'9" to 270'5".

The two best ever made sensational history ten days later in Ireland. Syedikh threw first and the ball and chain whipped through the air so long as to astound every witness. It measured 283'3", breaking Litvinov's world record by 6½ feet.

Litvinov, who fouled his first throw, threatened with 279'4". Syedikh answered with a mighty 282'2". Litvinov threw 278'4", and Syedikh threw 279'5". Apparently tiring, they next threw 274'9" and 276'3". A discouraged Litvinov fouled and Syedikh reached 273'3". Then both fouled. Thus, both titans threw a shorter distance on each succceeding turn in the circle.

When the amazing competition ended, the all-time list reeled. Syedikh's five throws ranked 1, 2, 3, 7, and 12 of all time, Litvinov's three throws ranked 4, 5, and 10 Syedikh's five throws averaged 278'10", more than two feet farther than the world record when the matchless day began!

In brilliant condition, Syedikh threw 280'10" in London ten days later, and in the Eastern bloc consolation Olympics, he won with another 280'10". At Budapest on August 20, he threw 278'11", with four other throws over 272'. He crushed Litvinov again in the Golden Gala in Rome with 275'3", and he finished his superlative season with a 277'7" victory at the Eight Nations meet. 1984 was Syedikh's answer to Litvinov.

In 1984, Syedikh threw farther than Litvinov's 1983 world record a total of 14 times, a remarkable accomplishment unmatched in track & field history. His incomparable year made up in part for his loss in 1983 and for missing the 1984 Olympic Games because of the Soviet boycott. For the sixth year, he ranked as best in the world. He also placed third in the balloting for *T&FN'S* Athlete of the Year, the highest placing for a hammer thrower since Bondarchuk's third place in 1969.

In 1985, he suffered another odd-year letdown as Tamm threw farther than Syedikh's best eight times. Syedikh's 271'4" fell 4½ feet short of the year's best, but he still had the satisfaction of defeating Tamm soundly in the dual meet against East Germany. Syedikh won with 270'9" and averaged 268'1" against Tamm's best of 268'11".

At season's end, Syedikh still owned the five best throws of all time, and nine of the best 14. At the age of 30, he is still a formidable force in the hammer world.

Daley Thompson, gold at Moscow, Helsinki and Los Angeles.

DALEY THOMPSON

The United Kingdom list of best performances by Youths in 1974 included an interesting 16-year-old sprinter and high jumper named Francis with marks of 11.1, 22.4, and 6'4". With no warning to anyone, Francis was really young Superman in disguise. Born July 30, 1958, to a Scottish mother, he was named Francis Morgan Thompson, but his amiable Nigerian father called him by the African name, Ayodele, shortened to Dele. And so Francis would later dazzle the track world as Daley Thompson.

Almost from the beginning, he wanted to win. "I just *had* to be first at everything, from catching the bus to finishing my lunch." His brother says, "Sport was life and death to Daley."

Sent to boarding school at the tender age of seven, Thompson grew up in an environment of discipline where his aggressive drive found an outlet in sports. He liked soccer at first, but some knowing force turned his desire to track and field.

In 1973, only 14 years old, he had the audacity to compete in an open meet. He put the 16-pound shot 23 feet for fifth place, placed third in both sprints with 11.9 and 24.1, and won the high jump at 5'7¾". He was on his way, though nobody dreamed how far he would go.

They began to wonder in 1975. On March 22, he sprinted along the boards to win the national junior indoor 60 in 6.9. He fancied himself a sprinter, but in late June, more or less as a lark, he entered the Welsh open decathlon.

He ran a fine 100 in 11 flat, and long jumped 22'11¼". He pushed the iron ball 35'3". In his third natural event, he high jumped 6'5½" for a good lead. A 50.2 400 ended his first day with 3764 points, and a few people looked at him with curiosity.

But the diabolical scheduling of the decathlon leaves the events requiring more skill and training the second day. Thompson hurdled a poor 16.8, wobbled the discus 103'1", vaulted only 9'6¼", and threw the javelin a fair 170'2". A 4:31.0 1500 completed his first decathlon, and although he scored only 2921 points on the second day, he won. And he enjoyed it. And he was captivated.

Nor was his total score all that bad. Still 16 years old, his 6685 was only 140 less than the 1948 Olympic gold medal total when Bob Mathias was almost a year older.

Thompson became a respectable sprinter during the summer. He won the English Schools 200 in 22.6 two weeks after his decathlon. Optimistically, he entered the 100 in the AAA junior championships against several more highly regarded sprinters. But such is his competitive ability that he won in 10.9. On August 30 he returned to Cwmbran, in Wales, for the AAA junior decathlon, his true love.

He scored 3880 the first day, with a wind-aided 10.7 and a jump of 23'8", close to his recent personal best of 23'11½". Then he bettered four PR's for 7008, best in United Kingdom history for 17 and 18 year olds.

As the third highest scorer in Britain for 1975, he became an international. Enthusiastically, he competed against France, again at Cwmbran, on October 4 and 5. Disappointed in the hurdles and discus, he came through with personal bests in the vault (11'1¾") and javelin (187'2") for a UK junior record of 7100. And he still had two more years as a junior!

In 1976 Thompson became a dedicated decathlete. "I can go into a competition in the long jump, say, and it is only a fraction above a training session in my mind, regardless of how big a meet it is. But put me in a competition where I'm getting some points at the end of it, and I'm a different man."

A student at Crawley College of Technology in physics, biology, and geography, he enjoyed competing for the Essex Beagles in some individual events, but he wanted to make the Olympic team in the decathlon. The most urgent goal in his life was an Olympic qualifying mark of 7650.

He began his crusade sensationally in the UK team trials, again at Cwmbran, with four personal bests: 10.8, 24'3½", 41'11½", and 6'6". After a 400 in 49.1 his first day total was 4092, but he needed 3558 more to qualify for the Olympics and his best previous second day totaled only 3214.

He hurdled in 15.5, and threw 127'3". "I was holding my chances of making 7650." But his hopes shattered when he vaulted only 12'5½". "I just wasn't riding with the pole after rocking back."

He threw the javelin about 177' on his first attempt. "Not bad, but I wanted more. If I could get a 60 meter (196'10") throw out, I'd only need to run 4:30 in the 1500, and if I can help it, I'd prefer not to absolutely kill myself in the 1500."

His second throw was a blooper. "I nearly fell apart. My face went white. I was near crying."

Now Thompson showed a glimpse of the truest part of his character, that remarkable competitiveness that was to stamp his whole career. "Somehow, I got myself determined again and went back out there to get that score together. I gave it a careful lob out and stayed loose." The javelin sailed 186'9", and he grinned. Now he needed only 4:25 to reach his goal.

His best 1500 was 4:30.9, but "I knew I could go quite a bit faster if it was called for." At 6'1¼", he weighed only 169 then, light enough for running. And he had support from everybody. The spectators yelled, the announcer screamed encouragement, and other decathletes paced him. He ran 4:20.3.

His 7684 shattered the record for a 17-year-old and was 849 points more than Mathias scored at the same age in the 1948 Olympics.

He rested for two weeks. "My body had taken a real caning, mentally and physically." Then, on June 13, he broke the UK junior long jump record with 24'7", and he trained hard again. "I try not to think too much about Montreal. It's exciting but frightening, too."

He competed in one more decathlon, in Copenhagen on June 26 and 27. After a good 10.6 and 23'10" start and a best of 48.6 in the 400, he had 4040 points. He hurdled in a PR 15.3, but he failed to clear a height in the pole vault. Shocked, he coasted in with only 6639 points.

At Montreal for the 1976 Olympic decathlon, Thompson "couldn't get enough of it. I was like a kid with a new toy. But it was a learning experience I'll never forget for the rest of my life. I was in total awe of almost all the others there in the decathlon."

He began his Olympic career with 10.79, his best automatic timing. He jumped 23'7¼", added a best of 42'11¾" in the shot, high jumped 6'3¼", and raced to another PR with a 48.15 400. The electronic scoreboard showed his 4055 in 11th place, not bad for someone still officially 17 years old.

The next day he celebrated his 18th birthday "out there to gain as much experience as I could." His experience was a dismal 15.98 and 119'3", but he came back with a PR vault of 13'9¼". Scoring well, he seemed on his way to an impressive finish, but "I was up and had so much adrenalin going that I tended to rush things."

He threw the javelin only 148'3", losing 158 points off his best. Discouraged, he ran the 1500 in 4:29.55 for a total of 7434 and 18th place. "I don't think I've ever felt so tired. It was emotional, mental, and physical fatigue, and I was totally wiped out."

Still excited about the decathlon, Thompson competed in France against Aleksandr Grebenyuk and Guy Drut, France's Olympic high hurdle champion. "The whole thing was being run just for Drut. They were treating him like some kind of film star."

Thompson surprised Drut in the 100, almost dead-heating in 10.5, hand timed. After a foul, Drut jumped 7.56 (24'9¾") and Thompson wanted to beat him even though he needed a personal best to succeed. "As I was charging down the runway all I was thinking was, 'Seven fifty-six. Seven fifty-six.' He had me going." He hit the board well and landed at 7.57 (24'10") for a new UK junior record—quite a competitive 18-year-old.

He stepped into the shot circle full of fire and put 44'7", his third consecutive PR. "I was very pleased." Drut was falling behind, and Thompson high jumped only 6'4¾". Then he fought down the stretch with his fourth PR of the day, 48.1 in the 400. His first day total was 4275, right up there with the men.

He hurdled in 15.4 into a 0.7 wind. "Good going." Then he slipped badly, spinning the discus only 123'8". Once again, he had to fire up his competitive juices. Playing safe, he started the vault at 12'1½" and he cleared each 10 centimeter raise (4 inches). "It went really well." He cleared until he made 14'5¼".

Exuberant, he threw the javelin with confidence. "I was on schedule for 8,000 plus." But he threw only 170'4". "My javelin throwing let me down. I throw it pretty badly. I bring it under too much and it gives me a lot of pain."

In the 1500, "I was getting really tired by that stage." He needed a PR to better 8000 points, but he ran only a 2:30 pace. "I stepped on the gas and ran the last 700 in around 1:55. So a 4:20 was definitely on if I'd gone harder at the start."

His total of 7905 disappointed him, but he broke the UK and Commonwealth records as well as the world junior best. Some experts attempting to predict the 1980 Olympics for *Track & Field News* were excited enough to pick him for the bronze medal at Moscow.

He sounded pessimistic about his future: "My throws are weak, and I count my high jump into that because I'm not improving. I'm putting some real hard work into the hurdles. I want a sub-15 next year." But he smiled about his point improvement for next year: "Oh, about say 200-250 points." Then he added a simple statement with awesome implications: "I feel I will be at my best at 27 or 28."

In spite of his preference for the decathlon, Thompson enjoyed many individual events during the 1977 indoor season. He placed third in the 200 meters of the indoor championships and worried the long jump winner. He long jumped in two international dual meets, then ambitiously entered four events in the junior indoor championships. He won the 60 in 6.9, the long jump at 23'7½", and the vault at 14'5¼" before barely toppling the bar at 15'1½". He finished second in the shot with a best ever 46'11¾".

He felt enthusiastic about his eighth decathlon, the annual international meet at Gotzis, Austria. Eager to score 8000 points, he began with a wind-aided 10.71 and 25'4" for another UK junior long jump record. He put only 43'10¾", jumped 6'6¾", and ran 48.35 for 4268, seven points behind his best from 1976. He hurdled 15.24 and spun the discus 122'4", but he vaulted only 13'9¼". His come-through javelin throw of 183' pulled him ahead of his own PR and he gained another seven points with his 4:23.8 for a personal best of 7921, but it left him unhappy.

Five weeks later, determined to improve, he competed against Spain, Denmark, and Italy in Madrid's hot weather. He sped a fast 100 in 10.5, disappointed because there was no auto timing. He jumped 24'11¼, his second best, then crashed through with three consecutive PR's. His 45'5¼" was only a decathlon best, but he high jumped 6'9½" and ran a 47.4 400. He raised his best score by 162 points, to 4437, third best ever scored.

He began the second day on the same impressive level, with a PR 15.1 in the hurdles and a decathlon best of 129'11" with the discus. Then he went slightly mad with a 15'9" vault. Excited about a great score, he pressed too hard and slipped to 165'1" in the javelin. Disappointed, he ran only 4:29.0, a lapse which cost him the best 1977 score in the world by three points. Still, his 8190 was the 17th highest ever, and he was still only 18 years old.

He celebrated his 19th birthday in the European Cup semifinal at Sittard. He fell slightly below his great Madrid scores, except for a PR of 47.31. His 4324 missed his best by 113 points. His excellent second day—15.26, 136'10", 15'5", 178'9", and 4:30.4—won with 8124, ninth best on the auto-timed list.

He had fun in the AAA Championships, vaulting 15'3" for ninth place and long jumping 24'8¼" for his first national title.

Thompson's goal for the year, the European Junior Championships, took him to Donetsk, USSR on August 19 and 20. He felt disappointed with his fifth in the open long jump, at 24'7". In the decathlon, he began with a discouraging 11.02 and jumped only 23'9½". Ashamed of himself, he put 45', high jumped 6'9", and ran 47.59 for a decent score of 4207.

He began his second day well with 14.95, his first race under 15, but, with no competition, he seemed to lose interest. The discus sailed only 125'5", careless vaulting left him at 12'5½", and he went through the motions with 163'1" and 4:35.53. He won with only 7647, not his proudest moment. Still a junior, he took some satisfaction from ranking No. 4 in the world for 1977.

With his decathlon season ended, he looked for fun in the GRE Cup Finals at Cwmbran on September 17. Instead of challenging the good individual athletes in his best events, he tried something entirely new—the intermediate hurdles. To the surprise of most, he placed third in 52.6.

In the UK Merit Rankings for 1977, he rated as best, of course, in the decathlon, but his individual event rankings were also impressive: ninth in the 100, eighth in the 400 and HJ, eleventh in the IH, sixth in the PV, and second in the LJ—a good prospect in all of them.

Training seven or eight hours a day by 1978, Thompson had little time for anything else, nor did he want much more. "It's my life. There isn't anything I want to do more than decathlon."

Despite liking it so much, he entered only three decathlon competitions in 1978, preferring quality over quantity. He wanted to train.

His main concentration was the annual decathlon gathering at Gotzis on May 27 and 28. Hoping to beat West German Guido Kratschmer, the silver medalist at Montreal, Thompson began with a good 10.77, then rode a friendly wind to 26'1". After a decathlon best put of 45'7", a clearance of 6'8", and a fine 47.76 he had 4385 points, close to his remarkable 4437 at Madrid.

He began the second day with a personal best of 14.85, threw a satisfactory 135'10", vaulted 15'1", and threw the javelin 186'8", and yet Kratschmer humbled him. His 4:29.11 gave him 8238 against

Daley Thompson

Kratschmer's 8410. He was a great teenager—twelfth on the all-time list and sixth best with auto timing—but he could not beat the best men.

Sprinting for fun, he ran 10.72 and 10.68 with wind. In the national championships, he ran 10.70 to place sixth against the top UK sprinters. But he fouled out in the long jump, a dishonor he would never tolerate in the decathlon.

A week after he became 20, Thompson stormed into the Commonwealth Games in Edmonton, Canada. On August 7, he ran 10.50, by far his best auto time, though wind-aided. "It wasn't bad, but I can do better." Supercharged, he burst down the runway and sailed 26'7¼". Elated with a mark better than the open long jump winner, he was also sobered by the wind of 6.29 meters per second, well over the 4 mps permitted for decathlons. He passed his last two jumps.

Even with no competition to excite him, he worked hard for a great score. He put the shot 47'4¼", his decathlon best, although below his 48'2¾" of five weeks earlier. "It was bad." He high jumped 6'9½". "My run-up went to pot. I've jumped 2.10 (6'10¾") in training and was expecting 2.14 (7'¼") today." He ran 47.85. "I lost maybe eight-tenths of a second because of the wind." In spite of his "failures," he scored 4550, only seven points below the best ever.

On the second day, he hurdled in 14.92. "I hit several hurdles." He threw the discus farther than he ever had before in a decathlon, 136'9", and equalled his best-ever vault of 15'9". He threw the javelin 185'8". "I was throwing really badly." Now a muscular 184 pounds, he ran a satisfactory 4:25.78.

His 8467 points, though wind-aided, became the sixth highest in history, third best with automatic timing. "I'm good now, but I will be great. I'd like to be another Bruce Jenner."

Thompson sounded cocky, but he knew his ability and he put his heart and soul into the European Championships at Prague on August 30-31. "This is the one that counts."

In his heat of the 100, he ran against Kratschmer, his most dangerous opponent. Thompson sped across the finish line in 10.69, his fastest legal decathlon mark, and looked back to see Kratschmer hobbling off with a pulled muscle.

In the long jump, Thompson sailed 25'7½". Not content, he improved to 26'¼" with a wind of only 0.5 mps, his best legal jump. He pushed the shot out to a personal best 48'2½". Then rain fell, and he high jumped 6'8¼", less than he hoped. His 47.77 gave him 4459, his best legal score.

He could smile about his 288 point lead over Aleksandr Grebenyuk, an 8161 man. "If I have the same sort of second day I got in Edmonton, I'm in for gold."

But disaster lurks at every step of a decathlon, and for Thompson it came at the second hurdle. He crashed into it and almost fell. He recovered well for a 15.28, but Grebenyuk's 14.43 gained 93 points and Thompson was in trouble.

He came through with a personal best of 142'8" in the discus, but Grebenyuk cut his lead to 105 points. Thompson cleared 13'9½" in the pole vault and hoped to go two feet higher, but he failed to adjust the standards and disaster caught him.

He showed his competitive fire with another PR, a javelin toss of 196'2", but Grebenyuk threw 222'2". Forty points behind, Thompson faced the hopeless task of beating Grebenyuk by six seconds.

In tears, Thompson wanted to quit. "I wasn't going to finish because it wasn't worth it to me." Brendan Foster encouraged him and he ran 4:22.80, his best since his lightweight days of 1976, but Grebenyuk stayed within ten meters and won the prestigious championship, 8340 to 8289.

"It was like the end. I've never felt so bad. I never want to feel like that again. It was such a low I couldn't believe it." But years later, Thompson said, "It was probably the best thing that ever happened to me. Even if only because at the time I was under the misapprehension that I was too good to be beaten. I was mentally getting too confident so I wasn't concentrating. It was only my fourth championship-level decathlon. I wasn't a bad athlete; I was just too young to be where I was. I was barely twenty and still learning."

In the spring, he explained why he did not want to compete more often in the long jump: "I don't think I could get the same fulfillment as a person. I do feel the decathlon is right for me. If I worked on it I could maybe get up among the best long jumpers. But I feel the decathlon can give a lot more personal satisfaction because I can get to the very top of it. I doubt very much that I could long jump 29˙2½", but I *know* I can score 8617 . . . and a lot more."

In spite of his love for the decathlon, he all but disappeared in 1979. But he trained hard and competed in individual events, and he liked his improvement toward a world record.

In the indoor championships, he flung his heavy body over crossbars at 6'8¾" for sixth and 15'9" for fourth. In the outdoor AAA, he vaulted only 14'11" for eighth place, but he sprinted well. Running heats, semis, and finals, he lowered his personal best three times, to 10.65, 10.56, and 10.49 for fourth place.

The only decathlon of his off year came at Flein, Germany, before his 21st birthday. Hoping for a great score, he dashed a best of 10.45, jumped 24'11¼", put a PR 48'7½", leaped over 6'9", and ran 47.30 for 4507 points. After another best in 14.39, and a near miss 141'6", he threatened the record.

But his vaulting poles were lost and he made the mistake of starting at 14'1¼" with a borrowed pole. To his dismay, he failed three times. Even a PR 203'2" in the javelin brought his total to only 6954 and he withdrew. He took small consolation from his four personal bests, and he competed in no more decathlons in 1979.

He regained some of his pride in the UK National Championships. He placed sixth in the high jump at 6'8¾" and collected his second long jump triumph with a wind-aided 25'2¾".

In spite of his poor decathlon season in 1979, he was pleased with his progress. He ran 200 meters in 20.89, vaulted 16'4¾", threw the discus 148'4", the javelin 203'5" and, indoors in November, put the shot 50'8¼", all personal bests. Thus, in 1979, without completing a decathlon, he set new PR's in seven events—the 100, 400, hurdles, vault, and all three throws.

In the 1979 UK Merit Rankings, he ranked fourth best in the 100, No. 5 in the 200, No. 9 in the hurdles, No. 5 in the vault, and No. 1 in the long jump. He placed 16th on the high jump list and 18th in the 400. His potential was awesome.

Thompson spent the winter in California, enjoying his outdoor training. He returned to England in time for the 1980 indoor championships and raced over the high hurdles for second place. Then he prepared for his greatest decathlon effort.

In superb condition, he entered the annual decathlon on May 18 and 19 in the small town of Gotzis in Austria near the Swiss border. I wasn't expecting to break the world record, but I was in good enough shape to do it."

His 10.55 was 0.10 behind his best. "I started well, but after about 80 meters I tied up. It was my first race of the year." Even so, he scored 919 points, 100 better than Jenner in his world record at Montreal.

Competing in his best event, Thompson long jumped 25'4". "I just wasn't hitting the board. Again, I think that was due to a lack of actually doing it." But he gained another 100 points on Jenner.

In the shot, "I tied up badly. In warmups I was throwing over 15 meters." (49'2½"). His 47'5¼" lost 53 precious points to Jenner's record.

Now Thompson felt wary of Kratchmer close behind, forgetting his dreams of a world record. Jenner's record included a 6'8" high jump and strength in all the remaining events. Kratchmer, second best of all time behind Jenner, was threat enough.

"The week before I only jumped 1.85." (6'¾"). "At this meet, I entered at 1.85 and the bar was going up three centimeters at a time. I took every single height." He did not miss until after he cleared a personal best of 6'11", a gain of 68 points on Jenner.

The 400 began at 7:15 p.m. "We had started at 9:30 [a.m.]. By then I was really tired, and there was a really strong headwind in the stretch." He ran too fast, 22.1 for 200 meters, and struggled home in 48.04. He gained on Kratschmer, but he lost 26 points on Jenner's record.

He felt satisfied with his 4486 points, 181 ahead of Kratschmer and 189 better than Jenner's record. "My spirits are good." Later, he admitted, "I was able to think seriously about the world record."

Jenner's second day gave Thompson a formidable, probably an unrealistic, target. For a world record he needed 4132, but his best was only 3917. Thompson said, "In the decathlon, nothing is won ahead of time. You can have one good event, but you'll never know how the next one turns out until you get to it."

Thompson began his second day well with a personal best of 14.37, in spite of hitting several hurdles. He gained 53 points on Jenner, but he lost 24 to Kratschmer.

He threw the discus only 141 feet, losing 139 points to Jenner's record and 68 to Kratschmer. He was now a precarious 89 ahead of his live opponent and 112 ahead of Jenner's ghost.

He could not forget the distress of his 1979 failure to clear a height in the pole vault, but fear is not part of Daley Thompson's nature. He waited until the bar reached 14'9¼" "the highest I've ever come in," and he made it on his first attempt. Supremely confident, he sailed over 15'5", equalled Jenner's 15'9", and cleared 16'1" on his first vault. His 1028 points gained 23 on Jenner and left Kratschmer 208 points behind. "I was really pleased."

He wanted a 100-point margin over Jenner before the 1500 meters, but he led by only 135 with a sure loss in the javelin. Jenner threw 224'9" in his world record and Thompson's best was 204'6". If he equalled his best he would lose 72 points and so his lead going into the 1500 would be only 63. This was more than a test of strength and skill for the 21-year-old. It became a fight against tension.

He strode down the runway in high spirits and sent the spear soaring 214'6", a personal record by ten feet. He led Jenner by 99 points. "That was good."

After 8:00 p.m. he toed the line for the 1500 meters. "I felt really good." He needed 4:26.1 for a world record and he had bettered it five times. He lumbered around the track, slower than necessary and knowledgeable spectators sagged with disappointment. "I felt awful. Never felt so bad in my life."

After three laps, his time was about 3:40, a 4:35 pace. Jenner's record looked safe. But Thompson heard the time and reacted as if jabbed by a cattle prod. His lumbering stride became a near-sprint. He sped down the backstretch and around the last curve and the crowd began to howl. He sprinted the entire homestretch, probably passing Jenner's ghost about 30 meters from the line.

His 4:25.50 brought his total to 8622, breaking Jenner's world record by the narrow margin of five points!

"That probably was the toughest thing I've ever done in my life... Now I can concentrate on the Games."

Thompson's glory lasted exactly 27 days. Kratschmer won the West German championship with 8649, 27 points ahead of Thompson's record. But Kratschmer was one of the unhappy athletes boycotting the Olympic Games, and so Thompson would go to Moscow as a strong favorite.

On July 12, a few days before he left for Moscow, Thompson had fun helping his Essex Beagles in six events in the GRE British League Division 1 meet, including a 45.8 anchor leg.

Although favored in the Olympics, Thompson took no chances in Moscow. He ran a formidable 10.62 on a cool and windy morning when only one other man could better 11 seconds.

He jumped 25'8¼" against a wind, but he was not satisfied. On his second jump, against a wind of 1.37 mps, he reached 26'3", a decathlon mark bettered only by his wind-aided jump in the Commonwealth Games.

He put his decathlon best of 49'9¾" in the shot, high jumped 6'9¾", and ran the 400 in 48.01 to total 4542, the best auto first day ever. He led by 264 points.

On the second day, rain fell in the morning, and he competed cautiously. He hurdled 14.47, and threw the discus only 138'7" from a slippery ring. In the afternoon he started vaulting early and worked up to 15'5". He threw the javelin 210'6", his second best ever, and victory was his. Needing 4:17.2 for a world record, he ran a more comfortable 4:39.9 for 8495 points.

Four days before his 22nd birthday, he stood on the victory stand in Lenin Stadium with the Olympic gold medal around his neck and listened to his national anthem. He was No. 1 in World Ranking for 1980, but his future was even brighter.

Everybody expected a new world record from Daley Thompson in 1981, but he wanted another kind of perfection.

"It's difficult to do a lot. With 1500's or 100's you can just go out to win. Decathlons have to be done well. It doesn't matter so much if you don't win as long as you do well."

He trained ruthlessly, and he competed as a weight man at Crystal Palace on May 6. He placed fourth in the shot with 49'3½" and third in the discus with a good 150'11".

On June 13 and 14 he was in Saskatoon, Canada, more enthusiastic than ever. "I am going to try to score more points than I ever have before . . . I am running faster. I have improved my discus and shot, and we've put in a lot of time on pole vault and hurdles . . . I'm in better shape than before last year's world record."

He began well, with 10.47, and he jumped 25'7¼". He was disappointed with his shot put of 47'8½" and his high jump of 6'8¾", but he ran 47.64 for a total of 4505. He felt hopeful.

Unfortunately, the weather changed. Saksatoon had suffered from a drought, with no rain for months. This began to change on the first day of the decathlon. On the second, the wind blew and Thompson hurdled only 14.81 and threw the discus only 136'8". Then the wind blew with gale force and rain fell in a cloudburst. They moved inside for the pole vault and Thompson equalled his PR of 16'4¾". He threw the javelin 205'1", but with no hope for a record, he withdrew from the 1500, leaving his score at 7936.

For the remainder of a mediocre year, he competed only in individual events for fun and training, sometimes as many as six in a meet, but he went unranked in his beloved decathlon.

Anyone who thought Daley Thompson was resting on his laurels had a surprise coming in 1982. He trained for three months during the winter in San Diego, California, and British coach Ron Pickering warned, "Watch out for Daley at Gotzis."

Daley Thompson

Thompson at Helsinki, 1983.

Dangerous competition at Gotzis on May 22 and 23 came from Jurgen Hingsen, a 6'6¾", 220-pound West German who was only six months older than Thompson and ranked No. 3 in the world in 1980 with a best of 8407.

Thompson began with a 10.49 100, only 0.04 off his personal record. But his fine 26'1" barely beat Hingsen, his personal best 50'2¾" in the shot lost to Hingsen's 52'4", and his 6'9¾" high jump was behind Hingsen's 6'11". Shocked, he found himself only 62 points ahead.

Charged up with his unquenchable spirit of competition, Thompson ran the 400 into a headwind in 46.86, a personal record by 0.44. Hingsen ran 47.86 and became the third man ever to score over 4500 points with his 4520, and yet he was 112 points behind Thompson's record 4632. He lamented, "I said that Daley was unbeatable right now and it looks like he might be."

Thompson did nothing to change Hingsen's opinion the next day, hurdling 14.31, his best ever. He threw the discus 145'6", vaulted 16'¾", and threw the javelin 198'7". Before the 1500, he had 8122 points, and Hingsen seemed slightly dazed.

To break Kratschmer's world record, Thompson needed only a 4:39.4 1500, but he lumbered along at a slow pace, placing the record in doubt. Concerned at last, on the last backstretch, he came alive with a frenzied kick and he finished in 4:30.55. He scored 8707, a world record by 58 points.

"This sort of score has been in me for a couple of years, so it's more a relief than a triumph to get it out. I don't feel like a conqueror because you never conquer this thing. I feel more a survivor, yes, to fight another day."

He was more prophetic than he wanted to be. In July, he lost his junior record to 8387 by an East German, Thorsten Voss. Then he slashed his arm when his fiberglass pole broke. And on August 15, Hingsen made up 109 points in the 1500 to break his world record by 16 points. Thompson said, "I'm truly happy for him. Now he's the favorite. Me, I like being the outsider."

Hingsen joked, "Daley was out fishing when he heard I got his record. At once he threw all his fishing stuff into the river and got to the track to start training. He keeps saying to me that to win is all, and records don't matter. He tells you that, but I know what he thinks deep inside."

The stage was set for the greatest decathlon competition of all time, record breakers Thompson and Hingsen facing each other in the

Daley Thompson

European Championships on September 7 and 8. Athens was hot and smoggy, but Thompson concentrated on this threat to his supremacy.

His explosive 100 in 10.51 beat Hingsen by 128 points, and his 25'7¼" gained another 43 points. He put the shot 50'11" for his best ever, but he high jumped only 6'6¾". Hingsen jumped 7'½" to cut Thompson's lead to a precarious 66 points.

Thompson's good 47.11 finished the long day with 4549, 80 points behind his former world record, but he was happy to lead Hingsen by 114 points.

Thompson hurdled 14.39 for a promising lead of 139, but after two throws in the discus he felt despair. He reached only 130'8" and he led by only 44 points.

He concentrated on his third throw, and felt joy as the disc sailed 149'2". This personal decathlon best almost guaranteed a victory with a lead of 152 points and it strengthened his reputation as one of the great clutch performers in history.

Not content, Thompson vaulted 16'4¾" and moved within 45 points of his world record pace. But disaster struck in the javelin. He slipped on his first throw and fouled. He slipped again on his second and reached only 194'4". The clutch situation only made him better. Changing to long spikes, he threw 208'6".

With 8110 points, he needed 4:26.5 in the 1500 to break Hingsen's record. His heavy stride left him five seconds behind pace at the bell. Urged by the crowd and Guido Kratschmer, he ran hard. "I thought I wasn't going to get around that last lap. I kept trying to think of things to make me angry and keep me going." He crossed the finish line and staggered to a stop. "When I looked at the clock I couldn't even read it, I was so dizzy."

His courageous last lap in 63.7 brought him home in 4:23.71. His European Championship victory in 8743 broke Hingsen's world record by 20 points.

Less than a month later, October 4 and 5, he defended his title in the Commonwealth Games at Brisbane, Australia. With no strong competition, he spent most of time on the field having a good time with other athletes. Almost casually, he ran 10.66, jumped 25'3½", put 49'9¼", leaped 6'8¼", and ran 47.59. On the second day, he continued his class act with 15.00, 146'3", 16'¾", and 206'7". He ran his usual confortable pace in the 1500 without the final kick, for 4:43.48. His total of 8410 won by 406 points.

For the second year, *Track & Field News* ranked him best in the world and he finished second in the voting for the magazine's Athlete of the Year.

"People have gotten the idea that I'm an outgoing guy, an extrovert. I'm not, but people expect me to live up to my image. When there are lots of people around, they expect me to be loud, jovial, silly, making pranks all the time."

In truth, Thompson trained as conscientiously as any athlete in history. He enjoyed the sunshine of another San Diego winter, planning only one low-key decathlon before his goal for 1983—the World Championships.

But fate was against him. In February, he injured his back and "couldn't really train." Next, he suffered a groin injury. Then he was startled by the results in the West German championship. Siegried Wentz, only 23, scored 8714 but lost to Hingsen's world record of 8777. Kratschmer, now 30 years old, scored 8456. Even without injuries, Thompson was in danger.

For the good news, Thompson raised his personal best in the discus, throwing 155'8". And in the Canadian Decathlon Championships at Toronto in early June, he scored a satisfactory wind-aided 8507, including a 16'8¾" vault. "I hoped that all the years I had been training would be like money in the bank."

Once again he went into a championship against a man with a higher score, and Wentz also threatened him. "I felt I wouldn't finish at Helsinki, but I would go out giving 110%."

Helsinki weather was cool, windy, and wet when the decathlon began on August 12. Thompson, favoring his groin injury, said, "If I can start with 10.60 and get through the long jump without trouble, I'll be all right."

His spirits rose when he ran exactly 10.60 and jumped 25'10¼", but Hingsen was close to his world record pace. Thompson put the shot 50'4-1/3", close to his best, but Hingsen was still projected as the winner.

Hingsen failed in the high jump, clearing only 6'6¾". Thompson flopped over 6'8" and smiled. "I've got it now."

In the 400, he went out fast, hoping to fool his opponents. He staggered home with a disappointing 48.12 to finish the first day at 4486, 120 points ahead of Hingsen, but the German giant had better second-day marks.

August 13 was colder, but dry. Thompson worried about the hurdles because of his lack of training, but he ran 14.37, losing only on one point to Hingsen. He improved with each discus throw, to 145'10", proving himself a better competitor than his tall opponent ... or almost anybody else.

Vaulters in the open championship failed because of the swirling wind, but Thompson equalled his best with 16'8¾". Mel Watman of *Athletics Weekly* wrote: "His sheer competitiveness and coolness under pressure is without parallel."

In two javelin throws, Thompson reached only 198'3", losing 83 points to Hingsen's PR. Cooly, Thompson whipped the spear 214 feet, his second best ever. Now he felt certain of victory. He ran 4:29.72 to score 8666 points, the sixth best total ever scored. Once again, he defeated Hingsen, this time by 105 points.

"I felt the strain," Thompson said. "My body tells me that it needs a long rest now and that's just when I intend to give it."

He ranked as best in the world for the third time.

Training in sunny San Diego during the winter of 1984, he competed in two indoor pentathlons in February. At Toronto on February 12, he high jumped poorly, only 6'2¾", and scored 4097, three points short of his world record of 1983. Worse, he lost both the meet and his record to Dave Steen of Canada. Never content with losing, Thompson competed again five days later, in Canyon, Texas. He ran the 55m highs in a respectable 7.48, jumped 25'2¾", put 50'4", high jumped 6'8", and ran 1000m in 2:44.93 for a world record 4219.

Intensely serious about the Olympic decathlon, Thompson spent six months in California over the winter. "The extra couple of hours I can put in every day might be reflected in my scores at the end of the year."

It is possible Thompson trained too much. "Every successive morning you wake up with some kind of residual tiredness in you. If you start day A at 100%, maybe at day Z you're feeling only 40%, yet you have to train harder. The tiredness just gets worse and worse ... from the total amount of what you do and the amount of hours you spend doing it. Because there really aren't enough hours in the day to do enough. I would like to be able to do more ... At least once or twice in every session I try to do an event very well so that even on my worst days I can throw a certain distance or jump a certain height."

His extra training impressed everyone in the open 100 at Modesto on May 12 where he placed sixth with a wind-aided 10.28.

As the only man in any event ever to win gold medals in the European Championships, World Championships, and Olympic Games and unbeaten in every decathlon he had finished since 1978, Thompson should have been an odds-on favorite to win his second Olympic title in Los Angeles. But there was Hingsen.

On June 8th and 9th, the awesome German raised his own world record to 8798. Even more threatening, Hingsen's best marks added up to a total 34 points higher than Thompson's.

Both superstars went to Los Agngeles with only one decathlon comeptition. Hingsen's was his world record, while Thompson's was incomplete. He competed well at Los Angeles on May 23 and 24, scoring 7938 in nine events, but he withdrew from the 1500. "I could have got a score of 8500, which is good for most people, but it was not what I was looking for." He wanted to train rather than recover from a 1500 meter run.

Thompson defeated Hingsen in all four of their previous competitions. In the first three, he broke the world record, and in the fourth he won the World Championship. Even so, Hingsen was a formidable opponent and Thompson knew the dangers of the decathlon. "With ten events, you have ten times the chances of things going wrong."

When the 1984 Olympic decathlon began in the huge Los Angeles Coliseum, Thompson focused on the gold medal. "Competition is my life. Winning is my only goal. Everything I do is directed toward that end."

For the public he maintained his happy face. When he heard Hingsen expected to win the gold medal, Thompson grinned. "The only way he will go home with a gold medal is to steal mine."

Down on the red track, there was no way he could take Hingsen lightly, and he exploded with a 100 in 10.44, as fast as he ever ran in a decathlon and only 0.06 slower than the best decathlon 100 ever. Hingsen slipped to 10.91, and Thompson led by 122 points. But since Hingsen had better personal records, Thompson's margin was really a precarious 17 points.

Thompson landed in the pit at 25'8¼" and 25'8¾", but Hingsen leaped 25'7¼". Alarmed, Thompson geared himself to a greater effort and sailed 26'3½", bettered in all decathlon history only by his own wind-aided jump. Still, Hingsen's projected score was right with him in their fierce battle.

Fighting as few other athletes can, Thompson responded with his best ever shot put in a decathlon, 51'7". When Hingsen put only 52'¾",

Daley Thompson

Thompson led by 155 points with a projected world record of 8891.

Thompson's only weakness comes when he is not despairing for points, and the high jump reversed his fortunes. He missed twice at 6'8". Desperately close to losing his lead, he cleared on his third trial, but Hingsen cleared 6'11½" and closed to within 78 points. Once again, Thompson could taste the danger of defeat.

Thompson fought savagely around the track in 46.97, only 0.11 slower than his best ever. Hingsen, though well back in 47.69, came within 0.04 of his best and within 46 points in the projections. Thompson's all time first-day record of 4633 did not ensure victory!

Beginning the second day, August 9th, Thompson hurdled more with ferocious power than with finesse. He hit nine hurdles and still ran 14.34 against a wind of 1.1 mps, only 0.08 slower than his best. And yet, Hingsen ran 14.29, still a threat.

Then came the discus, where disaster often struck. Thompson could throw only 124'4" on his first throw, 31 feet short of his best. Hingsen, smelling blood, whirled the platter 166'9", the best ever in an Olympic decathlon, and Thompson could feel the despair of second place.

Thompson's second throw sailed only 135'4". Hingsen was still 68 points ahead. Nervously, Thompson entered the ring for his last chance at the gold medal. Instead of throwing cautiously he whirled full speed and stayed in the ring. The discus sailed far beyond his marker, to 152'9", and he raised both arms in triumph.

Thompson led by only 32 points, and Hingsen projected a better finish. He was only 23 points poorer than Thompson in the vault and 24 better in the javelin. Hingsen threatened, "If it comes to the 1500 I'll blow him away."

Thompson passed confidently until the bar reached 14'9". Surprisingly, Hingsen also passed. Thompson cleared, but Hingsen, a 16-footer, needed all three attempts. Then, to Thompson's amazement and relief, Hingsen went out at the next height. Later, Hingsen said he was ill and vomited twice before the vault. There are those who say he became ill when he saw Thompson's great come-through in the discus.

But Thompson could give it all back by missing. He wanted to vault high enough to clinch his victory. He cleared 15'5" on his second try to gain 49 points. He missed at 16'¾", which would have given him an extra pad of 47 points. He missed a second time. Then, on his last attempt, he sailed high over the crossbar and celebrated with a backflip off the cushion.

Then he cleared 16'4¾". He led by 152 points and only a disaster could beat him now. Hingsen's world record was his for the taking. When he threw the javelin 214', close to his best, it was all over but the record.

He needed only 4:34.8 for a new world record and 4:34.6 to reach 8800. But he ran as if only to win, reaching the bell in 3:23.2. Still, he needed only a moderately good finish for the world record. He did not start his kick on the backstretch, nor around the curve, but a homestretch kick was all he needed.

With the crowd screaming for action, Thompson lumbered down the stretch and across the line in 4:35.0. He missed the world record by one point. Obviously, he had not made the effort, and he shrugged it off.

"At the end of the day, it's how badly *I* want it that is going to get me those extra few points, not a million people cheering for me.

"Hey, all I wanted to do is win. When Hingsen went out so low all my interest went out and I just tried to get through the next event with the least possible effort. I was having a good time and trying to enjoy it after that. There are other times to break the record.

Daley Thompson and his great rival Jurgen Hingsen (Helsinki 1983).

Daley Thompson

Thompson clowned his way through many interviews, and he ran a strong leadoff leg in the final of the 400 meter relay. He took a vacation in 1985, making an effort to start an acting career, but he still overwhelmed the other decathletes.

First, British timing expert Bob Sparks discovered an error in Thompson's hurdle time at the Olympics. If Thompson receives credit for 14.33 instead of 14.34, his score will tie Hingsen's record.

Second, under the new 1985 tables, Hingsen's world record increases to 8832. Thompson's mark will become 8846, another world record.

Even without a fourth world record, Thompson now claims more decathlon honors at the highest level than anybody before him. He is the only man, in any event, to win two Olympic golds and a World Championship. And he wants to win at least one more of each . . . and score 9000 points.

"I think I can break the world record in almost any other decathlon."

Sebastian Coe, the only Olympic 1500 repeat winner.

SEBASTIAN COE

On a sidewalk in Stratford-On-Avon in the year 1960, a tiny dark-haired boy of three jogged alongside his sister's pram, exuberant with the sheer joy of running.

His name was Sebastian Coe, and he cannot remember a time when running was not a pleasure. "It seems that from the time I could walk I preferred to run. It just seemed natural. I would regularly run two miles or so into town and back again on errands for my mother, never using a bicycle, preferring the feeling of runing. I never walked anywhere, it seems."

To go with his love of running he had abundant natural talent. His grandfather was a professional sprinter and his father raced as a cyclist, and so it seemed only natural when Seb wanted to begin racing at the age of 12.

His engineer father, an executive who believed in pushing hard for what he wanted, returned from a job in America so Seb could be born "at home," September 29, 1956, in Chiswick, West London. Always upwardly mobile, Peter Coe moved his growing family to Stratford-On-Avon. Pleased with a small son who loved to run, he took delight in discovering Seb was a rare child who allowed himself to be pushed.

The Coe family moved again, to a home on a hill near Sheffield University where Seb would do thousands of sprint repetitions. But Peter's first push was toward the Derbyshire Peak District. Seb says, "I've trained over the peaks from the age of 11 or 12."

A sunday ritual ever since, Seb's rigorous uphill training developed extra strength. Peter, learning to coach as he went along, established Seb's pattern early: "He always drives hard into the inclines, then takes it easy down hill." Peter was careful about Seb's condition and never allowed him to run through injuries. And most of the time, he followed Seb up the hill in a car and then drove him down to avoid strain.

Years later, the proud father said, "I've not heard of one athlete who is as dedicated as Seb." And Seb admitted, "Self motivation was never a problem." And it all began over those peaks where the self-taught coach pushed his small son into building leg strength which would amaze the world.

His mother, Angela, a former repertory actress, said, "I was amazed that Seb never complained at the routine, at the sheer pain in his hands from the cold when he came back from training sometimes in mid-winter up on the hills. His self-discipline was astonishing."

Seb joined the Hallamshire Harriers at 12, and his mother says, "Sports days were embarrassing. You could hear other mothers muttering, 'It's only going to be Coe again. I don't know why we bother to come.'"

When he was 13, Seb ran 1500 meters in 4:31.8, and they dreamed of his future as a 5000 meters runner. At 14, he ran in the 1971 Colts division of the Yorkshire cross-country, a scrawny, 90-pound champion.

Peter said, "At 14, I knew he was good," and the school sent two bus loads of supporters to cheer for Seb in the English schools junior division. But Peter had gone away on business and Seb disobeyed orders by racing a bus uphill in training. "I was so stiff I couldn't train for two days." He finished 24th, but he learned a great lesson. "I never again disregarded his training instructions."

On the track in 1971, he ran 2:08.4 and 4:18.0, promising times, but he was eliminated in a heat of the junior 1500, and a more promising junior by the name of Steve Ovett had run 2:00.0 at the same age. Seb Coe was far from sensational.

In 1972, at 15, Seb placed tenth in the Schools intermediates cross-country, a long 150 yards behind second-place Ovett, who was a year older. On the track, Seb did not win but he lowered his times to 1:59.9 and 4:05.9, and he ran 3000 meters in 8:50.0.

In 1973, after a 1:56.0, he went on a victory rampage, winning the Northern Youths 1500 in 3:59.5, the Schools intermediates 3000 in 8:40.2, and the AAA youths' 1500 in an excellent 3:55.0. Peter entered his 16-year-old son in an open 3000, and Seb placed sixth in 8:34.6.

Peter said, "I felt a strange kind of certainty that if I was patient I had a world beater."

Peter studied physiology and training methods, enjoying the intellectual challenge. Until now, he had been careful to bring Seb along slowly, avoiding injuries and burn-out. But now they discussed it and decided to train for speed. Later, Seb was to say, "Many people believe that to get results, you must run 75, 85, or even 100 miles a week. That's all wrong. For me, only one thing counts: speed, speed, speed... Modern 800m and 1500m running demands a considerable amount of leg speed and your're not going to get it from running slowly in training."

Sheffield lies near many hills, but one flat road has six consecutive half miles where Seb gradually developed his almost superhuman anaerobic powers by running all six with only a minute and a half of rest between runs. He also sprinted repeatedly on the university track near his backyard.

Once, Seb analyzed his father: "One of the most important features of our relationship, possibly the key, is that he knew nothing about coaching when he started. The fact that he didn't compete left him without mental barriers on what is physically possible."

Unfortunately, Peter learned a few hard lessons about speed work, for Seb ran 1:55.1 in training to start the 1974 season, then suffered stress fractures of both tibias and missed the entire season.

In 1975, at the age of 18, his training went well enough to win the national junior indoor 1500 in 3:54.4 and the outdoor in 3:47.1. He finished a good season at Athens in the European Junior Championships. He ran 3:45.2 with a 55.2 last lap but placed only third. Seb was a promising junior, but at the same age, Ovett had placed second in the *senior* European Championships with a 1:45.8 800.

In 1976, Seb was a 19-year-old senior and he placed no better than fifth in the national indoor 1500 with 3:51.0. Outdoors, he won the Yorkshire Championships with a personal best of 3:43.3. After a mile in 4:02.4, he led the AAA 1500 in 3:02.8 and he ran an excellent final 53.2, but he watched Dixon, Moorcroft, and Clement run past him. Still, he lowered his best to 3:42.67 and Peter remained confident.

Coe lowered his 800 PR to 1:47.7, but his best time came in the Emsley Carr Mile. Seb led in 59.2, and 3:00.4. With dismay, he saw seven runners pass him, but he would not quit, and his reward was a personal record 3:58.35.

Hoping to develop a faster finish, Peter gave him speed work during the winter, and in November, as a test, Seb ran an indoor 600 meters. His 1:19.7 was only 0.2 off the United Kingdom record, and they were delighted. Then he lost a month to a virus infection.

At the age of 20, Seb was regarded as a good prospect, but certainly not in the same class with Ovett. Secretly, Peter and Seb hoped to change that status with his winter speed work.

His 5'9" frame and light body adapted well to the tight curves of indoor tracks and he came through with a victory in the national indoor 800. His 1:49.1 was nothing sensational, but he ran an eye-opening 1:47.6 against West Germany for a UK record. Now Peter could smile at some tangible results.

Even with a sore throat, Seb beat France a week later in 1:47.5, and his indoor goal became the European Indoor Championships in Spain on March 13. He set a fast pace with 51.4 and 1:18.9 and triumphed in 1:46.54, only 0.17 behind the World Record.

Now a world-class 800 man, indoors, he suffered Achilles tendon pain, was able to train only four miles per day, and so his 1977 outdoor season began poorly. He lost to Milovan Savic of Yugoslavia in the AAA, lost to American Mark Enyeart at Gateshead, and placed only fourth in the European Cup with 1:47.61 after being shoved and spiked. On August 27, he ran a 49.1 400. The next day, against West Germany, he won the 800 in 1:47.78 and looked good enough to be invited to run in the next day's Emsley Carr Mile at Crystal Palace.

A year previously, as a novice miler, he had led for three laps and finished eighth. Now he trailed a 58.3 and 2:00.1 pace. Filbert Bayi, former mile record holder and still holder of the 1500 record, took over in 3:01.5. Seb trailed Bayi all the way to the homestretch and won in 3:57.67. His last 400 in 56.0 and 200 in 27.0 gave him his first important mile victory.

He closed the season on September 9 with a loss behind Boit's 1:44.76, but his 1:44.95 bettered Ovett's United Kingdom record. Now Peter *knew* he had been right four years earlier. His son was a world-class runner.

Seb, too, was enthusiastic about his speed training. "The basic reason I came down to 800 was to work on the leg speed for 1500... I've come down-distance from cross country, 3000 track, 1500, right down to 800, and I'm planning to do a few 400's."

On April 26, 1978, Seb won a 400-meter race in 48-flat, then ran a relay leg in 47.3, and they celebrated his increased speed. But another setback crushed their hopes for 1978. He stepped in a post hole while out training and severely ruptured his ankle tendons. He lost "about a month of flat-out preparation."

In spite of this blow, they still aimed for the European Championships. Seb says, "Peter worked brilliantly to get me back into some sort of shape." On August 18, in Brussels, he ran his first lap in 50.5 and lowered his UK record in the 800 to 1:44.25, less than a second from Juantorena's world record.

In the European Championships at Prague, Seb would race Ovett for the first time on a track. Ovett was now the #1 ranked miler in the world, and the two Brits were overwhelming favorites for first and second.

Seb's weight was down to 112 pounds and a stomach bug further weakened him. Added to his loss of training in the spring and the strength-sapping heats and semi-finals, Seb could have been expected to hang back and use his speed at the end. Instead, he wasted strength in the final with a sizzling pace of 49.3!

He led down the last backstretch and around the curve, but his legs were tiring and Ovett was close behind. Surprisingly, a third runner was still in contention. Olaf Beyer, a 21-year-old East German with a best time of 1:45.8, ran close behind Ovett.

Into the stretch, Seb struggled to hold his speed, but Ovett fought past. Then, shocking everybody, Beyer rushed past both Coe and Ovett, and Seb also lost his UK record to Ovett.

Peter, who separated his disappointment from a purely intellectual learning experience, said of Seb: "In spite of being miserable, he did not then or subsequently ever reproach me." Then, referring to Seb's role as a full-time student, Peter added, "The result wasn't bad for a part-timer in the fifth fastest race ever. We knew that in 1978 he was nowhere near the limit of his training schedules."

Seb wanted to run the 2-mile in the Coca Cola meet in London, but it was reserved for Ovett. Seb's answer was 1:43.95 to regain his prized UK record from Ovett.

Seb tried his only mile of 1978 at Gateshead on September 17, but annoying winds held him to 4:02.17, ahead of Henry Rono's 4:03.8. On October 1, he outsprinted Eamonn Coghlan in a 4-mile road race in 17:54.

"My premier aim in 1979 was to get a degree." His strenuous winter training covered only half the mileage of good distance runners and yet Peter timed him in 45 minutes for one 10-miler on the road, better than the world record at the correct distance. Afterwards, Seb was sick.

He won the indoor AAA 3000 in 7:59.8, then reduced his training until after his examinations in June. Training hard again after his exams and happily free of injuries, he wanted a world record in August.

His first international invitational race came in the Bislett Games in Oslo on July 5. On Tuesday, he loosened up for 40 minutes in the morning, ran ten warm-up 150's at noon, then, after two 400's and two 300's, he ran a series of 200's under 23 seconds. Pleased, he telephoned Peter the news, and that father-coach said, "Go out and have a go. Run through the first lap in 50–50.5, then hang on and see what happens."

Seb hoped to run near the European record of 1:43.7 if the wind died, but the wind was no problem in famed Bislett Stadium, nestled among high buildings in the center of Oslo. Running behind a rabbit, Seb passed 200 meters in 24.6, much too fast from a stationary start. Cautiously, he slowed to 26 seconds and passed 400 meters in 50.6.

He felt amazingly fresh and instead of "hanging on", he increased his pace, and he heard Coghlan, Dixon, and Foster shouting encouragement on the backstretch. "It was a strange feeling, like being on autopilot. I was mentally outside what my body was achieving, and it just felt beautiful."

Far in front, he passed 600 meters in 1:15.4, faster than any man before him. Now came the time for him to "hang on." His tiring legs could not hold that 24.8 pace, of course, but even though he slowed to almost 27 seconds he felt no difficulty.

To the astonishment and joy of almost everybody in Bislett Stadium, Seb's 1:42.33 broke the world record by 1.11 seconds. "I think I could have run even faster. I wasn't exhausted at all at the end."

One impressed observer was John Walker. "The way he ran was just unbelievable. He looked like he could run under 1:40. He never tied up at all."

Pleased beyond his expectations, Peter said, "It came a year earlier than I had reckoned."

Seb himself said, "I still believe the 1500 is my best distance."

He had a chance to find out, when he returned to Bislett twelve days later for the Golden Dubai Mile, a special IAAF race attracting almost every top miler in the world. He had run only three mile races in the past four years, and only one miler in the field had a slower personal record. Neither he nor Peter dreamed of a record. In fact, "I wasn't exactly sure what it was." On television, he said, "It calls for more specialized work than I've been doing."

But he was not overlooked. Walker, world record holder at 3:49.4, said, "Coe is the question mark, after his 800 meters. He's the danger. Nobody knows how good he can be. I just hope that with 200

Sebastian Coe, in the 1984 Olympic 1500 final.

meters to go I'll be there kicking past him."

The 16,100 rabid fans came to see what Seb called "an awesome field." Even so, as he stood with his father after his warmup, Peter said, "You can win this." And feeling better than ever, Seb answered, "I know."

The runners lining up on the red track at 8:20 p.m. included world record holder Walker, indoor record holder Coghlan, European record holder Thomas Wessinghage, Commonwealth champion Dave Moorcroft, and the fastest American, Steve Scott.

Seb ran in fourth place past 400 meters in 57.8. At 800, running comfortably in second place behind Scott in 1:55.3, Seb worried about the third lap. "I was prepared to hurt." Scott pushed the pace hard, leaving all but Seb behind, but Seb felt no strain. In fact, with a lap and a half to go he considered taking the lead.

Running with an elegant grace which must be disheartening to his opponents, Seb stayed behind Scott around the bend. In mid-stretch, approaching the bell, Seb sped smoothly past Scott and led at three-quarters in 2:53.4. "I was feeling very comfortable."

The crowd was noisy with excitement, clapping in rhythm and banging the tin fence at trackside. Seb had no idea what was happening. He kept looking back, expecting the worst. "I was afraid that someone would come surging up. I had a nagging doubt that I had done something wrong or unorthodox against a world class field, and that a big kicker would come through."

But Walker knew. Passing Coghlan ten meters behind Scott, he heard the time and thought of his record. "It's gone." He watched Coe's purple pants and white vest speeding around the curve, "knowing he was on the way to breaking my record."

Seb appeared astonishingly fresh down the backstretch and around the last curve. He passed 1500 meters in 3:32.8, and the crowd's roar beat down on him.

He broke the European 1500 record by 1.2 second and yet he ran the homestretch with good speed and no sign of strain. "When I looked back twice in the final straight it was fear, it was panic, not pain that I was feeling. I certainly wasn't in the slightest distress." He actually eased a bit before the tape, waving to the crowd.

Seb saw his father sprinting across the infield to him. "I was astonished when Peter said it was a world record. I had no idea it had been that fast."

Seb's 3:48.95 won the greatest mile ever run, for each of the first ten recorded the fastest time ever for his place!

Late that evening, when he entered the restaurant for the usual post-meet reception, the guests included many Olympic medalists and world record holders. When they saw Seb, barely known only a few weeks before, they stood and burst into applause.

Now he was a celebrity, hounded for interviews, and he went to East Germany as the favorite in the European Cup 800. Even though European champ Beyer was in the race, Seb stayed behind until the final 200. Then he blistered the track in 24.4 for an overwhelming victory.

Seb had agreed to run the 1500 in Zurich's famed Weltklasse invitational meet. Conflicting accounts reported Seb would or would not try for a record, but Seb himself wanted to try. He said later, "It was the only time I've ever gone consciously for a record."

Seb said his father had "thought out the lap times for a record *if* the weather was right. We both knew there was a chance for three in a row, which might never come again, but it depended on the weather because we reckoned that I was not going to get too much help from the field."

After Seb wakened from his afternoon nap, he heard thunder, and when they walked to the Letzigrund Stadium they were discouraged by wind which blew dust in their faces. But as the runners took their marks, the wind suddenly slackened. The record attempt was on.

Kenyan Kip Koskei set a faster pace than Seb wanted, but he stayed close in 54.3, and Peter shouted at him to slow down. "He didn't need to tell me."

The pace slowed to 59 and Seb went into the lead at 750 meters, passing 800 in 1:53.2. "I knew the record was there if I wanted it badly enough." His sudden increase in pace, to 13.2 for the next 100 meters made it a one-man race. "I can still today hear the roar from the Swiss crowd as I went in front, and it was that which lifted me."

He slowed to a reasonable pace, but he covered the lap in 56.3. Driven by his courage and the rhythmic clapping of the 26,000, Seb ran hard around the last curve. "I will never forget that draining run to the finish." He could not kick, but he held his speed to the end. "Physically it had been hard, but the mental exhaustion was total." His last three 100's were 14.4, 14.0, and 14.2.

Coe's hard-fought last lap in 56.9 brought him to the line in 3:32.03, his third world record in 41 days.

"It's the race of which I'm the proudest in terms of endurance... I don't think I've got anywhere near a peak this year in terms of training."

As a result of his three world records, Seb ranked as the world's best in both the 800 and 1500 and *Track & Field News* honored him as Athlete of the Year for 1979. Enjoying his new freedom from his university studies, he devoted full time to his running. He spent three winter months in sunny Italy running the long background distances he would need for six nerve-wracking races in nine days at the Olympic Games.

When he began to build his speed in the spring, he was bothered by a sore hamstring, the result of a pelvic tilt which made one leg shorter than the other. "By the beginning of July it was beginning to cross my mind that I might not make it to the Games."

He ran a slow 3:45.7, but 800's in 1:44.7 and 1:44.98 gave him hope. Then illness caused him to cancel a 1500 in June, and it seemed as if physicial ailments might stop him where opponents and the stopwatch could not.

Still, he was in increadible condition, claiming one workout of six 800's in 1:50 with three to four minutes rest between runs, and another of four 600's in 1:24 with only one minute of rest.

Coe's only real test before the Olympics was an assault on the World Record for 1000 meters on July 1 in friendly Bislett Stadium. The weather was cold, but Seb followed a rabbit in 51 seconds. All alone, he reached 800 meters in 1:45.0!

Now breathing was difficult and he strained around the last turn. "I tied up badly between 130 and 80 meters out." But he retained enough form to struggle down the stretch and across the finish line in 2:13.40, his fourth world record.

"I was pleased, because I wasn't well. In a way it was harder than running a hard 1500 meters. Whatever doctors say, antibiotics affect your system physically."

Seb's four world records did not last. An hour later, Ovett took away his mile record with 3:48.8. And, while Seb avoided racing in his final Olympic preparation, Ovett equalled Seb's 1500 record.

Thus, with Seb below par physically, most observers favored Ovett (undefeated in 41 consecutive 1500 or mile races) to win the Olympic 1500. But almost everybody, including Peter and Seb, picked Sebastian Coe in the 800. After all, he had run much faster than anyone else in history.

But in Moscow, Seb suffered from a bad case of nerves. "I've never known pressure like it... I had the worst night's sleep I've ever had just lying there listening to my own heartbeat... At lunch I knocked over my orange juice, and then dropped the cream carton into my cup of coffee."

Peter knew his son was too nervous. "Why, of all times, did I not prepare him properly?"

As they lined up in their lanes, a stiff wind flapped the flags around the high rim of the old concrete stadium. At the gun, Seb felt sluggish. "I was thinking of *nothing.*"

He drifted toward the rear, but he ran wide so as to be ready to move, even though he had 600 meters to go. The pace was slow, but he stayed back and wide for the entire race, a classic example of the fastest runner in history ruining his chances. He ran an extra 12 to 15 yards, wiping out most of his advantage.

Meanwhile, Ovett elbowed his way out of a box and pursued Nikolay Korov into the homestretch. As Ovett passed Kirov, Seb ran around the outside of the pack on the last curve, too far back to catch Ovett. In the stretch, he unleashed his great kick and managed to pass Korov a few meters from the finish line, but he finished more than three meters behind Ovett.

Even with his fast finish, his time was only 1:45.9. "I suppose I must have compounded more cardinal sins of middle distance running in 1-½ minutes than I've done in a lifetime."

Seb felt numb, glad it was over. At the press conference, Peter whispered, "You ran like an idiot," and Seb agreed with his father. "I knew all too well, and I knew how hard I'd hit him."

Fortunately, Seb read none of the scathing criticism in the British press. The pressure to win the 1500 was increasing, even without such humiliation. In the semi-finals, he ran another poor race tactically. Peter said, "If you do that tomorrow, you're dead."

But Seb was a different man now, with a quietly angry determination. He had ten hours sleep after his heat, and after his semi-final: "I slept very well. Instead of the nerves I had before the 800 meters, I was now excited by the final of the 1500 meters. I wanted to get out there and enjoy it."

In the final, nobody wanted to run fast, and so Jurgen Straub became a reluctant leader in a 61.6 pace. Seb ran close to him, determined to avoid any of the disastrous back-of-the-pack mistakes he made in the 800.

Straub slowed the pace even more on the second lap, running

63.3 for a dismal 2:04.9. Seb was alongside, and Ovett moved up on his shoulder, as if worried about giving him a head start in the coming sprint.

But Struab changed the funeral march into an exciting stampede, speeding around the third lap in a sensational 54.2. Coe followed smoothly, about two meters behind. "I was able to do what I can do best—that is, run freely." He had no more worries about being caught in the pack, for only Ovett stayed with them.

"I knew that sustained speed of this sort would play into my hands," Seb said later. "I'd always been confident, arrogant if you like, that I could maintain that speed longer than anyone." And his proud father added, "No one in the world can keep that speed the way Seb can."

Seb gained little on Straub down the backstretch and Ovett was poised behind him, ready for his final killing 200. Ovett swung wide on the curve to pass, but Seb glanced over at him and increased his speed. Seb ran the curve 100 in 13.3 while Ovett gained.

In the stretch, Coe caught Straub, but Straub found more strength and for a few strides they ran side by side. Close behind, Ovett was gaining again, and for a moment there was high drama and suspense while it appeared any one of them might win.

Suddenly, Seb's legs twinkled in one of the greatest kicks ever seen, speeding smoothly away with a final 100 in 12.1. He was, at last, the super racer his world records had promised.

He did not know how invincible he looked. "I tried to drive again at 40 meters out, and in the next few strides I knew I had nothing left if anyone came back at me. The anxiety over the last 20 meters was unbearable."

Seb's time was only 3:38.40, but his last 700 meters, averaged 53.37, an astonishing 1:46.8 800 meters pace. His actual time for the last 800 meters was 1:49.2. He ran his last 400 in 52.2, last 300 in 38.9, last 200 in 25.4.

Peter said, "I really gave him stick about the 800 meters, but he just came straight back and that makes the man."

After his Olympic victory, Seb said, "I was often asked before the Games whether I would swap my world record for an Olympic gold medal. I found it difficult to answer. I think the records of 1979 were in fact the truer indication of athletic ability and that's why it's my intention to get them all back at the earliest possible opportunity."

He spent several days relaxing in Switzerland, where he wanted to make a record attempt in the Weltklasse 1500 at Zurich on August 13. Before an anxious crowd of 26,000, Seb ran second in 54.6 and 1:52.9. Then he made the decision to run to win instead of pushing for a record. "It was too classy a race to take liberties," he said. "Every time

I turned my head I saw Bayi's face, or Walker's, or Scott's."

He led at the bell in 2:37.0, but a slow curve cost him a sure chance at a record. Even so, a sensational kick brought him home in 3:32.19, third fastest winning time in history. "It was a great race."

With the harrowing Olympics behind him, Seb spent the winter before the 1981 season torn between his graduate studies and quality speed work. "My intention is to get back the 1500 meters and mile records and improve the 800 meters."

His quality work paid off early with an world indoor 800 record of 1:46.0. On June 3, he ran 1:44.06, and he felt ready.

A week later, at 11:00 p.m. on a balmy, windless evening in Florence, Seb toed the starting line with the intention of showing the 15,000 spectators a record 800. For the first lap, he ran smoothly behind Billy Konchella, a young Kenyan with 400 speed.

Past the bell in 49.7, 0.6 seconds faster than in his world record run, Seb heard someone call, "Fifty." So strong were his intentions that he swung out and passed Konchella on the curve.

In his record race, he had run the third 200 amazingly fast, and once again he raced down the backstretch. He reached 600 meters in 1:15.0, 0.4 seconds ahead of his record pace, and he still felt strong.

He could not hold that pace. "It seemed like the track was turning uphill." Still, he managed to run slightly faster than in his 1:42.33 race, and he finished in 1:41.73, the fifth time he had broken a world record outdoors. Track fans shook their heads in wonder.

He won the European Cup semi-final in 1:47.57 with a spectacular sprint finish, and two days later the DN Galan meet at Stockholm on July 7 found him eager to break the 1500 record. Of this race, he said, "There are only a few races in an athlete's career when you are mentally ready for a world record. I was ready."

To spur him on. Seb had some choice competitors and the world's fastest rabbit. James Robinson, who ranked second in the world to Seb in the 800, set the most pitiless pace ever with 51.5 and 1:47.5. Unfortunately, no lap times were called, and so Seb, who had little knowledge of pacing, ran faster than he wanted - 52.4 and 1:49.2. With Robinson out, Seb passed 1000 meters in a sensational 2:18.8 and 1200 meters in a best-ever 2:48.3. A slow 43-flat for the last 300 would give him the world record.

But even Seb had his limits and he could barely increase his pace. His last agonizing 100 took him 14.3 seconds and he had to settle for a personal best of 3:31.95.

This was only the second time he had failed in a world record attempt, but that was no consolation. Determined, he tried for the

1000 record four days later in Oslo's Bislett Stadium where he had broken three world records in three attempts.

Running behind a rabbit, he put together 200's in 25.3 and 26.3 for 51.6, 0.4 behind his own record pace. A 26.7 left him 0.5 behind and he pushed the pace hard with a 26.3 200 which brought him to 800 meters in an awe-inspiring 1:44.56.

Now he began to tire and a broken blister hurt his foot, but he strained down the homestretch, forcing out all the speed he had. He could run only 27.6 for his final 200. "I didn't think I was going to get the record."

His time was 2:12.18, his sixth world record, and his fourth at Bislett. "There is something special with this stadium. The crowd is wonderful and lifts you beyond belief."

Then, wanting only to win, he won five 800's, including the AAA in 1:45.84 and the European Cup in 1:47.03 with a final 200 in 24.6.

Excitement pervaded the Weltklasse mile at Zurich on August 19, for Seb's goal was the world record in the mile, with the 1500 thrown in. Given his speed at 800 and 1000 and the brilliance of his few mile races, it was obvious that he could run much faster than ever before, and, indeed, he hoped for a time under 3:47.

The Zurich weather was excellent, the competition was strong, and two real milers agreed to help with the pace. Tom Byers led in a metric 56.13 with Seb close behind in 56.2. Byers circled the track evenly to pass 800 meters in 1:53.59. Eager to run, Seb was on his shoulder in 1:53.6.

Byers faded and Boit was supposed to lead, but Seb was too anxious to wait. He was already slipping behind his desired pace, and so he took the lead himself. He reached 1200 meters in 2:52.68 and his hopes for a 1500 record dimmed. He needed 300 meters in 39.62, a 52.8 pace.

Seb reached 1500 meters in 3:33.27, half a second slower than Ovett's world-record pace. "I had to dig in and concentrate on kicking."

His determination and speed resulted in a struggling 15.3 finish, a gritty final 120 which gave him his seventh world record. His 3:48.53 was only his fourth mile race in four years.

Although the overflow crowd of 25,000 left Letzigrund Stadium hoarse but happy, Seb said, "I'm disappointed I didn't take the 1500 meter record as well."

One week later, Ovett took Seb's mile record away with 3:48.40, and so, two days after that blow, Seb tried again. The yearly battle in the Golden Mile was fought in the Van Damme Memorial meet before

Sebastian Coe

48,000 spectators at Heysel Stadium in Brussels on August 28. Almost every famous miler competed except Ovett.

Byers ran an excellent pace of 54.92 and 1:52.67 with Seb almost too eager on his heels. Around the turn, into the backstretch, Seb caught Byers' heel and stumbled, but he regained his stride within three steps "I ran into the back of Tom. It was my fault."

Byers swung wide and Seb passed him 130 meters from the bell. Seb led in 2:52.00 and Boit's black shirt was only three meters behind. The pack trailed by 20 meters.

Seb led around the curve, and then Boit pulled a little closer and for a moment a sensational upset seemed possible. But Seb sped down the backstretch and began to increase his lead. "With 200 to go, I felt great." He gained another two meters, reaching 1500 in 3:32.94 to Boit's 3:33.67.

In the last 120 yards, the quietly furious competition between Coe and Ovett came to a head, almost as it had in their one meeting, at the Olympics. Seb was .04 behind Ovett's record pace, but he began his great kick, certainly faster than any other runner in history after a fast pace. At the head of the stretch, he glanced back to see Boit eight meters behind. His smooth form looked almost effortless, for only his face showed strain. Where Ovett had needed 15.5 seconds to finish, Seb sped down the homestretch in 14.39, the best finish in any mile faster than Ryun's 3:51.1. He said, "I felt tremendous."

Seb's time was 3:47.33! His last 200 was timed in 27.2 and his final 100 meters in 13.2. "I think it could have gone faster if Steve had shown up. There is more time to come off the mile yet, but it won't be done by finishing faster. It will be by going the three-quarters in 2:48."

Amazingly, both of Seb's mile races in 1981 were world records. Of his five mile races in four years, three of them were world records.

He completed an undefeated season with a tactical victory in the World Cup 800, covering the final 100 meters in 12-flat. He was again ranked #1 in the world in both events, and for the second time he was named *Track & Field News* Athlete of the Year.

Only 25 years old for the 1982 season, with wondrous possibilities still ahead of him, Seb's training received a rude jolt in early February from a stress fracture in his foot. He maintained good condition by swimming, but his running suffered and he never reached top fitness.

He ran no miles or 1500's in 1982, but he hoped for a world

record at 2000 meters on June 5 in Bordeaux. He circled the track in 57.8 and 1:57.4, but at 1500 meters in 3:42.8 he was three seconds behind John Walker's record pace. He won in a good 4:58.84, but he was obviously not in his marvelous condition of 1981.

In his favorite event, the 800, he ran poorly, for him, but he still managed to rank #1 in the world. His anchor leg of 1:44.01 helped Britain to a world record in the 4 x 800 relay, his tenth world record if you count relays and indoor records. He was encouraged by a 1:44.48 victory in Zurich on August 18 because he needed it to be selected for the British team. "I'm still not sure that I can produce three good races in as many days."

In the critical European Championships at Athens in early September, Seb led a slow 800 into the homestretch, and with his great kick he seemed a certain winner. But Hans-Peter Ferner sprinted past to win by two meters in 1:46.33. Stunned, Seb and Peter thought his defeat stemmed from his lack of endurance training, but the next day, when he withdrew from the 1500, they blamed mononucleosis. The full, devastating extent of his illness would stun them even more.

In March of 1983, Seb said, "I've been training well this winter and lost only three days due to influenza." And on March 12, he broke his indoor world record for 800 meters with 1:44.91. "I didn't really expect to do so well, but I always enjoy running indoors... I was surprised how easy I found it." A week later, he set an indoor record for 1000 meters, with 2:18.58.

Outdoors, in a special mile in the dual meet against the Russians on June 5, he ran away with a final 26 seconds in 4:03.37. A week later, he won an 800 in 1:44.99, and he seemed well on his way toward a World Championship at Helsinki.

Then came his first 1500-meter test, in Paris on June 24. He was pushed off the track near the start and lost ten meters, but he ran 56.5 and 1:55 and led at the bell in 2:39.9. Then Jose-Luis Gonzalez outkicked him, 3:34.84 to 3:35.17. Seb said, "No excuses. I got beaten. I'm happy with my time, but not my race."

It was his first loss in a 1500 or mile in seven years.

In the Bislett Games on June 28, Seb won an impressive 800 victory in 1:43.80 over new Dutch star Rob Druppers, and his future once again appeared bright.

In another 1500 at London on July 15 Seb looked sharp on the last curve in spite of a sore ankle, but when he asked "his legs for that final effort on the crown of the last bend, nothing was there." He lost to Dragan Zdravkovic of Yugoslavia, 3:35.28 to 3:36.03, and now his supporters felt genuine concern.

His training alarmed him. "One good session was followed by feeling rough for three days."

His next race was a special mile during the AAA championships at London on July 23. He made a strong effort, but he lost to Steve Scott, 3:51.56 to 3:52.93.

It was Seb's third straight disappointment, and he was obviously not himself. Eight days later he placed only fourth in an 800. "I feel like I was treading water out there."

He entered the hospital for a physical examination, and the doctors ordered immediate surgery. Lymph glands from his left armpit were grossly enlarged and dangerously infected. His illness was at last diagnosed as glandular toxoplasmosis, and a heavy drug treatment was required.

For the next month, while others won the honors at the first World Championships, Seb was in and out of the hospital. He could not train, and his future was gloomy. "My sole ambition was to get healthy again."

He could have retired with great honors. He had broken more world records than any man in this intensified era of the sport, the most since Ron Clarke. But the competitive fires still smoldered within, and as his health improved they burned once again.

In and out of the hospital for months, Seb worried more about his health than his running future. He could not train until December, and so the UK selection board forced him to prove his condition if he wanted to run in the Olympic 1500 at Los Angeles.

He trained well, and he ran 1:45.2 on May 19 and then 3:43.11 on a windy June 2. He said, "I have to be happy with my condition at the moment."

But in the British 1500 trials at the AAA on June 24, Peter Elliott outkicked him in a tactical race, 3:39.66 to 3:39.79. The British selectors had a difficult decision, for one of the greatest runners in history seemed near end of his career.

Seb himself said, "I wouldn't have complained if they hadn't selected me."

Anxious to defend his 1500 title in the Olympics, he ran 1:43.84 on June 28, and six days later he ran a 3:54.6 mile with his last 880 in 1:54. The selection board happily added his name to the 1500 team.

Almost three years had passed since his last great race, and so Seb began the four arduous days of Olympic 800's in the Los Angeles Coliseum in doubt about his condition. After winning his heat in 1:45.71, he said, "I'm not in bad shape, but I would have liked another year to train." In the quarter-finals, he looked comfortable, but he ran only 1:46.75 and placed third. In his semi-final, he finished first in 1:45.51. Now it became a question of his condition on the all-important fourth day.

Since his atrocious tactics at Moscow, Seb had become a "sitter," always racing close to the leader, even when it meant running a few extra meters. In the final, he was close to Brazilian Joaquim Cruz at the bell in 51.2. He followed closely all down the stretch and around the curve, and his fans hoped for another of his great finishes. But into the homestretch, Cruz pulled away and Seb had to fight off Earl Jones of the U.S.A. for another disappointing silver medal.

Perhaps more than anyone else, Seb admired Cruz's great ability in running 1:43.00 after three days of fast heats. "The guy is a supreme champion, worthy of an Olympic crown."

Worried about his condition, he had only two days of rest before his formidable task of three 1500's in three days.

He looked serenely swift in his heat, but his time was only 3:45.30. "I'm still a bit worn down from the 800. Actually, I haven't been feeling all that well this week. It must be a combination of the heat and smog. I suppose that fast 800 took more out of me than I first suspected."

In his semi-final, Seb led at 1200 meters in a fast 2:54.73, but he finished an uncomfortable third in 3:35.81 because this was the fastest trial heat ever run. With the fastest field of finalists in history, the suspense grew.

For the final, the high rim of the Coliseum shaded the red track, but the temperature was 75 degrees with noticeable humidity, not favorable for a fast pace. Because recent championships were run at disappointingly slow paces, nobody expected this one to be fast, but Seb grimly planned to "sit" on any pace they wanted.

Wearing the all-white of Great Britain with a red and blue band around his chest, Seb started fast, leading the other eleven, but he let Omer Khalifa go past into the turn. Down the stretch to the finish line, Coe tripped and came close to disaster, but he moved out on the leader's shoulder as Khalifa passed 300 meters in a quick 42.94, the fastest Olympic pace since 1968. In the middle of the backstretch,

Steve Scott strode quickly and surprisingly into the lead. Seb tripped again, but his luck held and he set out after Scott. Now the excitement became intense as Scott led past the 800 in 1:56.81 and down the backstretch with Seb close behind.

Jose Manuel Abascal of Spain swept past Scott on the turn, and Seb also slipped past, running so lightly he looked like a white ghost. Abascal passed the clanging bell in 2:39.04 and a fast time beckoned, as they gathered their strength and courage for the hard drive ahead.

Seb, with only Abascal in front of him, did not know Scott and Ovett were out of contention. He was ready to move, fearing the danger behind him. Abascal ran past the curved starting line in 2:53.21, the fastest ever run in the Olympic Games. Seb ran on his shoulder with an alert, eager look, unaware of World Champion Steve Cram (No. 1-ranked in 1983) striding purposefully close, ready for the kill.

Approaching 1300 meters, with about 40 meters left before the last turn of the race, Cram made the same move he used to win the World Championship. It was the last tactical moment of the race, before it became a fierce, all-out drive for the gold. Cram had said nobody was good enough to survive seven races in Los Angeles, and now he would put his famous countryman to the test.

Seb glanced at the runner alongside. Cram! Instantly, Seb accelerated so quickly and smoothly as to leave no doubt about his recovery from last year's illness and the previous week's 800. Not only did he hold off Cram, but he whizzed past Abascal to lead into the curve.

Abascal: "I was surprised how much Coe had left."

Cram: "Seb was just too much in control. He wouldn't let me past him on the bend. When I couldn't get by him, I knew that unless Seb's legs gave out, I wouldn't win it."

Seb ran the backstretch in 13.28 and now his speed increased around the curve 100 to 13-flat, a blistering 52-flat pace. Cram ran as fast as Seb but he had to run wide and he lost two feet around the turn. Abascal, running the greatest race of his life, lost about the same distance to Cram, and only those two threatened Seb.

Entering the homestretch with 100 meters to go, Seb led Cram by only four feet. Cram: "As we came around that final turn, I didn't think Seb had it in his legs." Now came the question: How much of his marvelous speed did Seb have left?

In answer, Seb raced for the finish feeling "the best I've felt for two years." He pulled away from Cram by five glorious meters to become the first man in history to win two Olympic championships at 1500 meters.

Seb's new Olympic record of 3:32.53 is the fastest anyone ever ran on the third consecutive day of racing. His final 200 in 26.1, 300 in 39.92, and 400 in 53.25 are all better than anyone ever ran in a 1500 of that speed or faster. His scorching 13.04 down the homestretch 100 is also the best known for this pace, but such times are rarely taken. Considering this was his third consecutive day of arduous races—and his seventh in nine days—his finishing burst must be regarded as the most remarkable in history.

"This whole year has been as much a mental battle as physical. To make a comeback within a year is something, but to do it in an Olympic year, with all the jitters that go with it. . . I am elated. This is a dream come true for me."

Cram said, "I was beaten by a better athlete on this day. . . Seb was brilliant. I'm happy for him."

Immediately after Seb crossed the finish line, throwing his arms high in triumph, he made some intense gestures toward the seats with the index fingers of both hand. Reporters interpreted this as a rebuke to the British press, but Seb said he only shared his elation with the rabid Brits waving their Union Jacks. But the fierce look on Seb's face was almost anger. This great champion, this man who had broken so many records, the only man ever to win the Olympic 1500 twice, his pride hurt by the cruel British press, felt himself bursting with requital. His words were, *"Now* believe in me."

Then he hugged his father, eyes closed, smiling with pure joy.

Seb ran only one post-Olympic race, at Zurich. His main competition came from Scott, who forced him past 1200 meters in 2:53.4. Once again Seb showed unsurpassed finishing speed. His last 200 in 25.1 and 300 in 39.0 are the fastest ever for any race better than 3:35.59.

With so much left in a 3:32.39 race. Seb was certainly in world record condition, but he suffered an injury to a ligament in his foot and he announced the end of his racing for 1984.

In early 1985, Peter began the careful process of training Seb for 5000 meters at 60 to 70 miles a week. "I can't afford the usual four months on a summer racing program which would contribute little to '86."

With such a long-term plan and little speed work, Seb's early season 800s produced a surprise—1:44.0 and 1:44.34—and he hoped for a good mile at Oslo on July 27 against Cram, the new 1500 record holder. "Because of a throat infection and a calf problem, my training and racing was a little sporadic. I was short a couple of races and short two weeks of hard training."

After a 2:53.4 pace, he seemed poised for another great finish, but Cram powered away to break Seb's record with 3:46.31, while Seb faded to third in 3:49.93. "I don't feel the record is out of reach yet, but he's certainly made it harder to get to."

His transition year and a sore lower back hampered his racing. He lost to Deleze, 3:56.70 to 3:56.89, and again, 3:31.75 to 3:32.13. "I'm still not strong enough. But then I think of how far I have come and where I was just a month ago and I tell myself after all that this isn't so bad."

He lost to Cruz in his third fastest 800, 1:42.54 to 1:43.07. "At least it was a world record for 29-year-olds."

Then his back injury forced him out of racing altogether, and he began his concentration on his new goal—a career at 5000 meters. "I'll go on training as long as I can win races and improve."

Edwin Moses—World Record at Koblenz, 1983.

EDWIN MOSES

In March of 1976, a certain "expert" listed 18 intermediate hurdlers with a good chance to make the American Olympic team, hoping he had included all the possibilities. He would have been wiser to wait another month, for on March 27 in the Florida Relays, second place in 50.1 went to a heretofore obscure hurdler named Edwin Corley Moses.

Probably the only people not surprised were the tall, lean hurdler and his coach, Lloyd Jackson. At high school in Dayton, Ohio, Moses struggled above 15 seconds in the high hurdles and 50 in the 440. "I was competitive, but nowhere near national class."

He chose to continue his education at Morehouse College in Atlanta, but primarily as a student, not a frivolous athlete. "I went to college on an academic scholarship. I wasn't even sure I'd go out for track." In an arduous engineering program, he earned a 3.57 grade point average on a 4.0 scale, but his track career suffered.

He drove 30 miles daily to a training track. When the part-time track coach quit, Moses and some others appealed to Jackson to coach them, and Jackson immediately opened coaching books to learn something about the intermediates. He says Moses "was only 150 pounds and he was running the 400 flat in 48 and the high hurdles in 14.2." Jackson's training system was wondrously simple: "No weights or stretching. Just work."

As a sophomore, in 1975, Moses showed promise by winning the conference 440 in 47.5, as well as the high hurdles. He began his career in the intermediates by qualifying for the finals with 52.0, but the final followed the 440 by only five minutes, and so he postponed his destiny.

Thus, his Florida Relays revelation was his first intermediates final. "I planned to run the intermediates ever since my freshman year, but I only got around to it this year." He widened a few eyes in the same meet by circling the track without hurdles in 46.1.

He hit the tape first at the Dogwood Relays in a slower 50.6, and Coach Jackson explained, "He is the kind of guy who will run just fast enough to win." If true then, Moses would change that particular trait radically in the future.

Moses was forced to run harder at the Penn Relays on April 24. His long, stretching strides took him over the first seven hurdles with only 13 steps between, but he hit the eighth hurdle, cutting his step to 14. He lost the lead to Harold Schwab and Mike Shine, but he resumed his long 13-step stride and won by four meters in 49.8. "I guess it seems kind of surprising to everybody else, but to me it isn't. I knew I had the basic talent and it was just a matter of putting everything together."

At the Tom Black Classic in Knoxville on May 8, Moses ran his heat in a personal best of 49.5. In the final, he excited fans all over the world with a victory in 48.9. When he won the King Games in 48.8 on May 22, his confidence grew. "I'm still working on the world record."

But even for an intelligent, dedicated trainer with surprising hidden talent, the intermediates is a difficult event with danger lurking at every three-foot barrier. The next weekend, in the NCAA Division III meet in Chicago, the danger caught him and he fell and failed to qualify with 53.52. He won a hastily organized race the next day in 49.8 but it was no consolation for missing the real final and certain advancement to the Division I NCAA Championships.

Moses's inexperience showed again in the AAU meet at UCLA on June 12. Excited, he ran his heat unnecessarily fast, a personal record 48.86, with 13 strides all the way. It was "real easy." In the final, he was running even faster when "I decided to look around and see what was happening behind me. That's when I lost concentration and started hitting hurdles."

He hit hurdles 8 and 10 and finished only fourth, although his time was 48.94. "When I saw my time it didn't bother me that much. I knew I was on my pace if I hadn't made those mistakes."

Nine days later in the Final Olympic Trials at Eugene, Moses was not so certain. He still had astonishing potential, but the dangerous event had stopped him twice in a row. He ran smoothly through his two heats in lane 1, winning in 50.03 and 49.02.

In the final, challenged by the fastest hurdlers in history, Moses ran calmly, avoiding mistakes. "I went out relaxed, but not too relaxed."

Most intermediates races are settled in the homestretch and this was no exception. Moses, no more than an enthusiastic beginner only three months earlier, turned on a burst of power which amazed and thrilled the crowd, and he won in American record time of 48.30. Some beginner.

Edwin Moses

In a pre-Olympic warmup at Montreal, Moses lost to Mike Shine, 49.2 to 49.3, but he felt no concern. In his Olympic heat, "I started decelerating right after the tenth hurdle," and yet his time was 49.95. In the semi-finals, "I thought I was running around 49-flat," but he lowered his own American record to 48.29.

"I was right where I was supposed to be. I was relaxed and not worried about the final. . . . All I had to do was not make any mistakes."

But when the gun sounded for the Olympic final, his mistakes began. "I had a slow reaction to the gun, one of the slowest I can remember. I must have lost at least a tenth at the start and another tenth getting to the first hurdle. I was off balance at the first hurdle."

Dismayed, he increased his speed and by the fifth hurdle he caught the leader. Around the last curve, he pulled away, but he did not know it. "All I could see was the rest of the hurdles. I just maintained my normal pattern."

He was far in the lead over the last hurdle. "After the tenth, I cut my stride down for more speed and just went on into the tape."

After a jubilant victory lap with silver medalist Shine, the official time flashed onto the huge scoreboard: 47.64. The first-year beginner was the new world record holder.

Through his joy, his analytical mind was critical. "I know I made at least five or sixth tenths worth of mistakes."

In less than four months Edwin Moses changed from complete unknown to Olympic champion and world record holder, and he ran three of the six fastest races of all time. He was 20 years old.

If any fans expected Moses to slip in 1977, he proved them wrong in his first meet, again the Florida Relays. He won in 49.1, doubling back with a good 13.6 over the high hurdles. In April, he won Dogwood in 48.9, and in May he won the Jamaica Invitational in 48.64 and the Ali in 48.68 on a dirt track. In the Jamaica meet, he also doubled in the high hurdles against the Olympic second, third, and fourth placers. He showed awesome talent by winning in 13.5.

He won a double in the NCAA Division III championships, in 13.7 and 49.59, but he passed up the NCAA. He entered the AAU championships with great confidence. I've been running 48's easing up this year." Not to mention a 44.1 relay leg.

On the fast track at UCLA, Moses started slowly, but down the backstretch he cut his stride to hold his 13-step pattern. Around the final turn, he pulled away powerfully, even though he hit the eighth hurdle, and he won by more than 12 meters.

"I knew it was fast," even though, "I made a lot of mistakes." Because of his mistakes, along with a case of 'flu two weeks before, and his concentration on final exams, he was surprised at his time—47.45, a new world record.

Supremely confident in a quiet, serious way, he said, "I didn't have to kill myself to get that time."

Now, as one of the great athletes of the world, European promoters wanted him for the summer season. He won easily at Cologne in 48.73, but he injured his foot and returned home for almost two months.

Eager for action, he returned, for the Van Damme in Brussels on August 16, but he ran the 400 flat race instead of his favored hurdles. He lost to Fons Brydenbach, the #2 runner in the world for 1977, but his 45.60 defeated three others who ranked in the top 10 for the year.

Not yet in top shape, he ran three races in five days. After winning in 49.05 and 48.60, he felt ill, but on August 26 he led over the ninth hurdle in Berlin. He missed his step and finished behind Harald Schmid, 49.07 to 49.29—an historic defeat.

Anxious to redeem himself against Schmid, he ran fast in the first ever World Cup at Dusseldorf on September 2. "I was hurting. I had a bad foot, a sore back, my knees were messed up, I was sick from not eating the right food."

With the West German crowd shrieking for Schmid, the poor sick American won by ten meters in 47.58, second only to his recent world record. Slyly, he said, "There was no competition to push me."

He finished the season with three more victories, giving him eight winning times faster than the second-best hurdler of 1977. He could take pride in the three fastest times in history and five of the fastest eight.

He ranked fourteenth in the high hurdles and fifteenth in the 400 because of limited competition. He barely lost the honor of Athlete of the Year, in the closest possible voting. He lost to Alberto Juantorena who was best in two events and had broken the 800 record, and Moses said, "I really don't know what I have to do to be considered Number One."

He towered too far above the other intermediate hurdlers to make it interesting. "There's no one thing in particular left for me to achieve in the intermediates." He could only set his sights on being the best of all athletes.

Moses returned from Europe and rested on his laurels while he studied for his degree in physics. He disappointed his fans by avoiding the 1978 U.S. season including the AAU, where he blamed the 'flu.

He ran a smooth 48.62 in Jamaica in May, then flew across the Atlantic for another European crusade. On June 22 in Cologne, his 48.20 crushed Schmid by seven meters. It was his fourth best time and the sixth best ever.

After his World Games victory in 48.6 in spite of missing some steps, he made a routine of sub-49 races—48.55, 48.34, 48.72, and 48.8. Routinely superb.

In the Weltklasse at Zurich on August 16, he flashed over the high hurdles in 13.64 for third, then returned half an hour later to run 47.94. He now claimed four of the five fastest of all time, and eight of the best ten.

His single high hurdle race gained a #12 ranking, obviously below his true level. He finished fourth in the voting for Athlete of the Year, a truly remarkable achievement for almost anybody, but disappointing to him.

Indoor promoters wanted Moses, and so he entered the 500 at the 1979 Ali meet, but he crashed to the boards. "This is the last race I'll ever run indoors. My stride is too long for the small curve."

In good shape earlier than usual, he powered to 47.69 in Durham, North Carolina, fourth best ever. "I could have run the record if I had wanted to, but I haven't trained that hard yet this year."

After he won his second AAU championship in 47.89, he began a hectic July in Europe. Nine times in 19 days, he circled the track and cleared ten hurdles ahead of all opponents, including 47.67 at Oslo.

He now had the five best times ever run, but on August 4 Schmid won the European Cup in 47.85 and suddenly Edwin felt a threat. His next race would be the World Cup in Montreal's beautiful Stade Olympique on August 24—against Harald Schmid.

Their confrontation aroused tremendous interest, and Moses obviously took it seriously. Four lanes inside Schmid, he gained with startling speed and caught Schmid on the backstretch. Around the curve, Schmid appeared shocked, Almost 20 yards behind.

Moses did not finish as well as he started. "I'm not as sharp as earlier in the season, and the humidity was bad. . . It's just hard to push yourself when the competition is 20 yards behind you. . .And then I came off the last hurdle off balance and not in good running position."

With all his problems, he crossed the line ten meters ahead of Schmid in 47.53, the second best ever run.

He completed a long season of 21 victories without so much as one close race. His routine superiority produced a magnificent record—the six best times in history, 14 of the fastest 17, 37 consecutive victories.

Still, he only placed third in the voting for Athlete of the Year. But he achieved some measure of satisfaction when the same voters, at the same time, voted him second best behind Soviet triple jumper Viktor Saneyev as Athlete of the Decade. In spite of missing the first half of the decade, Moses ranked higher than men whose one great season beat him for Athlete of the Year.

Moses's race is surely the most hazardous event in track. A high hurdler runs the same danger of hitting a hurdle with subsequent disaster, but an intermediate hurdler has the added peril of fatigue changing his leg speed and the length of his step. To maintain 13 steps all the way, as he did, seldom hitting a hurdle after his first two years, requires a control achieved by few athletes in any sport. And to exhibit such consistent control at his speed... Edwin Moses continued to stagger the imagination.

Unlike the coddled prizes of the Eastern Bloc, Moses was on his own. He finally found a generous sponsor for his bare living expenses, and he trained himself, usually all alone on the track. He worked as zealously as a middle distance champion, using his scientific mind to analyze and perfect his technique.

The year 1980 was to be a year of special triumph for Moses. He was the most highly favored of all trackmen for an Olympic victory, and he was ready for another world record. "I know I can do it anytime... When the time comes I'll do it."

Over the winter he ran "a lot of distance work, getting in good background, and I was looking forward to running under 47 seconds."

When the U.S. government decided to boycott the Olympic Games, "I was very disappointed that I wouldn't be going to the Olympics to defend my gold medal." His whole attitude deteriorated. Then, in February, he twisted an ankle stepping off a curb.

"It took quite awhile for me to feel emotionally ready to compete. Physically, too."

He did not race until the Final Olympic Trials, and he lacked confidence. "The only thing I was really concerned about was stepping on

the side of my foot the wrong way and messing up my ankle again...
When you get right down to it, I go into evey race with the same concerns I have had from the beginning: not tripping over a hurdle, getting the proper approach to each hurdle, coming off the hurdles with the proper technique and power."

When he went to his blocks in Eugene for the first heat, "I was nervous." But he ran a comfortable 49.23, and in his semi-final he ran 48.22, good reason to smile.

In the final, "I went out too fast over the first two hurdles and I had to chop my stride to the third or I would have crashed it. I just had to run a very cautious race because it was so wet. I couldn't think about a world record today."

Even so, he pulled away after the fifth hurdle and splashed through rain and puddles to make the phantom Olympic team in 47.90, his ninth race under 48 seconds. Even though it gave him eight of the ten fastest ever, he almost apologized for his time, "I just wanted to win here. There will be chances for the record later in the summer."

After a placid 49.10 at Oslo, Moses became excited about a night meet in Milan on July 3. "I thought about a record before the race.... The big thing, though, was that Harald Schmid was in it, which I didn't expect so early in my European tour. But I always love good competition."

Once again the two best in the world were four lanes apart, but this time Schmid was in lane two. He must have been discouraged to see his rival disappear in the dim light ahead, for Moses reached the fifth hurdle in a sensational 20.9.

Moses finished more than 15 meters ahead in 47.13, a world record by 0.32.

"I feel I'm at only about 70% of my maximum condition. I wasn't tired at the finish." Asked if he put his full effort into the race, he answered, "I can say that I haven't yet."

None of which helped improve Schmid's confidence.

Moses had sober thoughts about the Olympics he would miss. "I am 24 and to have to abandon my Olympic title is sad.... not to be there surely will make me sick."

He won routinely at five more big invitationals, with a best of 48.36, bringing his total to seven victories in 17 days. After a two-week layoff, he won at Rome on August 5. Then he faced another crucial test.

In the ISTAF meet in Berlin's 1936 Olympic Stadium on August

8, Moses felt dizzy and sick. Three years before, at this same meet, he had lost a race, and the man who beat him, Harald Schmid, threatened him again. "I was a little paranoid about meeting Schmid again here in Berlin."

Schmid tried courageously, running close to Moses for 150 meters, but Moses's pressure was relentless and he pulled away rapidly. He beat the discouraged German by well over ten meters in 47.17, only 0.04 from his latest world record. The Berlin crowd was duly impressed.

"I was running cautiously and correctly, but my stride was right on and everything worked out well. I eased up about 15 meters from the end because I just didn't realize how fast the race was. If I had known the time, I certainly could have broken the world record."

As in the first half of July, he competed insatiably, winning eight races in 12 days. He strode across the line at the Weltklasse on August 13 in 47.81 for his 50th consecutive victory, the longest winning streak in running event history.

He completed his 1980 season undefeated in 21 races. He was now the proud possessor of the nine fastest times ever run in the intermediates, as well as 15 of the top 20, 19 of 25, and 29 of the 50 best. His total number under 49 seconds rose to 55, an amazing 38.7% of the total ever run.

And, at last, he received the plaque as *Track & Field News'* Athlete of the Year.

Track fans wondered how well Moses could run 400 meters on the flat, or 800 meters, or the high hurdles. Moses said, "I think I can run right at 44 seconds." Surprisingly, he added, "I think my training is more suited to the 800 than the 400. At least what I've been doing the last four years."

Unfortunately, one of his strongest assets in the intermediates is his lunging 8½-foot stride, and the same overstriding is a drawback on the flat. Therefore, his awesome talent remained concentrated on the intermediates.

He began his 1981 season in poor condition at the Mount San Antonio Relays on April 26. "This was the first set of hurdles I have run all year, including practice."

He trailed Andre Phillips into the stretch. Worried, he ran hard to win by almost three meters in 48.61. "I shouldn't even be out here on the training I'm doing."

Edwin Moses

After two easy victories in 48.65 and 48.29, he said, "My training program hasn't been as intense as in past years. I'm pointing for the meets in late August and early September. I won't really attack the hurdles until then."

Eight days later he surprised himself. In the TAC meet at Sacramento, with the concrete stadium radiating 100-degree heat, he saw Phillips pass him at the eighth hurdle. "I could have run hard from the sixth hurdle but I decided to wait until the homestretch."

He charged down the stretch to win by four meters in 47.59, the sixth fastest race ever run. "I know my best races are a month or two down the line."

He flew to Milan, with fond memories of his world record 47.13. But rain fell as the race started and so he ran only 48.35. Then he began one of the greatest series in the history of track and field.

At Oslo on July 11, Moses won in 47.99, his 14th race under 48 seconds. Three days later, at Lausanne, in balmy evening weather, he came tantalizingly close to his own world record with 47.14. "Had I guessed I was so close to the record, I would have turned on the power after the final hurdle. It's a shame to miss the world record by a hundredth of a second."

Never before had he broken 48 in two consecutive races. He took a month off and returned full of enthusiasm for the Zurich Weltklasse on August 19. Overeager, he missed his step several times, but he managed to run 47.64, the ninth best ever.

Two days later in Berlin's Olympic stadium, Moses won in 47.27, the fourth best of all-time, and his fourth race in a row under 48. He seemed in top condition when he arrived in Rome for the meet of the year, the third World Cup.

"I'm not in the best of shape, as I've been hurt." After the race, he also lamented, "I thought the track was a bit soft, and I brought the wrong pair of glasses. I couldn't quite see the hurdles properly." Another mistake: "I was hoping to break the world record but I went out too fast."

All his misery resulted in a 15-meter gap between him and Olympic champion Volker Beck. His 47.37 was the fifth fastest ever and an amazing five in a row under 48.

He coasted to four peaceful victories, finishing with 14 won and none lost, his fourth straight undefeated season. His remarkable winning streak, not counting heats, rose to 72 races. He ranked No. 1 for the sixth year in a row.

The name of Edwin Moses occupied the top 14 lines on the list of the best intermediate hurdles races of all time. He also owned 18 of the fastest 20, and 28 of the best 33. No other runner has ever been so dominant.

An injury he first felt in the cold Berlin meet of 1981 refused to disappear, and in 1982 he once again began cautiously, waiting for late season races. His absence disappointed his fans throughout the entire American season, and then he caught pneumonia.

"I could have run in the last half of the European season, but that would have stressed my legs and my lungs and maybe hurt me for the future." Withdrawing from the remainder of his races, he smiled bravely. "I think it will be the best thing. I know I can come back stronger and much more."

While Moses was content to rest in 1982 and marry Myrella Bordt, an attractive German fashion designer, Schmid took over the No. 1 ranking and ran 47.48. A concerned Moses now had only the six best times ever run... and new motivation. "I know I have to go into all my races prepared to do even better than ever before."

He began training in November, rebuilding his great strength with two workouts a day, and sometimes three. Slowly, he worked into good shape, his goal the first World Championships at Helsinki.

His first race of 1983, after 20 months, came in the small, open-ended stadium at Modesto on May 14. He called his comeback, "Olympic Games type of pressure. Pressure like that isn't nearly as evident when you are in shape and have been competing all along."

Bothered by a strong wind on the backstretch, Moses ran only 49.02, but he won handily. "It felt like 48.5 in terms of effort."

On May 30, he won an 800 in 1:48.98, and he felt satisfied with 48.43 in the Elliott Memorial. "I think I'm really tuned for the TAC's."

A week later, the TAC championships at Indianapolis were especially important because athletes selected themselves for the World Championships team. Moses won by 12 meters in a trouble-free 47.84. "This was an easy race. I didn't press at all."

He collected five more victories before the Worlds. In a dual meet against East Germany on the New Olympic track at Los Angeles, he beat Volker Beck easily in a relaxed 48.46. In Moses' absence, Beck had taken the 1980 Olympic title. On July 3, in the mountain altitude of Colorado Springs, he won the USOC Sports Festival in 47.98. In

Los Angeles 1984: Moses on the victory stand, with Harris (left) and Schmid.

Europe, he won three unpressed races, and in August he went to Helsinki, keen on becoming the world champion.

In the 1952 Olympic stadium, now with a faster track and high temporary bleachers to hold the enthusiastic overflow crowd of Finnish fans, Moses won his heat in 49.54 and his semi-final in 48.11 from lane 1. He felt confident, in world record condition.

He drew lane 2 for the final and ran smoothly in spite of a loose shoelace. "I couldn't stop and tie it." At the seventh hurdle, he gained a narrow lead over Andre Phillips and then pulled away with awesome, long-striding power, winning in 47.50. Schmid finished second, ten meters behind.

Adding the world championship to his other honors (by a larger margin than in any Olympic race since 1924), he was not completely satisfied. "Nothing was really wrong with this race, but I feel I can just run a better race."

Schmid paid him a great compliment when asked if he felt frustrated by finishing second. "No, because the man is there."

After a 48.48 at the ISTAF meet, Moses tackled the best field ever assembled. Around the speedy track at the Zurich Weltklasse on August 24, his opponents ran faster than four losers ever ran, with a dismayed Schmid fifth in 48.63, behind David Patrick, Andre Phillips, and David Lee. But Moses won by more than five meters in 47.37. He said, "I know I have a world record in my legs."

Four days later, in Cologne, Phillips became a serious threat as the fourth man ever to run under 48 seconds. Edwin felt the pressure from Phillips and he ran too fast at first. Forced to adjust his stride, he ran 47.43, but he won by only three meters. Phillips ran 47.78. They were closing in on him.

Three days later, Moses celebrated his 28th birthday by running at Koblenz for the first time. At 7:05 P.M. in balmy weather, Moses started in lane 5 between Schmid and Phillips. Later, he said, "I didn't feel pressure like I have in other big meets," but he ran as if afraid of his two fast opponents.

He touched down after the fifth hurdle in 20.9 in spite of an adjustment to his stride. Phillips still threatened, but "I felt very strong." Phillips was still there at the seventh hurdle "and that gave me that little extra bit of mental pressure."

He used all his strength and skill to widen the gap back to Phillips and he won by ten meters. Edwin knew his time was good, but "I'm just like everyone else. I see the results when I cross the finish line."

Along with the 24,00 fans, he cheered the result—47.02, his fourth world record. "This is only the second time I have felt this strong... If I hadn't had to adjust early in the race, I might have been able to run 46.80."

After three consecutive races under 48, Moses relaxed for the rest of the season, although he ran 47.93 on the fast track at Rieti. In 1983, he triumphed in all 15 of his finals, became World Champion, recorded an astounding world record, took possession of the nine fastest times ever run, ran his winning streak to 87 finals and finished second to Carl Lewis in the voting for Athlete of the Year.

"Training is going very well," he said early in 1984. "I started training earlier than in past years. I'm even training on weekends."

Moses spent some time studying motion analysis on the screen, eager to learn even more about his form. He liked the idea of changing to 12 steps between hurdles. At the Pepsi meet, he chopped his stride twice on the backstretch in a 48.71 victory. "I almost took 12 steps between hurdles. I've tried it in training, but I didn't feel totally confident to do it in the race. So I cut my stride. I'll stick with thirteen."

In the TAC championships at San Jose he won heats in 49.61 and 48.25, but he withdrew from the final to avoid risks only ten days before the Olympic Trials.

The Trials were held in Los Angeles' 1932 Olympic Coliseum, and the loudest pre-race cheers were for Edwin Moses. After winning his heat in 48.83, he faced his greatest American threat in the semi-final. Danny Harris, an 18-year-old novice from Iowa State, ran faster than did Moses in his breakthrough year, and he wanted to finish ahead of Moses in the semi-final. Harris ran 48.02, a world junior record and faster than all except four other hurdlers in history, but Moses had his pride—and his streak. He stayed ahead in 47.58.

In the final, on June 18, Moses chopped his stride again over the first three hurdles before smoothing his form. He pulled away to win in 47.76, with Harris second in 48.11. "Anything anyone says about pressure in this meet is nothing like being out there."

Many athletes suffer from a psychological condition called "fear of winning." They feel more pressure when they are favored to win, and so they prefer to be underdogs. Opponents of Edwin Moses never feel this condition.

At the Olympics, Moses felt more than the usual pressure of

maintaining the longest winning streak in running history. "I know I certainly feel pressure, maybe more than anyone else. It gets more intense every day. But I know it's going to happen and I just try to relax and go with the flow."

Down on the hot track of the Coliseum, he loafed through his first round on August 3 in 49.33, and yet it was the fastest of the six heats. The next day, he won his semi-final in 48.51, again the best time.

When the huge crowd saw Moses entering the Coliseum on a hot and humid August 5th, they stood and applauded with unusual fervor. Moses showed his nervousness with a false start, blamed on clicking cameras. In an event with so many hazards, this important race could be the one great disaster of his life.

The gun fired again, and Moses started fast, gaining on everybody. With long and sure strides, he pulled away by four meters at the fifth hurdle. He ran powerfully around the curve, but in the homestretch he ran only to win, making certain he avoided disaster. Behind him, Harris outsprinted Schmid as both gained a little, but Moses smiled as he crossed the finish line almost three meters ahead in a comfortable 47.75—Olympic champion again.

"I had a feeling of total, absolute relief at the end... I really appreciated the support of the crowd. They were with me all the way."

Schmid, the last man to beat him, far back in 1977, said, "I don't think I will ever give up. Moses was not as fast today as he had been." Someday, Moses knows, he will lose again—unless he retires first—and the threats are creeping closer.

But in Europe, the fans recognize his superiority. In his first post-Olympic race, the ISTAF meet, 40,000 Berliners cheered him loudest of all before his easy 48.49. At Cologne, on August 26, 50,000 applauded his 47.95 victory.

Three days later at Koblenz, site of his 47.02 a year earlier, he won in 47.32, the sixth best ever. Two days later, on his birthday, he pleased 55,000 spectators at Rome's Golden Gala while beating Schmid by five meters in 48.01.

His usual undefeated year brought his amazing victory streak to 94. His opponents in 1984 ran faster than ever before, ten races between 48.02 and 48.19. But of the 35 races ever run under 48, Moses claimed 30. He had run 19 of the 20 fastest of all time, and, greatest of all, the ten best ever belonged to Edwin Moses.

Nobody in track history has dominated an event as long and as thoroughly as this lean, long-striding hurdler—#1 in all eight years of active competition, undefeated in his last six.

In 1985, an injury to his right knee prevented him from reaching top condition and he did not compete. But he assured his fans and rivals he is not through. He wants to win the 1988 Olympics.

Carl Lewis, winning the Helsinki 100 final, 1983.

CARL LEWIS

Frederick Carlton Lewis was born in Birmingham, Alabama, on July 1, 1961, to parents who were enthusiastic athletes and coaches. (His mother, as Evelyn Lawler, hurdled in the 1951 Pan-American Games.) Bill and Evelyn Lewis founded the Willingboro Track Club in New Jersey and aroused Carl's interest in practice sessions when he was only seven years old. He "did the sprints mostly," and he played soccer and practiced the cello, but he became a long jumper at 13, leaping a promising 18'1".

He improved to 19'11" the next year, and to a remarkable 22'9" in junior high school in 1976. As a high school sophomore in Willingboro, he leaped 23' 10", and he was a good junior with 23'11¼" indoors and 24'10" outdoors. But during the summer, he gave more than a hint of greatness with a 25'9" jump and an unsubstantiated 9.3 for 100 yards.

In 1979, as a powerful 6'2" senior, he won a 60 in 6.37 and matched his best previous indoor jump of 24'7". Two weeks later, he opened a few eyes with 25'5½", second best ever by a prep.

He also sprinted brilliantly, winning his state championship at 100 meters. He ran 9.5 for 100 yards and 20.9 for 200 meters.

Troubled by a bad knee, he conserved himself to such an extent that few people recognized his great ability. "I'm a right-footed jumper, and at the sectionals, the state meet, and everything leading up to that meet, I jumped off my left foot so I could preserve my right leg. I won the state meet and everything else off my left foot."

Then he let himself go, and the world noticed. At an Olympic training camp in Puerto Rico, he jumped 26'2" in an exhibition. On June 9, in the NPI meet in Naperville, Illinois, he sailed 26'6" for a national high school record. Then, in the national AAU championships at Walnut, California, on June 16, he startled the track world.

Lewis first surprised with a wind-aided 26'2½", behind Larry Myricks' 27'2". Then he showed impressive consistency with 26'3¾. He watched 1972 Olympic champion Randy Williams leap 26'5" and he felt disappointed, because only two jumpers qualified for the Pan American Games team and he wanted to go. Lewis had already impressed the experts, but this became a test of character.

His mother says, "He was always a competitor. He didn't like to lose at anything. He still doesn't." And he adds, "Trying to do better is what you live for, what you do sports for."

He sped down the runway, hit the board, and sailed 26'6½". Long jumpers watching him at Walnut, and, indeed, all over the world, felt a tinge of dismay.

Still only 17 years old, he said, "This may sound funny, but my goal is to be the best of all-time."

A week later, under less helpful conditions, he jumped only 24'5" and lost. And at the Pan American Games in Puerto Rico on July 7, he seemed mediocre. His first jump sailed 25'2¼", more than a foot and a half behind the two leaders.

On his last jump, once again, he showed more than great athletic ability. He shot out 26'8", to lose by only two inches. He was the only male high school athlete of 1979 competitive with the world's best in any event, and he ranked #5 in the world.

Lewis entered the University of Houston to be coached by Tom Tellez, an outstanding technician. With such a combination of talent, ambition, and coaching, his future should have been unlimited, but he had one obstacle.

"I have a knee problem and it's on my jumping leg. I injured the knee about seven years ago. I fell down one time and it injured a tendon. Then last spring, right after my high school senior year, I was jumping on a wet board with no spikes, and I reinjured it. I can run sprints all day, but once I start jumping, it starts bothering me. When I got here, we knew there was no way that I could keep jumping the way I was and stay healthy."

Lewis and Tellez tried various techniques and decided upon a variation of the double hitch-kick. "It was kinda tough for me out of high school, jumping as far as I had, to just want to stop and change almost all of the things I was doing in high school. I had to stop—pretty much forget what I had learned and start over. That was very hard."

Because of this retraining, Lewis's early collegiate efforts were less than sensational. Indoors, he won a 60 in 6.20 and long jumped 26'1½", but he was a disappointed third in the TAC championships with 25'9¾", and second to Giralt of Cuba in the Astrodome with a modest (for Carl) 25'8½".

His relative mediocrity continued through most of the indoor NCAA. A doctor lanced a boil on his left thigh on Monday, and then bad weather forced the Houston team to ride a bus to Detroit. "The way I was sitting left me almost paralyzed on my right side. I couldn't move my right arm or leg without throbbing pain, and I had a headache."

He complained to a teammate who was studying chiropractic. "He knocked my back around, and then he cracked it for me. When I woke up Friday morning I felt fine."

After four jumps, he found himself a poor third with a best of only 25'½", but he dug into the same reserve he used in his sensational come-throughs of 1979 and soared 26'4½" to win his first national championship.

Outdoors, Lewis competed well, for a freshman, but disappointing to himself. He alternated between sprinting and jumping, to avoid overworking. At the Jenner Classic in San Jose, he jumped 26'6¼" but lost by one inch. At the Mt. San Antonio Relays, he ran a windy 10.16 but lost by Harvey Glance's 10.07. Even so, "That told me, 'You can be a sprinter.'"

He won at Penn with 25'6¾" and lost to Glance again in Houston. In his conference meet, he won the sprints in 10.24w and 20.68, and at Berkeley on June 1, he won a 100 from undefeated James Sanford and Glance, but his 10.43 failed to impress.

Then, nearing the end of the season, he rocketed to a higher level of excellence.

In the NCAA at Austin on June 5, he began with 25'10¾", approched his best-ever with 26'7¼", then bounded into exciting new territory—a 27'4¾" victory with a barely illegal 2.2mps wind. "It was the first time I've really jumped well this year."

He passed up the TAC meet in favor of the Junior Championships at Knoxville, where he won sprint victories in 10.21 and 20.66.

The ill-fated 1980 Olympic team, not permitted to compete, chose itself at Eugene in late June. Lewis ran well in the cold and wet 100 final, only 0.06 behind winner Stanley Floyd and only 0.02 behind third place, and he made the honorary relay team.

Rain and a strong headwind hampered the long jump qualifying. Lewis jumped only 25'1½", but only three others jumped farther. The rain stopped before the final, on June 25, but a cold wind blew. Lewis watched Larry Myricks dominate the event with a first jump of

26'10½" and three better. Lewis fouled his first attempt, then bounded 26'3½" with the aid of the wind. He fouled twice more before his final jump, a legal 26'1". Still 18 years old, he made the Olympic team in two events.

He went to Europe and lost more 100's to Floyd. He returned to Philadelphia in mid-July, but "hyperenxtended my other knee in the long jump pit. The doctor said I was through for the season, but I came back. I have a chiropractor down here and I went to him six times in eight days, and I saw another doctor three times, and I was running in the swimming pool and I was working out with weights and everything else, and I got my legs back where I could do sprinting."

He returned to Europe in August as a top-notch sprinter. In the Golden Gala at Rome on August 5, he lost again to Floyd, 10.20 to 10.23, but he felt some satisfaction in beating the other two who finished ahead of him in the Final Trials. Three days later, in Berlin, he beat them again, losing only to Floyd, 10.25 to 10.33. He ran 10.23 and another good race, "and then I decided to all it quits because I didn't want to put any strain on the leg."

He ranked #6 in the world in the long jump, and #7 in the 100, excellent achievements for a junior.

Over the fall and winter, Lewis lifted weights conscientiously, gaining ten pounds of valuable muscle. "I feel I can go a long way. I have to learn technique and do things right. I'm going to establish myself a lot more this year than last year."

But during the early indoor season of 1981 he failed to please himself. After winning the 60 at Philadelphia in 6.17, he jumped a poor 25'11¾" at Los Angeles and lost to Myricks by almost a foot. He felt worse the next night in Dallas, failing to make the final of the 60. And in the Millrose 60, he lost Floyd, 6.21 to 6.15.

Track fans thought of Carl Lewis as a good athlete, but not the great athlete promised by his high school jumping. All such thoughts changed dramatically on the night of February 20 at Fort Worth when his hard work on strength and new techniques finally made him smile.

In the Southwest Conference Championships, he ran his 60 heat in a personal best of 6.12. Too tall to be a great starter, he stumbled in the final, but he surged into the lead near the end. His 6.06 missed Floyd's world record by only 0.02.

In his first long jump, he shot out 27'1½", third best on the all-time indoor list. "It was one of those days when everything was clicking. Coach Tellez told me I was out just a little bit too much, so I moved up on the next jump and my steps were right on. Once I hit the board, I knew it was a good jump."

Good, indeed! He leaped 27'10¼", more than four inches beyond Myrick's world indoor record. The 19-year-old "great prospect" became great for any age.

Tellez said, "People just didn't believe in Carl Lewis. I think they will now."

The TAC meet for the national indoor championships pitted Lewis against Myricks, but a short runway in New York all but ruined the contest. Myricks jumped 26'8¼" on his second and fouled five others. Jumping miserably, Lewis fouled, leaped only 25'3", quit in the middle of his third, fouled again, and jumped only 25'8". He seemed less than a superman after all.

But once again, he proved his competitive fire on his final jump, soaring 26'6¼". He lost by two inches, but he proved he could compete with anyone.

He practiced a short run-up, 118 feet instead of 134, for the NCAA in Detroit. "I've been looking foward to it all season." But he fouled his first two jumps and carefully cleared 25'8" to qualify. Then he ran his first heat in the 60 and his next jumped was aborted to 22'5¼". This was not what he wanted.

He gathered everything together and almost sailed over the whole pit, 27'10", one centimeter from his own world record. He prepared to break it on his last attempt, but he heard the call for his next heat of the 60. "I kind of rushed the jump and it hurt me a little bit." He jumped 27'2½", giving him 50% of the eight longest jumps in indoor history.

He won his quarter-final heat in 6.17 and his semi in 6.21. In the final, he started poorly. "I tried to stay relaxed and just keep working." He gained steadily on Georgia's Mel Lattany and nipped him at the tape in 6.16 for his fifth NCAA victory in a year and a half.

But being on top is hazardous. Five days later, he lost a close 10.1 100 to Jeff Phillips of Tennessee. Troubled by a sore leg, Lewis ran only in relays until the Penn Relays at the end of April, where he won at 26'9". Then, anxious to test himself in the long jump, he travelled to UCLA for the Pepsi meet on May 10.

His first jump carried 27'5½", and he felt great. His second was even better, but he fouled. Bothered by an erratic wind, he fouled his next two. Then he decided "to settle down and relax on my last two jumps and just jump."

His fifth jump sent him into the sand at 27'9½" and moved him to fourth place on the all-time list. Not content, and he proved himself once again as a sixth-jump competitor. He sped smoothly along the green runway, hit the white board, hitch-kicked twice, high in the air, and his body fell sideways after his feet landed. His distance: 28'3¾", second only to Bob Beamon's miraculous 29'2½" at high altitude. But the bad news came with a wind reading of 2.02, barely above the legal limit.

On May 16, in his conference meet in Dallas, Carl completed his progression into the ranks of the super athletes. He warmed up with an impressive anchor leg in the 4 x 100 relay. Then he took his marks in the 100 and started fast. "It was the best start I ever had. I knew I couldn't slack off. I had to go for it."

He went for it all the way through the tape, and his reward was 10.00, only 0.05 behind the world record. More significantly, no wind aided him and no other runner ever ran so fast except at high altitude. Some experts called it the best 100 ever run.

In this meet, so important to his team, Lewis had no time to rest on his laurels. He long jumped only once, but his now-commonplace 27'¾" gave him the best 100 and long jump double of all time. He finished his day with his first 200 of the year, a 20.73 victory.

The next week at the Tom Black Classic, he beat Phillips in 10.13 after stumbling again at the start, and he felt ready for a difficult double in the NCAA.

A hard rain in Baton Rouge flooded the NCAA long jump pit and so they all moved into the large field house. "I wasn't happy moving inside, because the pit wasn't as good as the outdoor pit."

He hoped to win on his first jump, but he cleared only 26'1". "I came up short." His second jump soared 27'¾", and he passed. "I wanted to try and rest for the 100, because I knew it would be demanding."

He went outside, where the rain had stopped, and ran the 100 against Phillips and Lattany. Nobody had won the 100 and long jump since Owens in 1936, and Lewis's chances looked bad at the start. Lattany rocketed out of the blocks while Carl started poorly.

Phillips charged into the lead, but Lewis's smooth drive caught him at 85 meters. Lewis moved ahead, but he leaned too soon and almost lost. The 2.6mps wind voided his 99.99. "At the end, I knew it was fast because I could feel the strain."

After a quick trip to Italy for a 10.13 victory, Lewis arrived in

Sacramento for the TAC championships. Temperatures over 100 degrees left the stadium hot even during the evening when Lewis qualified for the final. He fouled his first qualifying jump, when put a little of the Lewis determination into his second attempt.

The flag for an excessive wind of 4.6mps went up, and so did Lewis. He did not land until he reached 28'7¾" and he lost a few inches by dragging one hand. "It felt like a good jump, but it didn't feel like it was that far."

The next evening in the final, his great jump counted for nothing. He still wanted a long one to beat Myricks, who had won all eight of their meetings. On his first jump, he hit the board near the clay and hitched his way 28'3½". With a wind of 0.8, he now owned the second best legal jump in history. "Technically, the jump was better than my big one last night." He nodded solemnly. "Bob Beamon's world record can be broken at sea level."

In the 100, Lewis faced the fastest field ever assembled. The ten finalists averaged 10.10 for their personal records. He was off behind Lattany, but "I had a very good start. Right around the 10 or 15 meter mark I knew I had it."

He trailed for 60 meters, then, he brought a roaring exclamation from the crowd with a surge of speed seldom seen. He sprinted away to a full meter victory over Floyd in 10.13.

He returned his attention to the long jump pit, passing each jump but alert for more if Myricks pulled off a miracle. When Lewis had won by half a foot, few people believed they had seen anyone less than an all-time great.

Yet once again, an old truth surfaced. Athletes in most other events feel more secure than sprinters and long jumpers. The slightest physical ailment, unnoticed in most athletes can slow a sprinter by 1% or 2%. And so close is the competition that 98% is not enough for even the best sprinter. And the extended explosive effort required can so easily result in a diabling injury. The specter of doom always casts its shadow near sprinters.

Lewis began his European tour with uninspiring victories: 26'4¼", 10.4, and 25'9½". He might have been resting, but on July 8 in Milan, his 10.22 last decisively to 10.14's by Sanford and Floyd.

Jarred from complacency, Lewis won at Oslo on July 11. His 10.19 beat Sanford and Olympic champion Alan Wells, but he limped off the track with a cramp in his hamstring.

He returned to competition after three weeks, only to lose in Los

Angeles on August 1. He was left at the start and Sanford ran 10.08. "I wasn't ready. I jumped up and before I realized it, Sanford was way out ahead."

He nursed his sore leg carefully. The World Cup, in early September, loomed as the important meet of 1981. On August 19, Lewis jumped against Myricks in the famous Weltklasse in Zurich. He leaped 27'1¼", 27'11½" into a 2.0 wind, and 27'4¼", the first man ever to better 27 feet three times in a row.

With Myricks beaten, Lewis fouled his last three jumps, two of them close to 28 feet. After his last jump, he grabbed his hamstring and limped off, in the shadow of doom.

Lewis was nominated to run the 100, long jump, and anchor the relay team in the World Cup, but many people close to the scene were uneasy about his condition. Before the long jump, "I had a good warm-up and ran at full speed on the practice track." But he ran through his first attempt and appeared slow and awkward on his next. Even so, he managed 26'9", good enough to win, and he passed his remaining jumps.

In the 100 the same day, he started well and ran with the others for 50 meters, but instead of his marvelous free-flowing finish, his leg began to tighten and he eased off to place last in 10.96.

In spite of his poor record in Europe, he ranked #1 in World Ranking in both the long jump and 100 meters. *Track & Field News* honored him as the US Athlete of the Year.

"I've just turned 20 years old and I still have some maturing to do. I think that after this year I can be ready."

Lewis's first conflict of 1982 came at the Olympic Invitational on January 16. The exasperating buoyancy of the runway in the brand new arena in New Jersey's Meadowlands caused him to foul his first two jumps. "I was chopping my steps all night."

Afraid he would be eliminated from the competition if he fouled his third attempt, he took the advice of his sister Carol (fast becoming one of America's top female long jumpers) to "Just do a pop-up." Cautiously, he chopped his stride and sprang high into the air. "I thought it was a mid-26, but when I saw the judges standing around the pit I figured it was over 27 feet."

Imagine his surprise at his new indoor record of 28'1", the greatest pop-up in history. "I was totally shocked."

People wanted him for meets and promotions, and he traveled

too much. Unfortunately, he missed some school work and became ineligible to compete for Houston. "You have to make time for what you have to do. Maybe it's good I won't have the pressure of competing for the school. I'll just be running for myself, but I'll still train the same way."

Continuing his classes, and training under Tellez, Lewis jumped only 27'1-¾" in a poor pit and lost two sprints because of his mediocre start. His important indoor meet, TAC's championships in New York, began with more low-level results. He fouled twice and needed desperate measures to qualify. He hopped 26'5½" to go into second place. He bounced into the lead with 26'10", but Myricks' fifth round jump sailed 26'10½".

With his new superstar stature in danger, he overwhelmed Myricks once again with a fifth round jump of 28'¾", and he finished with 27'9¼". He took pride in the five longest jumps ever made indoors.

When people praised him as another Jesse Owens, Lewis said, "I just hope I can live up to his name and be a good a person as he was." Then he added shyly, "I'd like to be the first Carl Lewis."

Lewis won the Sullivan Award for 1981 as best amateur athlete in the United States. The prestige of the coveted award takes on new meaning with the latest interpretations of amateurism, and Lewis said, "Between now and next year, I'll be the most valuable athlete in the United States who is not accepting money."

He began his outdoor season with a good 10.16 at Tempe on April 3, and two weeks later at the Jenner meet in San Jose, he wanted to try his first sprint double in open competition. He won an untroubled 100 in 10.13. In the 200, he battled TAC champion Phillips to a dead heat in 20.27. "I've been told I'm a natural for the 200. I may run it two or three times this year. It will just help satisfy my curiosity."

After winning in 10.09 and 10.27, he wanted to begin jumping. "I've underemphasized my sprinting the last couple of weeks to get ready for the long jump." On May 15, he began an exceptional weekend.

At Modesto, his smooth power won the 100 in 10.00 to equal his own low-altitude record. "This 10.00 was a lot easier than my 10.00 at Dallas last year."

At UCLA the next day, Lewis hoped his new 163-foot approach would add distance to his jumps, but he ran too fast on his first and he fouled. On his second, his hand dragged, costing him precious inches, but it measured 28'3", with a wind of only 0.5. He cut his stride to avoid fouling his third, yet he jumped 27'8¾". His fourth sailed 28'3" again, the first time any man bettered 28 feet twice in one day. Running with great speed, he fouled his last two, but his sixth measured 28'10½", with no more than a ½" foul. "The last jump may have been the best jump I've ever had." His eyes twinkled. "Next time I'll have to wear shorter shoes."

His series bettered everything in previous history. "My steps would have been better if I had been able to jump in other meets."

His two 28-footers raised his total to 7—two indoors and two wind-aided. "I want 28 feet to be a typical day."

He won the USTFA meet at 27'6" on a spongy runway. "I never worked so hard for a 27-footer."

The national TAC meet, wasted on Knoxville during the World Fair, drew only about 1000 spectators. Everybody else in the world missed seeing the first two-year, 100-LJ double in 97 years. First, Lewis pulled away from Calvin Smith to win the 100 in 10.11, exceptional time on a slow track, against a headwind of 0.5, and using an upright finish with one hand flung high in triumph. "I would not have been beaten by anyone in world history in the 100 this weekend."

A few minutes later, still happy with his sprinting, he began defense of his long jump title with a foul. Then, jumping against the wind, he soared 27'1¼", 27'10", 27'2¾", and 27'½". He passed after becoming the first man to better 27-feet four times in one day. "I got so pleased with my running this weekend that I didn't think too much about my jumping."

Questioned about his opponents in the world of long jumping, he answered, "Beamon. Only Bob Beamon." Asked why he did not jump at a high altitude in quest of Beamon's record, he said, "I want the record, and I plan to get it, but not at altitude. I don't want that A after the mark."

His stature as a superstar, and perhaps his overconfidence, slipped a little in Durham, NC, against West Germany and Africa. He lost the 100 to Smith, 10.3 to 10.5, wind-aided. "Calvin's a good sprinter. I'm not displeased to run and lose to him."

He met his conqueror again the next week in the dual meet against the USSR at Indianapolis. He barely won, 10.09 to 10.10. According to *Track & Field News* editor Bert Nelson, who adjusts times for wind and altitude, those two times, against a headwind of 1.7 meters per second, were the two best in history.

Carl Lewis

After a 9.9 victory at Port-au-Spain on July 9, Lewis attacked Beamon's record in the USOC Sports Festival at Indianapolis on July 24. "I've been pointing for this meet in the long jump all year."

Without any doubt, Lewis jumped far better than anybody, including Beamon. His first jump fouled by more than an inch and he landed around 29'6". He ran a leg on the relay, then repeated his first foul, almost to the inch. Disgusted with himself, he missed his step on his third and ran through the sand. His fourth will be a legend forever.

He hit the board near the end and soared like no man. People looked at his mark in the sand with disbelief, excited even though the red flag signalled a foul. Competitor Jason Grimes said, "It was definitely 30 feet." Lewis said, "I figured it at 30'2"." The jump was not measured for posterity, even though TAC Rule 36 reads: "The Field Judges shall measure, judge and record each trial of each competitor in all field events."

Lewis walked back and examined the plasticine indicator beyond the board. There was no mark. The official told Lewis his toe had extended over the board by about a quarter of an inch. He said, "As long as you break the plane, it's a foul."

Nothing in the rules supports the official, and so what may have been the single greatest performance in the sport remains nothing more than a small f in the summary. Lewis said, "I'm disappointed, but now I know 30 feet is possible."

For his fifth jump, Lewis found himself in the curious position of jumping almost unbelievable distances without a mark to his credit. He dropped his feet too soon and landed short of his three previous jumps. With a legal aiding wind of 1.0, it measured 28'9", merely the greatest non-altitude jump of all-time. His sixth jump seemed a disappointment—only 28'¾".

After such sensational jumping, the rest of his season was anticlimactic. He won in Los Angeles with a windy 27'10¾", then began a European tour. He beat Smith with 10.25, but Smith jolted him in a 200, 20.35 to 20.49.

In the Weltklasse on August 18, Lewis jumped 28'1¾", his fifth legal outdoor 28-footer and tenth of all kinds. He owned seven of the best eight outdoor marks, including wind-aided, to go with his five best indoors.

In Berlin's ISTAF meet two days later, Lewis started fast in the 100 and led all the way to beat Smith, his only dangerous rival of the year, 10.08 to 10.13. They raced again two days later, in Cologne.

Alongside Smith for 10 meters, Lewis felt pain in his left thigh and slowed, losing with 10.24 to 10.12. "I just don't know how serious it it is."

A month later, he won the 8 Nations meet in 10.32. He ranked best in the world again in both the 100 and long jump and gained his first ranking, #6, in the 200.

Lewis regained his academic eligibility, but he gave up his scholarship. He wanted to compete as an open athlete, even though he continued as a Houston student. Above all, he continued to train under Tellez. "We're very good friends. We haven't finished yet. We still have goal: world records in the 100 and long jump."

Lewis apologized for his 27'4¼" in his first 1983 indoor meet. "The runway was too short." But in his second meet, the Millrose Games on January 28, he showed his awesome talent.

On his first attempt he missed his step and took off half a foot behind the 8-inch board, and yet his jump measured 27'11½". From takeoff to landing, he covered about the same distance as Beamon's record jump. Lewis' next five jumps all bettered 27 feet, with a winning jump of 28' ¼".

A week later in Dallas, he broke the world 60-yard record with 6.02. "My major goal is still to get the outdoor world record in the long jump, but something like this gets me really excited about sprinting, too."

At San Diego on February 18, he sailed past 27 feet four times, with two jumps at 27'9½". The ten best indoor jumps in history were all his.

In the TAC Championships, Lewis started especially well and won the 60 in 6.04. In his brief but brilliant career, he ran three of the six fastest auto times ever recorded. "I've had a chest cold and I didn't feel too strong tonight." He jumped 27'4¾" and passed, becoming the first man in 40 years to win this double.

In his final indoor appearance, he started pooly and could not catch Houston McTear. In the long jump, he leaped past 27 feet only twice out of five trials, but his 27'8¾" bettered every other man in indoor history.

Outdoors, at the Mt. San Antonio Relays in April, Lewis showed his smooth power with a 9.93 100, aided by a wind of only 2.3 mps. He won the Penn Relays 100 in 10.09, then ran 10.06 into a wind of 0.69mps at Houston. "I feel a little ahead of schedule right now, and that's even a little scary. But the Number One ranking is something I don't plan to relinquish without a dogfight." The next day in Columbus, Ohio, he ran 10.26 into a cold wind.

Next week, at Modesto with a friendly legal wind of 1.48. he ran away from Arizona State's Ron Brown in 9.97, second best ever and a new low-altitude record.

A day later, in UCLA's Pepsi meet, he fouled twice and jumped 27'6½", 27'1", 28'1", and 27'1¾"w. His series surpassed everybody else who ever jumped, but to Lewis it seemed almost disappointingly routine.

Lewis wanted his first double sprint victory in open competition at the Jenner Classic in San Jose on May 28. He ran well in the 100, but he failed to catch Brown at the tape, 10.02 to 10.03. "I lost concentration for a moment, and if you let Ron Brown get ahead of you, you don't catch him."

In the 200, Lewis raced neck and neck with Myricks, the world leader, until 30 meters from the line. Lewis won in 20.16, fastest time of the year.

He went to Indianapolis "trying to win all three events" in the TAC Championships, which also served as the all-important trials for the World Championships. In the 100, Brown and Lattany suffered injuries, and Lewis raced past Emmitt King to retain his championship by two feet. A hindering wind of 2.37 slowed his time to 10.27.

In the long jump qualifying, the same day, Lewis jumped 28'7¾" aided by a wind of 3.2. Curious officials measured the jump from his takeoff at 29'3". "I've got an even bigger jump in me for later this weekend."

But he developed sore muscles. "After the first day, I was okay, but the second and third days I was so sore I could barely move. I'd have to go out and start jogging real slow to get the pain out."

On the third day, Lewis wanted to take only one jump, saving himself for the 200. He hit the board well, splashed sand so far out that the crowd roared, and bounded up with his hands high in triumph. His jump measured 28'10¼", another low-altitude record. "It was such a great jump I decided to take another one and try to go over 29 feet."

On his second jump, he soared 28'7", the shortest of his three jumps in the meet. He passed the others, content with his record of nine of the ten longest outdoor jumps ever made. Counting wind-aided and indoor jumps, he now owned 15 of the 18 jumps over 28 feet.

Heats in the 200 showed exciting times because of the fast track, the wide curve, and an aiding wind near the legal limit. Lewis won his semi in 20.15 on the same day as the long jump and 200 finals. In the final he ran with amazing speed around the curve, catching Butler and Myricks before the straight. He pulled away powerfully to lead by three meters.

Near the end, he raised his arms in triumph and coasted across the line, obviously slowing. He failed to take advantage of a lean, and yet his time, 19.75, missed the world record by only 0.03. "I have no regrets about raising my arms near the finish. I figured I was under 20, but had no idea I was running so fast. The feeling I had crossing the finish is one I will carry with me until the day I die."

In a race where seven of the nine finalists set personal records, Lewis was happy with the American record and the fastest low-altitude mark ever run. "Coach Tellez tried to beat me over the head to keep me from running the 200."

In spite of being the first man to win the sprint-jump triple in 97 years, Lewis decided not to run the 200 at Helsinki in the World Championships. "I would have to compete on each of the seven days. The 200 is the last event and the hardest event and I would have to run four rounds in it."

Questioned about his success, Lewis praised his coach. "Tellez is the best in the world." Plus: "I'm a very hard worker. I've always been that way. I think it showed in the 200. A lot of people think it all comes naturally, that I don't train hard. But I do. I work very hard."

After a relaxed 20.27 before the World Championships, Lewis entered Helsinki's 1952 Olympic stadium on August 7 and won heats in 10.34 and 10.20. "The 100 concerns me the most of the three events. It's the most demanding because of the four rounds, and it's also my most nerve-wracking event."

The next day, Lewis won his semi-final easily in 10.28, then waited two hours for the final. His nerves received no help from a bee which buzzed around his face when he took his blocks. He slapped at the bee and stood up. A false start delayed them again.

At the gun, Lewis leaped from his blocks, then stumbled and lost a meter to King. He could not gain, and Smith was inching ahead of him. At 70 meters, Lewis accelerated with beautifully smooth power and moved past to win by more than four feet in 10.07. His finishing speed amazed track experts. 'I think I ran as good a race as I have ever run. I just tried to stay relaxed."

The first track man to win a World Championship, Lewis felt

quietly happy on the victory stand between Smith and King, watching the three American Flags rise high above the rim of the stadium and listening to his national anthem. "I believed in three medals for the USA because we are the best runners in the world."

The next morning, Lewis ran anchor on the 400 meter relay team's heat victory in 38.75, impressive for four sprinters competing together for the first time.

In the afternoon, he qualified with one jump of 27'5½", his first attempt since his great TAC jumping. "I have confidence in my technique. I have confidence in my coaching. I have confidence in my condition. So I don't need to compete a lot."

Even so, he had problems in the finals the next day. Frustrated because he was scheduled to jump and run the relay at 6:50 pm, he pleaded with officials for several minutes before they allowed him to jump later. Relieved, he anchored the relay team in the semis 38.50 after some ragged baton passing.

He felt the pressure of the relay final at 8:45, and so he was anxious to win the long jump in a hurry. Grimes led the 11 other jumpers with 27'2½", and Lewis wanted 28 feet on his first jump. He watched with interest as Mary Decker won the 3000, then he began his deceptively fast run.

His foot hit the red runway several inches beyond his last checkmark and so he shortened his last four strides, hitting the board where he wanted. He bounded out of the sand, arms thrown high, and spectators knew his jump was good. It measured 28'¾', enough to win his second World Championship.

He passed his second jump, then casually leaped 27'7½". "I took the second jump just to stay loose. After that, I just wanted to relax and rest for the relay final."

He socialized with the other jumpers, helping Mike Conley complete another medal sweep for the USA. Then he went under the stands and came out again with the relay team.

Standing on the curve before the homestretch, Lewis felt a little tension as he watched King sprint around the first curve. Poor passing was their only real danger. But when Smith slapped the stick into his palm and his fingers close on it, with no other team within his vision, he knew only an injury could beat them. He ran powerfully and broke into a smile before the finish, but he did not throw up his arms until he crossed the line. His anchor 100 was electronically timed in 8.98.

With his third championship in hand, Lewis slowed around the curve and looked up at the electronic clock. "I thought it said 38.8." Disappointed, he looked away. Then, disbelieving, he looked again and saw the world record time of 37.86. He grinned broadly, leaped into the air, and exchanged a series of handslaps and hugs with his teammates. "It was like a dream come true for me, my first world record."

His first official outdoor record, that is. He already owned indoor world records for the 60 and the long jump, and low-altitude records for the 100, 200, and long jump.

At the ISTAF meet on August 17, Lewis beat Smith in a good 100, 10.07 to 10.09. But at Zurich a week later, Smith tied Lewis's low-altitude 100 record of 9.97, then shocked Lewis in the 200, 19.99 to 20.21. Smith said, "I was really warmed up. . . I was really ready, while Lewis had passed the evening sitting in the stands. He didn't run that well."

Undefeated in the long jump since the indoor season of 1981, Lewis ranked as best in the world again. He also repeated #1 honors in the 100 and moved up to #2 behind World Champion Calvin Smith in the 200. "This past year I trained only about three or four months for the 200. . . I will train more."

He wanted to try for four gold medals in the Olympics. "If I can deal with the World Championships, I can deal with any meet. If I feel good and I'm 100% healthy, it's something I want to do, and I'll do it."

For the second year in a row, Lewis won the vote as Athlete of the Year, and his greatest problem became the shrill demand on his time. "Every single Olympic sponsor has called up wanting me to attend their banquet or function. Fund raisers for all kinds of things call. Joe Douglas constantly gets calls for advertising and commercial deals. At least ten foreign countries have called wanting me for an Athlete of the Year banquet or award ceremony. . . There is just no way I can attend."

Reluctantly, he cut out most contact with the press and television. This drew the ire of the media, with a predictable loss in popularity for Carl. But he wanted four gold medals in the Olympics above all else. "To me, the Olympics was my whole life and no one in the world could ruin that party."

In Japan for his first indoor meet, he lost at 60 meters. "It's the beginning of the season and I'm not as sharp as I could be."

Unfortunately, he proved himself right in the Millrose long jump. He opened with only 22'2½", 26'11¼", and 26'10½". "I expected to

The Los Angeles 200, 1984.

jump well tonight. On Tuesday, I had the best long jump workout of my life. I'm eight pounds lighter than I was last year, and that was helped me a lot. I'm stronger than I was in the past, too."

Leading the competition, he passed his fourth jump, but Myricks excited the crowd with 27'3¼". Lewis came back with 27'2¾", half an inch short. Then Myricks jumped 27'6". In danger of ending his three-year winning streak, Lewis consulted Tellez. "He said I was too close to the board, and told me to move the start of my run back a foot and run all-out."

With his superstar status threatened, he raced along the runway and hit the board close to a foul. "When a long jumper gets a good one, he knows it right away. You can feel it. As soon as I left the board I knew it was at least 28-6."

He flew 28'10¼", more than nine inches beyond his own indoor record and equal to his best outdoor jump. In addition to proving his condition, he once again proved his remarkable competitive ability. "Being able to come from behind is as important as winning."

He proved less than superior in the short sprints. Ron Brown beat Lewis's poor start at Dallas on February 4, 6.06 to 6.07. Two weeks later, in San Diego, Lewis lost two close sprints to Brown, who said, "It's still a long time before the Olympics." And Lewis said, "No one can intimidate me; no one."

In between his sprint losses. Lewis jumped well at the Olympic Invitational on February 11. His series—28'¾", 27'8¼", 27'10¾", pass, 27'1¼, and 27'4¾"—averaged 27'7½" for five jumps, longer than anyone else ever jumped indoors. Elated with his consistency, Lewis said, "This meet will make a difference outdoors."

He jumped in the TAC Indoor Championships in New York on February 24 because he wanted to pass the drug test and prove he avoided such aids. After two fouls, he came within an inch of fouling out, but his jump went 27'9¼", good enough to beat Myricks' best-ever 27'8¼". Lewis then jumped 27'2¾" and 26'8½" before soaring 27'10¾" for his third consecutive indoor championship.

Lewis felt eager to sprint in his first outdoor meet, the Mt. San Antonio Relays on April 28 and 29. He avenged his three indoor losses to Brown by winning the 100, 10.06 to 10.12. He charged from fourth place in the 400 relay and just missed catching Brown, who led from the pass. In a leg of the sprint medley, Lewis chastened Myricks, 19.6 to 19.9.

On May 5, Lewis's low-altitude record was broken by Lattany's

9.96 with a wind of only 0.06. The next day, in Houston, Lewis wanted to regain it with the legal aid of a 1.27 wind, but his time was 9.99, fourth fastest ever at low altitude. Then he ran an interesting relay leg. Starting out in 19.9, he hung on grimly to finish with 46.4. "It proved what kind of condition I'm in."

In the Pepsi meet, he wanted "to jump far." But the footing at the top of the world's pyramid is dangerously thin, especially with Lewis's new attitude. After fouling his first three jumps, he said, "I don't back off on any of my jumps, worrying about fouling or qualifying."

His fourth jump went 27'6½", but he trailed Myricks by 2½". Bearing down, with his competitive desire fully aroused, he shot into the sand at 28'7", calling it "very easy, even if I don't feel in meet condition right now."

In an excellent tune-up at San Jose, Lewis came from behind in the 100 to beat Brown, 10.00 to 10.07, aided by a wind of 2.06. In the 200, with a wind of 2.07, he ran a powerfully smooth 20.01. Barring injuries, he was ready.

Few sprinters hold their best form for more than a year or two. Even fewer rank at the top for more than one year. In 1984, Lewis wanted to be best in the world for the fourth consecutive year, a feat never surpassed. Aside from his quality performances, his durability is remarkable. Still, he entered three events in the Final Trials with most of the best speedsters in the world eager to beat him.

Unfortunately for Lewis's opponents, many of them suffered from some disability. Lattany, Smith, King, and Brown ran slower than their best. "I trained hard for this meet and skipped the TAC meet where everyone was injured. I think I did the right thing."

Beginning the Trials in the huge Los Angeles Coliseum, Lewis won two heats, in 10.29 and 10.14. In his semi-final the next day, he breezed in 10.15, excellent time against a wind of 2.1. His obviously great condition eased some of his tension, but his real test was yet to come. "You feel like your whole life is at stake, and it is, because you have put out your whole life for this one chance."

In the final, the same day, he started well, and at 40 meters he led all except NCAA champion Sam Graddy. He turned his head toward Graddy and accelerated, gaining two meters in the next 50. Elated, he threw his arms high, depriving himself of a few hundredths. Even so, he won by five feet in 10.06, great time against a wind of 2.2mps.

On the Olympic team in his most treacherous event plus the 400 meter relay, Lewis returned to the Coliseum on the third day for qualifying in the long jump. Unpredictable winds swirled around the runway, hindering all the jumpers, and Lewis needed a second jump to qualify with 27'6½", a foot and a half farther than Myricks.

On the morning of the fourth day, Lewis coasted through a heat of the 200 in 20.53. Two hours later, with six hours of welcome rest ahead of him, he unleashed his power in the quarter-finals. His 19.84, with a wind of only 0.2, beat all but three other times in history and was second best ever at low altitude.

In the long jump finals that evening, he jumped last, with Myricks' 27'¾" to beat. Carefully, Lewis observed the wind, anxious to win with his first jump. He hit the board and blasted through the air 28'7". More than successful, he leaped high with joy. He ran through on his second jump and then passed.

After a day of rest, he won his 200 semi-final in 20.09, now ordinary time for him but ninth best ever at low altitude.

Barring injury, nothing could block him from a fourth Olympic event, but he took no chances. He ran the curve hard in the final and led into the stretch. Only another Houston-trained runner, Kirk Baptiste, could stay close as Lewis powered smoothly down the red track. He won in 19.86 against a wind of 0.2, fifth best ever. He felt the pride of owning the three fastest low-altitude times in history. "I'm still a novice in the 200. The only thing holding back better times were the winds."

Halfway toward his goal, he said, "I'm happy because my whole year was geared to the Olympic Trials and the Olympic Games. It feels good to be able to say that the only thing I'm shooting for is the Games."

His only pre-Olympic competition came at Sacramento on July 21, where the cold wind limited him to a single jump of 28'1". On August 3, he felt the excitement of the first day of Olympic track competition. Beautifully relaxed in the first 100 heat, before the largest morning crowd in history, he loafed home in 10.32. "It felt great to be out there this morning. I practically walked through the whole race."

Later in the morning, he won his quarter-final in 10.04, best Olympic time ever at a low altitude. The next afternoon, he won his semi-final in 10.14, fine time against a wind of 1.5mps.

Favored in the final that evening. Lewis feared all of the dangers of the 100, and his first fear materialized in a mediocre start. Graddy led, and Lewis trailed badly for half the race. Then, over the last quarter, he accelerated with a startling burst of speed, probably faster than anybody ever ran, to win by more than two meters. His 9.99 with a wind of only 0.2 after a slow start compares well with any race ever run.

Sighing with relief over his first Olympic gold medal, Lewis said, "As far as I'm concerned, it's 60% over. When you compete in four events it's like going up a hill. Now that I've won the 100, I feel like I'm going down."

On the third day, Lewis tackled the comfortable task of qualifying in the long jump. He took care of that easily, his 27'2¾" sailing 11 inches farther than any of the others.

He felt more anxious on the fourth day, August 6, because he faced two heats of the 200 and the long jump finals. In mid-morning, he smiled about an easy 21.02 heat, and around noon he won his quarter-final in 20.48, saving himself for later.

The long jump runway lay in the evening shade when he took his first jump in the final. He hit the board a few inches from the end and shot into the sand at 28'¼", good enough to win by almost a foot.

He stepped over the line on his second attempt, and then, with the temperature dropping and the 200 and relay still to run, he passed. This so annoyed the ignorant crowd that they booed him on the victory stand. "I was shocked at first, but after I thought about it, I realized they were booing because they wanted to see more of Carl Lewis. I guess that's flattering."

After a welcome day of rest, Lewis returned on August 8 to win his 200 semi-final in 20.27. Hours later, he lined up in lane 7 for the final. Knowing Baptiste could run faster than most men in history, Lewis left nothing to doubt. He ran the curve as it has seldom been run. The Swiss timer caught him in 10.23, astounding for 100 meters around a turn. He led by two meters and even after his all-out curve, he held on to his lead over Baptiste as both gained on the others.

Lewis's triumph in 19.80 into a wind of 0.9 at sea level is surely the best 200 ever run. Now holder of the four best low-altitude marks of all time, he jogged a victory lap with the other American medalists, Baptiste and Thomas Jefferson. "We really celebrated our sweep of the race. It was great to jog around with two other guys and not just by myself."

With three Olympic gold medals to go with his three World Championship golds, Lewis rested on August 9 before beginning the relay. In their heat, the four Americans handled the baton carefully in 38.89, and in the semi-final the next day, they ran 38.44, still cautiously below their best.

In the final, there were a few minor problems. Graddy led off and he could not keep up with Canadian Ben Johnson on the curve even though he beat him in the 100 final. Next a mediocre pass left Brown behind. With his condition still in doubt, USA fans held their breaths, fearing an upset. But Brown showed his class with a burst which pulled them even, and, for once, an American team gained on the pass.

Smith sprinted into the turn with a slight lead and handed the baton safely to Lewis with more than three meters of breathing space. Lewis needed none, but he wanted the world record and he started 0.01 behind his Helsinki world record of a year before. He ran with all his relaxed power and leaned at the line to slice off a few more hundredths. His sizzling final 100 in 8.94 brought their time down to 37.83, the only track and field world record set at the 1984 Olympics.

"The world record at Helsinki last August was important because it was my first one, but being able to do this at the Olympic Games in front of American fans is ten times better."

Lewis toured Europe after the Olympics, competing every other day. At London on August 18, he ran too enthusiastically in the middle 100 of a 300-meter race and tied up, finishing fourth while Baptiste broke the all-time record. At Budapest, he won the 100 in 10.05. At Zurich he won in 9.99 with a wind of 0.9. At Brussels, he jumped 27'8¼" and 26'9¼". Then he passed, but Myricks, who had fouled twice, came through with 27'8¾". Lewis put his heart into it then, jumping 28'4½", 27'10¼", and 28'2¼". In Cologne for the last of his series, Lewis won the 200 in 20.21 and excited the crowd by coming from behind in a close relay. He closed his great year after a few weeks at home with a 10.13 victory in Tokyo.

Lewis was named Male Athlete of 1984 by several different international groups, he began acting lessons, sang for a recording, and his manager considered all sorts of offers, but Lewis was not distracted from his main goal. "I didn't have a personal record last year. I didn't concentrate on records. Winning the event was the entire emphasis." He wanted to change all that in 1985.

Indoors, he won the Millrose long jump at 27'10¾", and won short sprints in 6.10 and 6.15. In his first outdoor meet, he beat Baptiste, 10.05 to 10.17, remarkable time for March. Five weeks later, in the Mt.

Carl Lewis

SAC Relays, he jumped the gun once and started poorly yet ran 9.90 with a wind of 2.5mps. Then he ran a 400-meter relay leg in 45.4. At Modesto on May 11, he came from four feet behind to win in 9.98, and he appeared ready for another great year.

At UCLA for the Pepsi meet on May 18, he set out to break Beamon's record. Such is his reputation that his first jump of 27'10" caused disappointment. Eight minutes later, he jumped with an aiding wind of 2.4 mps and he soared 28'7¾", equal to the fifth longest jump in history. A strong cross wind aided him at 3.86 mps on his third jump after another 8-minute wait, and he shot out 28'9¼", fourth longest ever. His 28'7¾" thus became the longest non-winning jump of all time. He aborted his fourth jump, stepping down at 23'6", and he limped out of the pit with an injury at the base of his right hamstring, the beginning of a nightmare of losses.

At the TAC meet a month later, his 10.34 failed to qualify for the final, and he withdrew from six weeks of competition.

On August 9, in an all-comers at Houston, he ran a wind-aided 20.3 and he had high hopes for his European tour. But at Zurich on August 21, he ran only 10.31 for fourth place. Two days later, in Berlin, he ran 20.69 for another fourth place. "I feel like I'm in a twilight zone." At Cologne, on August 25, he improved to 10.27 and second place. "My legs are coming back. I was really going at the end."

Finally, at Brussels on August 30, he won the 100 from Baptiste in 10.24. In the long jump, he trailed Myricks until his fifth jump soared 28'3½". "My 100 race was fine, but above all I regained my good timing in the long jump. It has been a long time since I had such a good feeling."

Even with his injury, he won his fifth consecutive No. 1 rankings in the long jump and in the 100 (fortunately no sprinter with enough consistency emerged to challenge him). Only injury, the dark threat to every sprinter, knocked him off his pedestal. "Everybody thinks it comes easily for me. Nothing could be farther from the truth."

Lewis's remarkable career (at the end of 1985) includes 28 of the 33 jumps in history over 28 feet. Eliminating wind and altitude, he jumped 22 of the best 25, including the best 11.

The world's greatest sprinters ran under 10-flat nine times with automatic timing through 1984. Of the seven run at low altitude, Lewis ran five. On Bert Nelson's all-time list, adjusted for wind and altitude, Lewis owns five of the 10 fastest. Add his outstanding record of running the four fastest low-altitude 200's in history and you have the fastest sprinter of all-time to go along with the best long jumper. For added glory, he ran on two world record relay teams and holds the indoor records for 60 meters and the long jump.

Add his superior competitive record—seven gold medals in the Olympics and World Championships plus ranking as best in the world 11 times—and he had solid credits toward the title, Greatest Of All Time.

PROFILES OF OTHER TRACK & FIELD CHAMPIONS

KEY TO THE SYMBOLS

Each athlete's major honors are listed on the same line as his name, using the following symbols:

G   = A gold medal in the Olympics or World Championships ("2G" means two gold medals, etc.)
S   = A silver medal.
B   = A bronze medal.
r   = Indicates the medal was for a relay or team race.
WR = A World Record, outdoors, as approved by the International Amateur Athletic Federation or by the Association of Track & Field Statisticians which recognizes World Records in performances overlooked by or preceding the IAAF. Includes the marathon, but not relay records.
AOY = Selected as World Athlete of the Year by *Track & Field News*, 1963-85, or by Cordner Nelson, 1947-62 (see explanation and AOY list at end of this supplement). If a number precedes AOY it indicates the number of years the athlete was named AOY, 1947-85.
*   = An asterisk after "No. 1" or "AOY" indicates that, in the author's opinion, the athlete would have been No. 1 in an event or Athlete of the Year, prior to 1947 (before the *T&FN* or Cordner Nelson rankings).
** = Two asterisks after "No. 1" or "AOY" indicate the author believes the athlete would have been ranked No. 1 or Athlete of the Year several (undetermined) times, prior to 1947.

The second line indicates event(s), years of major competition, date of birth, height/weight, where known.

AKII-BUA, JOHN (Uganda) . . . . G, WR, 2 No. 1
    400 Hurdles, 1970-76. . . . . .12/3/48, 6-2/170

Akii-Bua burst into prominence in 1971 after running only 51.0 in 1970. He lost only once in 1971 and ranked No. 3 in the world with a best of 49.0. He won the 1972 Olympic 400 hurdles with a startling World Record of 47.82. He ranked No. 1 again in 1973, but he had to escape his native Uganda to save his life and his career suffered. He ranked No. 2 in 1975, but the African boycott kept him out of the 1976 Olympics.

ANDERSSON, ARNE (Sweden)..............4WR, 2 No.1*
  Mile, 1939-45.............10/27/17, 6-0/154

In 1939, at the age of 21, Andersson ran 3:48.8, only a second slower than the 1500 record, but then he ran in the shadow of Gunder Hagg. He lost half a dozen races through 1941. In 1942, he tied the World Record for the mile but lost to Hagg, he broke the 2-mile record while losing, and he broke the 2000 record behind Hagg. In a mile without Hagg, he tied Hagg's world record of 4:06.2.

In 1943, with Hagg competing in America, Andersson lowered the 1500 record to 3:45.0 and the mile to 4:02.6. In 1944, he defeated Hagg in 3:48.8, then ran the fastest-ever ¾ mile—2:56.6. Hagg beat him with a record 3:43.0, then Andersson won a slower race. Next in this greatest of all racing duels, Andersson beat Hagg in 4:01.6 and said, "If ever we could get together and help each other, the four-minute mile would be ours for the asking." He beat Hagg again in a slow Swedish Championships race to remain No. 1 miler for the second year. He beat Hagg later in a 2000 and a 3000. The climax of the great series came at Malmo on July 17, 1945, the greatest mile ever run. Side by side into the stretch, Hagg beat Andersson in 4:01.3, a record which lasted 9 years. Neither runner ran so well again, although Andersson ran 3:45.0 and 4:03.8. Both were suspended from amateur competition after 1945.

AOUITA, SAID (Morocco)...............G, B, 2 WR, 3 No. 1
  800-5000, 1980-.............11/2/60, 5-8¾/128

Aouita began as a promising steeplechaser in 1979 with 8:40.2 at the age of 18. He ran well at cross country in his native Morocco, and yet he proved remarkably fast in 1981 with a 200 in 22.8 and 400 in 46.9.

He ran 1500 meters in 3:37.08 in 1980 when he was only 19, and he was considered a great prospect. But he ran only 3:37.69 in 1981 and 3:37.37 in 1982, and so his 3:38.5 in April of 1983 seemed to be in his usual rut. Only insiders were prepared for his thunderbolt at Florence on June 8.

In the city where he now lived and trained, he finished with 54-flat for an eye-opening 3:32.54. Suddenly, everybody considered him a contender for the World Championships.

He won an 800 in 1:44.38, third best time of the year. Four days later, he placed only 6th in 1:46.33, but on July 17 at Casablanca, he ran 3:35.6. On July 27 he finished with a sizzling 38.8 to win in 3:33.95, making him a serious threat at Helsinki.

Profiles of Other Champions

Running in the green shirt and red pants of Morocco, Aouita qualified easily for the finals on August 14, and he lined up with 11 other finalists for the first big race of his life.

They ran at a friendly warm-up pace, and turning into the homestretch approaching the bell they were cozily bunched within 5 meters of each other.

Then Aouita burst into the lead in front of the covered stands. "I came here to win." He led around to the starting line, completing a sizzling 54.78 lap.

Steve Cram shot past him before the final turn. He followed Cram into the stretch and began to gain, but Steve Scott powered past.

Aouita won the bronze medal ahead of Ovett with 3:42.02. "I made a big tactical mistake by not taking the lead. I've been working on my endurance, not enough on speed. That was my mistake." He also lamented, "I fell into a trap."

He also ran 1000 meters in 2:15.75, third fastest of the year, and in the Golden Gala meet in Rome on September 1, he ran a mile in 3:52.97 for 4th, and he ranked No. 4 in the world in the 1500.

In April, 1984, he suffered an injury which forced him into distance training instead of speed work. His results shocked everybody. After a 3:36.31 on June 3, he ran the 5000 in Florence on June 13. His 13:04.78, second best of all time, proved he had a staggering combina-

Said Aouita

tion of speed and endurance, surely enough to run 1500 meters under 3:30.

On July 6, in Holland, Aouita ran 3:31.54, the third fastest 1500 all-time. On July 10 in Lausanne, Aouita won a 5000 in 13:12.51. He won the 1500 in the African Championships at Rabat on July 15 with a sizzling final 300 in 38.6, and three days later he ran 3:34.82.

Aouita now appeared to have the enviable choice of a gold medal at either distance, but competition in the 5000 was less fierce. Still, Aouita favored the 1500: "I think I might win too easily in the 5000. I love to fight it out on the track."

Finally, he chose the 5000. After an easy heat on August 8 in 13:45.66, he won a semi-final the next day in 13:28.39 and appeared amazingly fresh. In the final, two days later, he followed a swift pace by Antonio Leitao until the final backstretch. Then he sped away with ease to win the gold medal in 13:05.59.

His finishing speed equalled Viren's. He ran his final 400 in 55.0, last 800 in 1:55.2, last 1200 in 2:58.5, and the last four laps in 4:02.3.

His progression to the 5000 in 1984, running the second- and third-best ever and winning the Olympic gold medal most impressively, gave him the greatest combination of speed and endurance in running history. Some experts thought him good enough to win the Olympic 1500, and Aouita said: "It can't be said that [Coe's 3:32.53] would have been enough to beat me."

After the Olympics, Aouita pulled away in the homestretch of the Weltklasse mile to win in 3:49.54. This added the fastest mile of the year to Aouita's collection. Two days later, he won a 7:33.3 3000, the 4th-best ever. He was now the 1984 leader at four distances.

With the speed and endurance to break many records, he said, "The records will come next year."

Even though he did not run the Olympic 1500 he was ranked No. 1 in the event to go with his No. 1 in the 5000.

In 1985, after an easy start, he won a 2000 at Madrid on June 4 in 4:54.98. At Oslo on June 27, he ran 5000 meters in 13:04.52, last 200 in 28.8. At Nice on July 16, poor tactics left him five meters behind Cram in the homestretch of the 1500, but he almost overcame the deficit at the finish, clocking 3:29.71 to Cram's World Record 3:29.67.

Eleven days later in Oslo, Aouita won a hard-fought 5000 from Maree in 13:00.40, breaking the World Record by 0.01.

Profiles of Other Champions

After a rest, Aouita tried to break Cram's new mile record at Zurich on August 21, and his 3:46.92 missed by only 0.60. Undaunted, he came back two days later in Berlin to shatter Cram's 1500 record with 3:29.46. On August 30 in Brussels, Aouita won a 3000 in 7:32.94, only 0.84 from the world record. At Rieti on September 4, he ran 2000 meters in 4:54.02, 4th best ever.

ASHENFELTER, HORACE (USA)................G, WR, No. 1
    Steeplechase, 1952-56 ....1/23/23, 5-10/145

Ashenfelter won the 1952 Olympic steeplechase in 8:45.2, fastest ever run to that point.

ATTLESEY, DICK (USA)............... 2WR, 2 No. 1, 1/3 AOY
    110 Hurdles, 1950-52..........5/10/29, 6-3½/178

Attlesey ran the first 13.5 120y hurdles, at Fresno on May 13, 1950. He won the 1950 AAU in 13.6. On July 10, 1950, he ran the 110m hurdles in 13.5 at Helsinki. He ran 13.6 twice in 1951, giving him five of the six fastest ever run. He died on October 14, 1984, of leukemia.

AVILOV, NIKOLAY (Soviet Union).............G, B, WR, No. 1
    Decathlon, 1970-1980 ....8/6/48, 6-3/181

After ranking No. 6 in the world for 1970 and going unranked in 1971 with a best of 8096, Avilov exploded at the 1972 Olympic Games to win with a World Record total of 8454. He ranked No. 3 in 1975 and won the bronze medal at Montreal in 1976. He still scored 8062 in 1980.

BACON, CHARLES (USA)................... G, 2 WR, No. 1*
    400 Hurdles, 1908............1/9/85, 6-1/150

Bacon won the 1908 Olympic 400 hurdles in world record time of 55.9.

BANKS, WILLIE (USA)......................S, WR, 3 No. 1
    Triple Jump, 1975- 3/11/56, 6-3/170

Banks won the 1980 Olympic Trials, ranked No. 1 in the world for 1981, placed 2nd in the 1983 World Championships and 6th in the 1984 Olympics. On June 8, 1985, he triple jumped 57-11¾ at Los

Angeles, the longest low-altitude jump ever. Eight days later, he won his fourth TAC championship with a World Record 58-11½. By the end of 1985, he owned 5 of the 11 longest non-altitude jumps ever.

BANNISTER, ROGER (Great Britain) . . . . 2 WR, 2 No. 1
Mile, 1950-54 . . . . .3/23/29, 6-1½/154

Bannister ran few races, preferring to point for the important occasion while doing his medical studies. He was No. 1 in the 1951 World Rankings, at the age of 22, with a best mile of 4:07.8 in the AAA. Favored in the 1952 Olympic 1500, he ran only once before the Games. Lack of experience plus three races in three days relegated him to 4th. In 1953, he ran 4:03.6 and 4:02.0 and won the AAA in 4:05.2 to rank No. 3 in the world.

On May 6, 1954, on the Iffley Road track at Oxford, he became history's first sub-4:00 miler with a 3:59.4. He won the AAA in 4:07.6. He defeated Landy at the Empire Games in 3:58.8 in the so-called "Miracle Mile." He won the 1954 European Championships 1500 in 3:43.8.

Roger Bannister, the first sub-4 mile

Profiles of Other Champions

BARNES, LEE (USA) . . . . G, WR, 2 No. 1*
    Pole Vault, 1924-28 . . . . .7/16/06, 5-8/150

Barnes won the Olympic pole vault in 1924 before his 18th birthday and vaulted 12-11½ again in the 1928 Olympics for 5th. On April 28, 1928, he set a World Record of 14-1¾.

BAUSCH, JIM (USA) . . . . G, WR, No. 1*
    Decathlon, 1930-32 . . . . .3/29/06, 6-1/200

Bausch won the 1932 Olympic decathlon with a new World Record. He won the 1931 AAU pentathlon and the 1932 decathlon.

BAYI, FILBERT (Tanzania) . . . . S, 2 WR
    800-Steeplechase, 1972-80 . . . . . .6/23/53, 6/130

In 1974, at the age of 20, Bayi won the Commonwealth Games 1500 with a World Record 3:32.2. In 1975, he ranked No. 2 for the third consecutive year and broke the World Record in the mile with 3:51.0. Suffering from periodic bouts of malaria, he ran with less success for three years, then apparently retired. But in 1980, he came back in his original event, the steeplechase, and placed second in the Olympics with 8:12.48. He also ran 3000 meters in 7:39.27 and 5000 in 13:18.2.

BEAMON, BOB (USA) . . . . G, WR, No. 1, AOY
    Long Jump, 1965-69 . . . . .8/29/46, 6-2/155

Beamon long jumped 25-3½ in 1965 and set a national high school record of 50-3¾ in the triple jump. The next year, at 19, he improved to 25-7 and 50-8 and placed 4th and 9th in the AAU.

In 1967, he won the indoor AAU long jump at 26-11½. Outdoors, he was 3rd in the AAU and 2nd in the Pan American Games, with 26-5¾. He jumped a wind-aided 26-8.

Indoors in 1968, he showed it was only a matter of time until he became the longest jumper in history. He won the NAIA with a World Indoor Record of 27-1. He won the AAU at 26-11½ again (plus 52-7 for third in the triple jump). He won both events in the NCAA— 52-3 in the triple jump, lengthening the long jump indoor record.

Outdoors, he jumped a windy 27-4, won the AAU at 27-4, and leaped 27-6½ with a 3.2mps wind in the Final Olympic Trials.

At the Olympic Games, with the aid of Mexico City's high altitude,

Bob Beamon
THE jump

he was expected to better 28 feet. After nearly fouling out in the qualifying round, he put everything together in his first jump of the final.

A 9.5 sprinter and 6-5 high jumper, he hit the board exactly right without chopping his stride. His technique was his ultimate. The wind behind him was a helpful 2.0 mps. The altitude aided him by many inches. He landing was excellent, with his legs extended, and yet he shot across his feet and bounced twice without stopping.

His distance was 29-2½, probably the greatest single performance in the history of track and field.

Seemingly unable to compete against his own greatness, he ranked No. 4 in 1969 with a best of 26-11. In 1970 his best was 25-11½. After not jumping for two years, he turned pro in 1973 and jumped 26-9¼ indoors.

BECCALI, LUIGI (Italy) . . . . .G, B, WR, 2 No. 1*
    1500 1931-38. . . . . .11/19/07, 5-6½/139

    Beccali won the 1932 Olympic 1500 and was third in 1936. He set a World Record of 3:49.0 in 1933 and won the European Championships in 1934.

BEDFORD, DAVE (Great Britian) . . . . .WR, No. 1
    Distances, 1970-73 . . . . .12/30/49, 6-0/140

    Bedford ranked No. 1 in the 10,000 at the age of 20. In 1971, he

Profiles of Other Champions

set European Records for 3 miles, 5000, 6 miles, and 10,000, ranking No. 3 in the 5000 and No. 5 in the 10,000. After a poor Olympics, he returned in 1973 with a World Record 27:30.8 in the 10,000.

BERRUTI, LIVIO (Italy) .... G, =WR, 2 No. 1
  Sprints, 1959-68 .... .5/19/39, 5-10¾/145

Berruti won the 1960 Olympic 200 in a World Record Equalling 20.5. He placed 5th in 1964 and competed in 1968. He ran 10.2 when the World Record was 10.1.

BEYER, UDO (East Germany). . . . . G, B, 2 WR, 7 No. 1
  Shot Put, 1973-. 8/9/55, 6-4¾/265

Beyer put the shot 64-5¾ in 1973 while still 17 years old. He put 66-3¼ in 1974 and ranked No. 7 in the world the next year with a best of 68-9½. He won the 1976 Olympic championship and the next year he began a 6-year streak of ranking No. 1 in the world each year. He set a World Record of 72-8 in 1978, won the World Cup three times and the European Championships twice, and he won 34 consecutive meets until his surprising 3rd place in the 1980 Olympic Games. He raised his World Record to 72-10¾ in 1983 but his No. 1 streak ended because an injury held him to 6th in the World Championships. He ranked No. 1 again in 1984, bettering 70-0 in all his meets.

BIKILA, ABEBE (Ethiopia) .... .2 G, 2 WR, 3 No. 1
  Marathon, 1960-68 .... .8/7/32, 5-9¾/134

Bikila had no record of note before 1960. He had won two marathons (2:21:23 PR), but he had lost shorter trials. At Rome, running barefoot on the stones of the Appian Way, he pulled away at the end to win the Olympic marathon in a fastest-ever 2:15.17.

He won the 1961 Kosice Marathon in 2:20:12 and other marathons, but lost a 10,000 to Wolde at Berlin in 1962, where he ran 29:00.8 in his first race on a track.

In 1963, he led the Boston Marathon for 20 miles, but a leg cramp dropped him to 5th place at the end, his first loss in a marathon. In August 1964, he ran 2:16 in training, but in September, 40 days before the Olympic marathon, he had an appendectomy. Thus, he was not favored to win at Tokyo, in fact, no Olympic marathoner had ever won twice.

Running in shoes this time, he moved to the front at 20,000 meters in a swift 1:00:58 and pulled away. He won by over four minutes in 2:12:12, fastest marathon ever run. He appeared fresh and said, "I could run another ten kilometers." Ron Clarke said, "That was the greatest performance ever in track and field."

At the age of 36 in 1968, Bikila felt ready for his third Olympic championship as a high altitude runner, but he was forced to drop out with an incipient fracture of his left fibula. Early in 1969 he was partially paralyzed in an auto accident. He died in 1973 at age 42 from the effects of a stroke.

BOIT, MIKE (Kenya)........................... B, No. 1
   800-Mile, 1971-85............1/1/49, 5-10¾/150

A 1:47.5 runner in 1971, Boit won the bronze medal in the 1972 Olympic 800 and placed 4th in the 1500. For six years, through 1978, he averaged No. 3 in world ranking in the 800, with a No. 1 in 1975 when he ran 1:43.79, only 0.09 from the World Record. Politicians boycotted him out of two Olympic Games, and he let down in 1979 and 1980, but the next year he came back to rank No. 3 in both distances. As a born-again miler, he ran 3:49.74 and 3:49.45 while losing to Coe. He slowed after 1981, yet he ran a 3:52.72 mile in 1983 at the age of 34. He clocked a 3:33.91 1500 in 1985, his final year of top-level racing.

BOLOTNIKOV, PYOTR (Soviet Union) .... G, B, 2 WR, 3 No. 1
   Distances, 1955-64 ....3/8/30, 5-8/139

Bolotnikov placed 9th in the 1956 Olympic 5000 and 16th in the 10,000. He won the 1960 Olympic 10,000. On October 15, 1960, in Kiev, he broke the World Record with 28:18.8. On August 11, 1962, he lowered his own record to 28:18.2. A month later he won the 10,000 in the European Championships and placed 3rd in the 5000. He was No. 1 in the world rankings in 1959, 1960, and 1962. He finished 25th in the 1964 Olympic 10,000.

BONDARCHUK, ANATOLIY (Soviet Union) ... G, B, 2 WR, 3 No. 1
   Hammer, 1967-76...........5/31/40, 6/245

A 232-0 thrower in 1968, ranking No. 8 in the world, Bondarchuk whirled to No. 1 in 1969 with a World Record 245-0 in the European Championships and an improvement to 247-7 in his last meet. He lost his record and No. 1 in 1971, but he came back in 1972 as the unde-

Profiles of Other Champions

feated Olympic champion. His 248-11 was second-longest ever. Again No. 1 in 1973, he fell behind but managed a bronze medal in the 1976 Olympics. He now coaches the greatest hammer throwers.

BORZOV, VALERIY (Soviet Union) . . . . 2G, Sr, B, Br, 3 No. 1
    Sprints, 1968-76 . . . . .10/20/49, 5-11¾/174

Borzov set a European Record of 10.2 in 1969 and ranked No. 5. He improved to No. 2 in 1970. He won every race at both distances in 1971, including two European championships, but he ranked only No. 2 in the 200. He continued undefeated in 1972, winning both Olympic gold medals, equalling his European Record 10.0 twice, and he ranked No. 1 in both sprints. He all but disappeared in 1973, although he ran 20.6, but he won the European Championships 100 in 1974 to rank No. 5. He ranked No. 3 in 1975 and 1976, winning the bronze medal in the Olympic 100.

BOSTON, RALPH (USA) . . . . .G, S, B, 5WR, 8 No. 1, AOY
    Long Jump, 1959-69 . . . . .5/9/39, 6-1½/164

In 1959, Boston had a best long jump of 25-3 and placed 3rd in the NCAA and 4th in the AAU. One year later he had improved only 4¼ inches and placed 6th in the AAU, although he won the NCAA and NAIA.

Suddenly he turned into a great jumper. His winning 26-6¼ at the Final Olympic Trials was wind-aided, but he had a legal 26-4¼. On August 12, at Walnut, California, he broke Owens' 25-year-old record by leaping 26-11¼. He won the Olympic championship at 26-7¾.

In 1961 he set an indoor record of 26-6¼ in the AAU. Outdoors, he was undefeated until injured in September. He raised his World Record to 27-½ at Modesto, California, May 27. He jumped 27-¼ at Albuquerque, New Mexico, June 17. He won the AAU at 26-11¼. He broke his record with 27-2 against the Soviets at Moscow and was voted Athlete of the Year at season's end.

In 1962 he was undefeated outdoors. He won the AAU at 26-6 and jumped a windy 26-9 against the Soviet Union. In 1963, his best jump, 27-2¾, was wind-aided and lost to Phil Shinnick's 27-4. He won the AAU at 26-10 and the Russian dual meet at 26-10½. His best legal jump was 26-11¾.

In 1964 he jumped 27-2½ at Modesto, won the AAU at 26-7½, and cleared a windy 27-5½ in the semi-final Olympic Trials. He jumped

Track's Greatest Champions

Ralph Boston

27-3¼ on August 11. In the Final Trials at Los Angeles, September 12, he regained the World Record from Igor Ter-Ovanesyan with 27-4¼, but his winning jump was a wind-aided 27-10¼.

Rain and win held him to 26-4¼ in the Olympics at Tokyo and he lost to Lynn Davies.

In 1965, he lost only in his first meet. He cleared a windy 27-2 in Madrid. He raised his World Record to 27-4¾ at Modesto, May 29. He won the AAU at 26-3½.

In 1966 he had an ankle injury. He lost twice and had best jumps of 26-10 at Mexico City and a windy 27-0. He won the AAU at 26-3.

In 1967 he barely lost his AAU title, after winning six years in a row. He lost three other meets, but he jumped 27 feet in five meets, including 27-2½ in the Pan American Games, and he was No. 1 in the world rankings for the eighth consecutive year.

Profiles of Other Champions

In 1968 he started poorly, with a floating cartilage in his knee. He was second in the AAU at 26-7¾ and reached a windy 27-1 at the Final Trials. At Flagstaff, Arizona, a high-altitude site, he jumped a windy 27-5½. In the qualifying round at Mexico City he set an Olympic record of 27-1½.

In the final, his first jump of 26-9½ was good for 3rd place. On his fifth jump, he had a hairline foul close to 28 feet.

Boston was talented in several other events. In the high hurdles, he was undefeated in 1961 with a best time of 13.7, and he ranked No. 5 in the world. In 1965 he won the indoor AAU high hurdles. In the low hurdles, he ran 22.4 in 1960 and a windy 22.2 in 1961.

He high jumped 6-9 in 1960, placed 4th in the 1963 Pan American Games at 6-8¼, and cleared 7-0 in practice. In the triple jump, he led the U.S. list in 1963 with 51-8½ and jumped 52-1½ after the 1964 Olympics. In his 1961 conference meet, he won the javelin at 185 feet and vaulted 13 feet.

BOUIN, JEAN (France) . . . . S, 4 WR, No. 1*
    Distances, 1911-13 . . . . .12/28/88

Bouin set World Records for one hour in 1911 and 1913 (11 miles, 1,412 yards); he lowered the 10,000 record to 30:58.8 in 1911. In the 1912 Olympics he set a World Record in the heat of the 5000 and barely lost in the final.

BRAGG, DON (USA). . . . . G, WR, 2 No. 1
    Pole Vault, 1955-60. . . . . .5/15/35, 6-3/197

Bragg set a World Record of 15-9¼ in 1960 with a steel pole. He set an Olympic Record of 15-5. He set an indoor record of 15-9¾ in 1959. He won the 1955 NCAA and the 1959 AAU. He ranked No. 1 in the world in 1959 and 1960.

BUBKA, SERGEY (Soviet Union) . . . . G, 6 WR, 3 No. 1
    Pole Vault, 1982- 12/4/63, 6-0/165

Bubka vaulted 18-2½ in 1982 at the age of 18. At 19, he cleared 18-9¼ and won the World Championships at 18-8¼. Indoors in 1984, barely 20 years old, he raised the World Record three times, eventually to 19-1½. Outdoors, he improved the World Record four times, to 19-2¼ on May 26, 19-3½ on June 2, 19-4½ on July 13, and 19-5¾ on August 31.

Track's Greatest Champions

Sergey Bubka

Bubka lost several times in 1985, but on July 13 in Paris, he cleared an historic 6 meters (19-8¼). Three days later, in Nice, he cleared 19-6¼. He closed his season with 19-plus wins in the European Cup, Grand Prix final and World Cup, giving him nine 19+ meets on the year.

BUDD, FRANK (USA). . . . . 2 WR, No. 1
    Sprints, 1960-62 . . . . 9/20/39, 5-10/168

Budd ran the first official 9.2 in the 1961 AAU and tied the 220 straightaway record of 20 flat in 1962.

BURGHLEY, DAVID (Great Britain) . . . . G, S, Sr, WR, No. 1*
    Hurdles, 1927-32. . . . . 2/9/05

Lord Burghley set a World Record of 54.2 for the 440y hurdles in 1927. He won the 1928 Olympic 400 hurdles. He was 4th in the 1932 Olympics in 52.2 and placed 5th in the 110 hurdles. He won a silver medal in the 4 x 400 meter relay.

CALHOUN, LEE (USA). . . . . 2 G, WR, No. 1
    110 Hurdles, 1956-60. . . . . .2/23/33, 6-1/165

Calhoun is the only man ever to win two Olympic high hurdles titles. In 1946 he lowered his best time from 14.4 to 13.5. He won the indoor AAU, the NAIA, the NCAA, and the AAU before his narrow 13.5 victory over Jack Davis at Melbourne.

He repeated his four national championships in 1957. In 1958 he was suspended for being married on television and receiving wedding gifts. In 1959 he won his third AAU title.

Profiles of Other Champions

He won the 1960 Final Trials in 13.4. At Bern, Switzerland, on August 21, he tied the world record of 13.2. He won his second Olympic gold medal in 13.8.

CAMERON, BERT (Jamaica) . . . . .G, 2 No. 1
    400, 1979- 11/16/59, 6-2/174

Cameron ran 45.97 in 1979 before attending UTEP, where he won three NCAA championships. He won the Commonwealth Games in 1982 and the World Championships in 1983. An injury prevented him from qualifying for the semis in the 1980 Olympics, and in 1984 a muscle cramp cost him 10 meters although he recovered to run a sensational 45.10. He had to withdraw from the final. He ranked No. 1 in 1982 and 1983, and No. 2 in 1981 although he ran his fastest ever time of 44.58.

CAMPBELL, MILT (USA) . . . . .G, S, WR, 4 No. 1
    110 Hurdles, Decathlon, 1952-57 . .12/9/33, 6-3/208

Campbell placed second in the 1952 Olympic decathlon at the age of 18. He won the 120y hurdles in the 1955 NCAA and AAU and set a World Record of 13.4y in 1957. He won the 1956 Olympic decathlon.

CARLOS, JOHN (USA) . . . . B, 2 WR, 4 No. 1
    Sprints, 1967-70 . . . . .6/5/45, 6-4/198

Carlos won the Pan-American Games 200 in 1967 with 20.5. In 1968, he broke the World Record with 19.7 (19.92 auto) in the Final Trials at Lake Tahoe, then placed 3rd in the Olympics. In 1969 and 1970, he ranked No. 1 in both sprints, undefeated in the 200. He tied the WR of 9.1 for 100 yards in 1969 and equalled the indoor 60 yard record. He turned professional in 1970.

CARLTON, JAMES (Australia) . . . . WR
    Sprints, 1931-32 . . . . .2/10/08

Carlton ran an unofficial 9.4 in 1931. Later, in New Zealand, he won a double victory over George Simpson. On January 16, 1932, he ran 220 yards around a curve in 20.6, a mark that was unbeaten for 28 years. He retired to the priesthood before the Olympics.

Track's Greatest Champions

Lee Calhoun

Henry Carr

Profiles of Other Champions

CARR, BILL (USA). . . . . G, Gr, WR, No. 1*
  400, 1932 . . . . .10/24/09, 5-9/155

With a previous best 440 of 48.4, Carr defeated World Record holder Eastman (46.4) in 47.0 for the IC4A title. He beat Eastman again in the AAU with 46.9 for 400 meters. He won the Olympic championship in 46.2, a World Record, then anchored the World Record relay team. His career ended with a traffic accident.

CARR, HENRY (USA). . . . . G, Gr, 2 WR, 2 No. 1
  200-400, 1962-64 . . . . .11/27/42, 6-3/185

Only a 9.4 man for 100 yards, Carr ran 20.1 for a straightaway 220 and set a World Record 20.3 for 220 yards around a turn in 1963. He ran eight other races between 20.4 and 20.8. In 1964 he lowered his record to 20.2 and won the Olympic championship in 20.3. He anchored the U.S.'s gold medal 4 x 400 meter relay team. He ran 45.4 for 400 meters and won two AAU furlong titles.

CARR, SABIN (USA) . . . . G, WR, No. 1'
  Pole Vault, 1927-28. . . . . .9/4/04, 6-1/168

Carr became the first amateur to vault 14 feet in 1927. In 1928, he vaulted 14-1 indoors and won the Olympic championship.

CAWLEY, WARREN (Rex) (USA). . . . . G, WR, 2 No. 1
  400 Hurdles, 1959-65. . . . . .7/6/40, 6-0/165

As a high school boy, Cawley became the first hurdler ever to place in all three events in an AAU meet. He was 5th in the 120y hurdles, 3rd in the 220y lows, and 6th in the 440y hurdles in 1959. He ran the 110 hurdles in 13.9 that summer in Europe.

In 1960, he ran 50.6 for the 400 hurdles, placing 7th in the Final Trials. In 1961, ranked No. 4 in the world with 49.9; he also ran a 46.2 440 and 22.5 for the low hurdles before an injury forced him out. Injuries hobbled him again in 1962, but he moved up to No. 3 with a best of 50.6 for the 440 hurdles.

In 1963, he became No. 1 in the world with 49.6 to win the NCAA 440 hurdles. He also won the AAU title and placed 2nd in the NCAA 440 with 46 flat.

In 1964, he set a World Record of 49.1 in the Final Trials and won the Olympic championship in 49.6.

CIERPINSKI, WALDEMAR (East Germany) . . . . 2 G, B, 2 No. 1
    Marathon, 1976-83 . . . . .8/3/50, 5-7/130

Like Lasse Viren, Cierpinski boosted himself to superior efforts in Olympic years. In 1976, he emerged from obscurity to win at Montreal in 2:09:55. He was unheard from again in 1977, tried in 1978 but placed 4th in the European Championships, then disappeared in 1979. In 1980, he came back to win Olympic gold in 2:11:03. He ran well in the World Championships, placing 3rd in 2:10:37. The boycott kept him out of the 1984 Games.

*Ron Clarke,
the first sub-28 10K*

Profiles of Other Champions

CLARKE, RON (Australia) . . . . B, 18 WR, 7 No. 1
Distances, 1963-70 . . . . .2/21/37, 6-0/163

Clarke set a World Junior Record of 4:06.8 for the mile in 1956. After carrying the Olympic torch into the stadium at Melbourne, he ran 4:07.2 early in 1957 and retired.

He began training again in 1961 at the age of 24. On December 18, 1963, in Melbourne, he broke the World Records for 6 miles (27:16.6) and 10,000 meters (28:15.6).

In the 1964 Olympic Games, he led in the homestretch of the 10,000 but finished 3rd. In the 5000, he wore himself out with repeated surging and placed 9th. He ran the marathon in 2:20:26.8 for another 9th place.

On December 3, he broke the World Record for 3 miles (13:07.6), and on January 16, 1965, he lowered the 5000 meter record to 13:34.8. He took another 1.2 seconds off that record 16 days later in Auckland, New Zealand. He went on to run an astounding number of fast distance races.

On March 3, in Melbourne, he set a 10-mile World Record of 47:12.8. On June 4 in Los Angeles, he lowered his 3-mile record to two World Records in the same race—3000 in 7:51.0 and 2 miles in 8:24.8—though he lost the race and the records to Michel Jazy.

After losing a 3000 and two 5000s, he ran 3 miles in 12:52.4 at London, July 10. Four days later, at Oslo, he lowered the 6-mile and 10,000 record to almost unbelievable times of 26:47.0 and 27:39.4.

At Geelong, Australia, on October 27, he broke the World Records for 20,000 meters (59:22.8) and one hour (12 miles, 1006 yards).

In 1966 he made fast runs commonplace. On July 5, in Stockholm, he lowered the 3-mile record to 12:50.4 and his 5000-meter record to 13:16.6. In the Commonwealth Games he lost the 6-mile to Naftali Temu and the 3-mile to Kip Keino, even though he ran 12:59.2. He dropped out of the marathon after 19 miles.

In 1967, tired of losing to faster finishers, he improved his speed. He lowered the 2-mile World Record to 8:19.8 at Vasteras, Sweden, on June 27. His only loss of the year was to Keino in Los Angeles when he was injured. He won the British AAA 3-mile for the third straight year under 13 minutes. Two days later, he ran 12:50.0 to give him 7 of the 9 times ever run under 13 minutes.

In 1968, he took an 0.2 off his 2-mile World Record in London, August 24, and ran under 13:40 for 5000 meters on 9 occasions, but he lost 5 races before the Olympics. He could not cope with Mexico City's high altitude and placed 6th in the 10,000 and 5th in the 5000. He announced his retirement, but he ran well enough in early 1969 to set an indoor 3-mile record of 13:12.6 at Oakland, California.

Outdoors, he ranked No. 1 at both the 5000 and 10,000. In 1970, he placed 5th in the Commonwealth Games 5000 and 2nd in the 10,000.

Clarke broke World Records 18 times. He ranked No. 1 in the world for 5000 meters in 1967, 1968, and 1969, and for 10,000 meters in 1963, 1965, 1968, and 1969.

COCHRAN, ROY (USA) . . . . G, Gr, WR, No. 1
    400 Hurdles, 1939-48. . . . . .1/6/19, 5-10/155

A 23.1 220y low hurdler in 1939, Cochran won the AAU 440 hurdles in 51.9 as a novice. On April 25, 1942, at Des Moines, Iowa, he set a World 440 hurdle Record of 52.2. After the war, he ran 46.7 for third in the 1946 AAU 400 meters. He won the 1948 Olympics 400 hurdles in 51.1, a time bettered only by Glenn Hardin. He won a 2nd gold medal in the 4 x 400 relay.

COE, SEBASTIAN (Great Britain) . . . 2 G, 2 S, 8 WR, 5 No. 1, 2 AOY
    800-Mile, 1977- 9/29/56, 5-9¾/119

See chapter.

COGHLAN, EAMONN (Ireland) .G, No. 1
    1500-5000, 1974- 11/21/52, 5-8¾/139

Coghlan placed fourth in the 1976 Olympic 1500. In 1978, he ranked No. 2 and placed 2nd in the European Championships 1500. In 1980, he placed 4th in the Olympic 5000. He ranked No. 1 in the 5000 in 1981, won the World Cup, and set an indoor 1500 record of 3:35.6. In 1983, he set an indoor mile record of 3:49.78 and won the 5000 at the World Championships. He was injured in 1984.

CONNOLLY, HAROLD (USA) . . . . .G, 7 WR, 2 No. 1
    Hammer, 1953-69 . . . . .8/1/31, 6-0/220

Connolly won the 1956 Olympic hammer throw with an Olympic record of 207-3. He competed in three more Olympics, placing 8th in 1960 and 6th in 1964.

Profiles of Other Champions

He raised the World Record to 220-10 and 224-10 in 1956, to 225-4 in 1958, to 230-9 in 1960, to 231-10 in 1962 and to 233-2 and 233-9 in 1965, when he had to his credit seven of the eight longest throws ever made.

In World Ranking, he was No. 1 twice, No. 2 six times, and No. 3 three times. He won the AAU hammer nine years. He set a best-ever record with the 35 pound weight in the 1960 indoor AAU and won the title twice more.

CONSOLINI, ADOLFO (Italy) . . . . G, S, 2 WR, 4 No. 1
    Discus, 1938-60 . . . . .1/5/17, 5-11/220

Consolini placed 5th in the discus in the 1938 European Championships at the age of 21 and 17th in the 1960 Olympic Games at the age of 43. In between, he missed two Olympics because of war, won in 1948, was 2nd in 1952, and 6th in 1956. He won European Championships in 1946, 1950, and 1954. He set a World Record of 175 feet on October 26, 1941. He lost it in 1946 but regained it with 181-6 at Milan, October 10, 1948. His lifetime best, a European Record, was 186-11 in December, 1955, at the age of nearly 39.

COURTNEY, TOM (USA) . . . . G, WR, 2 No. 1
    400-800, 1955-58 . . . . .8/17/33, 6-2/180

Courtney won the 1956 Olympic championship at 800 meters. On May 24, 1956, in Los Angeles, he lowered the 880 World Record to 1:46.8. On August 9 in Oslo, he ran 800 meters in 1:45.8, 0.1 slower than the World Record. After the 1957 season he had five of the eight fastest 800s ever run. He was No. 1 in the World Rankings in 1956 and No. 2 in 1957 and 1958. He won the NCAA in 1955 and the AAU in 1957 and 1958. In the 400 meters, he ran 45.8 to win the 1956 AAU and ranked No. 1 in the world in 1957.

COVA, ALBERTO (Italy). . . . . .2 G, No. 1
    Distances, 1981- 12/1/58, 5-9¼/128

After a promising 13:27.20 5000 at the age of 22, Cova won the 1982 European Championships 10,000 in 27:41.03. In 1983, he ran 27:37.59 and won the World Championships. He won the 1984 Olympic 10,000 and ran 13:18.24 for 5000 meters.

In 1985, he ran 13:10.06 behind Aouita's World Record. He won the 5000 and 10,000 in the European Cup.

Track's Greatest Champions

Steve Cram

Joaquim Cruz

Profiles of Other Champions

CRAIG, RALPH (USA) . . . . 2 G, 2 WR, No. 1**
    Sprints, 1910-12 . . . . .6/21/89, 6-0/170

Craig twice equalled the 220 World Record of 21.2 in 1910 and 1911, also winning three IC4A sprints. In the 1912 Olympics, he won both sprints.

CRAM, STEVE (Great Britain) . . . . G, S, 3 No. 1
    800-1500, 1978- 10/14/60, 6-1¾/148

At the end of a long schoolboy career, Cram ran a 3:57.4 mile in 1978 while still 17 years old. He ran in the Olympic final in 1980, and in 1981 he ran a 3:49.95 mile. In 1982, he won the European Championships and Commonwealth Games at 1500 meters to rank No. 1 and ran the year's fastest 800 and 1000. He ranked No. 1 again in 1983, the undefeated World Champion. His 1:43.61 was the fastest 800 of the year and his 7:38.31 was second best 3000. He placed 2nd in the 1984 Olympic 1500 at the end of an injury-plagued season.

In 1985, Cram became one of the great runners of history. After losing a slow 800 to Coe in June, Cram raced Said Aouita over 1500 meters at Nice on July 16. Cram's superior tactics left Aouita more than 5 meters behind into the stretch. Cram held on to win by a foot in World Record time of 3:29.67. Eleven days later, in Oslo, Cram finished powerfully to break the mile record with 3:46.32. On August 4 in Budapest, running 10 seconds ahead of his competition, he broke John Walker's World Record of 4:51.4 for 2000 meters with a 4:51.39. Five days later, in cold, windy weather at Gateshead, Cram's 1000 meters in 2:12.85 missed Sebastian Coe's World Record by only 0.67. He won the European Cup 1500 on August 17 and on August 21 he outkicked Olympic champion Joaquim Cruz in a 1:42.88 800. Then a training injury on August 25 ended his great season.

CRUZ, JOAQUIM (Brazil) . . . . G, B, 2 No. 1
    800-Mile, 1981- 3/12/63, 6-2/170

Cruz began running at 11 when Luiz de Oliveira saw his great potential during a basketball game, and at 14, he ran 1500 meters in a sensational 4:02.3. The next year he ran 800 meters in 1:51.0. At 16, his 1:49.8 and 3:54.2 were much better than Ovett or Coe ran at the same age, and his 47-flat 400 promised great times ahead. In 1980, at 17, he won the Pan-American Junior Championships in 1:47.85 and 3:49.96, and he also ran 3:47.3.

In 1981, Cruz became more than a great prospect. First he ran a sensational 1:44.3, a World Junior Record. Then, in Venezuela for the selection of the World Cup team to represent the Americas, he defeated Alberto Juantorena, 1:46.24 to 1:47.72. In the World Cup at Rome, after an ankle injury, Cruz placed only 6th with 1:47.77.

In September, he moved to the United States to attend BYU, but a foot injury and subsequent surgery stopped him for five months. In 1982 he and his coach moved to Eugene and Cruz spent most of his effort learning English.

Competing for Oregon, he ran 1:45.37 in May and won the NCAA Championships with 1:44.91. He ran 1:44.8 in the Brazilian Championships but lost, and he lost twice more even though he ran under 1:45 three more times with a best of 1:44.04, plus a Collegiate Record 1000 in 2:15.28.

In the World Championships at Helsinki, Cruz led to the homestretch, then finished 3rd with 1:44.27. More than a promising 20-year-old, Cruz ranked No. 3 for the year.

In 1984, he began an interesting move into the 1500. Setting American collegiate dual meet records, he lowered his PR to 3:39.4, 3:38.43 and 3:37.72 before racing Steve Scott on May 13. He barely lost, running 3:53.0 in his first mile race ever.

In the NCAA, he ran all four days to win the 800 in 1:45.10 and the 1500 in 3:36.48. Then, preparing for the Olympic Games, he lowered his Collegiate Record for 1000 meters to 2:14.54.

The Olympic 800 required 4 races in 4 days, and Cruz ran 1:45.66, 1:44.84, and 1:43.82 before the finals. In the final, he pulled away from World Record holder Sebastian Coe in the homestretch to win in 1:43.00, a remarkable time after such fast heats.

He rested three days, then won his heat of the 1500 in 3:41.01. Many experts now picked him to win the gold medal, but he became ill and withdrew from the semi-finals.

Soon after the Olympics, he went to Europe. At Nice on August 20, he won the 1000 in 2:14.09, the 4th-fastest ever run. Only two days later, he followed a 49.8 pace and finished with 1:42.34. Two days later, at Brussels, Cruz ran 1:42.41, 4th-fastest ever.

Again with only one day of rest, Cruz then showed great power to finish in 1:41.77, only 0.04 behind Coe's World Record. In five days of sensational running, the Olympic champion ran three of the five fastest times ever recorded. He now owned four of the top six times. He retired for the year, ranked No. 1 at the age of 21.

Profiles of Other Champions

In his first 1500 of 1985, his 3:37.34 looked easy in beating Scott, and he beat him again in the Pepsi meet and in Eugene. He lost a tactical 800 to Johnny Gray at Jenner.

Out of action in July, his 1:43.23 lost to Cram on August 21, but he ran 1:42.98 two days later, and on August 25, he beat Coe in 1:42.54. Three days later, he edged Gray in 1:42.49, his sixth time under 1:43.

CSERMAK, JOZSEF (Hungary)....................G, WR
   Hammer, 1952-60...........2/14/32, 5-7/198

Csermak won the hammer in the 1952 Olympics with a World Record 197-11 at the age of 20. He threw 205-4 in 1956 and placed 5th in the Olympics. His best throw was 210-8 in 1960, but he failed to qualify for the final in the Olympics.

CUNNINGHAM, GLENN (USA)....................S, 2 WR
   800-Mile, 1932-40...........8/4/09, 5-9¾/165

Cunningham was 4th in the Olympic 1500 in 1932 and 2nd in 1936. He set a mile World Record of 4:06.7 in 1934 and an 800 meter record of 1:49.7 in 1936. He won six AAU championships.

DANIELSEN, EGIL (Norway)..................G, WR, No. 1
   Javelin, 1955-58............11/9/33, 5-11½/185

Undefeated in 1956, Danielsen won the Olympic javelin with a World Record 281-2. He ranked No. 2 in the world for the next two years and placed 2nd in the 1958 European Championships.

da SILVA, ADHEMAR FERREIRA (Brazil).....2 G, 4 WR, 5 No. 1
   Triple Jump, 1948-60..........9/29/27, 5-9¾/152

After an 11th place in the 1948 Olympics, da Silva triple jumped 52-6 on December 3, 1950 in Sao Paulo to equal the World Record. On September 30, 1951, he took sole possession of the record with 52-6¼. In the 1952 Olympics, he won the championship with a World Record 53-2½. He lost the record in 1953, but in the Pan-American Games, at Mexico City, March 16, 1955, he leaped 54-4 to regain the World Record. In the 1956 Olympics, he won again with 53-7¾. He jumped 53-3¾ in 1958, but he placed only 14th in the 1960 Olympics. He was undefeated from 1951 through 1956.

DAVENPORT, WILLIE (USA) . . . . G, B, 2 WR, 5 No. 1
    110 Hurdles, 1963-77. . . . . .6/28/43, 6-1¼/185

Davenport surprised in 1964 by making the U.S. Olympic team. Injuries eliminated him in Tokyo, but he was No. 1 in the World Rankings for the next four years. He won the AAU 120y hurdles three years, but injuries forced him out in 1968. He came back on August 31 at Knoxville, Tennessee, to equal the 110 hurdles World Record of 13.2. He won the Final Trials in 13.4. He won the Olympic title in 13.33. In 1969, he set several indoor records, and tied for first in the AAU. Outdoors, he tied the World Record of 13.2 and ranked No. 1 the fifth year in a row. He placed 4th in the 1972 Olympic Games and won the bronze medal in 1976. In 1977 he slipped to No. 6 in the world and retired. He competed in bobsled racing in the 1980 Winter Olympics.

DAVIS, GLENN (USA) . . . . .2 G, Gr, 6 WR, 4 No. 1, AOY
    400, 400 Hurdles, 1956-60 . . . . . .9/12/34, 6-0/165
    See chapter.

DAVIS, HAL (USA). . . . . 2 WR, 5 No. 1*
    Sprints, 1940-43 . . . . .1/5/21, 5-10/160

In his first year out of high school, Davis won both AAU sprints in 10.3 and 20.4, each only 0.1 off the World Record. The next year, 1941, he tied the World Record of 10.2 in the Compton 100 meters, but a poor start cost him his AAU title in the 100, his only loss of the year. He won the 200 in 20.4. He was undefeated in 1942, winning doubles in both the NCAA and AAU. He tied the World 100 yard Record of 9.4. In 1943, he won doubles again in both meets, including a wind-aided 20.2 in the AAU. He also ran a wind-aided 220 in 20.2. World War II ended his triumphs and cancelled two Olympic Games where he would have been favored for sprint doubles. He was undefeated after his high school years in the furlong, and he lost only three 100s during those 4 years (only one important race).

DAVIS, JACK (USA). . . . . 2 S, WR, 3 No. 1
    110 Hurdles, 1951-56. . . . . .9/11/30, 6-3/155

Davis won the NCAA high hurdles all three years, adding 3rd place in the 1951 lows, 2nd in the 1952 200 meters flat, and won the 1953 lows. In AAU meets, he was 2nd in the highs in 1951 and won the lows.

Profiles of Other Champions

In 1952, he was 2nd to Harrison Dillard in the highs. In 1953 and 1954 he won both hurdles. False starts eliminated him in the 1955 AAU and he placed only 3rd after a World Record 13.4 in his 1956 heat. He barely lost in both the 1952 and 1956 Olympic 110 hurdles. He ran 13.4 twice and 13.5 twice, giving him four of the six fastest times ever run. He ran 13.6 seven times, 13.7 nine times, 13.8 fifteen times, and 13.9 seventeen times. He once won 37 consecutive high hurdle finals, including all in 1953 and 1954.

DAVIS, OTIS (USA) . . . . .G, Gr, WR
400, 1959-61 . . . . .7/12/32, 6-1/164

Davis ran his first good 440 in 1959 at the age of 26. That 46.2 was improved to a 45.6 400 in 1960. He won in the Olympics with a World Record 44.9 (45.07). He anchored the relay team for another gold medal. His only AAU victory, in 1961, ended his brief career.

DAVIS, WALT (Buddy) (USA) . . . . G, WR, 2 No. 1
High Jump, 1950-53 . . . . .1/5/31, 6-8/210

Buddy Davis was crippled by infantile paralysis as a boy but became an All-American in basketball. He began high jumping with a 6-4½ in 1950 and jumped 6-9 in 1951 to rank No. 2 in the world. In 1952, he changed to the western roll, won the AAU at 6-10½, and the Olympic championship at 6-8¼ in cold weather. On June 27, 1953, in the AAU at Dayton, Ohio, he set a World Record of 6-11½.

DILLARD, HARRISON (USA) . . . . 2 G, 2Gr, 5 WR, 6 No. 1, 2 AOY
100, 110 Hurdles, 1947-56 . . . . . .7/8/23, 5-10/155

See chapter.

DIXON, ROD (New Zealand) . . . . B, No. 1
1500-Marathon, 1971- 7/13/50, 6-1/157

One of the most durable runners, Dixon surprised in 1972 by winning the bronze medal in the Olympic 1500. He began to lengthen his distance, and in 1975 he ranked No. 1 in the 5000 and ran the world's fastest times in the 3000 and 2-mile in addition to ranking No. 3 in the 1500. He placed 4th in the 1976 Olympic 5000. He competed steadily, although boycotting the 1980 Olympics, and won many road races. In 1982 he tried the marathon and ran 2:11:21. In 1983, he won the New York Marathon in 2:08:59. He finished 10th in the 1984 Olympic marathon.

DOUBELL, RALPH (Australia) . . . . .G, WR, No. 1
    800, 1966-70 . . . . .2/11/45, 5-11/145

Doubell won the 1968 Olympic 800 meters while equalling the World Record of 1:44.3 (1:44.40).

DRUT, GUY (France) . . . . .G, S, WR, 2 No. 1
    110 Hurdles, 1969-76. . . . . .12/6/50, 6-2½/172

Drut ranked No. 3 in 1970 and No. 4 in 1971, then won the silver medal in the 1972 Olympic 110 hurdles. He ranked No. 3 in 1973 and won the 1974 European Championships to rank No. 2. In 1975 he ran a hand timed World Record of 13.0 and ranked No. 1. In 1976 he won the Olympic title and again ranked No. 1. His career ended when he was declared a professional in 1977.

DUFFEY, ARTHUR (USA) . . . .?
    Sprints, 1900-02 . . . . .5/18/58, 5-7/138

Duffey won several titles in the IC4A and AAU sprints and set four World Records, but his name was removed when he was declared a professional. His 9.6, the first in history, in the 1902 IC4A also was removed.

DUMAS, CHARLES (USA). . . . . G, WR, 2 No. 1
    High Jump, 1955-64 . . . . .2/12/37, 6-1½/179

At age 18, Dumas cleared 6-10½. In 1956, at 19 he was undefeated. After winning the AAU at 6-10 he became history's first 7-footer in the Final Trials with 7-½. He won the Olympic championship at 6-11½ and ranked No. 1 in the world.

In 1957 he was undefeated and won the AAU at 6-10¼. In 1958 he won the AAU, tied for 2nd in the NCAA, and ranked No. 2 in the world. In 1959, he regained his No. 1 ranking, cleared 7-0, won the AAU, and lost only once.

In 1960, he jumped 7-¼, but he was hobbled by a leg injury and placed only 6th in the Olympic Games. He retired completely until 1964, when he appeared out of nowhere to clear 7-¼.

EASTMAN, BEN (USA). S, 6 WR, No. 1*
    400-800, 1931-36 . . . . .7/19/11, 6-1/158

Eastman tied Ted Meredith's 440 World Record of 47.4 in 1931. He lowered it to 46.4 on March 26, 1932. He ran 46.5 in May. On June 4 he broke the 800 and 880 World Records with 1:50.0 and 1:50.9.

Profiles of Other Champions

Charles Dumas

Adhemar da Silva

Lee Evans

Choosing the 400, he lost three times to Bill Carr, including the Olympic final.

In 1933 he set a world best of 1:09.2 for 600 yards. In 1934 he won the Princeton Invitational in 1:49.8, a World Record for 880 yards and a tie with Tom Hampson's 800 record. He won the AAU 800 in 1:50.8. In Europe he bettered his 600y mark with 1:08.8, ran the fastest 600 meters on record, 1:18.4, and set a world best of 1:02.0 for 500 meters. After a year of rest, he ran 1:50.1 for 800 meters in 1936. but humid, 100-degree heat sickened him and he failed to make the Olympic team.

EDWARDS, PHIL (Canada). . . . . .3 B, 2 Br
  800-1500, 1928-36 . . . . .9/22/07

A native of British Guyana, Edwards attended New York University and ran in three Olympic Games for Canada. In 1928 he placed 4th in the 800 and won a bronze medal in the 4 x 400 meter relay. In 1932 he won three more bronze medals, in the 800, 1500, and relay. In 1936 he took his 5th bronze medal, in the 800, plus a 5th in the 1500 and 4th in the relay. He won the AAU 880 in 1929 and the indoor AAU 600 from 1928 through 1931.

ELLIOTT, HERB (Australia). . . . . G, 3 WR, 2 No. 1
  800-Mile, 1957-61 . . . . .2/25/38, 5-11½/150

See chapter.

EVANS, LEE (USA) . . . . G, Gr, 2 WR, 4 No. 1
  400, 1966-72 . . . . .2/25/47, 5-11/172

Evans burst into prominence in 1966, his first year out of high school, with an undefeated season, No. 1 in the World Rankings, and the AAU championship. In 1967 he ranked No. 1 and won the AAU and Pan-American titles, but he lost to Tommie Smith's World Record plus three races after an injury. In 1968 he lost only two minor races and won NCAA, AAU, and Olympic championships plus a second Olympic gold medal in a World Record 4 x 400 meter relay. He lowered the 400 meter World Record to 44.0 (44.06) at South Lake Tahoe, California, in September and to 43.8 (43.86) in the Olympic final. In 1969 he won his 4th AAU title. He ranked No. 1 in 1970, suffered injuries in 1971, and won the AAU in 1972. He made the Olympic relay team, but no team ran at Munich. He turned professional in 1972.

Profiles of Other Champions

EWELL, NORWOOD (Barney) (USA) . . . . Gr, 2 S, WR, 4 No. 1*
    Sprints, 1936-48 . . . . .2/25/18, 5-11/158

Barney Ewell had the longest career of any good sprinter. He started by winning the junior AAU 100 meters in 1936. He won six AAU sprint championships, was runner-up four times, and placed in five other races, plus once in the long jump. In 1940 and 1941, he won NCAA sprint doubles. He won both sprints and the long jump in all three of his IC4A meets. An injury in the long jump eliminated him from the 1942 NCAA and AAU.

He won the indoor AAU long jump three times and jumped 25-2½ in an IC4A indoor meet. In 1948, after missing two Olympics because of the war, he won the Final Trials with a World Record equalling 10.2 (10.32). At London, he placed a close 2nd in both Olympic sprints and won a gold medal in the 4 x 100 meter relay.

EWRY, RAY (USA). 8 G, 3 WR, No. 1**
    Standing Jumps, 1898-1908 . . . . .10/14/73, 6-1/162

Ewry was paralyzed as a boy, but exercises developed tremendous strength in his legs. In 1898, at the age of 25, he began winning championships in the standing jumps, then official events. He won 15 AAU titles even though the events were not held from 1899 to 1905.

Ewry won 8 Olympic titles in 3 Games, and another 2 in the unofficial 1906 Games. In 1900 he won the high jump with a World Record 5-5, the long jump at 10-6½, and the triple jump at 34-8½. In 1904 he repeated his three triumphs, raising his long jump record to 11-4¾. This mark stood unbeaten on the World Record list until the event was discarded in 1938.

In the unofficial Olympics of 1906, Ewry won both the standing high jump and long jump, and he repeated in 1908 at the age of 34.

FEUERBACH, AL (USA). . . . . WR, 2 No. 1
    Shot, 1969-78. . . . . .1/14/48, 6-1/250

Feuerbach placed 5th in the 1972 Olympic shot. He set a World Record of 71-7 in 1973, ranked No. 1 and ranked No. 1 again in 1974. He placed 4th in the 1976 Olympics.

FINLAY, DONALD (Great Britain) . . . . .S, B
    110 Hurdles, 1931-51. . . . . .5/27/09

Unequalled for longevity, Finlay was 3rd in the 1932 Olympic 110 hurdles at the age of 23. He won the silver medal in 1936. He ran 14.1

and 14.2 in 1937, and won the 1938 European Championships in 14.3. He fell in the 1948 Olympics, but in 1949, at the age of 40, he won in 14.4 against France.

FLANAGAN, JOHN (USA). . . . . .3 G, S, 14 WR, No. 1**
       Hammer, 1895-1909 . . . . .1/9/73, 5-11/220

Flanagan set a World Record of 145-10 for the wooden handled hammer in Ireland in 1895. In the United States, he raised the record 13 times, eventually to 184-4, at New Haven, July 24, 1909. He won AAU titles in the hammer seven times and in the 56-pound weight six times. He won three Olympic championships, in 1900, 1904, and 1908, placed 2nd in the 1904 weight, and 4th in the 1904 discus.

FOSS, FRANK (USA) . . . . G, WR, No. 1*
       Pole Vault, 1920. . . . . .5/9/95, 5-8/145

Foss won the 1920 Olympic pole vault with a World Record of 13-5.

Anders Garderud

Walter George

Profiles of Other Champions

FOSTER, BRENDAN (Great Britain) . . . . B, 2 WR, 2 No. 1
1500-10,000, 1970-78 . . . . .1/12/48, 5-10½/147

Foster placed 5th in the 1972 Olympic 1500. In 1972, he set a 2-mile World Record of 8:13.8. In 1974, he broke the 3000 World Record with 7:35.2 and ranked No. 2 in the 5000, winning the European Championship and placing 2nd in the Commonwealth Games. He ranked No. 1 in the 10,000 for 1975. In the 1976 Olympics, he won the bronze medal in the 10,000 and placed 5th in the 5000. He ranked No. 1 again in the 10,000 for 1977. The next year, he won the Commonwealth 10,000 and placed 4th in the European Championships.

FOSTER, GREG (USA) . . . . .G, S, 2 No. 1
110 hurdles, 1977- 8/4/58, 6-3/195

Foster ranked No. 1 in the 110 hurdles in 1982 and 1983, and he ranked No. 2 four other years. He won the World Championship in 1983 and placed 2nd in the 1984 Olympics.

FUCHS, JIM (USA) . . . . 2 B, 4 WR, 3 No. 1, 1/3 AOY
Shot, 1948-52. . . . . .12/6/27, 6-2/205

Fuchs raised the World Record in the shot four times, to 58-10¾ in 1951. He won both NCAA and AAU in 1949 and 1950, and placed 3rd in the Olympics in 1948 and 1952. He also threw the discus 172-7, making him 14th best of all time in 1949.

GARDERUD, ANDERS (Sweden) . . . . G, 4 WR, 2 No. 1
Steeplechase, 1968-76 . . . . .8/28/46, 6-1¼/154

In 1972, Garderud set a World Record of 8:20.7, but he placed only 5th in the 1972 Olympic steeplechase. He ranked No. 2 for the next two years and placed 2nd in the 1974 European Championships. In 1975, he lowered the World Record to 8:10.4 and again to 8:09.70. He won the 1976 Olympic gold medal with a World Record 8:08.02. He also ran a mile in 3:54.45 and 5000 meters in 13:17.59.

GEORGE, WALTER (Great Britain) . . . . . . 8 WR, 14 No. 1*, AOY**
Mile-10 Miles, 1879-84 . . . . .9/9/58, 5-11/136

One of the greatest runners of all time, George won 14 British Championships from the 880 to 10 miles in the four years he entered.

In 1884 he set his third World Record in the mile (4:18.4) and records for 2 miles (9:17.4), 3 miles (14:39.0), 6 miles (30:31.5), and 10 miles (51:20). In 1885 he ran a well-documented practice mile in 4:10.2 on a course six yards long. The next year he ran his famous 4:12.8. He won a two out of three series from Lon Myers, losing only indoors.

GORDIEN, FORTUNE (USA). . . . . S, B, 2 WR, 4 No. 1, AOY
    Discus, 1947-56 . . . . .9/9/22, 6-½/230

Gordien set World Records in the discus of 186-11 in 1949 and 194-6 in 1953. At that date he had 16 of the 18 longest throws ever made. He won three NCAA and six AAU titles. He ranked No. 1 in the world in 1947, 1949, 1953, and 1954. He was 3rd in the 1948 Olympics, 4th in 1952, and 2nd in 1956. He lost only four times from 1947 through 1950, when he retired temporarily. In 1947 he was the No. 3 shot putter in the World Rankings.

GREENE, CHARLES (USA). . . . . .Gr, B, 2 WR, No. 1
    100, 1964-72 . . . . .3/21/45, 5-8/148

Greene tied the World Records of 9.1 for 100 yards (1967) and 9.9 for 100 meters (1968). He ranked No. 1 in the world in 1966. He placed 3rd in the 1968 Olympic 100 and won a gold medal in the 4 x 100 meter relay.

GUTOWSKI, BOB (USA) . . . . S, WR, No. 1, AOY
    PV, 1955-57. . . . . .4/25/35, 6-0/150

Gutowski placed 2nd in the 1956 Olympic vault and broke Cornelius Warmerdam's record in 1957 with 15-8¼, using a steel pole.

HAGG, GUNDER (Sweden) . . . . .15 WR, 7 No. 1*, 2 AOY*
    1500-5000, 1940-45 . . . . .12/31/18, 5-10¾/150

Hagg developed into a world-class runner in 1940 at the age of 22 four years of training in an unstructured method now called Fartlek. He tied the Swedish record for 1500 meters with 3:48.8 in 1940, only 1.2 second from the World Record.

In 1941, he ran 3:48.6, then defeated Arne Andersson by seven yards in World Record time of 3:47.5. He ran a mile in 4:09.2.

After nine months of hard Fartlek, he ran his first race of 1942 on July 1 at Goteborg. He defeated Arne Andersson in a 4:06.1 mile, a

Profiles of Other Champions

*Gunder Hagg
(and Arne Andersson)*

new World Record. Two days later, he lowered the World Record for 2 miles to 8:47.8. Two weeks later, at Stockholm, he defeated Andersson and lowered his 1500 meter record to 3:45.8. Four days after that, at Malmo, he broke the 2000-meter record with 5:16.4.

On August 23, 1942, at Ostersund, he lowered his 2000 record to 5:11.8. Five days later, in Stockholm, his 8:01.2 was a new World Record for 3000 meters. A week later, he took the mile WR down to 4:04.6. Another week later he broke the 3-mile record with 13:55.4.

Nine days later, September 20, in Goteborg, he bettered that 3-mile time by three seconds on his way to 5000 meters in 13:58.2. Those two records lasted 12 years.

In a period of 82 days he had broken 10 World Records at seven distances in 26 victorious races.

In 1943 he made a long, hazardous, war-time voyage to the United States and won all of his races without setting a World Record. In Sweden, Andersson lowered two of Hagg's records to 3:44.9 and 4:02.6.

On July 7, 1944, in Goteborg, Hagg recovered one record when he defeated Andersson by seven yards in 3:43.0. Eleven days later, at Malmo, Andersson managed his lone victory over Hagg in 4:01.6, while Hagg ran 4:02.0.

Hagg lowered his 2-mile record to 8:46.4 on June 5. On August 4, at Goteborg, he ran 8:42.8, a World Record which lasted eight years.

In 1945, Hagg made a rough voyage to the United States and ran without distinction, but by July 17 he was back in shape. At Malmo he defeated Andersson by six yards in a 4:01.3 mile, a World Record for the next nine years. Both he and Andersson were barred from amateur competition in November, 1945.

Hagg's best distance was undoubtedly longer than a mile. When he retired he had run the six fastest 2 miles of all time, plus five of the six fastest 3000 meters, all in separate races.

HAHN, ARCHIE (USA). . . . . 3 G, WR, 2 No. 1*
    Sprints, 1903-06 . . . . .9/14/80, 5-6/142

Hahn won three Olympic sprints in 1904, the 60, 100, and 200. He repeated in the 100 of the unofficial 1906 Games. He won three AAU championships.

HALBERG, MURRAY (New Zealand) . . . . G, 2 WR, 4 No. 1
    1500-10,000, 1954-64 . . . . .7/7/33, 5-11/136

Halberg, a 4:04.4 miler at the age of 21, placed 5th in the 1954 British Empire mile behind Roger Bannister and John Landy. In the 1956 Olympics, he was 11th in the 1500 meters. In 1958 he won the Empire 3-mile and ran a 3:57.5 mile behind Elliott's 3:54.5.

In March, 1960, he ran 27:52.2, the second-fastest 6-mile of all time, then won the Olympic 5000 and placed 5th in the 10,000. On July 7, 1961, he lowered the 2-mile World Record to 8:30.0. On July 25, in Stockholm, he bettered the 3-mile World Record with 13:10.0 and continued to 5000 meters in 13:35.2, only 0.2 off the World Record.

He won the British Empire 3-mile again in 1962. In 1964, after four consecutive years ranking No. 1 in the world at 5000 meters, he did not qualify in the Olympic 5000 and placed 7th in the 10,000.

HAMM, ED (USA). . . . . G, WR, No. 1*
    Long Jump, 1927-28 . . . . .4/13/06

Hamm won the NCAA long jump in 1927 and 1928. On July 7, 1928, in the AAU meet, he jumped 25-11 for a new World Record. He won the Olympic championship with 25-4¼.

Profiles of Other Champions

HAMPSON, THOMAS (Great Britain) . . . . G, WR, No. 1*
800, 1930-32 . . . . .10/28/07

Hampson won the AAA title three times before he set a World Record of 1:49.8 (1:49.70) in the 1932 Olympic 800 meters.

HANSEN, FRED (USA) . . . . G, 3 WR, No. 1
PV, 1962-64 . . . . .12/29/40, 6-0/167

Hansen ranked No. 8 in the world in 1963 with a best vault of 16-1. In 1964 he cleared a 17-1 World Record in Texas on June 5. He raised his World Record to 17-2 at San Diego on June 13. He won the AAU at 17-0. Against the Soviet Union, in Los Angeles, July 25, he raised the world record to 17-4. He won a dramatic Olympic victory at 16-8¾.

HARBIG, RUDOLF (Germany) . . . . 3 WR, 2 No. 1*, AOY*
400-800, 1936-42 . . . . .11/8/13

Unsuccessful in the 1936 Olympics, Harbig was deprived of two Olympics by World War II. He was undefeated in 1937, lost one 400 meters to Ray Mallott in 1938, and was undefeated in 1939. That year he ran 1:46.6 at Milan on July 15, a World Record 800 which lasted 16 years. On August 12 at Frankfurt, he ran 400 meters in 46.0, a World Record which lasted 10 years. In 1941, he set a World Record for 1000 meters, 2:21.5. In 1942 he lost two slow races and in 1944 he was reported missing on the Russian front. He was European 800 meter champion in 1938.

HARDIN, GLENN (USA) . . . . G, S, 5 WR, 5 No. 1*
400, 400 Hurdles, 1932-36 . . . . . .7/1/10, 6-2/170

As a freshman at Louisiana State in 1932, Hardin won the AAU 400 hurdles but he was disqualified. At Los Angeles, he set an Olympic record of 52.8 in the semi-final and finished a close 2nd in the final. Tisdall, the winner in 51.8, knocked down a hurdle and so was deprived of a World Record. Hardin, timed in 51.9, was credited with equalling the official World Record of 52.0.

In both 1933 and 1934, Hardin won NCAA doubles in the 440 and 220y low hurdles, plus the AAU 440 hurdles. His 47.1 in the 1933

Track's Greatest Champions

Bob Hayes

Uwe Hohn

Rudolf Harbig

Profiles of Other Champions

NCAA was the second fastest 440 ever run on two turns. His 22.9 broke the World Record for the low hurdles but it was not approved.

In 1934 he won a 440 in 46.8, second only to Ben Eastman's World Record. He improved both his NCAA marks with 47.0 and 22.7. Again his low hurdle record was not recognized, because an automatic timer showed a slower time. In the 1934 AAU, his 51.8 was a new World Record for the 400 hurdles.

He toured Europe in 1934. In Stockholm for three days, Hardin started with 47.8. On the second day he ran 300 meters in 33.7, half a second off Charlie Paddock's world best. On the third day, July 26, he ran the 400 hurdles in 50.6, which remained as the World Record for 19 years.

He was off form in 1935. He finished third in the NCAA 440 and lost to Jesse Owens in the 220 low hurdles.

In 1936, he won his third AAU title, in 51.6, giving him the five fastest times in history. He won the Olympic championship in 52.4, completing four years without a defeat in the 400 hurdles.

HARY, ARMIN (West Germany) . . . . G, Gr, WR, No. 1
    Sprints, 1958-60 . . . . .3/22/37, 5-11¼/156

Hary was a miraculous starter who ran the first 10.0 100 meters, at Zurich, June 21, 1960. He also ran two unofficial 10.0s. He won the 1958 European Championships in 10.3 and the 1960 Olympic championship in 10.2 (10.32).

HAYES, BOB (USA) . . . . G, Gr, 9 WR, 3 No. 1
    Sprints, 1961-64 . . . . .12/20/42, 5-10/178

Hayes' career lasted through his four college years at Florida A&M. In 62 100 yards or 100 meters finals he lost only twice, both in one week after he had been ill. Indoors, his only loss in nine races was to an admitted rolling start when he hesitated, expecting to be recalled. Lack of conditioning probably accounted for his 220 losses although they were mostly to great runners.

Hayes was No. 1 in the World Rankings his last three years in the 100. He ranked only No. 5 in 1961 because he was unknown and ran few races although he was undefeated and equalled the World Record of 9.3.

In the 220 he ran 20.1 on a straightaway in 1961 and twice tied the World Record of 20.5 around a curve. He ranked No. 2 in 1963 and

No. 4 in 1964.

Indoors, he ran only once before 1964, lowering the best for 70 yards to 6.9. In 1964, he again ran 6.9. In his seven 60-yard races, he ran 6.1 once, tied the World Record of 6.0 five times, and set a new World Record of 5.9 in the AAU meet of 1964.

His outdoor championships included the 200 in his only NCAA appearance and three AAU 100s. He lost his only AAU 220 to Paul Drayton. He won the 1964 Olympic 100 meters by 2 meters and won a second gold medal with an almost inhuman burst of speed on the anchor leg of the 4 x 100 meter relay.

His times at 100 yards and 100 meters were phenomenal. After 1961, the records were 9.2 and 10.1. He ran 9.2 and 10.1 in 1962. In 1963 he ran 9.1 for an official World Record plus a wind-aided 9.1, and he ran a windy 9.9 100 meters. In 1964 he ran three 9.1s and a 9.2. In the Olympic semi-final he ran a windy 9.9. His World Record 10.0 (10.05) in the final was hand timed at 9.9. He ran 9.3 or faster 19 times, plus three with excessive wind.

HEMERY, DAVID (Great Britain) . . . . .G, B, WR, No. 1
    400 Hurdles, 1966-72. . . . . .7/18/44, 6-1½/170

Hemery lived and trained in the United States, attending Boston University where there was no outdoor track and only a part-time coach.

In 1966, he won the IC4A 120 hurdles in 14.1 and ran 51.8 for second in the 440 hurdles. He ran 13.9 in the Soviet Union and won the Commonwealth championship in 14.1.

In 1968, he placed 2nd in the IC4A 600, indoors. In early outdoor meets, he ran 14.0, 13.9, and a windy 13.7. His progress showed even more in the 400 hurdles, where he clocked two 50.7s, 50.6, and 50.5 yards before winning the IC4A at 50.4.

In the NCAA meet at Berkeley, he won the 400 hurdles in the slow curb lane with 49.8. He won the AAU title of July 13 with 50.2 for 440 yards. On August 24, in London, he ran 49.6m.

In the Olympic Games, Mexico City's high altitude aided 400 runners by as much as a full second, but a hurdler had to maintain the correct step. In the final Hemery gambled on using only 13 steps between the first six hurdles. He built up an astounding lead, then changed to 15 steps. He won by 8 meters in a full second faster than the official World Record.

Profiles of Other Champions

He all but retired for two years, then came back to win the bronze medal in the 1972 Olympics.

HILLMAN, HARRY (USA) . . . . 3 G, S, WR, 3 No. 1*
400, Hurdles, 1902-08 . . . . .9/8/81, 5-11/145

In the 1904 Olympics, Hillman won the 400, the 400 hurdles, and the 200 hurdles. In 1908, he set a World Record of 56.4 in a heat of the Olympic 400 hurdles, then placed 2nd in the final.

HINES, JIM (USA) . . . . G, Gr, 4 WR, 2 No. 1
Sprints, 1966-68 . . . . .9/10/46, 6-0/180

Hines ranked No. 1 in the world for 100 meters in 1967 and 1968 and No. 2 in the 200 in 1966 and 1967. He won three AAU titles and the 1968 Olympic 100 (with the first official auto-timed World Record—9.95). His fast finish saved the gold in the Olympic 4 x 100 relay. He tied World Records with 9.1 and 9.9 and he ran a 20.3 curve 220.

HINGSEN, JURGEN (West Germany) . . . . 2 S, 3 WR
Decathlon, 1978- 1/25/58, 6-6¾/205

Hingsen broke the decathlon World Record with 8723 in 1980 at the age of 22, raised it to 8779 in 1983, and again in 1984, to 8798. Unfortunately, he competed against Daley Thompson and placed 2nd in the 1983 World Championships and 1984 Olympics, and he ranked No. 2 from 1981 through 1984.

HOCKERT, GUNNAR (Finland) . . . . G, 2 WR, 2 No. 1*
3000-5000, 1936 . . . . .2/12/10

Hockert won the 1936 Olympic 5000 meters in an Olympic record 14:22.2. On September 16, 1936, in Stockholm, he broke the 3000-meter World Record with 8:14.8. Eight days later, he broke the 2-mile record with 8:57.4.

HOHN, UWE (East Germany) . . . . G, WR, 2 No. 1
Javelin, 1982- 7/16/62, 6-5½/212

Hohn won the European title in 1982 with 299-8 while barely 20. Injured in 1983, he returned as a superstar in 1984. After throwing 326-6, second best ever, he astounded the world on July 20 with a World Record throw of 343-10. In 1985, he threw 311-6, 317-11, 313-5 (twice), 304-8, 309-8, 314-11 and 318-1 to rank No. 1 again.

HORINE, GEORGE (USA) . . . . .B, 2 WR, No. 1*
    High Jump, 1912. . . . . .2/3/90, 5-11/162

    Horine invented the western roll. Only 5-11 tall, he broke the high jump World Record with 6-6 on March 29, 1912. On May 18, he raised it to 6-7. Ill, he placed only 3rd in the Olympics.

HOUSER, CLARENCE (BUD) (USA) . . . . 3 G, WR, 4 No. 1*
    Shot, Discus, 1924-28 . . . . .9/25/01, 6-2/210

    Bud Houser, only 187 pounds, won the shot and discus in the 1924 Olympics. In 1928 he won the discus again. On April 3, 1926, he set a World Record of 158-2 in the discus. He won two AAU shot titles and three in the discus.

HUBBARD, De HART (USA) . . . . G, 2 WR, 6 No. 1*, 2 AOY*
    100, Long Jump, 1922-28 . . . . . . .11/25/03

    Hubbard won the long jump in the 1923 NCAA. He won the 1924 Olympic long jump after falling far back on a jump which measured 24-5. In the 1925 NCAA, he won the 100 and jumped 25-10 for a World Record. In 1926 he tied the World Record of 9.6 for 100 yards. In 1927, he jumped 26-2¼ but the landing pit was one inch too low. He won six AAU long jumps, 1922-1927. He was injured in 1928 and placed only 11th in the Olympics.

IHAROS, SANDOR (Hungary) . . . . .8 WR, 3 No. 1, AOY
    1500-10,000, 1954-58 . . . . .3/10/30, 5-11¼/132

    Iharos set a European Record of 3:42.4 for 1500 meters in 1954. In 1955, he set successive World Records for 3000 meters (7:55.6), 2 miles (8:33.4), 1500 meters (3:40.8), 5000 meters (13:50.8), 3 miles (13:14.2), and, in the same race, 5000 meters (13:40.6). In his first attempt at 10,000 meters in four years, he set a World Record of 28:42.8 (in 1956), passing 6 miles in 27:43.8. He missed the 1956 Olympics because of the Hungarian uprising.

INESS, SIM (USA) . . . . .G, WR, No. 1
    Discus, 1948-53 . . . . .7/9/30, 6-6/240

    Iness threw the discus 180-6 for a new Olympic Record in 1952. In 1953 he won his second NCAA title with a World Record of 190-0.

Profiles of Other Champions

ISO-HOLLO, VOLMARI (Finland) . . . . .2 G, S, B, WR, 2 No. 1*
　　Distances, 1931-36 . . . . .5/1/07

　　Iso-Hollo won two Olympic steeplechase championships, in 1932 and 1936. His 9:03.8 at Berlin was by far the fastest ever recorded. He placed 2nd and 3rd in two Olympic 10,000s. His 30:12.6 in 1932 placed him third on the all-time list. He was a close 2nd to Lauri Lehtinen's World Record 5000 in 1932, timed in 14:18.3. In 1933 his 8:19.6 was barely beaten by Lehtinen in the second fastest 3000 ever run. On July 20, 1933, he broke the world best for 4 miles with 19:01.0.

JARVINEN, AKILLES (Finland) . . . . .2S, 2 WR, No. 1*
　　Decathlon, 1928-34 . . . . .9/19/05

　　Son of a World Record discus thrower, Aki placed 2nd in two Olympic decathlons, 1928 and 1932. Under a later scoring system, he would have won them both. In 1931 he bettered the decathlon World Record and in the 1932 Olympics he broke the World Record but only held it for the 30 seconds it took Jim Bausch to finish the 1500 with an even higher score.

JARVINEN, MATTI (Finland) . . . . .G, 10 WR, 6 No. 1*, 2 AOY*
　　Javelin, 1929-38 . . . . .2/18/09, 6-¾/185

　　Brother of the World Record decathlon man, Matti had the longest throw in the world at the age of 20 in 1929, his first full year with the javelin. On August 8, 1930, he broke the World Record with 234-9. He raised his record nine times, eventually to 253-4 in 1936. He won the 1932 Olympic championship, but a back injury dropped him to 5th in 1936. He won the European Championships in 1934 and 1938. In 1949, at the age of 40, he threw 220-10. He won the Finnish Championship eight times. At the end of the 1937 season he had to his credit the 10 longest throws of all time.

JAZY, MICHEL (France) . . . . .S, 5 WR, No. 1
　　1500-5000, 1956-66 . . . . .6/13/36, 5-9¼/146

　　Jazy ran in the 1956 Olympics at the age of 20, and placed 10th in the 1500 meters of the 1958 European Championships. In the 1960 Olympics he ran 3:38.4 for 2nd in the 1500. In 1962, he set World Records of 5:01.5 for 2000 meters and 7:49.2 for 3000 meters and won the European Championships 1500 in 3:38.3.

Track's Greatest Champions

Michel Jazy

Matti Jarvinen

Bruce Jenner

Profiles of Other Champions

In 1963 he ranked No. 3 in both the 1500 and 5000 and lowered his 1500 meter best to 3:37.8. He set a 2-mile World Record of 8:29.6. He placed 4th in the 1964 Olympic 5000.

In 1965 he was undefeated at 1500 meters and the mile and broke the mile World Record with a 3:53.6. He lowered the 2-mile record to 8:22.6. He was undefeated and ranked No. 1 in the 5000, beating Kip Keino and Ron Clarke in 13:27.6, only 1.8 seconds behind Clarke's new World Record.

In 1966 he won the European Championships 5000 and was undefeated. In the 1500, he ran 3:36.3 twice and placed 2nd in the European Championships.

JENNER, BRUCE (USA) . . . . G, 3 WR, 3 No. 1
  Decathlon, 1971-76 . . . . .10/28/49, 6-2/196

Jenner finished 10th in the 1972 Olympic decathlon. He scored only 7770 in 1973, but in 1974 he began a strong effort and ranked No. 1, undefeated for the year. His 8240 took him to No. 2 on the U.S. list, and he won the AAU with 8245. His fourth victory scored 8308. In 1975, he won five decathlons and did not finish the AAU where he failed to clear a height in the vault. He set a hand-timed World Record of 8524 in 1975, and an auto-timed WR of 8538 in the 1976 Final Trials. He won the Olympics with a World Record 8617, and finished 2nd in voting for Athlete of the Year.

JEROME, HARRY (Canada) . . . . B, 2 WR
  Sprints, 1959-68 . . . . .9/30/40, 5-10/170

Jerome tied World Records at 9.2 and 10.0 and ran in three Olympics. He pulled a muscle in 1960, placed 3rd in the 100 and 4th in the 200 in 1964, and 7th in the 1968 100.

JIPCHO, BEN (Kenya) . . . . S, 2 WR, 3 No. 1, AOY
  1500-5000, 1968-74 . . . . .3/1/43, 5-10/159

Jipcho appeared in 1968 as the pacesetter in the Olympic 1500. He returned in 1971 to rank No. 3 in the 1500, but in 1972 he ran the steeplechase, winning the Olympic silver medal. In 1973, he became Athlete of the Year with superior performances in three events. He ranked No. 1 in the 1500, and finished undefeated in the 5000 but ranked only No. 6. In the steeplechase, he broke the World Record with 8:19.8, and lowered it to 8:13.91. He won 1974 Commonwealth championships in the steeplechase and 5000 and placed 3rd in the World Record 1500. He turned professional shortly afterward.

JOHNSON, CORNELIUS (USA) . . . . G, WR, 2 No. 1*
        High Jump, 1932-38 . . . . .8/28/13, 6-4/172

"Corny" Johnson tied for the 1932 Olympic championship at 18. Under present rules he would have been 2nd, but he placed 4th in a jumpoff. He was never beaten, though tied, in the AAU from 1932 through 1936. He won indoor titles in 1935, 1936, and 1938.

In 1936 he set an indoor record of 6-8. At the outdoor AAU in Princeton, he arrived late and cleared 6-7 on his first jump. He won at 6-8. The next week, in the Final Trials, he set a World Record of 6-9¾. He won the Olympic championship at 6-8 without a miss.

JOHNSON, RAFER (USA) . . . . G, S, 3 WR, 3 No. 1, AOY
        Decathlon, 1955-60 . . . . .8/18/34, 6-3/200

See chapter.

JONES, HAYES (USA) . . . . .G, B, 4 No. 1
        110 Hurdles, 1957-64. . . . . .8/4/38, 5-11/169

Jones was a Dillard-type hurdler, short (5-11), fast (9.4), and consistent. He set a World Junior Record of 13.7 at age 18 in 1957. The next year he ran 13.6, won the AAU, and ranked No. 1 in the world. In 1959, he was 2nd in both the NCAA and AAU and won the Pan-American championship in 13.6. He won the NCAA 220 low hurdles in 22.5 and lost narrowly to Charles Tidwell's World Record 22.6 around a curve in the AAU.

In 1960, after running 13.5, he placed 3rd in the Olympics. He ranked No. 1 again in 1961 with an undefeated season. In 1962 he ran 13.4 in the AAU but lost to Jerry Tarr. In 1963, Jones ranked No. 1 again, and won the AAU in 13.4.

In 1964 he ran 13.4 in the semi-final Olympic Trials and won his fifth AAU championship. He won the Olympics in 13.6.

Indoors, Jones was unbeatable. His last loss was in March of 1959, after which he won 55 consecutive major races. He lowered the 60 yard hurdles record to 6.8 in his final race in 1964. He also won sprint races indoors.

Profiles of Other Champions

JUANTORENA, ALBERTO (Cuba) . . . . . 2 G, 2 WR, 6 No. 1, 2 AOY
400-800, 1974-80 . . . . .3/21/51, 6-2/185
See chapter.

KEINO, KIP (Kenya). . . . . .2 G, 2 S, 2 WR, 6 No. 1
1500-10,000, 1964-72 . . . . .1/17/40, 5-10/146

Keino placed 5th in the 1964 Olympic 5000. In 1965 he ranked No. 2 in the world with a 5000-meter World Record of 13:24.2 at Auckland, New Zealand on November 11. He set an outstanding World Record of 7:39.6 for 3000 meters. He ranked No. 2 in the mile with 3:54.2, third best ever. In 1966, he ranked No. 1 in the 5000 and No. 2 in the mile. He ran a 3:53.4 mile and won both the mile and 3-mile in the Commonwealth Games. In 1967 he was No. 2 in the World Rankings in both events and lowered his mile best to 3:53.1.

Kipchoge Keino

In 1968, Keino ran 10,000 meters in 28:06.4, a time bettered by only two men in history. In the Olympic Games he was a contender in the 10,000 meters until pain from a gall bladder ailment forced him out near the end. In the 5000, he finished a close 2nd. In the 1500 meter final, his sixth run in eight days, he shocked everybody with the fastest race of his carrer, at 7350-foot altitude. He won by almost three seconds in 3:34.9, an Olympic record.

Keino ranked No. 2 in 1969 even though he lost no races in the 1500 and mile. In 1970, he ranked No. 1 with a victory in the Commonwealth Games, and he ranked No. 4 in the 5000. He ran the year's fastest 2000 and 2 mile. He ranked No. 2 and No. 4 for 1971 in the 1500 and 5000. In the 1972 Olympics, he ran as a novice in the steeplechase, but he won the gold medal. Then he lost a close 1500. He ran some professional races with little distinction.

KING, LEAMON (USA)........................Gr, 3 WR
    Sprints, 1955-57.............2/13/36, 5-11/142

King was the first to run two official 10.1s for 100 meters. This came in 1956 after an injury kept him out of the Olympic sprints. He won a gold medal at Melbourne in the 4 x 100 meter relay. He ran WR equalling 9.3 and won the 1957 AAU 100.

KINGDOM, ROGER (USA) ....G, 2 No. 1
    110 Hurdles, 1983- 10/26/62, 6-0/185

A football player, Kingdom surprised by winning the NCAA 110 hurdles in 1983. Then he won the Pan-American title with 13.44. In 1984, he won the Olympic gold medal with 13.20. In 1985, he ran 13.14 and ranked No. 1 a second year.

KLIM, ROMUALD (Soviet Union)............G, S, WR, 3 No. 1
    Hammer, 1963-71...........5/25/73, 6-1½/227

Klim won the 1964 Olympic championship and barely lost in 1968. He won the 1966 European Championships. He threw 241-3 in 1968 and was undefeated from 1966 to the 1968 Olympics. On June 15, 1969, at Budapest, he reached a World Record distance of 244-6.

KOLEHMAINEN, HANNES (Finland) ....4G, 4 WR, No. 1**, AOY*
    Distances, 1912-20 ....12/9/89

In the 1912 Olympics, Kolehmainen won the 10,000 meters by 46 seconds and the cross country by 33. Jean Bouin of France led the 5000 meters at 3 miles in 14:07, 10 seconds under the World Record. Kolehmainen fought past in the homestretch to win by a yard in

14:36.6, a World Record by almost half a minute. He also set a World Record for 3000 meters (8:36.8) in a heat of the team run.

In the United States, Kolehmainen ran an indoor 4-mile faster than Alf Shrubb's world best and came close to Shrubb's times in two long runs. After missing a chance for more gold medals in the cancelled 1916 Olympics, he won the 1920 marathon in the rain by 13 seconds in 2:32:36.9, the fastest ever run. On October 10, he set a World Best of 1:26:29.6 for 25,000 meters.

KOZAKIEWICZ, WLADYSLAW (Poland) . . . . G, WR, 4 No. 1
Pole Vault, 1973-82. . . . . .12/8/53, 6-1½/190

Kozak placed 2nd in the European Championships in 1974 and ranked No. 3 with a best vault of 17-7¾. In 1975, he ranked No. 1 with a best of 18-4¾, and he was favored in the 1976 Olympics with a mark of 18-5¼. But injures held him to 11th place. He ranked No. 1 in 1977, vaulting 18-6¾, but he slipped to No. 4 in 1978, placing only 4th in the European Championships. He regained his No. 1 ranking in 1979, and he won the 1980 Olympic championship with a World Record 18-11½.

KRAENZLEIN, ALVIN (USA) . . . . . . .4 G, 3 WR, 5 No. 1*, 2 AOY*
Sprints, Hurdles, Long Jump, 1897-1900
12/12/76, 6-0/165

As a freshman at Pennsylvania in 1897, Kraenzlein won the AAU 220 low hurdles in a meet record 25.0. In 1898 he won both hurdles in the IC4A and AAU. His IC4A low hurdle time of 23.6 remained as the World Record for 25 years. His 15.2 in the AAU 120 hurdles was a World Record.

In 1899 he again won the hurdle double in each meet. He finished 2nd in the AAU 100 but is credited with the championship because Arthur Duffey was suspended. Kraenzlein also won both long jumps. His 24-4½ in the IC4A was a World Record.

In 1900 he won his third IC4A hurdles double and took the 100 in 10.2. At the Olympic Games in Paris, he set four Olympic records: 60 meters (7.0), 110 hurdles (15.4), 200 hurdles (25.4), long jump (23-7).

KRIVONOSOV, MIKHAIL (Soviet Union). . . . . S, 6 WR
Hammer, 1953-56 . . . . .5/1/29, 6-2-3/8/198

Krivonosov raised the World Record in the hammer throw six times, eventually reaching 220-10 in 1956. He won the 1954 European Championships and placed 2nd in the 1956 Olympics.

KRZYZKOWIAK, ZDZISLAW (Poland) . . . . G, 2 WR, 4 No. 1
  Distances, 1955-61 . . . . .8/3/29, 5-7¾/130

Krzyzkowiak placed 4th in the 1956 Olympic 10,000 and qualified for the steeplechase final, but an injury prevented him from running. He won both the 5000 and the 10,000 in the 1958 European Championships.

On June 26, he set a steeplechase World Record of 8:31.3. In the Olympics, he won the steeplechase and placed 7th in the 10,000. He lowered his steeplechase record to 8:30.4 on August 10, 1961.

KUCK, JOHN (USA) . . . . G, 3 WR, 2 No. 1*
  Shot, 1926-28. . . . . .4/27/05, 6-3/225

Kuck won the NCAA shot in 1926 and the AAU in 1927. On April 28, 1928 at Fresno, he broke the World Record with 51-½. He raised it a week later in Los Angeles to 51-2, but he lost it the same day to Emil Hirschfeld's 51-9¾. At the 1928 Olympic Games, Kuck won with a World Record of 52-¾.

Vladimir Kuts

Profiles of Other Champions

KUSOCINSKI, JANUSZ (Poland). . . . . .G, WR, No. 1*
Distances, 1931-36 . . . . .1/15/07

Kusocinski won the Olympic 10,000 in 1932 in 30:11.4, second only to Paavo Nurmi's World Record. Kusocinski lowered the World Record for 3000 meters to 8:18.8 at Antwerp on June 19, 1932. In the 1934 European Championships, he finished 2nd in the 5000.

KUTS, VLADIMIR (Soviet Union). . . . . .2 G, 6 WR, 6 No. 1
Distances, 1953-57 . . . . .2/7/27, 5-7¾/159

In 1953, at the age of 26, Kuts ran 5000 meters in 14:04.0 and 10,000 meters in 29:41.4. In 1954, he ran away from Emil Zatopek and Chris Chataway to win the European Championships in a World Record 13:56.6, plus a 3-mile record of 13:27.4. In a great race at London's White City on October 13, Kuts led Chataway at 3 miles in a record 13:27.0, but he lost by two feet to Chataway's WR 13:51.6. Ten days later, at Prague, Kuts regained the 5000 record with a 13:51.0.

He lost his 5000 record to Sandor Iharos on September 10, 1955. Eight days later he recovered it with 13:46.8 at Belgrade, only to lose it a third time to Iharos's 13:40.6 on October 23. Kuts also ran 10,000 meters in 28:59.2.

The next year, Kuts ran 5000 meters in 13:39.6 but lost to Pirie's record 13:36.8. On September 11, at Moscow, Kuts lowered the 10,000 World Record to 28:30.4. In the Olympic Games, he won the 10,000 in 28:45.6 and the 5000 in 13:39.6.

Stomach problems assailed Kuts in 1957, but in October he returned to form. On October 6 in Prague, he barely missed the 5000 record with 13:38.0. A week later, in Rome, he broke it for the fourth time with 13:35.0.

In his five years of international racing he was No. 1 in the World Rankings three times at each distance. After 1957 he had run four of the five fastest 5000s of all time.

KUZNYETSOV, VASILIY (Soviet Union). . . . . . .2 B, 2 WR, 2 No. 1
Decathlon, 1956-60. . . . . .2/7/32, 6-1/184

Kuznyetsov broke Rafer Johnson's decathlon World Record in 1958 and again in 1959. He won the bronze medal at the Olympics of 1956 and again in 1960.

LADOUMEGUE, JULES (France) . . . . S, 4 WR, 2 No. 1*
   800-Mile, 1926-31 . . . . .12/10/06

Ladoumegue placed 2nd in the 1928 Olympic 1500. In 1930, he lowered the 1500 World Record to 3:49.2, and two weeks later he broke the 1000 record with 2:23.6. In 1931 he set a 2000-meter record of 5:21.8 and in September he ran the fastest ever ¾ mile, in 3:00.6. Three weeks later, he broke Paavo Nurmi's mile record with a 4:09.2. Then he was barred from amateur competition because of excessive expense payoffs.

LARRABEE, MIKE (USA) . . . . G, Gr, WR, No. 1
   400, 1956-64 . . . . .12/2/33, 6-1/170

Larrabee was an in-and-out quarter-miler at the age of 30. His best World Ranking had been No. 2 in 1957 when he ran a 46.2 440. He ran 45.8 in 1959. In 1964, his patient determination paid off with a record tying 44.9 400 meters in the Final Trials and the Olympic championship. He won a second gold medal in the 4 x 400 meter relay.

LAUER, MARTIN (West Germany) . . . . .Gr, WR, No. 1, AOY
   110 Hurdles, Decathlon, 1957-60 . .1/2/37, 6-1¼/165

Lauer lowered the 110 hurdle record to 13.2 in 1959 and also ranked No. 2 in the decathlon. In the 1960 Olympics, he hit three hurdles and finished 4th. Then he anchored West Germany's 4 x 100 meter relay team to victory.

LEHTINEN, LAURI (Finland). . . . . G, S, 2 WR, No. 1*
   Distances, 1931-37 . . . . .8/10/08

Lehtinen took 11.3 seconds off Paavo Nurmi's 5000 World Record with 14:16.9 on June 19, 1932, at Helsinki. He also set a 3-mile record of 13:50.6. He won the Olympic 5000 at Los Angeles. He placed 2nd in 1936 after a collision in the last kilometer. His 8:19.5 for 3000 meters was second-fastest ever, in 1933. In 1937, he ran a losing 10,000 in 30:15.0, fifth-fastest ever.

LEMMING, ERIK (Sweden) . . . . .3 G, 2 B, 8 WR, 2 No. 1*
   Javelin, 1899-1912 . . . . .2/22/80

Lemming set a javelin World Record of 161-9 at the age of 19 in 1899. He broke it seven times, reaching 204-5 in 1912. He won the javelin at the Olympics of 1908 and 1912, and the unofficial Games of 1906. He also

Profiles of Other Champions

placed 3rd in the 1906 shot and pentathlon. He won a second gold medal in 1908—the javelin "held in middle." He was 5th in the 1900 high jump.

LEWIS, CARL (USA) . . . . 5 G, 2 Gr, 11 No. 1, 3 AOY
 Sprints, Long Jump, 1979- 7/1/61, 6-2/176
See chapter.

LIPPINCOTT, DON (USA) . . . . S, B, 2 WR
 Sprints, 1912-13 . . . . .11/16/93, 5-10/160

Lippincott set an Olympic and World Record of 10.6 for 100 meters in 1912, then finished 3rd in the final. Second in the 200 final, he came back in 1913 to tie the 220 World Record of 21.2.

LITVINOV, SERGEY (Soviet Union) . . . . G, S, 3 WR, 2 No. 1
 Hammer, 1976- 1/23/58, 5-11/196

A sensational teenager, Litvinov threw 237-5 in 1976 at the age of 18 and 243-10 in 1977. He improved to 250-10 in 1978 and ranked No. 1 in the world in 1979 when he won the World Cup and threw 261-10. In 1980, he set a World Record of 267-11 in May and placed 2nd in the Olympics. He slipped to 261-2 in 1981, but he raised the World Record to 275-6 in 1982. He won every competition in 1983, including the World Championship and threw a new World Record of 276-0. In 1984, he threw 279-4 while losing to Yuriy Syedikh's World Record. The boycott kept him out of the Olympics.

LONG, DALLAS (USA) . . . . G, 10 WR, 3 No. 1
 Shot, 1958-64. . . . . .6/13/40, 6-4/260

Long astounded track fans with a 61-½ put while he was still 18 years old in 1958. With a 2nd place in the AAU, he was No. 2 in the World Ranking. As a freshman at Southern California in 1959, he bettered the World Record with 63-7 and was again No. 2 in the world. He raised the World Record to 64-6½ on March 27, 1960, but lost it to Bill Nieder. He won the NCAA and Final Trials and placed 3rd in the Olympics.

In 1961, Long improved to No. 1 in the World Ranking. He won the NCAA and AAU and was undefeated with a best mark of 64-7¾. He broke Nieder's World Record with a 65-10½ in the 1962 Coliseum Relays. He won the NCAA with 64-7, then slipped to 63-1¼ in the AAU and lost to Gary Gubner. He ranked No. 1. Now busy as a dental

Carlos Lopes, the fastest marathon

Profiles of Other Champions

student, he slipped to No. 6 ranking in 1963 with a best of 63-9 in two meets.

Training intensively in 1964, he bettered his World Record by one inch on April 4. At Fresno on May 9, he raised it to 66-7¼ in a rimless ring. He put 66-3½ on May 29, then declined and put only 63-4¾ in the AAU, losing to Randy Matson. Against the Soviets, on August 11 in Los Angeles, he threw 67-10. His great series also included puts of 65-6¼, 66-5¼, and 67-1. At Tokyo, he came from behind to win the Olympic championship at 66-8½.

LONG, MAXIE (USA) . . . . G, WR, 3 No. 1*
   400, 1898-1900 . . . . .b. 1878

Olympic 400 meter champion in 1900, Long set a 440 World Record of 47.8 on September 29, 1900, at Travers Island, N.Y. On October 4, in New Jersey, Long ran a straightaway 440 in 47.0. He won the AAU 440 three times (1898-1900) and the 1899 220.

LOOMIS, FRANK (USA) . . . . G, WR, No. 1*
   400 Hurdles, 1917-20. . . . . .8/22/96

Loomis won the 1920 Olympic 400 meter hurdles in World Record time of 54.0. He won 2 AAU 220 low hurdles plus one 440 hurdles.

LOPES, CARLOS (Portugal) . . . . G, S, WR, No. 1
   5000-Marathon, 1973- 2/18/47, 5-6/123

A gradual progression brought Lopes to times of 13:33.78 and 28:30.6 in 1975 at the age of 28. Then he broke through to win the IAAF cross country run. In the spring, he ran 7:48.8 for 3000 meters, plus 13:24.0 and 27:45.8. In the Olympics, he lost only to Lasse Viren and afterwards he ran 27:42.65. Then, much like Viren, he slipped back into obscurity for four years.

In 1981, at the age of 34, he began his comeback to the top with 27:47.8. The next year, he ran 13:17.28 and 27:24.39 but he placed only 4th in the European 10,000. In 1983, he broke into the marathon with 2:08:39 and ranked No. 3 in the world. He lowered his 10,000 best to 27:23.44 and placed 6th in the sprint-finish World Championships. In 1984, he won the IAAF cross country again, increased his speed with 13:16.38 and bettered the World Record with 27:17.48 while finishing 2nd. He won the Olympic marathon in 2:09:21. He won the 1985 Rotterdam marathon in the best-ever time of 2:07:12.

Track's Greatest Champions

Janis Lusis

Dallas Long

Jack Lovelock

Profiles of Other Champions

LOVELOCK, JACK (New Zealand) . . . . .G, 2 WR, No. 1*
   Mile, 1932-36. . . . . .1/5/10,   /133

Lovelock attended Oxford and set a British Record for the mile of 4:12.0 in 1932. After a 9th place finish in the 1932 Olympics, he set a mile World Record of 4:07.6 at Princeton, July 15, 1933. He won the British Empire Games mile at London in 1934 and the 1935 Princeton Invitational. In the 1936 Olympics, he set a new 1500 meter World Record of 3:47.8.

LOWE, DOUGLAS (Great Britain) . . . . 2 G, 2 No. 1*
   880, 1924-28 . . . . .8/17/02

In the 1924 Olympics, Lowe won the 800 and was 4th in the 1500. In 1928, he won again in the 800 and his team placed 5th in the 4 x 400 relay. In 1926 he was under the World Record while losing an 880 to Otto Peltzer in 1:51.6.

LUNDKVIST, ERIK (Sweden). . . . . .G, WR, No. 1*
   Javelin, 1928-36 . . . . .6/29/08

Lundkvist improved 26 feet in 1928 to win the Olympic javelin championship. Thirteen days later he broke the World Record with a 232-11. He retired because of mental illness but came back in 1936 with 233-5.

LUSIS, JANIS (Soviet Union) . . . . G, S, B, 2 WR, 9 No. 1
   Javelin, 1961-74 . . . . .5/13/39, 5-11/198

Lusis used great strength and excellent technique to be the greatest of all time in the sport's most erratic event, the javelin.

From a best throw of 265-9 in 1961, he progressed to No. 1 in the World Rankings for 1962. He had a best mark of 282-3 and was undefeated, including the European Championships at 269-2.

In 1963 he scored 7342 points in a decathlon. His best javelin throw was 274-5, but he was again undefeated. In 1964 his best mark was only 270-11 and he lost three times before the Olympics. He led at Tokyo with his second throw, 264-4, but he did not improve and placed 3rd.

In 1965 he lost three times, early in the season. Then he returned to form and won all the rest to regain his No. 1 position in the World Rankings. He threw over 280-0 in five meets with a best of 284-0. In 1966 he was an undefeated No. 1 again, with a best of 281-4. He won his second European Championship title at 277-2.

In 1967, a sore shoulder caused five early defeats, but on September 7, at Odessa, he threw 298-4 and 298-6, 2nd- and 3rd-best ever.

In 1968 he was over 280-0 in 17 meets. Of all the javelin throwers in history, only Terje Pedersen's throw of 300-11 had gone over 290 feet, but Lusis did it in 11 meets!

On June 23, at Saarijarvi, Finland, he broke the World Record with a throw of 301-9.

And yet, in the Olympic Games, he trailed Jorma Kinnunen's 290-6 until his last throw when Lusis won with 295-7.

The '68 season was his sixth as No. 1 in the World Rankings. In 1969 he won his third European Championships with a throw of 300-3 and ranked No. 1 again. He slipped to No. 6 in 1970, but returned to No. 1 in 1971 with his 4th European championship.

In 1972, at the age of 33, he raised the World Record to 307-9. In the Olympics, he lost by a mere 2 centimeters. He ranked No. 2 in 1973 and No. 7 in 1974.

MAKI, TAISTO (Finland). . . . . 6 WR, 5 No. 1*, AOY*
    Distances, 1938-39 . . . . .12/2/10

Maki set a World Record of 30:02.0 for 10,000 meters in 1938 and won the European Championships 5000. He set five World Records in 1939. On June 16 at Helsinki, he ran 3 miles in 13:42.4 and 5000 meters in 14:08.8. On July 7 he lowered the 2-mile record to 8:53.2. On September 17, still in Helsinki, he ran the 6-mile in 28:55.6 and the 10,000 in 29:52.6. The war ended his career.

MALINOWSKI, BRONISLAW (Poland). . . . . .G, S, 3 No. 1
    Steeplechase, 1971-80 . . . . .6/4/51, 5-11¼/154

Internationally interesting in 1971 at the age of 20, Malinowski ran a steeplechase in 8:28.2 and the 5000 in 13:39.4. He placed 5th in the 1972 Olympic steeplechase. He ranked only No. 6 in 1973, but he won the European Championships steeplechase in 1974 and ranked No. 1. In 1975, he ran 8:12.62 while placing 2nd to Anders Garderud's World Record and ranked No. 2. He won the silver medal in the 1976 Olympics in 8:09.11. Unranked in the 1500 and 5000, he ran a 3:55.40 mile, 4th-best in the world, and 13:17.69, the year's 6th-best 5000. Injured in 1977, he came back to No. 2 in 1978 with 8:11.63 and a European championship. He ranked No. 1 in 1979 even though injuries held him

Profiles of Other Champions

to three races, and he won the 1980 Olympic title with 8:09.70. He claimed 4 of the 10 fastest steeples ever, and 7 of 20 fastest, at the time of his death in an auto accident in 1981.

MARTY, WALTER (USA) .... 3 WR, No. 1*
    High Jump, 1933-34 .... 8/15/10

Marty set a high jump World Record of 6-8½ in 1933. The next year he tied for first in both the NCAA and AAU and raised his World Record to 6-9 and again to 6-9½.

MATHIAS, BOB (USA) .... 2 G, 3 WR, 4 No. 1
    Decathlon, 1948-1952 .... 11/17/30, 6-3/200

See chapter.

MATSON, RANDY (USA) .... G, S, 4 WR, 5 No. 1, AOY
    Shot, Discus, 1963-72 .... 3/5/45, 6-6½/270

Matson was the best high school junior of all time with a shot put of 64-7 and a discus throw of 186-6 in 1962. As a senior, in 1963, he put the 12-pound shot 66-10½ and the 16-pounder 60-6. He threw the high school discus 193-1 and lost a national record of 199-4 because of sloping ground. He threw the heavy discus 169-7, making him the 2nd best high school thrower of all time with all four weights. He placed 4th in the AAU shot at 59-1¼ and toured Europe.

As a freshman at Texas A&M in 1964, he gained new strength through weight training. He concentrated on the shot, but he threw the discus 182-11. Indoors, he improved his shot best to 62-5 five days before his 19th birthday.

Outdoors, he kept improving to 64-10½. He beat Dallas Long for the AAU title at 64-11. He put 65-5½ on September 5 and made the Olympic team with 63-10. At Tokyo, he put 66-3¼ and nearly won the gold medal.

In 1965 he put 66-2¼ indoors and won the NCAA. In the discus he was undefeated and set a Collegiate Record of 201-1. In the shot, he became the greatest ever. He broke the World Record with 67-11¼ on April 9. He raised it to 69-¾ on April 30. Eight days later he put 70-7.

In 1966 he played basketball and lost weight and strength. He ranked No. 1 in the shot and No. 5 in the discus in the World Rankings, but his bests were 69-2½ and 197-11. He won both events in the NCAA. He won the AAU shot and was third in the discus.

In 1967, his first loss since the Olympics was to Neal Steinhauer, indoors. He put the iron outdoor shot 70-7½ indoors, but it was ineligible for record consideration.

In April, 1967, he had one of the greatest performances in track and field history. He had not trained much with the shot for a month because of a hand injury. For the first time in his life he had concentrated on the discus. On April 9, at College Station, Texas, he put the shot over 70-0 three times, with a best of 70-5½. Then he threw the discus over his own Collegiate Record three times with a best of 213-9, only 2 inches from the World Record.

Two weeks later, he put 71-5½, probably the greatest single mark ever made to that date in track and field. He reached 70 feet again, then won a double at the NCAA and took the AAU shot. He won the Pan-American Games title at Winnipeg.

In 1968 he started with a sprained hand and never reached his potential. His best put was 69-10½. He won his fourth AAU championship and won the Olympic gold medal at 67-4¾.

He let down in 1969, competing in only four meets with a best of 66-7½, but he reared back in 1970. Undefeated, with a near-record 71-4¼, he won the award as Athlete of the Year. His record now included the 25 longest puts in history and 52 of the 53 longest. He ranked No. 2 in 1971 and faded to No. 6 in 1972, placing 4th in the Final Trials. He became a professional soon afterward.

McDONALD, PAT (USA) . . . . 2 G, S, 4 No. 1*
    Shot, 1909-20. . . . . .7/29/78, 6-6/250

McDonald won the Olympic shot in 1912. In 1920, he won the 56-pound weight and placed 2nd in the two-hand shot at the age of 42. At 56, he won the 1933 AAU weight throw.

McGRATH, MATT (USA). . . . . .G, 2 S, 2 WR, 6 No. 1*
    Weights, 1906-35. . . . . .12/18/78, 6-0/248

McGrath broke the World Record in the hammer with 173-7 in 1907 and again on October 11, 1911, with 187-4. He threw 190-0 in an exhibition in 1913. He set World Records for the 35-pound weight (53-11) and 56-pound weight (40-6¼) in 1911 and later threw 61-8 (1918) and 41-3 (exhibition). McGrath won seven AAU hammer titles from 1908 to 1926, and seven 56-pound weight titles. He placed in four Olympic hammer throws: 2nd in 1908, 1st in 1912, 5th in 1920 (with a twisted knee), and 2nd in 1924.

McKENLEY, HERB (Jamaica). . . . . Gr, 3 S, 4 WR, 4 No. 1
   100-400, 1945-52 . . . . .7/10/22, 6-1/159

McKenley attended Boston College and the University of Illinois and won NCAA 440 titles in 1946 and 1947. He won the AAU in 1945, 1947, and 1948. On June 1, 1946, he lowered the 440 World Record to 46.2, then ran a 20.6 220. He tied his 46.2 in the 1947 NCAA and lowered it to 46.0 at Berkeley, June 5, 1948. He won the AAU 400 in a record 45.9. In the 1948 Olympics, at the age of 26, McKenley lost the 400 meters to Arthur Wint's 46.2.

McKenley ranked No. 1 in the world for 1947 and 1948, but his career was one of fast 2nd places in big meets. He was 2nd in the AAU in 1946, 1949, 1950, and 1951. In the 1952 Olympics, he was a close 2nd in the 100 and 400. He finally won a gold medal with a 44.6 relay leg, fastest ever recorded to that time. Strangely, he never developed his 220 talent, although he ranked No. 2 in the world in 1950.

MEADOWS, EARLE (USA) . . . . G, 2 WR, No. 1*
   Pole Vault, 1935-42. . . . . .6/29/13, 6-1/160

Meadows tied for 1st in the 1935 NCAA and AAU and the 1936 NCAA. In 1936 he won the Final Trials and the Olympic gold medal, with a record 14-3¼. In 1937 he tied with Bill Sefton for a World Record 14-8½ at Palo Alto, California, on May 8. Three weeks later, in Los Angeles, they both cleared 14-11.

Meadows won the indoor AAU in 1940 and 1941. He set an indoor World Record of 14-7 in 1941.

MENNEA, PIETRO (Italy) . . . . G, Sr, 2 B, Br, WR, 3 No. 1
   Sprints, 1971-84 . . . . .6/28/52, 5-10/150

A promising 10.2 and 20.7 sprinter in 1971 at the age of 19, Mennea developed rapidly to become one of the world's most durable sprinters. He ranked among the top 10 in the world six years in the 100 and 11 years in the 200, in spite of "retiring" in 1981 and 1982. He made the Olympic 200 finals in 1972 through 1984, placing 3rd, 4th, 1st, and 7th; he placed 3rd in the 1983 World Championships, and he won both European titles. In 1979, he set a World Record 19.72 at Mexico City, and the next year he ran the fastest ever at a low altitude—19.96.

MEREDITH, TED (USA) . . . . .G, Gr, 5 WR, 5 No. 1*, AOY*
400-800, 1912-20 . . . . .11/14/91, 5-9/155

Meredith was probably the greatest middle-distance runner of all time until the 1930s. In 1912, he came out of obscurity to win the Princeton Interscholastics in 49.2 and 1:55.0, far under the old High School Records. The 5-9, 155-pound 19-year-old made the Olympic team in both events.

In the Olympic 800 at Stockholm, Meredith fought past Mel Sheppard in the homestretch to win in World Record time of 1:51.9, continued to 880 yards and set a new World Record of 1:52.5. In the 400, he started too fast and placed only 4th. He won a second gold medal on the World Record 4 x 400 meter relay team.

A freshman at Pennsylvania in 1913, he set an indoor record of 1:13.8 for 600 yards. In 1914, he won the IC4A 440 in 48.4, then lost the 880 to Dave Caldwell's Collegiate Record 1:53.4. He won the AAU 440.

In the 1915 IC4A, he tied the Collegiate Record in the 440 with a 48.0 and won the 880 in 1:54.4. In the AAU meet in San Francisco, he won the straightaway 440 in 47.0.

In 1916, he set an indoor record of 1:21.4 for 660 yards. In a dual meet with Cornell, Vere Windnagel equalled Meredith's World Record 880 but Meredith beat him in 1:52.2. In the IC4A he set a new World Record of 47.4 in the 440 and then won the 880 in a Collegiate Record 1:53.0.

After a mediocre 1917 season he retired, holding High School, Collegiate, American and World Records for 400 meters, 440 yards, 800 meters, and 880 yards. His 880 record lasted 20 years, his 440 record 27 years. A comeback in 1920 saw him eliminated in his semi-final of the Olympic 400 meters.

METCALFE, JACK (Australia). . . . . B, WR, 3 No. 1*
Triple Jump, 1934-36. . . . . .2/3/12

Metcalfe won the 1934 British Empire Games triple jump at 51-3. He set a World Record of 51-9¼ the next year, and placed 3rd in the 1936 Olympics.

METCALFE, RALPH (USA) . . . . .Gr, 2 S, B, 10 WR, 6 No. 1*, AOY*
Sprints, 1930-36 . . . . .5/29/10, 5-11/180

In high school, Metcalfe won a sprint double in the Illinois state meet three times, and he placed 4th in the AAU 220 (1930). As a freshman at Marquette in 1931, he was 5th in the AAU 100 and second in the 220.

In 1932, the 5-11, 180-pounder won the metric sprints in the NCAA in 10.2 and 20.3. Neither World Record was considered by the AAU. He won both sprints in the AAU, but in the Los Angeles Olympics he had bad luck. His chest touched the tape first in the 100 meters, but under existing rules Tolan was the winner because his back crossed the line first. In the 200, Metcalfe's lane was measured wrong and he ran five feet too far, finishing 3rd. In Canada, he ran a wind-aided 220 in 19.8.

In 1933, he won doubles again in both the NCAA and AAU, and added the indoor AAU title. His 9.4 and 20.4 in the NCAA were not recognized. In Budapest, August 12, he entered the record books twice, with a 10.3 100 meters and a 20.6 200 meters. The latter was amazing because it was around a half turn.

In 1934 he became the only man ever to win three NCAA doubles. He again doubled in the AAU and won his second indoor title, even though he was a notoriously slow starter. In Japan, he ran 200 meters in a windy 20.2.

In 1935 he lost his AAU 100 championship to Eulace Peacock, but he won the 200. In 1936 he won his third indoor AAU and his fifth AAU 200 meters. No other sprinter has ever won five times in one event. He made the Olympic team behind Jesse Owens in the 100, but for the only time in his life he failed in the 200, placing 4th after leading into the homestretch. He was 2nd to Owens in the 100 meters at Berlin, gaining two yards after a poor start. He finally won his gold medal in the 4 x 100 meter relay.

Metcalfe tied the 100 meter World Record of 10.3 10 times and broke it once. He received credit for only three of the 10.3s. He broke the 220 record twice without recognition. In five years of competition he lost only five times in the 100 and three times in the 200.

Jesse Owen's coach, Larry Snyder, said of Metcalfe: "He had no adequate coaching in how to start properly...but how he could fly at the finish!.. I am convinced that Metcalfe was potentially the best of them all."

MICHEL, DETLEF (EG) . . . . G, No. 1
Javelin, 1975- 10/13/55, 6-¾/209

Michel threw 277-5 when he was only 19, in 1975, but he im-

Track's Greatest Champions

Ralph Metcalfe   Randy Matson

Bobby Morrow, winning 1956 Olympic 200 over Andy Stanfield (left)

Profiles of Other Champions

proved only 5 feet in four years. In 1979, he added 20 pounds of muscle and threw 294-5. Improving steadily, he threw 317-4 in 1983, second-best ever, and won at the World Championships.

MILBURN, ROD (USA) . . . . .G, 5 WR, 3 No. 1, AOY
110 Hurdles, 1969-83 . . . . 5/18/50, 6-0/176

Milburn set a High School Record of 13.7 for the 42" hurdles in 1969, and ranked No. 6 in the world for 1970 as a freshman at Texas Southern. After a winter of intense technical training, he became the fastest hurdler in history. Undefeated in 15 meets, he won the NCAA, AAU, and Pan-American Championships and lowered the 120 hurdles record to 13.0. He was voted Athlete of the Year. In 1972, he won the Olympic championship in 13.2 (13.24), equalling the 110 hurdles record. In 1973, he tied his 120 record of 13.0, broke the 110 record at 13.1 and then equalled it. He turned professional and then retired, never to be heard from again. . . until 1980 when he made a remarkable comeback to run 13.40 and rank No. 5 in the world. In 1981, he set an indoor 50 yard hurdles World Record of 6.02 and ranked No. 8. After ranking No. 4 in 1982, he went unranked in 1983 although he ran 13.60, and he retired once again.

MILLS, BILLY (USA) . . . . .G, WR, No. 1
Distances, 1960-68 . . . . .6/30/38, 5-11/152

Mills won the 1964 Olympic 10,000 and placed 14th in the marathon. In 1965, he set a World Record of 27:11.6 in the AAU 6 mile, plus an American Record of 28:17.6 for 10,000 meters.

MIMOUN, ALAIN (France) .G, 3 S, No. 1
Distances, 1950-56 . . . . .1/21/21

Mimoun, an Algerian, ran 2nd to Emil Zatopek in five major races: 1948 Olympic 10,000, 1952 Olympic 5000 and 10,000, and the 1950 European Championships 5000 and 10,000. In 1956 at the age of 34, he won the Olympic marathon in 2:25:00. He won the International Cross Country four times.

MOGENBURG, DIETMAR (West Germany) . . . . G, WR, 2 No. 1
High Jump, 1978- 8/15/61, 6-7¼/161

One of the most promising young athletes in history, Mogenburg jumped 7-3¾ in 1978 while barely 17 years old. In 1979, he cleared

7-7¼ before his 18th birthday and ranked No. 1. In 1980, he broke the World Record with 7-8½, but the boycott kept him out of the Olympics and he ranked No. 3. He fell to No. 8 in 1981 and No. 4 the next two years, winning the European title in 1982. Apparently a fading morning glory at the age of 22, he came back strongly in 1984, clearing 7-6½ 15 times. He won the Olympics at 7-8½ and raised his PR to 7-8¾, 4th best ever. Indoors in 1985, he jumped 7-10.

MOORCROFT, DAVE (Great Britain). . . . . .WR, No. 1
    1500-5000. . . . . .4/10/53, 5-10¾/146

Moorcroft placed 7th in the 1976 Olympic 1500, and ranked No. 3 in 1978, after winning the Commonwealth Games 1500. Bothered by injuries, he added the 5000 in 1980, ranked No. 5 in 1981 as European Cup champion, and broke the World Record with an astounding 13:00.41 in 1982. He also ranked No. 6 in the 1500 with 3:33.79 and a 3:49.34 mile. Injuries stopped him again and he ran poorly in the 1984 Olympic 5000 final.

MOORE, CHARLEY (USA) . . . . .G, Sr, 2 WR, 3 No. 1
    400, 400 Hurdles, 1942-52 . . . . . .8/12/29, 6-0/170

Moore won the NCAA 440 in 1949 and the 220 low hurdles in 1951. He won four AAU titles in the 440 hurdles. He was first in the World Rankings in 1949, 1951, and 1952. He won the 1952 Olympic 400 hurdles in 50.8. In 1952 he equaled the 400-meter hurdles World Record of 51.9 and then improved it to 51.6 five days later.

MORRIS, GLENN (USA) . . . . G, 2 WR, No. 1*
    Decathlon, 1936 . . . . .6/18/12, 6-2/185

Morris, in his single year as a decathlon man, won the 1936 AAU with a World Record and raised it 20 points with his victory in the Olympic Games.

MORROW, BOBBY (USA) . . . . 2G, Gr, 5 WR, 5 No. 1
    Sprints, 1955-60 . . . . .10/15/35, 6-1½/165

Morrow was the best all-around sprinter of all time before his injury in 1959. He was undefeated as a high school senior in 1954, and he continued undefeated in his freshman year at Abilene Christian until after he had won the AAU 100. His only loss was his 4th place in the AAU 220.

Profiles of Other Champions

He had won 30 consecutive 100s when Dave Sime caught a flyer and defeated him in the 1956 Drake Relays. Morrow was undefeated that year in the 200/220. He won both sprints in the NAIA, NCAA, and Final Olympic Trials, plus the AAU 100.

In the Olympic Games at Melbourne, he won both sprints and anchored the winning 4 x 100 meter relay team. He ran 9.4 three times and 10.2 four times, each within 0.1 of the World Record. Also in 1956, he ran 20.6 around a curve three times, tying the best ever recorded.

In 1957 he tied the World Record of 9.3 three times and ran another 20.6. He lost only one race all year, winning the NAIA and NCAA doubles again. In 1958, he ranked No. 1 in the world for the third straight year, but he slipped to No. 2 in the 200. He won both sprints in the AAU.

In 1959 he ran 10.2 and three 9.4s before his injury. In 1960, hobbled by injuries, he barely missed making the Olympic team in the 200.

MOSES, EDWIN (USA) . . . . 3 G, 4 WR, 8 No. 1, AOY
    400 Hurdles, 1976- 8/31/55, 6-1/170

    See chapter.

MYERS, LAWRENCE (LON) (USA). . . . . . . .14 WR, No. 1**, AOY**
    100-Mile, 1879-87 . . . . .2/16/58, 5-8/112

Lon Myers was one of the most versatile and remarkable runners in history. A thin 5-8, 112-pounder, he beat the best in both the United States and Britain in races from 50 to 1000 yards, setting American Records at all those distances. He was the first man to run 440 yards under 50 seconds.

Myers won 15 AAU championships—two in the 100, four in the 200, six in the 440 (1879 to 1884), and three in the 880. In 1880 he won all four distances in one afternoon and repeated in the Canadian Championships. In 1881, after winning three AAU titles, he went to England to run in the biggest international meet available. He won the AAA championship in 48.6, fastest time on record. His 6.4 for 60 yards, his 35.0 330, and his 2:13.0 1000 yards lasted more than 25 years.

Myers equalled the World Record of 10.0 in the 100 yards, ran 22.5 in the 220, and a 4:27.6 mile. In 1884 he lowered his 880 World Record to 1:55.4; in 1885 he tied it and won a 440-880 double in the AAA.

He turned professional in 1885. As an amateur, he had raced the great Walter George in a series consisting of 880, mile, and ¾ mile, witnessed by crowds totaling 130,000 at the New York Polo Grounds. Myers won only the 880 (1:56.4). As professionals, they raced in two more series. Indoors, in New York in 1886, Myers won all three. In 1887, in Australia, Myers won only the 880. His best pro mile was 4:22.6.

His most amazing professional race came at Rochdale, England, on August 19, 1885. After a 1:57.0 880, he came back two hours later and spotted England's best professional quarter-miler. Mason, a 24-yard handicap. The race ended in a tie in 46.4.

MYYRA, JONNI (Finland) . . . . 2 G, 5 WR, 4 No. 1*
    Javelin, 1912-25 . . . . .7/13/92

Myyra placed 8th in the 1912 Olympic javelin, then broke the World Record with 205-3 in 1914. He bettered it four times, ending with 216-10 in 1919. He won the javelin in the Olympic Games of 1920 and 1924. He had an unofficial throw of 224-11 in 1925.

NAMBU, CHUHEI (Japan) . . . . G, B, 2 WR, 2 No. 1*
    Long Jump, Triple Jump, 1928-32 . . .5/27/04

Nambu placed 4th in the 1928 Olympic triple jump and 9th in the long jump. On October 27, 1931, in Tokyo, Nambu, a 10.5 100 meter man, broke the long jump World Record with 26-4¼. In the 1932 Olympics, he placed 3rd in the long jump, and he won the triple jump with a World Record 51-7.

NEHEMIAH, RENALDO (USA) . . . . 3 WR, 4 No. 1
    110 Hurdles, 1977-81 . . . . .3/24/59, 6-¾/157

A sensational high school athlete in 1977 in several events including a 13.89 for the 110 meter international hurdles, Nehemiah concentrated on the 110 hurdles and ranked No. 1 as a Maryland freshman in 1978. At the age of 19, he placed 2nd in the NCAA, won the AAU, and ran 13.23, only 0.02 from the World Record. The next year, he won the NCAA, AAU, and Pan-American Games, lowered the World Record to 13.16 and then 13.00, and ran the 4 fastest of all-time. In 1980 and 1981, he ranked No. 1 although injured, and he lowered his World Record to 12.93. Then he retired to professional football, owning 9 of the 11 fastest races ever run.

Profiles of Other Champions

NEMETH, IMRE (Hungary) . . . . G, B, 3 WR, 3 No. 1
   Hammer, 1939-52 . . . . .9/23/17

Nemeth set a hammer World Record of 193-7 on July 14, 1948. Ten days later he won the Olympic championship. He raised the World Record to 195-5 in 1949 and to 196-5 in 1950. He placed 3rd in the 1952 Olympics.

NEMETH, MIKLOS (Hungary) . . . . G, WR, 2 No. 1
   Javelin, 1968-80 . . . . .10/23/46, 6-0/190

Son of Imre, Miklos won the 1976 Olympic javelin with a World Record 310-4. He threw 308-9, 2nd-best ever, in 1977 and ranked No. 1 again. He placed 8th in the 1980 Olympics.

NIEDER, BILL (USA) . . . . G, S, 2 WR, 2 No. 1
   Shot, 1955-60. . . . . .8/10/33, 6-3/225

The first high school 60-footer with the 12-pound shot, Nieder was set back by a severely damaged knee. He won the 1955 NCAA at 57-3, then became history's second 60-footer with 60-3¾ in 1956. He placed 2nd to O'Brien in the 1956 Olympics.

In 1957 he beat O'Brien with 62-2 and ranked No. 1 in the world. In the army in 1958, he slipped to No. 4 in the World Rankings. In 1959 he improved to No. 3 with a best of 62-9.

He started 1960 with a World Record 65-7 in the Texas Relays. An injured leg dropped him to 4th in the Final Trials. His leg healed, and after four meets around 64 feet, he improved the World Record to 65-10 at Walnut, August 12. He won the Olympics with 64-6¾. At his retirement he owned 12 of the 13 longest puts ever made.

NIKKANEN, YRJO (Finland) . . . . S, WR, No. 1*
   Javelin, 1935-46 . . . . .12/31/14, 5-10½/170

Nikkanen set a javelin World Record of 258-2 in 1938, which lasted 15 years. He was 2nd in the 1936 Olympics and in the European Championships of 1938 and 1946.

NORDWIG, WOLFGANG (East Germany). . . . . . G, B, 2 WR, 2 No. 1
   Pole Vault, 1966-72. . . . . .8/27/43, 6-½/160

Nordwig won the bronze medal in the 1968 Olympics. In 1970, he raised the World Record to 17-10½ on June 17 and again, to 17-11 on

September 3. He won the 1971 European championship and, undefeated, he ranked No. 1 again. He won the Olympic championship in 1972 but ranked No. 3.

NURMI, PAAVO (Finland) . . . . . 9 G, 3 S, 24 WR, 13 No. 1*, 3 AOY*
  Distances, 1920-34 . . . . .6/13/97
See chapter.

O'BRIEN, PARRY (USA). . . . . .2 G, S, 16 WR, 8 No. 1, AOY
  Shot, Discus, 1951-66 . . . . .1/28/32, 6-3/235
See chapter.

O'CALLAGHAN, PATRICK (Ireland). . . . . 2 G, WR, 4 No. 1*
  Hammer, 1927-37 . . . . .1/28/06

In 1928, O'Callaghan came from behind on his fourth throw to win the Olympic championship. In the 1932 Olympics, he came from behind on his last throw to win another gold medal. He raised the European record to 183-11 in 1931 and to 186-10 in 1933. He was ineligible for the 1936 Olympics because of a federation "war." In 1937, throwing from a circle five inches too small and with a hammer six ounces too heavy, he bettered the World Record with 195-4, a mark not beaten officially for 12 years.

ODA, MIKIO (Japan). . . . . G, WR, 2 No. 1*
  Long Jump, Triple Jump, 1924-32 . . .3/30/05

Oda placed 6th in the 1924 Olympic triple jump and won the Olympics in 1928. Injured, he placed 12th in 1932. He raised the Asian record to 50-6¾ in 1928. On October 17, 1931, in Tokyo, he set a World Record of 51-1½. His best long jump was 24-8.

OERTER, AL (USA) . . . . .4 G, 4 WR, 6 No. 1
  Discus, 1956-84 . . . . .9/19/36, 6-3½/228
See chapter.

OLIVEIRA, JOAO (Brazil) . . . . 2 B, WR, 3 No. 1
  Long Jump, Triple Jump, 1974-81 3/28/54, 6-2½/165

Oliveira entered 1975 as a 53-7¾ triple jumper and finished as the No. 3 long jumper at 26-10¾ and the No. 2 triple jumper with an altitude-aided World Record of 58-8½. He placed 3rd in the 1976 Olympic triple jump. He won the 1977 World Cup and ranked No. 1. In 1978 he equalled the sea level best in the triple jump with 57-2¾ to hold his No. 1 ranking as well as No. 6 in the long jump. In 1979, he won every triple jump, including the Pan-American Games at 56-8 and the World Cup. He ranked No. 1 and added a No. 3 ranking with a best long jump of 27-5¼. In the 1980 Olympics, questionable judging held him to 3rd. In 1981, he won his third World Cup and ranked No. 2. His career ended with an auto accident which cost him his leg.

OSBORN, HAROLD (USA) . . . . .2 G, 2 WR, 5 No. 1*
High Jump, Decathlon, 1922-36. . .4/13/99, 5-11/172

Dr. Osborn was one of the most remarkable of all athletes, with national placings for 15 years.

In 1922, he tied for 1st in the NCAA and AAU high jumps. He lost the AAU title in a jumpoff. He also placed 2nd in the triple jump and decathlon. In 1923 he won the AAU indoor high jump and the decathlon.

In 1924, after winning the indoor AAU high jump, he set an outdoor World Record of 6-8¼ at Urbana, Illinois, on May 27. In the Olympic Games, he won the high jump with an Olympic record of 6-6. Then he won the decathlon with a World Record score. No other man had ever won an Olympic decathlon with a World Record score. No other man ever won an Olympic decathlon plus an individual event.

In 1925, in the indoor AAU, he won four championships and placed 4th in the shot. He won the 70 yard hurdles in a good 8.6, the high jump, and the standing high and long jumps. In that same indoor season, he set an indoor World Record of 6-6¼ and a standing high jump record of 5-5¾, equal to the outdoor world best.

Outdoors in 1925, he jumped 6-8¼ but it was not accepted as a World Record. He won the AAU high jump (6-7) and the decathlon. In 1926 he won the indoor AAU high jump and standing long jump, plus the outdoor high jump and decathlon. In 1927, his only title came in the indoor standing long jump.

In the AAU high jump, he placed 3rd in 1927 and 1928, and tied for 4th in 1935. In the indoor AAU, he was 4th in 1927, won in 1928, and placed in 1929 and from 1931 through 1935.

He competed in his second Olympic Games in 1928, but placed only 5th in the high jump.

Charley Paddock

Steve Ovett

Profiles of Other Champions

Indoors, he won the AAU standing high jump three more years until it was abandoned after 1931. He was 2nd in the indoor standing long jump in 1930. In 1934 he tried the pentathlon and placed 2nd in the AAU. He was 5th in 1935.

In 1936, at the age of 37, Osborn climaxed his career indoors at St. Louis on April 4 when he cleared 5-6 in the standing high jump. This is still the best on record, indoors or out.

Thus, he won 18 AAU championships in six different events, and won 35 AAU medals in a total of nine different events.

OVETT, STEVE (Great Britain). . . . . G, B, 5 WR, 3 No. 1
800-5000, 1974- 10/9/55, 5-11¾/152

Ovett placed 2nd in the 1974 European Championships 800 at 18. In 1976, he finished 5th in the Olympic 800. In 1977, now 21, he ranked No. 1 in the 1500 with a World Cup victory in 3:34.45. In 1978, he ranked No. 2 in the 800 with another 2nd in the European Championships, and he repeated as an undefeated No. 1 in the 1500, including a European championship. His 8:13.51 2-mile victory over Henry Rono was the best ever outdoors. He won the 1980 Olympic 800, placed 3rd in the 1500 and set world marks of 3:31.36 and 3:48.8. He cut the mile mark in 1981 to 3:48.40 and also ran a 3:31.57 1500. Injured in 1982, he came back in 1983 with a 4th in the World Championships 1500 and then a World Record 3:30.77. Ill in 1984, he still made the Olympic final in both the 800 and 1500.

OWENS, JESSE (USA). . . . . 3G, Gr, 8 WR, 7 No. 1*, 2 AOY*
Sprints, 220, Hurdles, Long Jump, 1933-36. . . 9/12/13, 5-8/156

See chapter.

PADDOCK, CHARLEY (USA) . . .G, Gr, 2 S, 11 WR, 2 No. 1*, AOY*
Sprints, 1919-28 . . . . .8/11/00, 5-8/160

Paddock dominated the sprints in the 1920s although he lost many races. He won AAU 100s in 1921 (9.6) and 1924. He won the 220 in 1920 (21.4), 1921, and 1924 (20.8). He won the Olympic 100 in 1920 and placed 5th in 1924. He was 2nd in the 200 in both Olympics. He won a gold medal in the 1920 4 x 100 meter relay and ran unplaced in 1928.

In 1921 he tied the World Record of 9.6 for 100 yards and broke the 220 record with 20.8. A few weeks later he ran a World Record 100 meters in 10.4, then ran 300 yards in 30.2 and 300 meters in 33.2. The 30.2 was not official because only the time for the full distance could be accepted as a World Record. Two months later he ran 110 yards in 10.2 but it was not accepted as a 100 meter World Record because it was a longer distance! He entered the record books with six official 9.6s, but one, on May 15, 1926, in Los Angeles, was the first official 9.5.

PATTON, MEL (USA) . . . . .G, Gr, 4 WR, 5 No. 1 AOY
    Sprints, 1947-49 . . . . .11/16/24, 6-0/148

Patton was regarded as the fastest sprinter of all time but he was reluctant to compete. He won all five NCAA sprints he entered, but he ran no AAU races after he came into prominence in 1947. He placed 5th in the 1948 Olympic 100 meters and won the 200. He won a second gold medal in the 4 x 100 meter relay.

He tied the 100 yards World Record of 9.4 in 1947 and ran the first 9.3 in 1948. On May 7, 1949, in Los Angeles, he ran 9.1 with a wind of 2.9mps, then broke Jesse Owens's 220 record with a legal 20.2. His 20.7 around a curve in the 1948 Final Trials equalled Owens's American Record. He ran 20.4 four times, giving him half of the 10 fastest 220 times ever run. He lost only three races in three years.

PEACOCK, EULACE (USA) . . . . 2 WR, No. 1*
    Sprints, Long Jump, Pentathlon, 1933-48 . . . .8/27/14, 5-11/180

Peacock had unlimited potential but leg injuries defeated him. Second best in history only to Jesse Owens in the high school and indoor AAU long jumps, he won the national AAU pentathlon in 1933 and 1934. On tour in Europe, he tied the 100m World Record with 10.3 at Oslo.

After losing the NCAA 100 and long jump to Owens in the 1935 meet, he beat Ralph Metcalfe and Owens in the AAU 100 meters. His 10.2 was aided by a wind of 3.4 mps. His 26-3 long jump victory over Owens was the 2nd-longest in history. He defeated Owens in two 100s in the next week.

When he won a 1936 indoor 50 at Cleveland for his fourth consecutive victory over Owens, he seemed to be a certain Olympian, and his 6.0 World Record 60 yards at Toronto confirmed it. But he pulled a muscle and he was never again a contender.

He won four more AAU pentathlons, in 1937, 1943, 1944, and

Profiles of Other Champions

1945. He placed in indoor AAU 60s in 1939, 1940, and 1941, the outdoor 100 in 1940, and in the outdoor long jump in 1944. He won the Metropolitan AAU long jump in 1948.

PELTZER, OTTO (Germany) . . . . 3 WR, 2 No. 1*
  500-1500, 1924-32 . . . . .3/8/00, 6-1¼/159

Dr. Peltzer outkicked Douglas Lowe to set a World Record of 1:51.6 in the AAA 880 in 1925. In 1926, his stretch sprint defeated Edvin Wide and Paavo Nurmi in a World Record 3:51.0 1500 meters. His speed is indicated by his world best of 1:03.6 for 500 meters in 1926.

In 1927 his famed kick beat Sera Martin at 1000 meters in a World Record 2:25.8. Illness caused him to miss the 1924 Olympics. Injured, he failed to qualify in 1928. In 1932, at age 32, he finished last in the Olympic 800-meter final.

PENNEL, JOHN (USA) . . . . 9 WR, 2 No. 1
  Pole Vault, 1961-70. . . . . .7/25/40, 5-7¼/132

Pennel broke or tied the World Record in the vault nine times, raising the record from 16-2½ to 17-10¼ in a seven year span, 1963-69 but placed only 5th and 11th in his two Olympics. He was ranked number one in 1965 and 1966. He was the first vaulter to clear 17ft.

Eulace Peacock

355

Track's Greatest Champions

PETRANOFF, TOM (USA). . . . . S, WR
    Javelin, 1977- 4/8/58, 6-1¾/216

Petranoff progressed to a World Record 327-2 in 1983. He placed 2nd in the World Championships and 10th in the 1984 Olympics.

PIRIE, GORDON (Great Britain) . . . . S, 3 WR, No. 1*
    1500-10,000, 1952-60 . . . . .2/10/31, 6-2/144

Pirie placed 7th in the 1952 Olympic 10,000 and 4th in the 5000 at the age of 21. He set a World Record 13:36.8 for 5000 meters, June 19, 1956, in Bergen, Norway. Three days later, he tied the 3000-meter World Record with 7:55.6. On September 4, at Malmo, he beat the great Hungarians in 7:52.8. In the 1956 Olympics he tried to beat Vladimir Kuts in the 10,000 and finished 8th. In the 5000 he placed 2nd.

PORHOLA, VILLE (Finland) . . . . G, S, No. 1
    Shot/Hammer, 1920-36 . . . . .12/24/97

Porhola won the shot put in the 1920 Olympics and placed 7th in 1924. He turned to the hammer and was a close 2nd in the 1932 Olympics, won the 1934 European Championships, and placed 11th in the 1936 Olympics.

PORTER, BILL (USA). . . . . G, No. 1
    110 Hurdles, 1947-48. . . . . .3/24/26, 6-4/170

Porter won the 1948 Olympic 110 hurdles in 13.9. He ran two other 13.9s in 1948. He beat Harrison Dillard three times, including the 1948 AAU and Final Trials and a 22.7 220 low hurdles race in 1947. He ran 22.5, equal to the 2nd-fastest of all time, behind Dillard's 22.3.

POTGIETER, GERHARDUS (South Africa) . . . . 2 WR, No. 1
    400 Hurdles, 1955-62. . . . . .4/16/37, 5-10/163

Potgieter, at 19, fell over the last hurdle in the 1956 Olympic intermediates when he was in 3rd place. He won the Commonwealth title in 1958 with a World Record 49.7 for 440 yards. On April 16, 1960—his 23rd birthday—he broke the World Record for the 440 intermediates with 49.3. Undefeated for four years and No. 1 in 1959 in the World Rankings, he was eliminated from the 1960 Olympics by an automobile accident.

Profiles of Other Champions

PRINSTEIN, MYER (USA). . . . . 3 G, S, 2 WR, 6 No. 1*
 Long Jump, Triple Jump, 1898-1906 . . . . b. 1880

Prinstein, of Syracuse, set a long jump World Record of 23-8¾ in the 1898 IC4A meet, and won the AAU at 23-7. In the 1900 Penn Relays, he raised the World Record to 24-7¼. He led the qualifiers in the Olympic long jump with 23-6½, but he would not jump in the final because it was on Sunday, and he lost the championship by ¼". He won the triple jump on Monday.

He won the AAU long jump in 1902 and 1904. In the 1904 Olympics, he won both the long jump (24-1) and the triple jump on the same day, three days after placing 5th in the 400 meters.

In 1906, he won the AAU long jump. In the unofficial 1906 Olympics he sprained his ankle on the first jump, but it was 23-7½ and it held up for the championship. In the triple jump three days later he could place only 11th.

PUTTEMANS, EMIEL (Belgium) . . . . .S, 4 WR, No. 1
 3000-10,000, 1970-81 . . . . 10/8/47, 5-7¼/132

Puttemans set a European Record 7:39.8 for 3000 meters in 1971 and ran a World Record 8:17.8 for 2 miles. In the 1972 Olympics, he placed 2nd in the 10,000 and 5th in the 5000. After the Olympics, he set World Records in the 3000 (7:36.6), 3-mile (12:47.8), and 5000 (13:13.0). Indoors in 1973, he set records for the 3000 (7:39.2) and 2 mile (8:13.2). Undefeated outdoors in the 5000 with a best of 13:14.6, he ranked No. 1. In 1975, he ranked No. 2 in the 5000 and No. 5 in the 10,000. Indoors in 1976, he set World Records for 3 miles (12:54.6) and 5000 (13:20.8). Injuries ruined his Olympic hopes. For the next five years he ran 5000s between 13:23.2 and 13:26.9.

QUARRIE, DON (Jamaica). . . . . G, S, Sr, B, 2 WR, 4 No. 1
 Sprints, 1968-84 . . . . .2/25/51, 5-8/155

Quarrie ran in 5 Olympics, beginning in 1968 at the age of 17. Injured in the 1972 200 semi-final, he won the silver medal in the 1976 100 and won the 200. In 1980, he placed 3rd in the 200, and in 1984, after finishing 7th in his 200 semi, he won another silver medal in the 4 x 100 meter relay. He ranked in the top 4 in the 100 five times, including No. 1 in 1976 when he equalled the World Record of 9.9. In the 200, he ranked in the top 10 from 1971 to 1980, missing only 1979. He ranked No. 1 in 1971 when he set a World Record of 19.8 (19.86), and in 1975 and 1976.

357

QUINON, PIERRE (France) . . . . G, WR
   Pole Vault, 1981- 2/20/62, 5-10/161

Quinon vaulted 18-8¼ in 1982 when he was 20. In 1983, he set a World Record of 19-1 but cleared no height in the World Championships. He won the 1984 Olympics with 18-10¼.

REIFF, GASTON (Belgium) . . . . G, 3 WR, 6 No. 1
   1500-5000, 1947-52 . . . . .2/24/21

Reiff won the 1948 Olympic 5000 meters. He set a World Record of 5:06.9 for 2000 meters at Brussels in 1948. He set a 3000-meter record of 7:58.7 at Gavle, Sweden, in 1949. In 1952, after dropping out of the Olympic 5000, he went to Paris on August 26 and set a 2-mile World Record of 8:40.4. He ran 1500 meters in 3:45.8 in 1949 and 5000 in 14:10.8 in 1951.

RHODEN, GEORGE (Jamaica) . . . . .G, Gr, WR, 3 No. 1
   200, 400, 1949-52. . . . . .12/13/26, 5-10/150

Rhoden set a 400-meter World Record of 45.8 in 1950. He won the 1952 Olympic 400 and won another gold medal in the relay. He won three AAU 400s, three NCAA 400s, and an NCAA 220.

RICHARDS, BOB (USA) . . . . 2 G, B, 10 No. 1, AOY
   Pole Vault, Decathlon, 1946-58 . . .2/20/26, 5-10/165

Richards was the second man in history to vault 15 feet and he cleared it a total of 126 times. Only 5-10, he was not tall enough to vault higher with a steel pole, and his best vault was 15-5 outdoors and 15-6 indoors.

In college he managed to tie for first in the NCAA only once. He improved enough to win the AAU nine times, including two ties. He won the indoor AAU eight times, including one tie.

He vaulted in three Olympics. Third at London in 1948, he won in 1952 and 1956 to become the only man to win two gold medals in the Olympic pole vault.

He also competed in the decathlon. He won the AAU all-round in 1953 and the decathlon in 1951, 1954, and 1955. He made the Olympic team in 1956, but an injured tendon caused him to finish 12th.

He was first in the World Rankings for eight consecutive years between his No. 3 of 1948 and his No. 2 of 1957. He was undefeated for three years in a row, 1953-55. He ranked No. 1 in the decathlon in 1951 and 1954.

Profiles of Other Champions

RIEHM, KARL-HANS (West Germany). . . . . S, 4 WR, 2 No. 1
    Hammer, 1971- 3/31/51, 6-1½/236

In 1975, Riehm raised the World Record to 257-6, breaking the old mark in 7 different meets. He bettered the old mark on 12 consecutive throws. He placed 4th in the 1976 Olympics, then ranked No. 1 again in 1977 with a World Cup victory. He ranked No. 2 for the next four years, bettering the World Record with a throw of 265-1 in 1980. He placed 7th in the 1983 World Championships and 2nd in the 1984 Olympics.

RITOLA, VILLE (Finland). . . . . 5 G, 3 S, 2 WR, No. 1**
    Distances, 1921-28 . . . . .1/18/96

Ville Ritola won three Olympic championships, plus two gold medals for team championships. He won three silver medals, all behind Paavo Nurmi. In the 1924 Olympics, he won the steeplechase and 10,000 meters, both in World Record time. He was 2nd to Nurmi in a close 5000, and the cross country. In 1928, he lost a close 10,000 to Nurmi, but he beat Nurmi in the 5000.

Ritola won 14 AAU championships as a resident of the United States, from the time he was 17. He placed 2nd in the (short) 1922 Boston Marathon in 2:21:45. Indoors on February 24, 1925, he bettered all records for 3 miles and 5000 meters. His 13:56.2 was 15 seconds faster than Nurmi's 5000 record. Five weeks before, he had bettered Alf Shrubb's 5-mile world best by 11 seconds with 24:21.8 indoors.

ROBERTS, DAVE (USA). B, 2 WR, No. 1
    Pole Vault, 1970-76. . . . . .7/23/51, 6-2½/185

Roberts won three NCAA titles, then came back two years later, in 1975, with a World Record 18-6½ before injuries ended his season. In 1976, he raised his record to 18-8¼ in the Final Trials and placed 3rd in the Olympics on more misses.

ROBINSON, ARNIE (USA) . . . . .G, B, 4 No. 1
    Long Jump, 1969-81 . . . . .4/7/48, 6-2/165

Robinson ranked No. 1 in 1971 and placed 3rd in the 1972 Olympics. He won the 1976 Olympics with 27-4¾, his lifetime best.

Track's Greatest Champions

Bob Richards, winning at Helsinki

Gaston Roelants

Henry Rono

Profiles of Other Champions

ROELANTS, GASTON (Belgium) . . . . G, 4 WR, 5 No. 1
    Distances, 1960-68 . . . . .2/5/37, 5-8½/128

    Roelants placed 4th in the 1960 Olympic steeplechase. He won the 1962 European Championships. On September 7, 1963, he broke the World Record with 8:29.6. He won the 1964 Olympic championship in 8:30.8. In the 1965 Belgian Championships on August 7, he lowered his World Record to 8:26.4. He also ranked No. 2 in the World Rankings in the 10,000 with the 2nd-fastest ever run—28:10.6.

    In 1966 he ran under 8:30 twice but placed only 3rd in the European Championships, plus 8th in the 10,000. At Louvain, Belgium, on October 28, he amazed the track world by running 20,000 meters in 58:06.2. His second World Record of the day came when he ran 12 miles 1474 yards (20,644 meters) in one hour. In 1967 he lost his second steeplechase in six years but regained his No. 1 in World Ranking. In 1968, an injury and Mexico City's altitude knocked him back to 7th in the Olympic steeplechase.

RONO, HENRY (Kenya) . . . . .5 WR, 4 No. 1, AOY
    3000-10,000, 1976-82 . . . . .2/2/53, 5-7/139

    In one incredible year, Rono became the fastest distance runner of all time. After ranking No. 8 in the 10,000 in 1977, he became Athlete of the Year in 1978. He ranked No. 1 in the steeplechase, 5000, and 10,000, setting World Records of 8:05.4, 13:08.4, and 27:22.4. He won the Commonwealth Games at the two shorter distances and set a fourth World Record at 3000 meters with 7:32.1. He made an astounding comeback in 1981 to lower his 5000 record to 13:06.20.

ROSE, RALPH (USA) . . . . .3 G, 2 S, B, 5 WR, 5 No. 1*
    Shot, Discus, Hammer, 1904-12 . . .3/17/85, 6-6/225-286

    Rose broke the World Record and won the Olympic championship in the shot put at the age of 19 with 48-6 in 1904. He regained the record in 1907 (49-7¼), raised it to 49-10 in 1908, to 50-6 in 1909, and 51-¾ one week later. This was the official World Record for 19 years.

    On June 26, 1909, in an unsanctioned meet at Healdsburg, California, he put the shot 54-4, a mark not bettered until 1934, and he threw the hammer 178-5, better than the World Record. His best official hammer throw was 164-4.

    Rose set a record for the shot put with both hands, totaling

91-10½ in 1912. This was the official record for 19 years. He won the AAU shot put four times. The third time, in 1909, he also won the discus and javelin. His first AAU championship came in the 1905 discus.

Rose won six Olympic medals. In 1904 he won the shot, took the silver medal in the discus, and the bronze in the hammer. In 1908, he repeated his shot put triumph. In 1912, he lost the shot by 3½ inches, but he won the shot for both hands.

RYAN, PAT (USA) . . . . G, WR, 8 No. 1*
    Hammer, 1913-21 . . . . .1/4/98, 6-2/250

Ryan broke the World Record with a hammer throw of 189-6 on August 17, 1913, in Celtic Park, Long Island. It lasted 24 years. He won eight AAU hammer titles and two with the 56 pound weight. In 1920, he won the Olympic hammer throw.

RYUN, JIM (USA) . . . . .S, 4 WR, 3 No. 1, 2 AOY
    800-2 Miles, 1963-72 . . . . .4/29/47, 6-3/170

Ryun set an age-16 mile record of 4:07.8 in 1963. In 1964, he ran 3:59.0 and 1500 meters in 3:39.0. Youngest ever to make the U.S. Olympic team, he was ill at Tokyo. In 1965, he won the AAU from Peter Snell in 3:55.3 and ranked No. 4 in the world.

In 1966, at the age of 19, he won the 2-mile at the Coliseum Relays from Jim Grelle and Kip Keino in 8:25.2, an American Record. At the Compton Invitational, he missed the mile World Record by one tenth with 3:53.7. A week later, at Terre Haute, Indiana, he broke Peter Snell's 880 World Record with a surprise 1:44.9. He won the AAU in 3:58.6.

On July 17, at Berkeley, he set a World Record of 3:51.3. A week later he ran the third fastest 880 ever run—1:46.2.

In 1967, he ran 3:53.2 at Compton, and he won the NCAA championship. In the AAU meet at Bakersfield, he paced himself to 3:51.1, another World Record.

On July 8, in the Los Angeles Coliseum, Ryun smashed Keino by 20 yards in the 1500 meters. His last 880 in 1:51.3 brought him under Herb Elliott's World Record with 3:33.1. He beat Keino again in London in 3:56.0. On August 17 he sprinted away from Bodo Tummler and Harald Norpoth to win a 3:38.2 1500 by 30 yards. His last 400 was 50.6, his last 300 was 36.4, and his last 200 was 24.8.

Injuries to his back and ankle slowed him but he won the 1968 NCAA indoor 2-mile from Gerry Lindgren and doubled in the mile.

Profiles of Other Champions

Mononucleosis kept him out of the 1968 spring season, and high altitude training prevented fast times. He ran 3:55.9 in August.

In the Olympics, he lost to an incredible altitude run by Keino, finishing second in 3:37.8, faster than he thought possible.

He never ranked high again, although in 1972 he ran the year's fastest mile in 3:52.8. He was knocked down in an Olympic heat. He turned professional, but he continued to suffer from allergies and ran few good races.

SALING, GEORGE (USA) . . . . G, 4 WR, No. 1*
   110 Hurdles, 1930-32. . . . . 7/24/09, 6-3/170

Saling won the 1932 NCAA high hurdles in the unrecognized World Record time of 14.1. He won the 1932 Olympics in 14.6.

SALMINEN, ILMARI (Finland) . . . . G, 2 WR, 2 No. 1*
   Distances, 1934-39 . . . . 9/21/02

Salminen won the 1936 Olympic 10,000 meters, then fell in the 5000 and finished 6th. On July 18, 1937, in Kouvola, Finland, he broke Paavo Nurmi's 10,000 World Record with 30:05.5 and broke the 6-mile record en route. Salminen won the 10,000 at the European Championships in both 1934 and 1938, and placed 3rd in the 1934 5000. His fastest 5000 was 14:22.0 in 1939.

Jim Ryun, 3:51.3 at Berkeley

Track's Greatest Champions

SANEYEV, VIKTOR (Soviet Union) . . . . 3 G, S, 3 WR, 9 No. 1
    Triple Jump, 1965-80. . . . . .10/3/45, 6-2/174
See chapter.

SCHMID, HARALD (West Germany) . . . . S, B, 2 No. 1
    400-800, 400 Hurdles, 1975- 9/29/57, 6-1¾/172

    Schmid, the last man to beat Edwin Moses before the latter's long winning streak, ranked No. 1 in the 400 hurdles only in 1982, the year Moses did not compete. Still, his 47.48 in 1982 while winning his 2nd European championship, has been bettered only by Moses. Schmid ranked No. 1 in the 400 flat in 1979, with a time of 44.92, and he ranked No. 5 in the 800 the same year, with 1:44.9. He placed 2nd in the 1983 World Championships and 3rd in the 1984 Olympics.

SCHMIDT, JOZEF (Poland) . . . . 2 G, WR, 5 No. 1
    Triple Jump, 1957-68. . . . . .3/28/35, 6-1½/170

    Schmidt improved from a triple jump of 51-2½ in 1957 to win the 1958 European Championships with 53-11. On August 5, 1960, in the Polish Championships, he leaped 55-10½ for a World Record. Then, even though injured, he won the Olympic championship at 55-1¾.

    In 1961, a weak ankle reduced him to 2nd in the world with a best of only 53-9¾. He won the 1962 European Championships with his best jump of the year, 54-3½.

    In 1963, undefeated, he reached 55-9 twice in the Polish Championships, a windy 55-¼ against the U.S., and 55-4½ in September. He long jumped 26-1½. In 1964 he was injured and jumped in only two meets, including the Olympic Games, where he won again with 55-3½.

    In 1965, his best was 54-11 and he ranked No. 1 for the sixth year. In 1966, injuries continued to hobble him and he ranked No. 5. His best was 54-7¼ and he placed only 5th in the European Championships at 53-11¾.

    In 1967 he slipped to 6th even though he won the Polish Championships at 55-3. In 1968, a bad leg held him to a best of 54-3½ in his World Games victory. Injured again, he managed 55-5 at Mexico City's altitude for 7th in the Olympics.

SCHMIDT, WOLFGANG (East Germany) . . . . .S, WR, 4 No. 1
    Shot, Discus, 1973-80 . . . . .1/16/54, 6-5½/237

    Son of national coach Ernst Schmidt, Wolfgang became a teenage

Profiles of Other Champions

phenomenon. In 1973, at the age of 18, he put the shot 62-11½ and threw the discus 201-1. He won the European Junior discus but he lost the shot to Udo Beyer and so he concentrated on the discus. In 1974, he threw 210-4, and in 1975, at the age of 20, he threw 219-2 and ranked No. 1 in the world. He placed 2nd in the 1976 Olympics, but he regained the No. 1 position in 1977 while winning the World Cup. In 1978, he raised the World Record to 233-5 and won the European Championships. He won the 1979 World Cup and ranked No. 1 again. He slipped to 4th in the 1980 Olympics, but returned to No. 2 in 1981. Political problems ended his career prematurely.

SCHOLZ, JACKSON (USA) . . . . G, Gr, S, WR, 2 No. 1*
Sprints, 1920-28 . . . . .3/15/97, 5-8/135

Scholz placed in three Olympic Games: 4th in the 1920 100, 2nd in the 1924 100, 1st in the 1924 200, and 4th in the 1928 200. He won a gold medal in the 1920 4 x 100 meter relay. He claimed an advantage over Paddock in their career competition, but he won only one AAU title. He ran an unofficial 9.5 in 1925 and an official 10.6 in 1920.

SEAGREN, BOB (USA) . . . . G, S, 6 WR, 3 No. 1
Pole Vault, 1965-72. . . . . .10/17/46, 6-0/175

From a best of 16-4 in 1965, Seagren developed to a World Record 17-5½ at Fresno, May 14, 1966. He lost the record two months later, and regained it with 17-7 at San Diego, June 10, 1967. He lost that one 13 days later, and regained it with 17-9 in the Final Trials at South Lake Tahoe, September 12, 1968.

He won the 1968 Olympic championship with 17-8½. He set indoor records six times, beginning with 17-¾ in 1966. He cleared 17-6 in 1969. Injured in 1970, he all but retired. In 1972 he set a World Record of 18-5¾ and placed 2nd in the Olympics even though deprived of his favorite pole. He turned professional and vaulted 17-7 indoors in 1973.

SEXTON, LEO (USA) . . . . .G, WR, No. 1*
Shot, 1931-32. . . . . .8/27/09, 6-3/240

Sexton won the 1932 Olympic shot put, then broke the World Record with 53-½.

Josef Schmidt

John Pennel and Bob Seagren

Profiles of Other Champions

SHEPPARD, MEL (USA) . . . . 2 G, 2 Gr, S, WR, No. 1**
　　800-1500, 1908-12 . . . . .9/5/83, 5-8½/165

　　Sheppard won the 1908 Olympic 1500 and doubled with a World Record 1:52.8 in the 800. In the 1912 Olympics he barely lost in a World Record 800. He won relay golds in 1908 and 1912. He won five AAU titles.

SHERIDAN, MARTIN (USA) . . . . 3 G, B, 4 WR, 6 No. 1*
　　All-round, 1902-12 . . . . .3/28/81, 6-3/195

　　Called "the world's greatest athlete," Sheridan won the AAU all-round championship in 1905, 1907, and 1909. He also won the shot put in 1904, 1906, 1907, and 1911.

　　His greatest feat was winning two Olympic discus championships in 1904 and 1908, plus the discus title in the unofficial 1906 Olympics. He placed 4th in the shot in 1904 and won in 1906. In 1906 he also placed 2nd in throwing the 14 pound stone and in the standing long jump. He tied for 2nd in the standing high jump, was disqualified in the Greek style discus, and was expected to win the pentathlon until his knee went bad.

　　In the 1908 Olympics, he also won the Greek style discus and was 3rd in the standing long jump, bringing his Olympic total to five gold medals, three silver, and one bronze (if you include the unofficial Games).

　　He held the World Record in the discus from 1902 to 1912, with a best of 143-3 in 1905. He threw the hammer 162-8 in 1906 when the World Record was 175-1. He placed 9th in the 1908 triple jump.

SHORTER, FRANK (USA). . . . . .G, S, 3 No. 1
　　5000-Marathon, 1969-79 . . . . . . .10/3/47, 5-10/135

　　Developing rapidly after his senior year at Yale, Shorter became No. 2 in the world for 10,000 meters in 1970. Turning to the marathon in 1971, he ranked No. 1. In the 1972 Olympics, he placed 5th in the 10,000 and won the marathon. He ranked No. 1 in the marathon for the third year in 1973, and earned No. 2 honors in 1974. In 1976, he placed 2nd in the Olympic marathon.

SHRUBB, ALFRED (Great Britain) . . . . 9 WR, No. 1**, AOY*
　　Distances, 1903-05 . . . . .12/12/78, 5-6½/115

　　Shrubb became the world's best distance runner in 1903 at the age of 24, winning the British AAA mile and cross country, the International Cross Country, and set World Records of 9:11.0 for 2 miles and

14:17.6 for 3 miles. In the spring of 1904 he ran four World Record races: 5 miles (24:33.4), 3 miles (14:17.2), 2 miles (9:09.6), 4 miles (9:23.4).

On November 5, 1904, he ran 11¾ miles in 1:00:2.2 and put his name into the official record book six more times: 6 miles (29:59.4), 7 miles (35:04.5), 8 miles (40:16), 9 miles (45:27.6), 10 miles (50:40.6), and one hour (11 miles, 1137 yards). His unofficial 31:02.4 was better than the 10,000 meters World Record. His 6-mile record fell to Nurmi after 26 years, while his 7-, 8-, and 9-mile records lasted 33 years until they were removed from the official list. Shrubb was declared a professional in 1905 and he ran successfully in the United States and Canada until he was 42.

SIDLO, JANUSZ (Poland) . . . . .S, WR, 5 No. 1
Javelin, 1952-70 . . . . .6/19/33, 5-11½/180

The most durable of competitors, Sidlo threw in the 1952 Olympics and in four more. He set a World Record of 262-11 at the age of 20 in 1953. He won the European Championships in 1954 and 1958. He placed 2nd in the 1956 Olympics, 8th in 1960, 4th in 1964, and 7th in 1968. He ranked No. 1 in the world five times and No. 2 five times.

SILVESTER, JAY (USA) . . . . S, 4 WR, 2 No. 1
Discus, 1961-80 . . . . .8/27/36, 6-3¼/251

Silvester first set a World Record in the discus with 199-2 in 1961. He won AAU championships in 1961, 1963, and 1968. He was 4th in the 1964 Olympics and 5th in 1968. He raised the World Record to 218-3 in May of 1968. After many long throws, he reached 224-5 in a high wind at Reno, Nevada, September 18, 1968.

He ranked No. 1 in 1970, and in an early 1971 meet under special wind conditions, he raised the World Record to 230-11. Later, in Europe, he also bettered the official record with 229-9. He placed 2nd in the 1972 Olympics. After a semi-retirement, he placed 8th in the 1976 Olympics. Another comeback in 1980 fell short when he threw 197-8.

SIME, DAVE (USA) . . . . S, 9 WR
Sprints, 220 Hurdles, 1956-60 . . . .7/25/36, 6-2/180

Sime won no major championships, but he ran three 9.3 100s when that was the World Record. He ran 10.1 for 100 meters. He set a World

Profiles of Other Champions

Record of 20.0 for a straight 220 on June 9, 1956. That same year he ran 20.1, 20.2, 20.3 twice, and 20.4. He tied the World Record of 22.2 in the 220 low hurdles, on May 5. He was a close 2nd in the 100 meters of the 1960 Olympics.

SIMPSON, GEORGE (USA) . . . . S, WR, No. 1*
    Sprints, 1929-32 . . . . .9/21/08, 5-11/165

Simpson ran the first 9.4 100, while winning an NCAA double in 1929, but the use of starting blocks nullifed his record. He won the 220 in both NCAA and AAU in 1930. In the 1932 Olympics, he was 4th in the 100 and 2nd in the 200. His unofficial 20.6 in 1929 equalled the World Record.

SMITH, CALVIN (USA). . . . . G, 2 Gr, S, WR, No. 1
    Sprints, 1981- 1/8/61, 5-9/145

Ranked No. 2 in both sprints in 1983, Smith set a World Record of 9.93 at altitude in 1983 and won the 200 in the World Championships (after silver in the 100) to rank No. 2 in the 100 and No. 1 in the 200. In both the 1983 World Championships and the 1984 Olympics, he ran on World Record 4 x 100 relay teams.

SMITH, TOMMIE (USA) . . . . G, 9 WR, 3 No. 1
    100-400, 1966-68 . . . . .6/5/44, 6-3/185

Smith tied the World Record for 200 meters on a straightaway in 1965. In 1966 he lowered the 200/220 record to 19.5 and gained a 200/220 record of 20.0 around a curve. He also ran 9.3, 10.1, 45.3 for 400 meters, and long jumped 25-11. In 1967 he set World Records of 44.5 for 400 meters and 44.8 for 440 yards on May 20. He won AAU furlong titles in 1967 and 1968, and the 1968 Olympic championship in 19.8 (19.83-the first auto-timed WR). He ranked No. 1 in the world for 200 meters in 1966, 1967, and 1968.

SNELL, PETER (New Zealand) . . . . 3 G, 5 WR, 7 No. 1, 2 AOY
    800-Mile, 1960-65 . . . . .12/17/38, 5-10½/176
    See chapter.

SPIRIDONOV, ALEKSEY (Soviet Union) . . . . .S, WR, No. 1
    Hammer, 1963-83 . . . . .11/20/51, 6-3½/260

Spiridonov won the European championship and set a World Record of 251-6 in 1974. He placed 2nd in the 1976 Olympics.

Track's Greatest Champions

STANFIELD, ANDY (USA) . . . . G, Gr, S, WR, 2 No. 1
   Sprints, Long Jump, 1949-56. . . . .12/29/27, 6-1½/175

Stanfield won a sprint double in the 1949 AAU (10.3 and 20.4) and took the 200 title in 1952 and the 220 in 1953. At Philadelphia, in 1951, he ran a turn 220 in 20.6, equal fastest ever and long jumped 25-9. Injuries kept him out of fast-start 100s, but he won the Olympic 200 in 1952 and placed 2nd in 1956. He also won some 220 low hurdle races and ranked No. 4 in the lows in the World Rankings for 1951. He was No. 2 in the 100 for 1949 and 1950 and in the 200 for 1949 and 1951. He was No. 1 in the 200 in 1952 and 1953.

STEERS, LES (USA). . . . . .3 WR, 2 No. 1*
   High Jump, 1938-41 . . . . .6/16/16, 6-1½/190

Steers broke the World Record with a high jump of 6-10¾ on April 14, 1941, at Seattle, Washington. That year he had the five highest jumps of all time, raising the record twice by one-eighth inch to 6-11, but he lost the AAU after clearing 6-9¾. He won the AAU in 1939 and 1940 and the NCAA in 1941.

STERNBERG, BRIAN (USA) . . . . 3 WR, No. 1
   Pole Vault, 1962-63. . . . . .6/21/43, 6-1/167

After setting a World Junior Record of 15-8 at 18 in 1962, Sternberg set World Records of 16-5, 16-7, and 16-8 at age 19 in 1963. He won the NCAA and AAU and was undefeated. His last competition was the AAU victory on his 20th birthday. Shortly after, he was paralyzed in a trampoline accident.

STONES, DWIGHT (USA) . . . . .2 B, 3 WR, 4 No. 1
   High Jump, 1971- 12/6/53, 6-5/165

Stones placed 3rd in the 1972 Olympic high jump at the age of 18. In 1973, he set a World Record of 7-6½ and ranked No. 1. He ranked No. 1 for the next two years even though he lost 10 meets each year. In 1976, his World Records of 7-7 and 7-7¼ gained him a fourth straight No. 1 ranking even though he placed 3rd in the Olympics. After ranking No. 1 and No. 3, he eased off for two years but returned with a 7-7 and No. 4 in 1981. He placed 6th in the 1983 World Championships. In 1984, he regained the American Record with 7-8 and placed 4th in the Olympics to earn a No. 5 ranking.

Profiles of Other Champions

SYEDIKH, YURIY (Soviet Union) . . . . 2 G, S, 4 WR, 6 No. 1
Hammer, 1975- 6/11/55, 6-¾/243
See chapter.

TAIPALE, ARMAS (Finland) . . . . G, S, 2 WR, 2 No. 1*
Discus, 1912-24 . . . . .5/18/28

Taipale won the 1912 Olympic discus, placed 2nd in 1920, and 12th in 1924. He was 10th in the 1920 shot. In 1913 he twice bettered the discus World Record with an unrecognized best of 158-4.

TAJIMA, NAOTO (Japan) . . . . G, B, WR, No. 1*
Long Jump, Triple Jump, 1936 . . . .8/15/12

Tajima had the best jumps of his life in two events in the 1936 Olympics. His 25-4¾ placed 3rd in the long jump, and he won the triple jump with a World Record 52-6.

TAYLOR, F. MORGAN (USA) . . . . G, 2 B, WR, 2 No. 1*
400 Hurdles, 1924-32. . . . . .4/17/03, 6-1/165

Taylor won the 1924 Olympic 400 meter hurdles in a World Record time of 52.6, but a fallen hurdle nullified the record. His earlier 52.6 was only an American Record. On July 4, 1928, in Philadelphia, he set a record of 52.0. He finished 3rd in both the 1928 and 1932 Olympics. He won a 48.2 440, won the 1925 NCAA 220 hurdles, and once long jumped a wind-aided 25-2. He won four AAU championships in the 400 hurdles.

TER-OVANESYAN, IGOR (Soviet Union). . . . . 2 B, 2 WR, No. 1
Long Jump, 1956-72 . . . . .5/19/38, 6-1¼/172

Ter-Ovanesyan competed in four Olympics and won two bronze medals. In 1962 he set a World Record of 27-3¼ and in 1967 set another of 27-4¾. He ranked No. 2 six years and No. 3 four years before reaching No. 1 in 1969 at the age of 31. He became the Soviet Union national coach.

THOMPSON, DALEY (Great Britain) . . . . .3 G, 4 WR, 4 No. 1
Decathlon, 1977- 7/30/58, 6-¾/190
See chapter.

THOMSON, EARL (Canada). . . . . G, 4 WR, 3 No. 1*
110 Hurdles, 1916-22 . . . . .2/15/95, 6-3/185

Thomson, a 6-3, 185-pounder, attended Dartmouth after running the first 14.8 in the 120 hurdles, in 1916. He set another World Record in the IC4A with 14.4 at Philadelphia on May 29, 1920. He won the Olympic championship in 14.8, a World Record for 110 meters. In 1921, he tied his record of 14.4 and it lasted until 1931. He won three AAU titles in the 120 hurdles and one in the 220 hurdles.

THORPE, JIM (USA). . . . . 2 G, 2 WR, No. 1*, AOY*
Decathlon, 1908-12 . . . . .5/28/88, 5-11¼/183

If Thorpe had concentrated on track and field he might well have been the greatest of all. A legendary hero in football and a professional baseball player, he fitted track into his schedule only during the short season.

Five-eighths Indian, Thorpe spent his boyhood hunting, working, playing, and breaking wild horses. He is reputed to have run 18 miles at 10. At 19, he came under the influence of the famous coach, Pop Warner, at Carlisle Indian School.

The next year, 1908, he competed in the 120 and 220 hurdles, high jump, long jump, and shot put. He high jumped 6-0 to tie for 1st at the Penn Relays and again to win the State Intercollegiates.

In 1909, he competed in nine meets. Against Syracuse, he entered 8 events, winning his usual five and placing in the sprints and hammer throw. He won four in the State Intercollegiates and 5 in the Middle Atlantic AAU. In 1910 and 1911, he was out of school and took no part in track and field.

In 1912, he competed in many early-season meets, improving his high jump to 6-2¾ and his shot to 46-3½, half a foot better than the 1912 Olympic bronze medalist. On May 18, he won the pentathlon Olympic Trials with 3 firsts and 2 seconds. He was also chosen for the decathlon team without competition.

"I may have had an aversion for work," Thorpe admitted, "but I also had an aversion for getting beat. I was always in condition, and I never left my best performance on the practice field."

After winning six events against Lafayette on May 25, he entered the Final Trials on June 12. He won the high jump over Alma Richards, soon to be Olympic champion, and George Horine, the World Record holder. Thorpe's height was 6-5, only 5/8" from the official World Record.

Profiles of Other Champions

At Stockholm on July 7, he won a gold medal in the Olympic pentathlon. He won four events and placed 3rd in the javelin with 153-3, 29 feet less than the bronze medalist. The next day, he could high jump only 6-1½ and tied for 4th. Four days later, he placed 7th in the long jump with 22-7¼.

On July 13, he began his first decathlon with 11.2 compared with 10.8 for the Olympic 100 champion. He pulled away from his competition with 22-3½, 42-3½, 6-1, and 52.2. His second day marks of 15.6, 121-4, 10-8, 149-11, and 4:40.1 were all personal records except for his javelin mark set in the Olympic pentathlon. He won by 688 points, and his World Record was not bettered for 15 years.

The King of Sweden called Thorpe to his wooden box and said, "Sir, you are the greatest athlete in the world. I consider it an honor to shake your hand."

Thorpe smiled in appreciation and said, "Thanks, King."

In France, eight days later, Thorpe beat Olympic 110 hurdles champion Fred Kelly in 15.6. He finished his limited career on September 2 in New York by winning the AAU all-around with a World Record of 7476.

TISDALL, ROBERT (Ireland) . . . . G, No. 1*
   400 Hurdles, Decathlon, 1932 . . . . .5/16/07

Tisdall won the 1932 Olympic 400 meter hurdles in 51.7 (51.67) but did not receive an official World Record because he knocked over a hurdle. He also placed 8th in the decathlon.

TOLAN, EDDIE (USA) . . . . 2G, 8 WR, 4 No. 1*
   Sprints, 1929-32 . . . . .9/29/08, 5-7/145

In 1929, Tolan tied the World Record of 9.5 while winning the NCAA 100. He won the AAU sprint double. He tied the 100-meter World Record of 10.4 in Europe. In 1930 he did not reach his peak until the college season ended. In Canada, he ran an unofficial 10.2 and barely lost to George Simpson in 20.6, both World Record times. He won the AAU 100 but lost to Simpson in the 220.

In 1931, Tolan lost the NCAA 100 to Frank Wykoff, but he won the 220 by four yards. In the AAU he was 3rd in the 100, but he won the 220. In the 1932 AAU, he made the Olympic team by placing 2nd to Ralph Metcalfe in both sprints. In the Olympics, he barely beat Metcalfe in a World Record equalling 10.3. Then he came from behind

Track's Greatest Champions

Eddie Tolan

Tommie Smith

Bill Toomey

Profiles of Other Champions

Simpson in the homestretch of the 200 to win. All-told, he ran 100m in World Record clockings no less than eight times.

TOOMEY, BILL (USA) . . . . G, WR, 3 No. 1, AOY
Decathlon, 1959-69 . . . . .1/10/39, 6-1½/192

Lacking the natural talent of Bob Mathias, Milt Campbell, Rafer Johnson, and C.K. Yang, Toomey outscored all of them by developing himself over many years. At Colorado University, he long jumped 24-8½ and ran the 400 meter hurdles in 51.7, but he never placed in the NCAA.

He tried the pentathlon in 1959 and placed 6th in the AAU. In 1960 he won it, and in 1962, on his home track at Boulder, Colorado, he won again with an American Record of 3482. He also won in 1963 and 1964.

In 1963 he placed 5th in the AAU decathlon. In 1964, he placed 5th in the AAU and 4th in the Final Trials. After winning the 1965 AAU (7764) for No. 3 in the World Rankings.he spent six months in Germany coached by Friedel Schirmer. He became ill, returned to the United States, and spent six weeks in a hospital. On April 2, 1966, he began training again.

On July 2 and 3, in Salina, Kansas, his AAU marks included personal records in the first four events: 10.3, 25-6, 45-8¾, and 6-4. His 47.3 400 gave him a first day record of 4430. On the second day he ran his fastest ever 110 meter hurdles (14.8) and set a personal record of 147-5 in the discus. He finished with 13-0, 198-11, and 4:30.0 for a World Record 8234 which was never ratified.

Three weeks later, he scored 8219 and lost by 11 points to Russ Hodge, but he was No. 1 in the World Rankings.

In 1967, Toomey was injured, but he won the AAU (7880), lost in Los Angeles (7779), won the Pan-American Games (8044), and won against West Germany (7938). But he lost to Kurt Bendlin's 8319 and was No. 2 in the World Rankings.

In 1968 he won at Mt. San Antonio (7800) and the AAU (8037). He was ill in Germany (7628) and lost to Bendlin and Hans-Joachim Walde. He won in London (7985) and the final Trials (8222).

At Mexico City, in the Olympic Games, his first day marks were 10.4 (10.41), 25-9¾, 45-1½, 6-4¾, and an amazing 45.6 (45.68) for the highest ever score of 4499. An injured leg slowed him the second day but he won the championship with 8193 points. It was his sixth decathlon score over 8000 points. (For comparison, Johnson's best was 8063.)

He won his fifth AAU title in 1969, and scored 4123 points in a pentathlon in London, best in history. In December, at Los Angeles, he scored 8417 points to gain the World Record. He had 8 of the 12 best scores of all time.

TOWNS, FORREST (USA) . . . . G, 6 WR, No. 1*
    110 Hurdles, 1935-37. . . . . .2/6/14, 6-2/172

"Spec" Towns, a 9.7 sprinter, had one great year. With the 110 hurdles World Record standing at 14.2, he ran 14.1 nine times in 1936. He won the Olympic title in 14.2. On August 27, in Oslo, he shocked the track world with a 13.7 World Record, which lasted until 1948.

TUULOS, VILHO (Finland) . . . . G, 2 B, No. 1*
    Triple Jump, 1920-28. . . . . .3/26/95

Tuulos won in the 1920 Olympic triple jump and was 3rd in both 1924 and 1928. In 1923 he jumped 50-9½, only half an inch from the World Record.

VIGNERON, THIERRY (France). . . . . ½ B, 5 WR
    Pole Vault, 1978- . . . . .3/9/60, 5-11¼ /157

Vigneron twice vaulted to a World Record of 18-10¼ in 1980, then placed 7th in the Olympics. He raised the record to 19-¼ in 1981—becoming the first man to clear 19-feet—and set an indoor record of 19-2¼ in 1982. In 1983, he broke the record again with 19-1½, but he lost in 11 meets including a tie for 8th in the World Championships. He tied for 3rd in the 1984 Olympics and later vaulted to a record 19-4¾ while losing to Sergey Bubka.

VIREN, LASSE (Finland). . . . . 4 G, 2 WR, 4 No. 1, AOY
    Distances, 1970-80 . . . . .7/22/49, 5-11/130

See chapter.

VOLKOV, KONSTANTIN (Soviet Union) . . . . 1½S, No. 1
    Pole Vault, 1978- 2/28/60, 6-½/163

Volkov vaulted 18-4½ in 1979 at the age of 19. He tied for 2nd in the 1980 Olympics and cleared 19-2 in an exhibition, better than the World Record. He won the World Cup in 1981. He placed 2nd in the 1983 World Championships.

Profiles of Other Champions

WALKER, JOHN (New Zealand) . . . . .G, 2 WR, 3 No. 1, AOY
  800-5000, 1973- 1/12/51, 6-¼/163

Walker broke through early in 1974, running under the 1500 World Record for a close 2nd in the Commonwealth Games. Fast miles ranked him No. 1 for the year and he also ranked No. 5 in the 800 and ran the 2nd-fastest 3000 for the year. In 1975, he lowered the mile record to 3:49.4 to become the first under 3:50, ran the 2nd best ever 2000, and was voted Athlete of the Year. In 1976, he won the Olympic 1500, ran a sensational World Record 4:51.4 for 2000 meters, and ranked No. 1 for the third consecutive year. Injuries slowed him for two years, but he returned to No. 5 in 1980 and has been ranked ever since. He ran in the 1984 Olympic 5000 final. Early in 1985, he became the first man to run 100 sub-4:00 miles.

WARMERDAM, CORNELIUS (Dutch)(USA)...7 WR, 6 No. 1*, 2 AOY*
  Pole Vault, 1935-44. . . . . .6/22/15, 6-0/160

See chapter.

WEFERS, BERNIE (USA) . . . . 6 WR, 6 No. 1*
  Sprints, 1895-97 . . . . 6-0/175

Wefers won three AAU sprint doubles, 1895-97. He equalled the 100 record three times at 9.8, held the 220 record at 21.2 for 25 years and the 300 yard record at 30.6 for 39 years. He had two other World Records in the 220.

WELLS, ALLAN (Great Britain) . . . . G, S, No. 1
  Sprints, 1978-84 . . . . .5/3/52, 6-0/170

A mediocre long jumper at the age of 25, Wells suddenly was transformed into a world class sprinter. He won the Commonwealth Games 200 in 1978. In the 1980 Olympics, he won the 100 and placed 2nd in the 200. After ranking No. 1 in the 200 for 1981, he placed 4th in both sprints in the 1983 World Championships.

WESSIG, GERD (East Germany) . . . . .G, WR, No. 1
  High Jump, 1980- 7/16/59, 6-6¾/181

In 1980, at 21, Wessig won the Olympics with a World Record 7-8¾.

Track's Greatest Champions

WHITFIELD, MAL (USA) . . . . 2 G, Gr, Sr, B, 3 WR, 7 No. 1
400-1000, 1946-56 . . . . .10/11/24, 6-0/169

Whitfield was one of the greatest competitors of all time and the best doubler among middle-distance runners of his day. After early 2nd places in the 1946 NCAA and AAU 880s and the 1947 NCAA 880 and AAU 400, he became invincible in the 800.

He lost no championship races from 1948 through 1954, including two NCAAs, five AAUs, two Final Trials, and two Olympic Games. In the 400, he won the 1952 AAU, both Final Trials, placed 3rd in the 1948 Olympics, and made the Olympic final in 1952. He won a gold medal on the Olympic 4 x 400 meter relay team in 1948 and a silver medal in 1952.

He was No. 1 in the World Rankings in the 800 from 1948 through 1953, except for 1951. That year he was No. 6 while losing only one race after five months as a tail gunner in Korea. In the 400, he ranked No. 1 in 1949 and 1953 and 3rd in 1948, 1950, and 1952 in the World Rankings.

Indoors, he was No. 1 four times at 600 yards and twice at 1000 yards. He won an AAU title at each distance.

Mal Whitfield

Profiles of Other Champions

He seldom ran for time, but he set World Records in the 880 (1:48.6) and 1000 meters (2:20.8). His 45.9 at 400 meters was only 0.1 off the World Record. His indoor World Records were for 500 yards (56.6), 500 meters (1:02.9), and 600 yards (1:09.5). He set additional American Records for 400 meters (45.9), 440 (46.2), 500 meters (1:01.0), 600 meters (1:17.3), and 800 meters (1:47.9). Before 1954, he ran 9 of the 16 fastest 800/880 times ever recorded. He had faster times from the 100 through the mile than any runner in history (10.7 100 meters, 4:12.6 mile).

Perhaps his greatest accomplishments came as a doubler. In one day of the 1948 Final Trials, he won the 800 in 1:50.6, ran a heat of the 400 in 47.3, and won the final in 46.6. Indoors in 1953, he set a Madison Square Garden 880 record of 1:50.9 and came back little over an hour later with a World Record 600 in 1:09.5. On July 29, in Cologne, he ran a 1:48.4 800 and came back in 45 minutes with a 46.2 400. In Finland on August 16, he broke the 1000-meter World Record with 2:20.8. One hour later he ran his American Record 440 in 46.2.

WILKINS, MAC (USA). . . . . G, S, 4 WR, 2 No. 1
   Shot, Discus, 1971-84 . . . . .11/15/50, 6-4/255

An all-around weight man at Oregon, Wilkins eventually specialized in the discus. He won the NCAA and AAU in 1973 and world ranked three years in a row before exploding in 1976. He began the year with an indoor shot put of 68-4½. He added 3 inches to the discus World Record on April 24 with 226-11. A week later, in San Jose, he threw 229-0, improved to 230-5, and topped a brilliant day with 232-6—three World Records in one day. In a long season of 37 meets, he lost only twice. He set a new Olympic record of 224-0 in the qualifying and won the final with 221-5. His 10 longest throws averaged 228-10, farther than any other thrower in history under legal circumstances. He claimed 5 of the 7 longest throws ever.

He ranked No. 1 again in 1980 although the U.S. boycotted the Olympics. He "retired" but returned in 1982 to rank No. 3. He placed 8th in the 1983 World Championships and 2nd in the 1984 Olympics.

WILLIAMS, ARCHIE (USA). . . . . G, WR, No. 1*
   400, 1936 . . . . .5/1/15, 6-0/176

Williams won the 1936 NCAA in 46.5 and was timed in a World Record 46.1 at 400 meters. He won the Olympic 400 in 46.5.

Arthur Wint

WILLIAMS, PERCY (Canada) . . . . 2 G, WR, 2 No. 1*
    Sprints, 1928-30 . . . . .5/19/08

Williams won a double sprint victory in the 1928 Olympics. On August 9, 1930, at Toronto, he ran the first official 10.3.

WILLIAMS, STEVE (USA) .5 WR, 3 No. 1
    Sprints, 1972-80 . . . . .11/13/53, 6-3½/175

Williams equalled the 100-yard World Record of 9.1 in 1973 and ranked No. 1 in both sprints. He ranked high each year, but injuries prevented top performances.

WINT, ARTHUR (Jamaica) . . . . G, Gr, 2 S, No. 1
    400-800, 1948-52 . . . . .5/25/20, 6-4½/170

Wint won the 400 meters in the 1948 Olympics and was 2nd in the 800. In 1952, he was 5th in the 400 and 2nd in the 800, and he won a prevented top performances although he did tie the 100-meter World Record four times.

WINTER, ARCHIBALD (NICK) Australia) . . . . .G, WR, No. 1
    Triple Jump, 1924-28 . . . . .born 1894

Profiles of Other Champions

Winter won the 1924 Olympic triple jump with a World Record 50-11¼. He was 12th in 1928.

WOHLHUTER, RICK (USA). . . . . B, 3 WR, 2 No. 1, AOY
        800-Mile, 1972-76 . . . . .12/23/48, 5-9/130

Wohlhuter fell in the 1972 Olympics, but in 1973 he set an 880 World Record of 1:44.6. In 1974, he earned Athlete of the Year honors during an undefeated season. He lowered his 880 record to 1:44.1, broke the 800 American Record three times, including two 1:43.9s, broke the World Record for 1000 meters with 2:13.9, and ranked No. 5 in the mile with 3:54.4, again undefeated. In the 1976 Olympics, he placed 3rd in the 800 and 6th in the 1500.

WOLCOTT, FRED (USA). . . . . 4 WR, 3 No. 1*
        Hurdles, 1938-42. . . . . .11/18/17, 5-11½/170

Wolcott was the greatest hurdler of all time before Dillard. In his three collegiate seasons he lost only three races, one a 100-yard dash in which he ran 9.5. He also lost the 120 hurdles in the 1939 AAU and the 1940 NCAA.

Wolcott equalled the American Record with 14.0 in 1938 and 13.9 in 1940. At Stockholm, in 1938, he became the second man ever to run under 14.0. His 13.7 in the 1940 Texas Relays was a Collegiate Record but it was not recognized by the AAU. His 13.7 in the 1941 AAU officially equalled the World Record.

In the 220 hurdles, Wolcott won everything (three of his five NCAA titles and four of his seven AAU titles). His 22.9 in the 1940 AAU was the fastest ever around a curve but it was wind aided. At the 1940 Princeton Invitational, he broke Jesse Owens' 220 hurdles record with 22.5 and set a 220-meter record of 22.3 which lasted 16 years.

Indoors, Wolcott set high hurdle records at four distances plus a 60-yard low hurdle record of 6.9. He won the 1942 AAU indoor highs in 7.2. The war kept him out of Olympic competition.

WOLFERMANN, KLAUS (West Germany) . . . . .G, WR, No. 1
        Javelin, 1968-76 . . . . .3/31/46, 5-10/187

Wolfermann won the javelin in the 1972 Olympics. In 1973, he set a World Record of 308-8.

WOODERSON, SYDNEY (Great Britain). . . . . .3 WR, 3 No. 1*
800-5000, 1936-46. . . . . .8/30/14, 5-6/125

Wooderson was a successful internationalist from 800 meters to 5000. On August 28, 1937, at Motspur Park, London, he set a mile World Record of 4:06.4. Then he won the 1500 meters in the 1938 European Championships. On August 20, 1938, at Motspur Park, he set World Records for 800 (1:48.4) and 880 (1:49.2).

After the war had eliminated him from two Olympics (an ankle injury stopped him in 1936), Wooderson made an amazing comeback. He went to Sweden in 1945 and lost a close mile to Arne Andersson with a time of 4:04.2. In 1946, he won the European Championships 5000 in 14:08.6, second only to Gunder Hagg's World Record.

WOODRUFF, JOHN (USA) .G, 3 No. 1*
400-800, 1936-40 . . . . .7/5/15, 6-2½/165

As a freshman at Pittsburgh in 1936, Woodruff lost the AAU title by one foot through inexperience. In the Final Trials he ran 1:49.9, 3rd-fastest of all time, in his heat. He won the final and his superior talent blundered through to a tactical Olympic victory at Berlin.

He won the difficult 440-880 double in three consecutive IC4A meets, running 47.0 in all three 440s. He won the NCAA 880 each year. His only AAU victory came in 1937.

In 1937 he defeated new World Record holder Elroy Robinson in 1:47.8 at a distance five feet short of 800 meters. In 1940 he ran 1:47.0 for 800 meters and 1:47.7 for 880 yards on Dartmouth's five lap indoor track. In the Compton Invitational, he won the 800 meters in 1:48.6, an American Record.

WOTTLE, DAVE (USA). . . . . .G, WR, No. 1
800-Mile, 1970-73. . . . . .8/7/50, 6-¾/140

Wottle tied the 800 record with 1:44.3 in the 1972 Final Trials, then won the Olympic championship.

WYKOFF, FRANK (USA) . . . . 3 Gr, 2 WR, 2 No. 1*
Sprints, 1928-36 . . . . .10/29/09, 5-10/152

Wykoff was credited with the first 9.4 100. He won three IC4A 100s, two NCAA 100s, and two AAU 100s. He ran 200 meters in 20.8

Profiles of Other Champions

at age 18 in 1928. He ran in three Olympic Games, winning a gold medal in the 4 x 100 meter relay each time. He placed 4th in the 100 in 1928 and 1936. He was the only man before Jesse Owens to run two 9.4s, both in 1930.

YANG CHUAN-KUANG (Taiwan) . . . . S, WR, 2 No. 1, AOY
Pole Vault, Decathlon, 1958-64 . . .7/10/33, 5-11/176

C. K. Yang competed in the 1956 Olympics as a 6-7½ high jumper and placed 8th in the decathlon. In May, 1958, he set an Asian Record of 7319 in the decathlon. In late May, he won the decathlon in the Asian Games. He also placed 2nd in the 110 hurdles (14.8) and long jump (24-6¾), and 3rd in the 400 meter hurdles (53.0). In June, at the age of 26, he moved to the United States for training. He placed 2nd to Rafer Johnson in the AAU decathlon. His 7625 placed him 7th on the all-time list.

In 1959, he ran in the big California meets as a high hurdler, with a best of 14.2. In August, he scored 7835 and ranked No. 3 for the year in the World Rankings. He enrolled as a freshman at UCLA to train with Johnson and recorded marks of 13.9, 25-5, 14-1¼, and 233-2. He raised his decathlon best to 7892 in April, then exceeded the World Record with 8426 while placing 2nd to Johnson in the AAU. In the Olympic Games he pushed Johnson all the way, finishing a close 2nd with 8334.

In 1962, Yang won the AAU decathlon with 8249 and was No. 1 in the World Rankings. In 1963 he developed suddenly with the fiberglass pole into a near-record vaulter. He cleared 16-3½ for an indoor World Record and he cleared 16-5 outdoors. He was No. 6 in the World Rankings.

He used his vaulting ability to such an extent that he caused the adoption of new tables in 1964 when he shattered Johnson's World Record with 9121 points. In his record decathlon, he vaulted 15-10½, ran 10.7 and 47.7, and hurdled in 14-flat.

He won the 1964 AAU decathlon with 8641. Then the new scoring tables were issued, lowering his world record from 9121 to 8089. Discouraged and injured, he placed only fifth in the Olympics.

YASHCHENKO, VLADIMIR (Soviet Union) . . . . 2 WR, No. 1
High Jump, 1977-80 . . . . .1/12/59, 6-3½/183

Yashchenko burst on the world scene as a junior in 1977 when he broke the World Record with a jump of 7-7¾ in the U.S.-Soviet Union Junior dual meet. The next year, while still a junior, he cleared indoor World Records of 7-7¾ and 7-8½ while winning the European Indoor Championships, then set another outdoor WR of 7-8 on June 16, in Tbilisi. He ranked No. 1 in 1978, but his career waned after leg injuries sidelined him in 1979. Comebacks were never successful enough to bring him back to the top.

YIFTER, MIRUTS (Ethiopia) . . . . 2 G, B, 4 No. 1
        5000-10,000, 1961-80 . . . . .6/8/47, 5-6¼/128

Yifter ran little internationally. He placed 3rd in the 1972 Olympic 10,000, but Africa boycotted the 1976 Games. He won the 5000 and 10,000 in the 1977 and 1979 World Cups. In 1980, he won both events in the Olympics with sensational finishing speed.

YRJOLA, PAAVO (Finland) . . . . G, 4 WR, 3 No. 1*
        Decathlon, 1924-32 . . . .

Yrjola set a World Record in the 1928 Olympic decathlon and three other times. He placed 9th in 1924 and 6th in 1932.

ZATOPEK, EMIL (Czechoslovakia) . 4G, S, 18WR, 13 No. 1, 2 1/3 AOY
        Distances, 1947-56 . . . . .9/19/22, 5-8½/148

See chapter.

ZHU, JIANHUA (China) . . . . 2B, 3 WR, No. 1
        High Jump, ...3/29/63, 6-4/152

Zhu jumped 7-6½ in 1981 at the age of 18, ranked No. 6 in 1982, and set World Records of 7-9¼ and 7-9¾ in 1983. He placed 3rd in the World Championships. In 1984, he jumped 7-10, his third WR, but placed only 3rd in the Olympics.

ZSIVOTZKY, GYULA (Hungary) . . . . .G, 2 S, 2 WR, 3 No. 1
        Hammer, 1960-72 . . . . .2/25/37, 6-2¾/198

Zsivotzky was 2nd in the 1960 and 1964 Olympic hammer throws and he won in 1968. He won the 1962 European Chamionships and was 2nd in 1966. He set a World Record of 241-11 in 1965 and raised it to 242 feet in 1968. He ranked high for 4 more years and placed 5th in the 1972 Olympics.

Profiles of Other Champions

ATHLETES OF THE YEAR, 1947-85

World Track & Field Athletes of the Year have been selected by *Track & Field News* since 1959. In the February 1967 issue of *T&FN*, Cordner Nelson offered his personal list of AOYs, 1947-58, retroactive to the founding of the magazine.

1947	Harrison Dillard (US)	1965	Ron Clarke (Aus)
1948	Harrison Dillard (US)	1966	Jim Ryun (US)
1949	Fortune Gordien (US)	1967	Jim Ryun (US)
1950	Tie between	1968	Bob Beamon (US)
	Emil Zatopek (Cze)	1969	Bill Toomey (US)
	Dick Attlesey (US)	1970	Randy Matson (US)
	Jim Fuchs (US)	1971	Rod Milburn (US)
1951	Emil Zatopek (Cze)	1972	Lasse Viren (Fin)
1952	Emil Zatopek (Cze)	1973	Ben Jipcho (Ken)
1953	Mal Whitfield (US)	1974	Rick Wohlhuter (US)
1954	Parry O'Brien (US)	1975	John Walker (NZ)
1955	Sandor Iharos (Hun)	1976	Alberto Juantorena (Cub)
1956	Vladimir Kuts (SU)	1977	Alberto Juantorena (Cub)
1957	Bob Gutowski (US)	1978	Henry Rono (Ken)
1958	Glenn Davis (US)	1979	Sebastian Coe (GB)
1959	Martin Lauer (WG)	1980	Edwin Moses (US)
1960	Rafer Johnson (US)	1981	Sebastian Coe (GB)
1961	Ralph Boston (US)	1982	Carl Lewis (US)
1962	Peter Snell (NZ)	1983	Carl Lewis (US)
1963	C.K. Yang (Tai)	1984	Carl Lewis (US)
1964	Peter Snell (NZ)	1985	Said Aouita (Mor)